THE
REICH INTRUDERS

RAF Light Bomber Raids
in World War II

MARTIN W. BOWMAN

Pen & Sword
AVIATION

First published in 2005
and reprinted in this format in 2019 and 2021 by
Pen & Sword AVIATION
An imprint of Pen & Sword Books Ltd
Yorkshire – Philadelphia

Copyright © Martin W. Bowman, 2005, 2019, 2021
ISBN: 978 1 52676 083 8

A CIP catalogue record for this book is available from the British Library

Printed and bound in the UK on FSC accredited paper by 4edge Ltd, Essex, SS5 4AD

Pen & Sword Books Limited incorporates the imprints of Atlas, Archaeology,
Aviation, Discovery, Family History, Fiction, History, Maritime, Military, Military
Classics, Politics, Select, Transport, True Crime, Air World, Frontline Publishing, Leo
Cooper, Remember When, Seaforth Publishing, The Praetorian Press, Wharncliffe
Local History, Wharncliffe Transport, Wharncliffe True Crime and White Owl.

For a complete list of Pen & Sword titles please contact
PEN & SWORD BOOKS LIMITED
47 Church Street, Barnsley, South Yorkshire, S70 2AS, England
E-mail: enquiries@pen-and-sword.co.uk • Website: www.pen-and-sword.co.uk
Or
PEN AND SWORD BOOKS
1950 Lawrence Rd, Havertown, PA 19083, USA
E-mail: Uspen-and-sword@casematepublishers.com
Website: www.penandswordbooks.com

Contents

Acknowledgements

I must first thank Jim 'Dinty' Moore DFC and the late John Bateman, both of whom graciously made available their precious squadron albums and photographs on more than one occasion; Mike Bailey, for his guidance, proofing and loan of photographs and reference books; Bob Collis, for his invaluable input of research material and advice; Paul McCue, Dr Theo Boiten, Kees Rijken and Paul Schepers, joint authors of *Operation Oyster*, in Holland and Eric Mombeek in Belgium; Les Bulmer; Jan Kloos in Switzerland; Julian Horn and Paul Lincoln of the Wartime Watton Museum; Ole Rønnest in Denmark; and last but by no means least, Sister Laurence Mary. All of these filled many gaps with valuable photographs and material. I am no less indebted to the following: Arthur Asker; Eric Atkins DFC* KW (*Krzyz Walecznych*)*, Chairman, Mosquito Aircrew Association; Gerald Baker; Ralph Barker; Jack Bartley; the late Gordon Bell-Irving; The Rt Hon. Tony Benn MP; Philip J. Birtles, Leslie Bond; Roy J. A. Brookes JP, Chairman, 88 Squadron Association; Nigel Buswell; Arthur Butterworth; Michael Carreck DFC; Squadron Leader Ray Chance; Wilf J. Clutton; Maurice A. Collins DFC DFM; W. G. 'Bill' Cooper, 137/139 All Ranks Association; William F. 'Bill' Corfield FRICS FAAV ACIArb; Tom Cushing; Squadron Leader Mike Daniels; Rene Deeks; Reg Everson; John Foreman; Bob Gallup; GMS Enterprises; Ken Godfrey; Ted Gorman; Peter B. Gunn; Hans de Haan; Nicholas Heffer; Dudley Hemmings; H. C. 'Gary' Herbert RAAF DFC; Wilf Jessop; Bernard M. Job; Jack Lub; Jock MacDonald; Graham 'Digger' Magill; Peter Mallinson; Squadron Leader Hugh Milroy RAF; Eric Mombeek; Norma Moore; P. D. Morris; W. J. Morris; Aubrey Niner; Simon Parry; Squadron Leader Charles Patterson DFC DSO; Jack and Freddie Peppiatt; Chief Technician Steve Pope; Tony Rudd; Peter Saunders; Squadron Leader Malcolm Scott DFC; Steve Snelling, EDP, Norwich; Jerry Scutts; Mrs Vera Sherring; A. M. J. Smith; Steve Smith; Herbert E. Tappin; Group Captain Bill Taylor; Andy Thomas; 'Slim' Trew; Henk F. Van Baaren; Colin 'Ginger' Walsh; Kenneth A. I. Warwood; Colin Waugh; and Tony Wilson.

Martin Bowman Norwich, 2005.

CHAPTER ONE

Full Cry

Out of England, over France,
Three by three, in swift advance,
Eager as at the first cock-crow,
Let the hunting Blenheims go!

'Full Cry' by Flight Lieutenant Anthony Richardson RAFVR,
Adjutant, 107 Squadron

'There is quite a panic on here. We are going away today to WATTON. About twenty miles from Norwich. The reports of the place are not so hot. Will write soon as we get settled down now. Cheerio. We are off in about 1 hour. With love…'

So wrote 18-year-old Leading Aircraftsman (LAC) Freddie Thripp of 82 Squadron, in an urgent postcard home in August 1939. His squadron was one of ten in 2 (Bomber) Group, which had been formed on 20 March 1936. Now, in August 1939, war with Germany, which had been avoided at Munich in 1938, loomed large and 2 Group would be in the front line long before a large part of the rest of Britain's armed forces. With headquarters at Wyton, Cambridgeshire, the group numbered five wings: 70 Wing at Upper Heyford controlled 18 and 57 Squadrons; 79 Wing at Watton, 21 and 82 Squadrons; 81 Wing at West Raynham, Norfolk, 90 and 101 Squadrons; 82 Wing at Wyton, 114 and 139 Squadrons; and 83 Wing at Wattisham, 107 and 110 Squadrons. All 2 Group squadrons were equipped with the twin-engined Bristol Blenheim Mk I or Mk IV (21, 18 and 57 Squadrons were still in the process of converting to the IV). Britain and her allies were, however, ill equipped to prevent a repetition of the fate that had already befallen Poland. Four of these wings formed the 2nd Echelon of the Advanced Air Striking Force while 70 Wing was earmarked for service in France supporting the British Expeditionary Force (BEF) along with squadrons of obsolete single-engined Fairey Battles. The Battle and Blenheim monoplane bombers were a vast improvement on the Hind biplane bombers that had equipped 2 Group in the mid-1930s but the Air Ministry seemed to have little conception of modern fighter tactics. A Blenheim cost £20,000 and sadly was about to be exposed as an expensive machine in terms of lives spent for little offensive reward (it could only carry 1,000 lb bombs internally). Apart from a fixed forward-firing gun in the wing operated by the pilot and another under the nose, there was a rather ancient Vickers gas-operated .303 machine gun in a dorsal turret, which was fed from circular ammunition pans, each of which contained 100 rounds. Spare pans were clipped on to the side of the turret. The crew of three comprised the pilot (an officer or flight sergeant), observer (normally a senior NCO) and upper gunner (usually an aircraftsman 1st or 2nd class, leading aircraftsman or corporal). AC1 (later sergeant) Jack Bartley, a wireless operator/air gunner (WOp/AG) on Blenheims, recalls.

> The pilot, navigator and the air-gunner lived in three entirely separate social worlds. The only time the SNCOs and the officers met was once a month on invitation to the opposite mess. The airmen only met the officers at the annual airmen's Xmas dinner when the officers traditionally served the meal. The SNCOs and officers enjoyed a high standard of living in their respective messes, while the Wireless Operators/Air Gunners lived in barrack rooms together with the lowest ACHs who might have cleaned the toilets. Even when waiting for take-off during a stand-by we would be in separate crew rooms in the hangar. Prior to June 1940 (when all operational aircrew below the rank were promoted to Sergeant), WOp/AGs were 'other ranks' (AC2, AC1, LAC and Corporal). As such they were subject to normal station duties including guards, which could mean you were flying by day sitting behind a machine gun and slinging a rifle for four-hour spells patrolling the dispersed aircraft through the icy nights that the 1939–40 winter produced. The one privilege we enjoyed apart from the princely sum of an additional shilling [5p] per day flying pay plus sixpence [2p] a day for the Flying Bullet Air Gunner badge, was a monthly two-day leave pass.

New recruits were blissfully unaware of all this. During the summer of 1939 19-year-old Jim 'Dinty' Moore had been accepted as a wireless operator and he was advised to report to the recruiting depot at Bradford, Yorkshire. On Monday, 28 August he caught the train from his home in Hawes at the head of Wensleydale and set off on the first leg of a journey that would last six years and five months. Aircraftsman Second Class (AC2) Moore's feelings were a mixture of excitement and

Blenheim I aircraft of 21 Squadron at RAF Watton in June 1939. L1345 went on to serve with 90 and 114 Squadrons and 13 OTU until it went to Finland on 21 July 1940. The Finnish air force acquired ninety-seven Blenheim Is and they were used in the war with the Soviet Union, which began in November 1939. (*Wartime Watton Museum*)

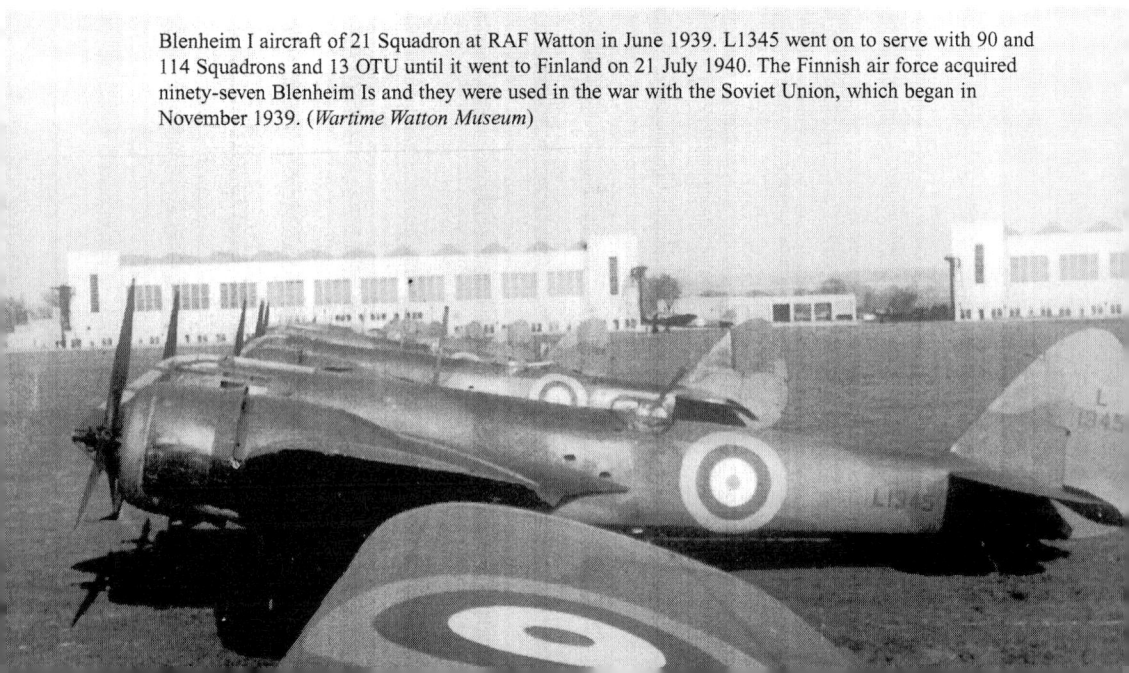

apprehension, and he certainly had no idea that within twelve months he would be flying over Western Europe as a member of the crew of a Bristol Blenheim. He was at Padgate, a training establishment on the outskirts of Warrington, when on Sunday morning, 3 September, the wireless in his hut was switched on and instead of the normal programmes serious music was being played. Moore recalls:

> It was then solemnly announced that the nation was to be addressed by the Prime Minister, Neville Chamberlain. His address began, 'This morning the British Ambassador to Berlin handed the German Government a final note saying that unless we hear from them by 11 o'clock that they were prepared, at once, to withdraw their troops from Poland, a state of war would exist between us. I have to tell you that no such undertaking had been received and that, consequently, this country is at war with Germany.' The remainder of his speech was drowned by cheers and excited conversation for, it must be remembered, we were all youngsters who were actually excited at the prospect of being at war with our old enemy. Considering that the last war, the war to end all wars, had ended only twenty years earlier with an appalling loss of life, we should have had a clearer idea of the reality of war. I suppose those who were actually involved were reluctant to talk of their experiences and our attitude had been influenced by books recording the heroics.

At the time of Chamberlain's historic broadcast, a Blenheim IV of 139 Squadron, piloted by Flying Officer Andrew McPherson (killed in action KIA 12.5.40) was preparing to take off from Wyton. His crew was Commander Thompson RN acting as observer and his WOp/AG Corporal V. Arrowsmith (KIA 24.9.40). A minute later they were airborne heading out over the North Sea to reconnoitre the German battle fleet at Wilhelmshaven. As they gradually gained height through haze and a freezing mist, which caused the camera and the radio to freeze up, they must have had doubts as to whether they would be able to see their objectives. On reaching 24,000 ft they flew on to Wilhelmshaven, where Commander Thompson was able to sketch details of the location of the enemy fleet. Finally, after the first operational flight of the war, which had lasted five hours and fifty minutes, they landed safely back at Wyton.

The following day, 4 September, despite appalling weather conditions, McPherson and his crew again took off to repeat their mission. On this occasion, due to the weather, he was forced to fly under the cloud at a height of about 250 ft. This time the camera was operational and they returned, after a flight of four hours, with the desired photographs. Awaiting McPherson's return were fifteen Blenheim crews, five each from 107, 110 and 139 Squadrons, and ten Wellingtons. They had been briefed to attack ships of the German fleet in the Schillig Roads and nothing else. Further, their approach to the target must be made from over the land in order to avoid the possibility of any civilian casualties. Without waiting for the results of McPherson's second reconnaissance to be evaluated, the three formations of five aircraft took off independently on the first bombing raid of the war. They flew across the North Sea through blinding rainstorms, but miraculously the Blenheims of 110 Squadron led by Flight Lieutenant Kenneth Doran made their intended landfall at Heligoland before changing course for their target. On approaching their quarry the cloud base had lifted to 500 ft when a cargo ship came into view and just beyond it the battleship *Admiral Scheer*. The *Kriegsmarine* was obviously quite unprepared for the assault – the aircrews reported seeing washing hung out to dry – so Doran led his formation straight into the attack. Three hits were claimed on the battleship, although it is now known that they failed to explode. Their attack brought no reaction and they flew off unscathed, although one Blenheim failed to return to base, becoming the first RAF casualties of the war.

The five aircraft of 107 Squadron led by Flight Lieutenant W. F. Barton arrived over the target ten minutes later to find the enemy very much alert, their gunners throwing up a murderous curtain of flak through which the Blenheims had to fly. One crashed onto the cruiser *Emden*, causing some damage but losing its entire crew, while another three were shot down. The only survivors were Flying Officer W. J. Stephens and his crew, who became lost in the low cloud and rain and never found the target. Some bombs bounced off the armour plating, while others exploded on the ships and may have accounted for the loss of at least one of the Blenheims. First-hand information on the raid was later gleaned by an escaping prisoner of war (PoW) in a train compartment in northern Italy. He overheard a sailor talking to his companion, remarking on the gallantry of the aircraft crews and the close attack of the aircraft. He also recounted how he saw one of the aircraft blown to pieces by the blast of a bomb burst. Only one crew of the Blenheims shot down lived to tell the tale, although the pilot, Sergeant A. S. Prince of 107 Squadron, died from his wounds five days later. Sergeant George Booth, his observer, and the WOp/AG, AC2 Lane Slattery, had the dubious distinction of becoming the first prisoners of war in this conflict. The third squadron, 139, perhaps fortuitously but understandably in view of the weather conditions, failed to find the target and returned with their bombs. This was indeed a disastrous start to the war, with the loss of five of the ten aircraft that had found and attacked the target.

Wing Commander Haylock, who had taken over command of 107 Squadron in April 1939, was posted within a few days and there arrived at Wattisham on 15 September Wing Commander Basil E. Embry DSO AFC, who was described by aircrew as a 'little ball of fire'. He was just the type of leader who was needed to instill urgency into what so far was almost a non-event, with neither side anxious to provoke the other. These conditions suited the Germans, as they were content to carry on preparing and planning for the *Blitzkrieg* that they were now about to unleash with staggering success. The Allies, on the other hand, would not allow themselves to believe that the war would ever really start in earnest. Leaders like Chamberlain seemed to believe that his appeals to the German people for peace would be accepted. The period became known as the 'Phoney War', when little aggressive action was taken by either side in the conflict.

Aircraftsman First Class (AC1) D. M. Merrett, an armourer in 107 Squadron at the time, wrote:

For us the 'Phoney War' never existed due in large part to Embry's terrific drive. He realised right from the start that the war would have to be pursued relentlessly and within his powers as a squadron commander he ensured that this was done. Embry expected everyone to match his own fierce energy and enthusiasm: a tall order. He commanded the greatest respect and admiration but not in my view at least, affection. 'Battle Orders' were issued almost daily and the squadron was constantly on operations, although this did not invariably result in bombs being dropped because targets were not always reached or located. This increased the armourers' work, for aircraft returning with bombs had to be de-bombed and there was considerable changing of bomb loads as different targets were selected by 2 Group. The meagre armament of the Blenheim left a large blind spot when attacked from below and astern. Embry demanded a quick remedy of his Engineer Officer, Flying Officer Edwards. Working together, Maintenance Flight and Armament Section provided a solution. Aft of each engine in the nacelle was found sufficient space to accommodate a rearward-firing .303-inch Browning gun and ammunition box. Each gun protruded through a hole cut in the nacelle and was fired by a fantastic length of Bowden cable leading to a huge firing lever mounted in the dorsal gun turret. In addition, a Vickers Gas Operated (VGO) gun was inverted and fitted into the stern frame aft of the tail wheel, with a further Bowden cable running up to the fuselage lever. This gun was very exposed and immediately before take-off the armourer would secure a magazine to it. As this was in the pre-runway era, when conditions were wet the tail wheel lathered the gun and magazine with mud during take-off, to the detriment of both, so the scheme, though welcome, was not an unqualified success. The Brownings were successful, however, and may have saved several aircraft but it was never possible to equip the whole squadron. Increasing armament did not rest there, for the same team perfected a twin .303-inch Browning gun installation to replace the single VGO in the turret and this was officially adapted for all Blenheim IVs. Forward of the nose, the escape hatch position was used to add first a single then twin underslung rearward firing .303-inch Brownings, fired by the observer and jettisoned if use of the escape hatch became necessary. The bomb doors were not hydraulically operated. They merely flew open when the weight of a bomb fell on them and were returned to the closed position by bungy cords. When 4 lb incendiaries were required, the doors were removed altogether.

Embry led twelve Blenheims on 27 March when he sighted a German cruiser and four destroyers about 70 miles north-north-west of the Hrons Reef in the Heligoland Bight. The formation followed the ships and four minutes later sighted most of the German fleet on its way to support the invasion of Norway. An attack was made out of the sun, engaging the *Scharnhorst* and *Gneisenau* and a message was sent giving the position and course of the fleet. Because of poor communications, however, this information only reached the authorities when the aircraft landed back at Wattisham some hours later.

On 9 April Norway was invaded by the Germans and on the 14th in response to a request from the Norwegian government for military assistance an advance party of an Allied expeditionary force was landed at Narvik in north-western Norway. The problems facing the bombers of the RAF in giving much-needed support were to an extent overcome by placing two Blenheim squadrons, 110 and 107, on temporary detachment to RAF Lossiemouth, from where they could attack shipping and the German-held airfield at Stavanger in southern Norway. On 17 April Stavanger was attacked from low level by twelve of 107 Squadron's Blenheims, their bombs causing a great deal of damage to enemy aircraft on the ground. A fierce firefight developed when they were attacked by a number of German fighters, a combat that lasted for sixty-five minutes and from which two Blenheims and their crews failed to return. Another of these sorties took place in the late afternoon of 30 April when six Blenheims of 110 Squadron led by Kenneth Doran, now a squadron leader, attacked enemy shipping. They in their turn were descended upon by a host of Bf 109s, which shot down two of the Blenheims. Flight Sergeant R. Abbott piloted one of those lost while Doran, who became a PoW, flew the other. During this short campaign seven Blenheims and their crews were lost before the two squadrons returned to their bases in East Anglia.

On 10 May the 'Phoney War' ended. In the early hours German troops crossed the frontiers of Holland and Belgium in force, supported by paratroops, glider-borne troops and hordes of bombers and fighters. Everyone listened anxiously to the radio to try and keep in touch with events, which were to change with astonishing rapidity. Reserves were posted to France to reinforce the squadrons. The medium-bomber squadrons there comprised six squadrons of Blenheim IVs and eight squadrons of Fairey Battles supported by the seven Blenheim squadrons in East Anglia. The Battles went into action within an hour of being given authority to do so by the French High Command but their losses were high (twenty-three were shot down during the day), and would remain so throughout the short campaign.

Meanwhile, at 0905 hours on the morning of 10 May the first of several operations was carried out by two Blenheims of 40 Squadron at Wyton, with Squadron Leader Paddon and Flying Officer Burns reconnoitring the Dutch-German border. Burns crash landed after being hit by flak, and he and his crew were made PoW. Paddon's aircraft, while damaged, made it back to Wyton with one engine smoking. At noon nine Blenheims of 15 Squadron, also from Wyton, bombed Waalhaven amid heavy flak and while several were damaged they all returned safely. During the afternoon 40 Squadron sent twelve crews to attack Wypenburg airfield near The Hague. Flight Lieutenant R. H. Batt (KIA 9.7.40) led the first of the attacks and dropped his bombs without reply but once the defences were alerted the other vics did not fare so well. Three Blenheims were shot down by flak, and Flight Lieutenant Smeddie's machine returned badly damaged and with the crew suffering injuries.

The next day, 11 May, German armour and motorized infantry were pouring across the River Meuse at Maastricht, where the bridges over the Albert Canal were still intact. The Belgian High Command considered the destruction of these bridges to be vital and at first light Blenheims of 114 Squadron, based at Conde Vraux near Soissons, were briefed to bomb them. The aircraft were lined up on the airfield and the crews were ready to take off when nine Dornier 17s surprised them, making first a bombing then a strafing run, destroying the squadron in forty-five seconds. After the Fairey Battles and the *Armée de l'Air* had failed to destroy the bridges, twelve Blenheims of 21 Squadron from Wyton carried out one further attack that evening. They approached the target at 3,000 ft in the face of a tremendous flak barrage and heavy fighter opposition. Four were shot down and the rest were severely damaged.

At dawn on 12 May eight Blenheims of 139 Squadron at Plivot tried to attack a German column on the road from Maastricht to Tongres but they were attacked *en route* by fifty Bf 109s, who shot down seven of the bombers. Three of the victims fell in quick succession to the guns of the *Staffelkapitän*, of 2./JG1 *Oberleutnant* Walter Adolph.[1] Only the Blenheim flown by Wing Commander Louis W. Dickens AFC made it back to Plivot, and it was declared a write-off. Meanwhile twelve Blenheims of 107 Squadron led by Wing Commander Embry took off from Wattisham at 0810 hours and headed for the bridges, which were to be bombed from 6,000 ft, a height that Embry considered would be the most effective. Fifteen miles before the target they too were fired at by anti-aircraft fire, which continued all the way to the target. However, despite this they flew on and dropped their bombs. One of the bridges was damaged but the Blenheim piloted by Pilot Officer S. G. Thornton was shot down and every other aircraft was damaged during the run-in. Then the Bf 109s attacked, shooting down three of the remaining Blenheims; eight survivors, severely damaged, managed to make it back to Wattisham.

An attack by six Fairey Battles of 12 Squadron later that morning resulted in all the attacking aircraft being shot down. Twelve Blenheims of 15 Squadron at Alconbury, which had been standing by since 0530 hours, lost six of their number before the survivors, all badly damaged, limped back across the Channel towards England. Twelve Blenheims of 110 Squadron reached the bridges and eleven claimed to have hit their targets but one aircraft was shot down and another crash landed in Belgium after being attacked by Bf 109s. Blenheims of 82 Squadron, meanwhile, which had been standing by at Watton since 0730 hours, took off at 1930 hours for an attack on the Albert Canal near Hasselt. The raid was successful and all the crews returned safely. Finally, nine Blenheims of 21 Squadron flew the last operation of the day, also from Watton. Their target was a road at Tongres, which they bombed at 2040 hours from 7,000 ft. At least two were damaged by flak but they were able to take advantage of cloud cover for their withdrawal and all of them returned safely. The RAF losses had been such that only a daylight raid by a few Battles of 226 Squadron was possible on 13 May.

In the afternoon of 14 May, when the Dutch government surrendered following the raid on Rotterdam by fifty-seven Heinkel He 111s, seventy-one Battles flew an operation against pontoon bridges across the Meuse. No fewer than forty were shot down, though six crews did manage to evade capture and return to their lines. Then it was the turn, in the late afternoon, of twenty-eight Blenheims from stations in East Anglia. AC1 Jack Bartley, WOp/AG in Sergeant Johnny J. Outhwaite's crew in 21 Squadron at Watton, wrote.

> On the morning of 14 May we looked up at the clear blue sky with not a little apprehension. We all knew the Germans were advancing with amazing rapidity through the Low Countries. We also knew that cloud cover or no cloud cover, we should be required to attack and bomb some sector of the enemy columns that day in an attempt to stem their advance at that point. Throughout the morning we were standing by while our sister squadron [82] made a short two-hour trip to attack the victorious *Panzers* in Northern Holland, carrying out the raid without loss.

Jack Bartley, WOP/AG in Sergeant Johnny J. Outhwaite's Blenheim crew in 21 Squadron at Watton (*Jack Bartley via Theo Boiten*)

At last the long-awaited summons to the Ops Room was announced and received with the quickening of the pulse that it never failed to effect in me and sighs of genuine relief from all in the crew room. We had been 'standing by' since 4 a.m. and activity of any sort was infinitely preferable to that tedious occupation. With assumed nonchalance we trooped into the crew room to receive the 'gen'. Our target, as it had been at Maastricht on the 10th and Tongres on the 11th, was the advancing mechanized columns, with the additional attraction of an important crossroads at Sedan, near the Luxembourg frontier. We were to make a dive attack for accuracy but to repair quickly to formation after the attack for protection against the Jerry fighters, whose presence was regarded as inevitable. Take-off was at 4 p.m. and at that hour twelve sleek and shining Blenheims were lined up on the 'drome awaiting the order to start engines.

I was standing near my machine, a little nervously, laughing with the ground crew who had been mercilessly ragging me the night before to the effect that it was my 'turn', as it undoubtedly was if the previous alphabetical sequence of losses of air gunners was to be adhered to. 'Tich' Birch had never returned from a Heligoland 'recco'. Johnny Ball had been killed in action a fortnight back. Paddy B had died on landing from the Maastricht raid after getting the only bullet that hit his aircraft through his lung and 'Butch' Burgess had piled straight in from 15,000 ft over Tongres the day after when his machine received a direct hit from flak. I had been flying No. 3 to his leader at the time and after seeing pieces of his tailplane flying past my turret, had watched as if hypnotized the crippled machine's devastating plunge down on to the target culminating in a terrific explosion. I was the only remaining 'B', so I was forced to agree that it was my turn, though privately I had other views on the subject.[2]

The signal to run up was given and the engines roared into life, when down the line of machines came the CO's car. Stopping at our machine he yelled out that a fighter escort of thirty Dewoitine machines had been arranged to patrol the target area from 6 to 6.30. I have often wondered since if that information was for the benefit of our morale, or indeed if the French even possessed thirty Dewoitine fighters. The fact remains that rendezvous was destined never to take place.

We took off just after 4 p.m. in a cloud of dust. As I saw the faces of my friends amongst the ground crews rapidly receding I began to wonder – but I'd had those doubts before and returned safely. So I fought down that feeling of over-excitement mixed with a little fear that seems to bring your heart into your mouth and keep it there. My services weren't needed for a little while, so I rested my forehead on the chin-rest of the gun mounting and closed my eyes to allow the excitement to die off and to get my thoughts into order for the approaching zero hour. When I again looked up we were just about to cross the coast and I watched the chalk cliffs slowly grow indistinct in the summer haze. I'd often had the experience before, yet never before had I felt quite so wistful towards them, or realized more fully how much they really meant to me as on that lovely still afternoon in May.

Followed the boring flight over the Channel, the monotonous ripples broken only at one spot by the ugly hull of a merchant vessel that reared almost vertically out of the water, presumably the victim of an enemy bomb or mine. We at times came across mines on the return trip when pilots would put machines' noses down to nought feet and cut the wave crests with spinning 'props', giving one a most exhilarating sensation of speed that was not entirely without foundation. I often thought the trips well worth while if only for that exultant flight home, careering over the wave tops. The French coastline appeared out of the haze (it might have been Holland – discipline would not allow the pilot or sergeant navigator to discuss where they were with the AG!) and our presence sent a small convoy of merchantmen zigzagging frantically. We had climbed to 12,000 ft so perhaps there was some excuse for their failing to identify us. But the same cannot be said of the AA gunners at different points along the whole of our journey across France, whose fire, though sparse and rather inaccurate, was at the same time infuriatingly misdirected. However, it served considerably to relieve the monotony of that seemingly endless flight across France, for we kept to 15,000 ft and could not improve our knowledge of the countryside from that height.

At long last Johnny yelled out that we were approaching the target area, whereupon I gave the magazine of 'ammo' on the gun a reassuring slap to ascertain its being properly fixed and forsaking my comfortable pose for a more alert attitude, kept my eyes skinned. I set the turret buzzing around and looked ahead but could make out no sign of activity. It was 6 o'clock and we had five minutes before being due over the target. We flew on. I began to have misgivings about our fighter escort, which were by no means decreased when I caught sight of two machines 2,000 ft or so above and flying across our track, their square wing-tips almost spelling out the word Messerschmitt. Holding myself in readiness and watching them like a hawk, I wondered why they made no attempt to attack us, when suddenly the reason was forming all about us in the shape of hundreds of black puffs and we were going down in a dive.

For a moment I thought we had been hit but a glance showed me that the rest of the squadron were with us in our descent, though the formation was loosened to go through the flak. Ack-Ack fire is always rather awe-inspiring, especially when you know you are the object of its attention. Big black blobs appear all over the sky with not a sound to announce their arrival, or so it seems after one's helmeted ears have listened to the roar of the engines for an hour or so. Even those that burst close enough to set the machine staggering drunkenly appear to make as much noise as a penny demon on 5 November, though there is more significance in the sharp report of shrapnel piercing the metal fuselage.

We straightened out at about 8,000 ft, leaving behind us the large artificial black cloud that was ack-ack. A jubilant shout through the phones compelled me to lower my eyes and see that Sergeant Broadland, our observer, had landed his bombs smack on the crossroads. Looking around for the remainder of the squadron my eyes were arrested by the sight of a Blenheim in flames about 2,000 ft below and going down. But before there was time to watch for the crew's escape my attention was riveted on a 109 fighter approaching from above and on the port quarter. Yelling out the 'gen' to Johnny, I saw that one of the Jerries had singled me out for attention and swiftly got him in my sights, until at 200 yards he started firing, giving the appearance of blowing smoke rings from his leading edges. Tracers were zipping a little over my head and I gave a short burst in reply to see where my tracer was going. He closed in further and I held on until I really had the weight of him, as he evidently had of me, for I felt a couple of slaps on my legs and holes were appearing in the fuselage around my turret. Then I gave him all I had as he neared fifty yards range, keeping my trigger depressed. I saw my tracers going into his port wing, then raking his fuselage, as clearly as I saw his streams of tracers coming straight at me and seeming to veer off at the last moment.

Unwaveringly he kept on until at thirty yards it seemed he was intent on ramming us, when suddenly his nose dropped and he was gone. The unorthodoxy of the dive led me to believe I had him. I was leaning out to catch some glimpse of him when I felt a terrible pain in my back as if a red-hot poker had been thrust into it. I turned to see a second Me about to break off his attack, made from the opposite beam simultaneously with the first machine.

Immobilized with pain for a second or two, I recovered too late to get a smack at him. In any case my ammo was expended, so with a twist of my turret control I lowered myself into the fuselage, hurriedly removed the empty pan and reloaded before elevating myself again, to be greeted with the sight of a fighter dead astern at 400 yards. Jagged holes appeared in the tailplane while I manipulated foot and hand levers till the gun was in position for shooting alongside fin and rudder. He closed in until his machine guns sounded like a much-accentuated typewriter tapping in my ears above the engine noises and in between my own bursts of fire.

Attempting to follow him down after his break away, my heart missed a beat or two when I found that my turret would no longer respond to pressure on the hand bar – the hydraulics were evidently severed. Desperately I grasped the pillars of the turret and shoved but to no avail; the turret just would not budge. I was, in effect, disarmed. Fortunately at this juncture there was a lapse in the attack. Placing my hand to my aching back I brought it away covered with blood and a feeling of nausea swept over me. Blood was also streaming from a wound in my thigh, so I decided to leave the cordite-reeking atmosphere of the useless turret and have my wounds attended to, pressing the emergency lever that would lower my seat and allow my exit.

To my horror I felt no lowering of my seat in answer to pressure there and realized that I was virtually trapped in my turret. I doubled my body down in an effort to slip off my seat and fall into the fuselage and was rewarded only by a shower of petrol in my face as it came below the level of the fuselage. It must have been leaking in through the wing roots from the severed feed pipes. I became aware that we were diving steeply and for the first time in the action I had time to be frightened. Feverishly I relieved myself of my parachute harness, tore at the strings of my Mae West and fumbled with the Irvin zip until with a manoeuvre worthy of a contortionist, I at last managed to extricate myself.

With the machine still roaring earthwards I donned my harness, this time with parachute attached in readiness. I re-plugged my phones in the midships socket and, wondering if Johnny had given the order to jump, or indeed if he were still alive, yelled down the mike, 'I'm out of action, Sarge. I'm out of action, Sarge!' There was no reply but my increasing fears were allayed by the gradual straightening out of the machine and through the camera hatch I saw that we were flashing over forest land, barely clearing the tree tops. Then my hopes of survival recently cherished were dashed to the ground as more jagged rips appeared in the already riddled fuselage, bullets whipped inside the machine, clanging against metal and above it all, nearer and nearer, the terrifying tapping of those lethal typewriters. A couple of bullets smacked into the parachute fastened to my chest. Deciding that I had not much longer to live, the mortal fear I had of being wounded in the stomach forced me to double up and point my head towards the tail, resignedly hoping for a mercifully quick end. The fact that I presented a small target in that position was purely incidental, though it was probably responsible for saving my life. Though I received two ricocheting splinters in my side during the next few seconds, live through the inferno I did; much to my surprise, though the ache from my wounds and the infuriation at my inability to retaliate knew no bounds.

The firing stopped as suddenly as it had begun and all went comparatively quiet. I fervently hoped that was the last of the fighters to pay us its unwelcome attentions. My wishes in this respect were borne out, though we were still not out of the wood. Wriggling over the bomb well and peeping over the pilot's seat, I could see that Johnny was having one royal time endeavouring to keep the machine on some sort of course and to check her pitching. The difficulty arising, we found afterwards, was from the fact that half the tailplane was non-existent and that the rudder resembled a tattered rag, fluttering in the breeze. I managed to attract my observer's attention and he placed a shell dressing over the worst gash in my back from which blood still oozed in a steady stream.

Johnny yelled out that he would have to lob her before the remaining fuel supply gave out and after flying over seemingly endless forests covering the slopes of the Ardennes we perceived through the cabin perspex, which had not escaped the onslaught unscathed, a comparatively flat stretch of grassland. Banking steeply, Johnny prepared to put her down. Realizing that even if the attempt were successful the landing would be a very bumpy affair owing to the unserviceability of the undercarriage from both tactical and practical points of view, I rolled myself up in the bomb well, the strongest part of the aircraft. I gripped the nearest fuselage rib as if my very life depended on it.

I saw the ground approaching through the rips in the metal fuselage. I heard the swish of air as the flaps lowered and a crash that shook every bone in my

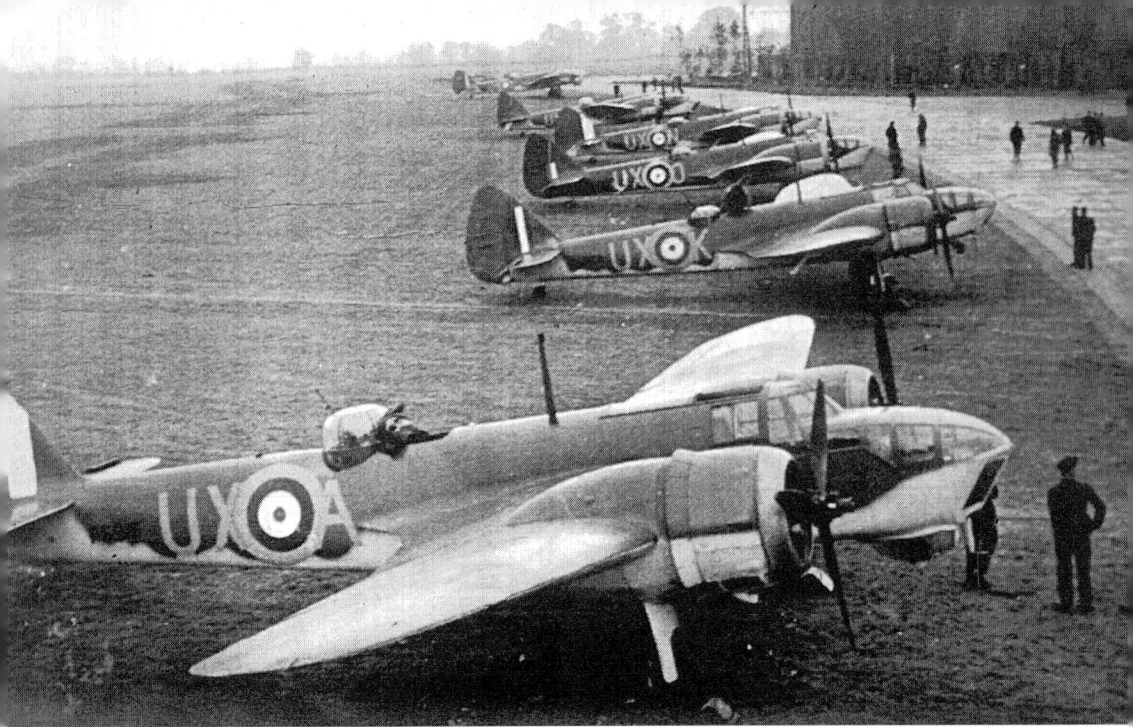

Blenheim IVs of 82 Squadron at RAF Watton photographed by Sergeant 'Bish' Bareham from the Watton watch office. On 7 June 1940 Sergeant A. E. Merritt and P6915 UX-A (which had one of the first rearward-firing nose guns) returned to Watton so badly shot up by Messerschmitt 109s that it was declared beyond repair. Note the asphalt applied to the grass behind the Blenheims to simulate hedges. Merritt was KIA six days later. (*Wartime Watton Museum*)

body. I was torn from my grip of the rib, dashed against the ceiling of the fuselage and down again two or three times, until with a scraping and rending the battered machine came to a halt. All was curiously quiet. Here let me pay tribute to Johnny's grand show in landing that crippled machine on that rough and steeply sloping grassy stretch in the Ardennes without so much as scraping a wing tip, though of course the propeller tips and bomb doors were buckled. The possibility of the kite firing spurred me in my opening the hatch and scrambling on to *terra firma*, over which I stumbled for twenty yards or so, followed by Johnny and Sergeant Broadland until my injured leg refused to carry me any further and buckled beneath me. I fell to the ground, weak, sick and exhausted but with that triumphant feeling of exhilaration that only those who have passed through the Valley of Death and survived can ever know.

Outhwaite's Blenheim came down in woods to the west of Givonne in the Ardennes to the north of Sedan. Jack Bartley was hospitalized at Reims, Epernay and finally Bordeaux, and was operated on to remove the bullets from his body. On 11 June Outhwaite was KIA. Bartley was evacuated to England on 21 June, the day France fell. In all, 114 Squadron lost four out of six crews to Bf 109s of I and III./JG53. Of the twenty-eight sorties flown by 21, 107 and 110 Squadrons into the Sedan sector in the evening of 14 May, six of the Blenheims, including five from 110 Squadron, were shot down by Bf 109s of III./JG2 and I./JG53 and Bf 110s of II./ZG26.[3]

On 15 May twenty-four Blenheims were despatched to attack communications and bridges in Belgium. Three aircraft of 40 Squadron, piloted by Wing Commander

E. C. 'Kekki' Barlow, Flying Officer J. E. Edwards and Sergeant Higgins, bombed a bridge at Dinant and were then attacked by Bf 109s, which broke up their formation. Barlow's gunners fought off the fighters but Edwards' and Higgins' crews were never seen again. Blenheims from 15 Squadron also bombed the bridge, approaching from 10,000 ft and diving to 5,000 ft before releasing their bombs. Pilot Officer Harrison's aircraft was hit by flak and he was forced to crash-land in Belgium.

At 0400 hours on the morning of 17 May twelve crews of 82 Squadron gathered in the briefing room at Watton to be told to attack an enemy column near Gembloux. Their expected fighter escort did not materialize and they ran into a severe flak barrage, which split up the formation, allowing Bf 109s of 1./JG3 to attack with great effect. *Oberfeldwebel* Max Bucholz claimed four Blenheims destroyed. Only one, flown by Sergeant A. F. 'Jock' Morrison on one engine and shot to pieces, got back to Watton, the rest being shot down. The squadron was now non-operational but the Commanding Officer (CO), Wing Commander the Earl of Bandon (known to all as 'Paddy' and to some as the 'Abandoned Earl') made sure it was re-formed and it resumed operations just three days later. (Morrison was KIA on 13.8.40). Also on the 17th, three out of six Blenheims of 15 Squadron were lost during an attack on German troop concentrations and two were damaged beyond repair. By the end of this, the eighth day of the campaign, the RAF had lost 170 medium bombers.

On 18 May four Blenheim squadrons, 15, 21, 40 and 110, dispatched thirteen aircrews to attack enemy troops approaching Le Cateaux. No.15 Squadron, which contributed six aircraft and crews, quickly lost three Blenheims to Bf 109s of 3./JG2, while two aircraft were so badly damaged that they had to be written off back at Wyton. Next day the remnants of the RAF squadrons flew back to England, the remaining surviving personnel following by boat. On arrival at Watton, three crews from 18 Squadron volunteered to fly with 82 Squadron in a raid by forty-seven Blenheims on 20 May against a *Panzer* division which was threatening to encircle the BEF from the south. One of the 18 Squadron aircraft captained by Pilot Officer 'C' Flight was mistaken for a Ju 88 and shot down by a Hurricane.

On 22 May fifty-nine Blenheims attacked the German columns advancing to the French coast, and three were lost. Wing Commander Embry led 107 Squadron in an afternoon attack on troops closing in on Boulogne, hitting vehicles in the fields. The squadron mounted a second attack that day in the same area and Embry led a third with 110 Squadron, making a dual attack on a German headquarters (HQ) at Ribeaucourt. With darkness and fog at Wattisham, landings were made at Manston in Kent. On 23 May twenty-seven Blenheims were sent to bomb German troop concentrations south of Arras. Three, including one flown by the commander of 40 Squadron, Wing Commander J. G. Llewelyn, the second CO lost by the squadron in eight days, were shot down. The next day sixty-nine Blenheims attacked German troops surrounding the British garrison at Calais with no losses. On 25 May forty-two Blenheims bombed German troops and vehicles and vital bridges just behind the enemy front line, which was fast closing in on the main body of the BEF with their backs to the wall at the French coast. Four failed to return. On 26 May it was decided to evacuate as many troops as possible from Dunkirk, so operations were directed at supporting the beleaguered BEF forces around the town.

On 27 May, the day the Belgians surrendered, twelve Blenheims of 107 Squadron led by Wing Commander Embry flew into the expected curtain of flak *en route* to bomb German troop concentrations near St Omer. Embry was on his last sortie as CO of 107 squadron before handing over to W/C L. R. Stokes. Embry's Blenheim (L9391) was severely damaged and Corporal G.E. Lang DFM, his WOP/AG killed. Embry and Pilot officer T.A. Whiting DFC, his observer, baled out and Whiting was captured. Embry's loss was a shattering blow to everyone in the group. But the 'little ball of fire', three times captured but never made a PoW (the second time, unarmed, he fought his way out, then, with a 'borrowed' German rifle, killed three Germans), eventually returned to England by way of the Pyrenees, Spain and Gibraltar. He landed at Plymouth on 2 October after this epic journey and subsequently became involved in night

LAC Freddie Thripp, Flying Officer Harries and Sergeant Harold J W. 'Bish' Bareham, observer of 82 Squadron, early in 1940. On 11 March Squadron Leader Miles V. Delap of 82 Squadron with 'Bish' Bareham as navigator, sank U-31 in the Schillig Roads, thus becoming the first British pilot to sink a German submarine in the second World War. Bareham volunteered to go on the first aircrew decompression tests at Farnborough and on 1 April 1940 during his three-day' absence from Watton Sergeant H. H. Kelleway took his place when nine Blenheims of 82 Squadron were detailed to carry out a raid against enemy shipping off Denmark. Harries's aircraft, P8867, was hit by fire from four flak ships in the Heligoland Bight after bombing and Kelleway was KIA. Twenty-year-old Flight Sergeant Freddie Thripp survived fifty-five Blenheim operations in 82 and 110 Squadrons (the latter as gunnery leader). He was KIA when Wing Commander Theo 'Joe' Hunt DFC, CO of 110 Squadron, and crew flying from Malta were shot down by a Fiat CR.42 Falco biplane fighter off Tripoli on 18 July 1941. (*Wartime Watton Museum*)

fighting before making a tour of command posts in Operation Crusader in the Western Desert and in Fighter Command in England.

On the last day of May, as the evacuation from Dunkirk reached its climax, the Blenheims in East Anglia flew by far the greatest number of operations on any one day during the campaign. These missions were directed at enemy troops massing for an all-out attack on the evacuation area, and it was largely due to their efforts and those of RAF fighter pilots, that this attack was halted and the BEF could be evacuated so successfully. AC2 Jim Moore had

Sergeant D. R. C. 'Jock' MacLagan, a WOP/AG in 21 Squadron, has his photo taken in the pilot's seat of his Blenheim at Watton. Prior to take-off on 8 June 1940 Jock shook hands with a member of the ground crew to say goodbye. He had a feeling he would not be coming back. His premonition came true. From 7 to 13 June 1940 Blenheims of 2 Group attacked German troop columns and communications in northern France flying 355 sorties and losing twenty-three aircraft. (*Wartime Watton Museum*)

listened to the accounts of the 'Miracle of Dunkirk', during which the remnants of the British Army were rescued from the French beaches.

We had also been told of the magnificent efforts of the RAF in covering the withdrawal. It was, therefore, a sobering experience when on the train to Upwood I met some of the survivors from the Dunkirk beaches who made some very uncomplimentary remarks about the lack of air support that they had received. Neither they nor I had any idea how few operational aircraft were available to the RAF at that time.

Freddie Thripp, now promoted to flight sergeant in 82 Squadron, tried to explain it all in a letter home on 3 June.

Here we are all safe and sound. Boy, what a week I have had. From last weekend, I made eight raids in nine days, then a little rest and three times in 24 hours and they say that we have been harassing the movements of the enemy but believe me, they want three RAFs to stop that mob. My one fear is having to swim the Channel, as it is quite a way and there is rather a lot of dirty-looking oil floating about – it is a change to see the sea. It is all very well saying that the BEF are a fine lot of blokes but I should think they should know a Blenheim when they see one. They shot one of the other squadron's down, then apologised, after killing the observer; the other two are back now. We have one of our operators back and his observer and the pilot of my pal. He says that he did not feel much, as he was dead before the machine fell to pieces. And two officers have returned a while before and one observer. It is nothing unusual now to hear guns blazing away on the coast. If only you knew what the Gerrys [Sic] have been doing round this district in the flat parts for quite a while before war started and the AM has only just realised it and what panic it would cause if released. . .

Overall losses of Blenheims now totalled at least 150 aircraft, roughly equivalent to nine fully established squadrons. They had been thrown into the Battle for France without any clear idea of how to conduct their operations, and had experienced many bitter lessons from which they had learned a great deal. Now they maintained better formations, operated at more appropriate heights, either low level or at heights that made the task of the anti-aircraft (AA) gunners more difficult, and they were afforded more fighter support. On 5 June, for example, enemy supply columns were bombed by twenty-four Blenheims of 107 and 110 Squadrons, followed the next day by 15 and 21 Squadrons, which with fighter escort bombed four railway bridges over the River Seine without loss. On 9 June, however, eighteen Blenheims of 107 and 110 Squadrons, with fighter escort, lost two to flak while bombing enemy troops in the Forest of Boray, near Poix. Twelve Blenheims were lost over three days in support of the beleaguered 51st Highland Division, who were aiming for the sea at St Valery-en-Caux. Battles flew their last major daylight operation on 13 June, when forty-eight bombed German troop concentrations for the loss of six aircraft. During June Blenheims began a new phase of operations by bombing *Luftwaffe* airfields, and losses began to rise again.

In July the twelve Blenheim squadrons of 2 Group lost thirty-one aircraft in action, with three written off because of battle damage and four in accidents. One of them was flown by Flight Lieutenant Bill Keighley, one of twelve despatched by 82

Blenheim IV R3800 UX-Z of 82 Squadron hidden beneath the trees at Great Wood, Bodney during the summer of 1940. Flown by Flight Lieutenant T. E. Syms, R3800 failed to return on 13 August 1940 when it was hit by flak and fell blazing into Limfjord, 50 yards offshore by Aalborg See, the *Luftwaffe* seaplane base at Aalborg. Sergeant Wright survived, but Sergeant F. V. Turner was killed. (*Wartime Watton Museum*)

Squadron to the oil refineries at Hamburg that day. Lack of cloud cover forced Keighley to divert and bomb Leeuwarden airfield instead but Bf 109s of II./JG27 based at the Dutch airfield intercepted him over the Friesian coast. *Leutnant* Herbert Kargel opened fire before Keighley could reach the safety of a cloudbank and killed his gunner, Sergeant Keith MacPherson. Keighley crash landed in a cornfield on Texel Island and he and Sergeant J. W. H. Parsons, his observer, scrambled to safety and were taken prisoner. It was Kargel's sole victory of the war, which he survived.

During July three wing commanders, fifteen other officers and forty sergeants were killed and losses continued on operations in August. On 1 August the Blenheim flown by Pilot Officer John Goode of 114 Squadron was shot down by Bf 109Es of 4./JG54 from Flushing with no survivors. The next day, when thirty-six Blenheims were sent to bomb *Luftwaffe* airfields in Germany and the occupied countries, 4./JG54 claimed another. Sergeant John Davies had just made a successful attack on

Blenheim IV YH-D of 21 Squadron at Watton. The early Blenheims carried a rather ancient VGO .303 in. machine gun in a dorsal turret, which was fed from circular ammunition pans, each of which contained 100 rounds. Spare pans were clipped onto the side of the turret. Initially the upper gunner was usually a lowly AC1, AC2, LAC or corporal. The rank depended on his trade rank as a wireless operator. (*Wartime Watton Museum*)

Haamstede airfield when *Leutnant* Malischewski shot him down. There were no survivors. On 19 August *Unteroffizier* Richard Woick of 7./JG54 from Bergen shot down the Blenheim of 114 Squadron piloted by 19-year-old Sergeant Kenneth H. Dobb, which crashed in flames in Middenbeemster.

The *Luftwaffe*, however, did not have it all its own way. On 28 July Sergeant Beeby, the WOp/AG in Wing Commander E. C. de Virac Lart's Blenheim shot down a Bf 109E of II./JG27. On 2 August Sergeant Reg Bassett, the gunner (who had had no gunnery training) in Sergeant George Parr's crew from 18 Squadron who were flying their first operation, shot down a Bf 109 flown by *Hauptmann* Albrecht von Ankum-Frank of 5./JG27, who was killed. This *Geschwader* also lost three Bf 109s on the ground during an attack by 110 Squadron Blenheims on 1 August.[4] However, because of the recent high losses it was decided to withdraw most of the Blenheims from daylight operations and to employ them in night attacks, initially on the Channel ports in support of the Hampdens, Whitleys and Wellingtons of Bomber Command.

After brushing up their gunnery skills at Squires Gate aerodrome, near Blackpool, on 12 August Jim 'Dinty' Moore, now a sergeant, was posted with his crew to 18 Squadron at RAF West Raynham in Norfolk. Sergeant Roger Speedy was 'a very competent pilot who came from Worcester' and Sergeant Bob Weston, from Coventry was 'an extremely good navigator'. Squadron Leader Deacon, 'a rather reserved, fatherly figure', was in charge of 'A' Flight, to which the crew were allocated. Like every other, 18 Squadron had been badly mauled in France, losing nine aircraft and their crews during the month of May. Personnel had arrived in England in just the clothes they stood up in and, with only three Blenheims left, they had finally decamped to West Raynham in June, where the painful task of rebuilding the squadron was taking place. Jim Moore and his crew were unaware of the

Shirt-sleeved fitters carry out a double engine change to a Blenheim IV at Bodney on a warm summer's day in 1940. Between July and September 1940 seventy-eight Blenheims of 2 Group were lost in raids using cloud cover and under cover of darkness on enemy barges and ports prior to Operation *Sealion*, the planned German invasion of Britain. (*Wartime Watton Museum*)

appalling losses being suffered. They also had no idea that the 'powers that be' had decided that most of the squadrons in 2 Group were to go over to night operations. 'Dinty' was acutely aware that he had just fifty-six hours day flying and just three hours and fifty minutes at night under his belt.

In anticipation of the expected invasion of England by the Germans, the following battle order was issued: 'Attacks will be pressed home regardless of cost. Each aircraft should aim to hit one vessel with one bomb and machine-gun the enemy whenever possible. Squadrons equipped with gas spray are to be ready to operate with this at the shortest possible notice but it will only be used as a retaliatory measure.'

Until the threat of invasion receded, as soon as an aircraft returned from an operation it was immediately rearmed and refuelled ready for take-off. Ground crews were also immediately available, some staying near the aircraft for twenty-four hours a day, while aircrew were kept on stand-by.

At Watton on Tuesday, 13 August, a bright clear day, twelve crews of 82 Squadron were briefed to attack Aalborg airfield in Denmark, occupied by Major Fritz Doensch's Ju 88s of I./JG30, which were making sporadic raids on Scotland and northern England. (The *Luftwaffe* flew 1,485 sorties on a day that would go down in their history as *Adler Tag* (or 'Eagle Day'). The Blenheims were to be used as bait to stop fighter *gruppen* moving westwards to join the mass attacks on 11 Group's already beleaguered airfields. They were also to forestall raids by *Luftflotte* 5 on the northern sector stations. The squadron was under no illusions: it would be a one-way trip. The target was at the extreme limit of the Blenheims' range and pilots were told that if they used their 9 lb of boost to evade fighters, the best they could hope for was to head for Newcastle and put down as near as possible to the coast.

At 0845 hours Wing Commander E. C. de Virac Lart DSO led 'A' Flight off from Watton, while 'B' Flight took off from the Bodney satellite field. Pilot Officer Donald M. Wellings' crew gained an eleventh-hour reprieve when, taxiing out, they were recalled because their posting had just come through! Pilot Officer E. R. Hales'

Blenheim IV R2772 UX-T of 82 Squadron lies wrecked in the sea off Aalborg on 13 August 1940 following the disastrous operation that cost eleven of the twelve Blenheims dispatched from England. Incredibly, Sergeant W. Greenwood WOP/AG, and Sergeant D. Blair, pilot, were only slightly injured. After the crash, Sergeant W. I. Q. 'Bill' Magrath, observer was found barely conscious floating on his back held up by his Mae West. Magrath spent a year in hospital before he escaped from a PoW camp at Rouen late in 1941 and after crossing the Pyrenees in the depths of winter in January 1942 he eventually reached England and was awarded the MM. He lost his flying pay (which he would have kept had he remained in PoW camp) when he failed a medical! (*Wartime Watton Museum*)

From left Sergeant Don A. W. McFarlane, observer, Pilot Officer Donald M. Wellings and Sergeant Peter K. Eames, WOP/AG in front of Blenheim IV R3821 NU-X of 'B' Flight, 82 Squadron at Bodney, a satellite of RAF Watton, Norfolk, in the summer of 1940. The crew were plucked from the jaws of death on 13 August, when, at the eleventh hour, they were pulled out of the twelve-ship formation while taxiing out, to be told that they were posted! Pilot Officer E. R. Hale, Sergeant R. G. Oliver and Sergeant A. F. Roland, who took their place and flew in R3821 were one of the eleven crews who failed to return from the catastrophic operation to Aalborg, Denmark (they crashed on Aalborg airfield and all the crew were killed). Flight Sergeant Eames DFM was KIA during a shipping strike on Schiermonnikoog on 26 April,1941 when he was serving with the crew of Wing Commander George A. Bartlett DFC of 21 Squadron. Pilot Officer Wellings DFC, who flew a second tour on Mosquitoes (see Chapter 9), was killed on 9 October 1944. Flight Lieutenant McFarlane DFM retired from the RAF in 1947. (*via Theo Boiten*)

crew took their place; they would not return. Over the North Sea the two formations veered slightly off course, taking them many miles south of their intended landfall. At this point Sergeant Baron decided that he would run short of fuel if he continued and he aborted (he was subsequently court-martialled but found not guilty). Unfortunately the formation had been identified and its intention correctly deduced. Flak batteries were alerted and eight Bf 109Es of 5./JG77 from Stavanger-Sola, which had just flown an escort mission, landed at Aalborg, refuelled and were in the air again as the Blenheims approached. Five Blenheims were shot down by flak then, led by *Oberleutnant* Friedrich, the *Staffelkapitän* of 5./JG77, the Bf 109Es attacked the survivors, shooting down five of them between Kaas and Pandrup. Sergeant John Oates survived but was hopelessly low on fuel and badly damaged, so he turned around and crash landed in a field. Oates, Pilot Officer R. M. N. Biden, the observer, and Sergeant T. Graham, the gunner survived, although Oates had a fractured skull, a broken back and both his legs were paralysed. In all, twenty of the thirty-three

Blenheim crewmen (including Lart) were killed and were later buried in the cemetery at Vadum with full military honours.

Despite the Blenheim crews' best efforts, three days later, on 15 August, fifty Ju 88s of KG30 from Aalborg attacked Driffield, Yorkshire, and from 25 August I./JG77 formed the nucleus of the IV *Gruppe*, JG51, being redeployed to St Omer in the Pas de Calais. In 2 Group over the next two years there would be many braver, yet futile, ventures like the attack on Aalborg and often the sacrifices made by Blenheim crews would be just as great.

Luftwaffe ground crew replenish ammunition at Rordal airfield following the successful action by eight Bf 109Fs of 5.*Staffel* JG 77, which shot down five of the eleven 82 Squadron Blenheims lost in the operation to Aalborg, Denmark, on 13 August 1940. Only one Blenheim returned to Watton. (Ole Rønnest via Jorn Junker)

CHAPTER TWO

The Night was Evil

The night when you went in low, the moon was grey,
Like an old nun's face a-dying,
And the wind was high and shrilling
Calling for the day,
Moaning for the day, because the night was evil
And intent for killing.

'Derek' by Flight Lieutenant Anthony Richardson RAFVR

On 16 August 1940 Jim 'Dinty' Moore, in 18 Squadron at West Raynham, looked at the battle order.

There were our names at the top of the list of six crews detailed to fly on operations that night. I don't know about Roger and Bob but I do know my feelings were a strange mixture of excitement and apprehension. This was it, this was what we had been preparing for and above all there was a feeling of expectancy. Time almost seemed to stand still though eventually we were called to the Operations Room where there was a buzz of conversation as we awaited our briefing. Behind a raised dais was a curtain which was unveiled, after the CO took his place to reveal, not surprisingly, a map of Western Europe indicating that our target was the *Luftwaffe* aerodrome at De Kooy in Holland. After the CO's opening address, the Met Officer gave us his weather forecast including details of the winds we could expect which were so important to the observer. It was then the turn of the intelligence officer to advise us about known anti-aircraft concentrations and so on. The actual course to and from the target was left to the individual crew as we shared the skies over Western Europe throughout that winter with a limited number of Wellingtons, Whitleys and Hampdens, which represented the heavy bombers of the RAF. Those of us who had the privilege of flying in the Blenheim developed a real affection for these machines.

This was the first time the squadron had operated at night so it was a new experience for all concerned. We were due to take off at 9 p.m. During the evening we got our flying gear together, emptied our pockets of any item, which might be of interest to the enemy and as we would be flying at heights of up to 10,000 ft, put on sufficient clothing to keep warm. The minutes ticked slowly by until the flight truck was ready to take us out to the dispersal point where our aircraft '*L-Leather*' was waiting for us. She was still painted with daylight camouflage although the underside of the wings were later painted a non reflective black. The ground crew fussed around, making sure everything was in order, whilst we climbed in, Bob and I stowing our parachutes and settling into our positions. I switched on the radio and we conversed in the intercom to make sure it was working. Roger started up the engines in turn, revving them up to a healthy roar, to make sure they were in order. At a signal from him, one of the ground crew removed the chocks from the front of the landing wheels. We then taxied out to the boundary fence, turning into wind to await our signal to take off. On seeing the signal from our flight controller Roger revved up the engines again before releasing the brakes, when we started to move, gaining speed as we headed across the field until we lifted off over the far hedge. Roger flew back over the aerodrome before turning on to the first course Bob had given him, gaining height as we flew towards the coast. It was still daylight and looking down at the fields, houses and villages, they seemed to assume a special significance. I still felt the thrill of flying but this was something new, an adventure which for us was into the unknown. What exactly was waiting for us on the other side of the North Sea? As I looked back at the coast of Norfolk I couldn't help wondering if I would ever see it again.

We droned on over the sea, gradually losing height on the course dictated by Bob, as the daylight faded. My responsibilities were to search the sky for enemy night fighters and to listen out on the radio in case there were any messages for us. I had, after checking with Roger, fired a short burst from my machine gun, once we were over the sea, to make sure it was working satisfactorily. In due course I heard Bob say we could see the Dutch coast and we were making our correct landfall. Turning the turret around to look ahead I could clearly see the coastline in the moonlight just as if I were looking at a large map. Our arrival had not gone unnoticed and soon we could see the beams of searchlights probing the sky looking for us accompanied by bursts of inaccurate flak. The light flak was multi coloured, rather like some of the rockets on bonfire night, whereas the heavy flak bursts left ominous looking small black clouds.

Bob had given Roger a new course in crossing the coast so we were now heading for the target, where, we hoped to dish out treatment to the *Luftwaffe*, in the same way they had been bombing our aerodromes in East Anglia. On the final run up to the target Roger kept the aircraft in a straight run responding to Bob's instructions: 'Steady – steady – left – steady' and so forth until I heard him say, 'Bombs Gone!' Our aircraft lifted, relieved of the weight of our four 250 lb bombs. It had been, as it always would be, an uncomfortable few minutes on the bombing run, as there was no question of taking evasive action to avoid the flak and we were at our most vulnerable. Having delivered our bombs, feeling very relieved' we turned onto another course for home. To my surprise, I saw the silhouette of a single engined fighter in the moonlight behind and slightly above us. It was the accepted policy to avoid combat with fighters if possible so, resisting the natural temptation to open fire, I gave Roger directions to take evasive action and we soon lost him. This brief encounter made me appreciate how absolutely vital it was for me never to relax and to keep searching the sky.

We crossed the Dutch coast, heading for home, when Bob asked me to get a radio fix so I contacted the wireless station at Bircham Newton, near Hunstanton. On receiving an acknowledgement, I was required to press my Morse key for a few seconds, during which time two ground stations took bearings on our position. Where these two bearings crossed fixed our position on the map and the operator sitting comfortably on the ground supplied these details to me. I passed on this information to Bob who could then check if we were on course or whether we needed to make any correction. Soon I heard Bob say he could see the coast of Norfolk and shortly afterwards he asked me to contact the operator at West Raynham to get a bearing which would give us the course which would take us home. I must confess to feeling rather pleased with myself for getting the necessary information on my radio on this, our first operational flight.

Finally, we could see our aerodrome identification letters being flashed in Morse code from the beacon near the field and on the ground the lights of the kerosene lamps which had been lit on the edge of the runway to guide us in. Roger made a perfect landing, taxiing to our dispersal point where our ground crew was anxiously waiting to greet us. It was a marvellous feeling to climb out of the kite, feeling stiff, after a flight of three hours and fifteen minutes but we had really made it; were now an operational crew. No sooner had we left the aircraft than the ground crew were refuelling and bombing it up again, a practice which was to continue until the threat of invasion faded. We were looking forward eagerly to our first operational breakfast of bacon and eggs in the sergeant's mess, which no doubt would be accompanied by a great deal of excited conversation going on over the events of the night but first we had to attend debriefing. We gave the Intelligence Officer details of the operation. He was particularly interested in the fighter I had seen. We then discovered that we were the only aircraft which had been on operations as the trip for the other five crews on the Battle Order had been cancelled after we became airborne!

During August 2 Group lost twenty-eight Blenheims and eight were damaged beyond repair. 'Dinty' added:

The squadron dispatched 62 aircraft on operations, losing four aircraft and their crews, none of whom we had the opportunity to really get to know. During the latter part of the month we moved our squadron's aircraft to a temporary aerodrome at Great Massingham, three miles from West Raynham, to spread our aircraft to minimize the damage that could be caused by attacks from enemy bombers. Apart from the landing field, there were none of the buildings one found on a permanent 'drome, only a few Nissen huts. It was necessary, therefore, to find accommodation for us in the lovely little villages of Great Massingham and Little Massingham, which adjoined the airfield. They were so close, in fact, that the roofs of one row of cottages were damaged from time to time by the trailing aerials of Blenheims when the WOp/AG had forgotten to wind them in as, of course, he should have done before coming in to land. The larger village of Great Massingham was built around two large ponds and a village green and had two or three public houses, which were to be popular with one and all. The problem of accommodation was solved by literally taking over both villages, the Sergeants' Mess being housed in a rather dismal, rambling old vicarage in Little Massingham. Another building was taken over as a theatre, dance hall or church as required, another as our Operations Room and so on. On 9 September leaving 101 Squadron to the delights of West Raynham, all air and ground crews followed our aircraft and moved into whatever accommodation had been found for us.

On 1 September at briefing we were informed that we were to make our first visit to the Ruhr, the industrial heart of Germany. The Met Officer advised us that the weather would be clear all the way to and from the target. At 2130 hours we took off as planned, climbing steadily to our operational height of between 10,000 and 12,000 ft, droning steadily along the North Sea. At the Dutch coast we were flying over a pretty solid bank of cloud, which rendered their searchlights useless, although some bursts of flak lit up the sky. Roger flew on in the faint hope of finding a gap in the cloud through which Bob could identify our target. We stooged around for ages without any luck before turning for home. Finally, in the region of Schiphol in Holland, we at last found a gap in the cloud through which a bunch of searchlights did their best to latch on to us. Not wishing to take our bombs home Bob lined up the aircraft on to the source of this nuisance and dropped our full load on them. We flew into cloud again and our true position became a matter of guesswork so the radio fix I was able to obtain from Bircham Newton was particularly helpful. We found our way back over the North Sea and were looking forward to touching down at Massingham when I received a signal informing us that due to the weather this was not practicable. We were directed to Honington, not far from Massingham, the home of a Wellington squadron where we were thankful to land after being in the air for four hours forty minutes. We were made very welcome and were able to get a little sleep before flying home.

Within a few days after the fall of France, the Germans started moving hundreds of barges, each 300 ft long, along the canals of Western Europe towards the North Sea and the Channel ports. These enormous barges were essential to the invasion force, which they intended to land on the shores of our

Sergeant Sid R. Merrett, air gunner, Pilot Office Frank Metcalfe, pilot and George Martin, observer, of Blenheim IV *The Crocked Jerry* in 82 Squadron pose cheerfully for the camera at Bodney in September 1940. On the night of 10/11 November, while returning from a bombing raid, the crew ditched in the North Sea after running low on fuel in a gale. Merrett perished but Martin managed to pull the badly injured Metcalfe into a life raft. They were picked up by HMS *Vega*, a navy minesweeper, which then hit a mine and sank. An ASR craft from Felixstowe picked them up and Metcalfe survived, spending several weeks in hospital. Sent home on rest and recuperation, the train he was on crashed, killing 16 people! (Wartime Watton Museum)

embattled island. These concentrations of barges were to be the focus of the attention of all the squadrons in Bomber Command during September. As a nation we were preparing, within our limited resources, to prepare a welcome for these unwanted visitors. On the squadron we were briefed as to the type of attacks we would be required to make on German naval vessels and troop carrying craft. We were also advised that, should the invasion take place, we would be moving to an aerodrome near Exeter. The Germans had, either installed, or seized from the French, some heavy naval guns at Cap Gris Nez on the French coast, which had formed the unpleasant habit of shelling shipping passing through the Straits of Dover and the town of Dover itself. We made three trips in August-September to bomb these guns and followed with attacks on barge concentrations in the ports of Dunkirk, which we visited three times, Flushing, Boulogne, Ostend and Calais. On these trips, which took approximately three hours, the defences were very alert with large concentrations of searchlights and pretty spectacular displays of anti-aircraft fire. We only trusted we were doing the maximum amount of damage to these barges, which represented such a threat to our island.

On one of these trips it was still daylight when we clambered into our aircraft to prepare for take-off. Roger hadn't started the engines when the anti-aircraft gunners on the 'drome opened fire at some low flying Junkers 88 medium bombers who were paying us a visit. Roger and Bob shot out of their hatch like corks out of a bottle whilst I, hampered by heavy clothing, followed a poor third to take refuge under a heavy log. Not very heroic, although, with the engines switched off my turret couldn't be operated, so I was unable to fire at the intruders who flew on to West Raynham where they dropped their bombs inflicting little damage. During the month the squadron flew 127 sorties with thankfully the loss of only one aircraft and crew.

At the beginning of October the weather was less kind to us and a number of operations had to be cancelled. In fact the squadron flew only fifty-one sorties. Roger, Bob and I did, however, make another visit to Cap Gris Nez on 8/9 October followed by an attack on the docks at Boulogne on 12/13 October. By now the Battle of Britain was over and the immediate threat of invasion had receded, at least for the winter, so the efforts of Bomber Command could be directed at targets of industrial importance in Germany. Without wishing to take anything away from the heroic efforts of our fighter pilots during the Battle of Britain, one should not disregard the efforts of the crews of Bomber Command. As a whole, bombing the ports and concentrations of barges was a persuasive argument to the German High Command in postponing their plans to invade the United Kingdom.

We now had more spare time and while Fakenham and King's Lynn were within easy reach, the most popular venue was the beautiful city of Norwich, thirty miles away. A number of us would share a taxi to spend the evening doing what came naturally. Norwich had already been the subject of attacks by German bombers both by day and by night, though at that time it was still relatively undamaged. After one such low-level attack carried out in daylight, 'Lord Haw-Haw', in his English broadcast from Berlin, informed us that the crews involved in this raid had reported that the clock on the city hall was slow.

At 2240 hours on 24 October, in accordance with the Command's new policy, we took off for an attack on the railway yards at Haltern in the heart of the Ruhr. It was a trip that lasted for four hours and five minutes and we found that the Germans had been very busy improving their defences. The concentration of flak was not only heavy over the target area but at intervals all the way from the Dutch coast. Nevertheless, we were able to deliver our bomb load on schedule – everything, including the weather report, going according to schedule. We had been warned that German intruders were attacking our bombers as they were coming in to land after operations. It was, therefore, evident the WOP/AG could never afford to relax from searching the sky at any time during an operation. The only time I wasn't doing so was when it was imperative to use the radio to get a fix or a bearing. [Three days later, on 27 October, Massingham and West Raynham were indeed raided by German intruders. Three aircraft thought to be Ju 88s attacked three times, dropping ten bombs which destroyed one Blenheim and damaged eleven others, although these were soon repaired. Four personnel were killed and seven injured; three seriously].

Our next operation was on 29 October. On this occasion our target was another railway yard, this time at Krefeld, in the Ruhr or, as it was popularly known, the 'Happy Valley'. It was identical to our attack on Haltern and we returned 'in one piece' after a flight lasting three hours and fifty minutes. Many aircrew returning from operations over Western Europe were forced to ditch in the North Sea, where some of the more fortunate ones, were able to get out alive and climb into their inflatable dinghies. On the 31st we were briefed to fly at low-level over the North Sea, in daylight, searching for any aircrew who had managed to survive in this way and were awaiting rescue. We took off at 10.55 a.m. flying to within sight of the Dutch coast, feeling very much alone and searching the area, which had been allocated to us. It seemed strange to be operating in daylight, over a sea, which looked both cold and cruel without, sadly, having any success. We landed back at Massingham after a flight, which had taken us three hours and twenty minutes. It was at least comforting to know should the same fate befall us we would not be forgotten and there was a chance of us being rescued. There can be no figures to say how many aircraft and their crews were lost due to faulty weather forecasts but there must have been many of them.

The first three operations in November took place in weather which, much to our surprise, was as predicted by our Met Officer and we were able to identify and bomb the targets allocated to us. On 5/6 November our target was the oil works at Antwerp, 7/8 November the Krupps armament factory at Essen and on 10/11 November, the docks at Le Havre. As the weather became colder the 'boffins' came up with a variety of bright ideas to make life easier for us aircrew. One, which applied to all of us, was what we would call 'Wakey-Wakey' tablets. We took one tablet before take-off and another in flight and these were supposed to help us stay alert. This was fine, except on occasions when, having taken the first tablet the operation was cancelled and you were unable to go to sleep. Another idea, was a tot of rum on returning from an operation to 'help the circulation'. We were also encouraged to eat plenty of carrots, which were supposed to improve our night vision and to take a variety of capsules for the same reason. We were also issued with flight rations of which, barley sugar was the most popular.

The WOP/AG had the coldest position in the aircraft, with temperatures down to ten degrees below zero, so they devised a woollen lined leather suit, with electrically heated gloves and boots. They worked very well although they were so cumbersome you felt as if you were dressed for deep sea diving and made it especially difficult to operate a wireless set. Whenever possible, rather than wear this outfit we wore three pairs of gloves, the first silk, the second wool and the third, leather, thick woollen underwear, flying suit and boots with thick woollen stockings.

On 13 November we were briefed for another trip to the Ruhr, so at 0210 we took off and headed for the continent following our usual plan in climbing steadily as we crossed the North Sea. On our arrival over the Dutch coast we encountered dense cloud, over which Roger managed to climb, keeping to the course Bob had worked out for us. We flew on and on searching, in vain, for a gap in the clouds through which we could identify the target. Finally, we did find a small gap in the clouds, through which we could see some searchlights on which we dropped our bombs, although where exactly these were is doubtful. We finally turned for home flying over mountains of enormous white clouds, passing between some of them as if we were flying through a valley and watching the sunrise, which was truly beautiful. Wandering about over Western Europe in daylight was not to be recommended and we watched the sky anxiously in case any *Luftwaffe* fighters had managed to find their way up through the cloud. We were beginning to wonder where the cloud would end when well out over the North Sea on our way home we left it behind. I was able to raise the wireless station at Bircham Newton where the operator provided us with a fix for which Bob was more than usually thankful. Arriving over the Norfolk coast I contacted West Raynham and obtained the necessary bearing to get us home.

By the time we were coming in to land we had been in the air for five hours 45 minutes and Roger was so very weary he must have allowed his concentration to lapse because we landed very heavily. The undercarriage collapsed and we skated merrily across the airfield before coming to a stop. There was always a risk of fire in these circumstances, although we could not have had much fuel left, so we wasted no time in getting out, more than thankful we had dropped our bombs somewhere over Germany. The fire tender and sundry ground crew were quickly on the scene and seemed rather frustrated to find us all in one piece. Thankfully, there was no fire and the aircraft was soon repaired and back in action. Sitting in one position in cramped conditions, subjected to the severe cold, the noise and smell of the engines, never able to relax and ever conscious of the dangers of flak and enemy fighters, made great physical demands of all three of us. But this was especially true of the pilot. There was no automatic pilot, so there was no opportunity for him to relax. We managed to get some sleep before spending an hour carrying out some take-offs and landings, which was the usual practice, after this kind of incident. Despite this bumpy landing Bob and I had complete faith in Roger and would not have wanted to fly with anyone else.

In the early afternoon of 14 November, as 437 *Luftwaffe* crews prepared to raid Coventry, 18 Squadron at Great Massingham, 105 Squadron using Wattisham as their base, 101 Squadron at West Raynham and 110 at Horsham St Faith were briefed for a counter-operation called *Cold Water*. Plans for the large-scale attack on Coventry were known in advance because of *Ultra* intelligence but the knowledge had to be kept secret from the Germans so no additional measures were taken to repel the raid. However, squadrons from 2 Group were directed to attack aerodromes from which the enemy bombers were operating, in order to cause as much disruption as possible, and the heavies would simultaneously retaliate against a German town. That night, as the *Luftwaffe* devastated the city centre of Coventry with 56 tons of incendiaries, 394 tons of HE and 127 parachute mines, killing 380 people and injuring 800 seriously, thirty-five Blenheims were despatched to bomb airfields in northern France and Belgium. 'Dinty' Moore recalled:

At our briefing we were instructed to attack the aerodromes at Flers and Lesquin spending some time over their airspace to deter them from using their landing lights. At 1910 hours it was our turn to take off. We were soon climbing away from the airstrip and turning onto course. On this occasion the weather was exactly as predicted, so despite the attention of the anti-aircraft gunners and searchlight operators, we were able to find both aerodromes. We stooged around for a while without seeing any signs of activity, before dropping our bombs and turning for home. We certainly hoped we had been able to dissuade some of the bombers from taking off to deliver their bombs over our country. In a similar attack, during November, on the *Luftwaffe* base at Melun our Pilot Officer Reg Buskell made two attacks from a relatively low level causing a great deal of damage. He was awarded the DFC, the first 'gong' to be given to a member of the squadron since our arrival. This attack is another illustration of how the route to and from the target and the manner of attack were, at this stage of the war, generally left to the individual crew.

All the Blenheims, including one flown by Sergeant Edgar Costello-Bowen of 105 Squadron, who had an engagement with a Heinkel He 111 returned safely. Costello-Bowen was one of nine 105 Squadron crews, part of a counter-operation involving fifty-six twin-engined aircraft (mainly Blenheims but also Wellingtons and Whitleys) who were briefed on the afternoon of 15 November to attack returning German night bombers over their airfields at Antwerp and Brussels. Bad weather, however, prevented all but five Blenheims from taking off and only four attacked Dieghem airfield. Flying Officer D. Murray DFC and Sergeants C. D. Gavin and T. Robson were killed when their Blenheim was downed by intense flak and the aircraft exploded in a fireball. The crew had returned from a raid on Etaples on 25 October on one engine after the propeller and reduction gear on the starboard engine fell away over the French coast. On that occasion Murray had managed to land safely at Deboler.

'Dinty' Moore recalled:

The attack on Coventry seemed to me to bring about a change of policy for the bombers of the RAF, who up to that point had generally been instructed to aim for targets of industrial or military importance. In our case, at our briefing on 16 November we were initially briefed to bomb the docks at Hamburg. Later, we were recalled to the briefing room to be directed to drop our bombs on the city itself. War in the air is impersonal but in the case of Bob and others from Coventry, or other English towns which had been bombed, they may well have felt differently as their families and friends were likely to be killed. In their case could you blame them if they felt this was an act of retaliation although, to be fair to Bob Weston, he never spoke about it in this way.

At 1905 hours we took off on this operation, which was to last for four hours twenty-five minutes, against a target which was particularly well defended. The city being on an estuary was relatively easy to find, although the reception we received by way of flak and searchlights was pretty impressive. Bob picked up the target on to which he directed Roger, the seconds ticking away like hours as we flew straight on the bomb run, before these magic words, 'Bombs Gone!' and we were able to take some evasive action. Following this operation we were granted leave. My brother Peter was still at home, though he was eagerly awaiting his call-up into the RAF as an electrician.

On the night of 26/27 November eight crews of 105 Squadron were dispatched to Cologne. Six aircraft got their bombs away before the weather deteriorated and one Blenheim returned with engine problems before reaching the target. Pilot Officer L. T. J. Ryan RNZAF arrived back late at 2325 hours and was given permission to land but flew off at low altitude towards the aerodrome beacon at Foxley Wood near the airfield where the Blenheim crashed and burst into flames. Ryan and Sergeants S. W. Slade and R. Meikle were killed. Sergeant Edgar Costello-Bowen, meanwhile, was above dense cloud and completely unable to find Swanton Morley. Looking for a gap in the cloud, he finished up near Liverpool, 200 miles away! He flew around desperately calling for help until there was no fuel left. Finally he, Sergeant Tommy J. Broom and Sergeant Cameron baled out at Harrup Edge near Stockport while the Blenheim flew on to crash at Mottram in Longdale on the eastern outskirts of Manchester.[5]

During December operations were again curtailed by the weather. The targets, both airfields and industrial areas, were often blanketed by low cloud. 'Dinty' Moore takes up the story:

On return to Massingham we were soon in action again, our first operation being on 6 December when we took off at 2325 to attack and disrupt the *Luftwaffe* aerodromes at Harkamp and Rotterdam. Apart from dropping our bombs we loitered around over these aerodromes for some time in order to prevent their use. We landed back after a flight lasting three hours forty minutes hoping we had caused the German bombers as much discomfort as possible. Two days later [8/9 December] it was back to the 'Happy Valley' with an attack on Düsseldorf, where we found the defences had been greatly improved, as they had at all targets in Germany. At one stage we were caught by the searchlights, which is a terrifying experience, feeling like a fly caught in a spider's web.

Roger, by changing height and direction, was able to shake them off and we were able to bomb the target. On our way back to Massingham Bob asked me to get the usual fix but when I went to let out the trailing aerial I found it was missing. Thankfully, the weather was being kind to us and Bob was pretty confident of our position so he was able to manage with the assistance of some bearings I was able to get from the wireless station at West Raynham. As always, we were thankful to touch down at Massingham after a flight which, on this occasion, had lasted four hours twenty-five minutes.

During our flights to targets in Germany the intelligence 'boffins' at Air Ministry had found us an additional pastime. This was to act as 'litter louts' scattering propaganda leaflets across the countryside, advising the Germans they ought to make peace. In order to drop these leaflets it was necessary to open the escape hatch and some of my friends hit on the idea of dropping empty beer bottles at the same time. On the night of 11/12 December, as a spot of light relief, we made yet another trip to bomb our old friends, the heavy naval guns at Cap Gris Nez, an operation that went off without incident. A tour of operations was thirty trips. This was our 27th together so we were looking forward to a rest. Nevertheless, having got this far one began to feel rather anxious, hoping your good luck would continue. On 21 December at 0320 hours, when all good people should be in bed, we took off and headed once again for the Ruhr to an oil refinery at Gelsenkirchen. We need not have worried for everything worked perfectly, being able to bomb, returning and landing at Massingham at 0730 as it was becoming light.

On 22 December we attended what was to be our last briefing together, although we were not to know this at the time, when we found our target was to be the railway yard at Wiesbach. Again we took off at 0315 hours for an operation which was to last for five and a half hours. There were the usual searchlights probing the sky and the bursts of light and heavy flak along our route and especially over the target but our luck was in and having bombed the target, we flew back over the Dutch coast unscathed. Returning over the North Sea it was becoming daylight and we felt very exposed although no enemy fighter appeared on the scene.

During our partnership we had flown nearly 100 hours in completing our 28 operations. During that time we had suffered no battle damage, had always dropped our bombs and found our way back to base even though, on one occasion, we were directed to land elsewhere. Many were less fortunate, some of these suffering from inaccurate weather forecasts, for example, one crew were so far off course they landed at Acklington, north of Newcastle, instead of East Anglia. Another crew having flown over continuous banks of cloud across the North Sea first saw land over Norfolk when the observer believed he was over Holland. Further, he would not accept the wireless bearings obtained by his WOp/AG as being correct until they found themselves over the Irish Sea. Being concerned, those of us who had already landed were in the wireless station at West Raynham listening to the exchange of signals. They finally landed at an airport near Liverpool, with about enough fuel to fill a cigarette lighter left in the tanks. This crew was taken off operational flying, the only one to come out of the incident with any credit being the WOp/AG. These are just two of the many examples of the problems which faced Bomber Command during the winter. On the 28th we were briefed for another operation and I duly put on my flying suit in readiness for take-off, although I was feeling far from well, going alternately hot and cold. Thankfully, the operation was cancelled and the next morning my friends sent for the squadron medical officer. He diagnosed pneumonia and I was duly despatched by ambulance to the RAF hospital at Ely. I felt terrible and had hardly any recollection of the journey or of my first few days in the hospital.

In my absence Roger and Bob, without flying on any further operations, were told that their first tour was over and they were to be posted 'on rest'. This was the term used to describe the periods between operational tours, which, normally, would be duty as an instructor. However, in their case they were to go to Takoradi in West Africa where they were to fly Blenheims, as they were delivered by sea, across the African continent to our forces in Egypt. Apart from being an unpleasant place to fly from, it was a really hazardous duty as it meant flying over wild and uncivilised country where they could ill-afford to force land. We had no opportunity to say goodbye nor have I met them since but I sincerely hope that they both survived the war. Roger was a truly competent pilot, ideally suited for the type of operations in which we had been engaged, whilst Bob was a first class observer and I was truly sorry we had to part company. However, whilst I hardly enjoyed my period in hospital, someone up there spared me from this distinctly unpleasant duty in Africa.

Bad weather dogged operations in England throughout December and although operations were briefed every day only a handful of sorties were flown. When they were losses were incurred. On 11/12 December Flight Sergeant P. R. Richardson and crew of 105 Squadron were killed when they were shot down at Zedelgem near Bruges. On Christmas Eve Wing Commander Cyril K. J. Coggle, the CO of the squadron, had to hand over command to Squadron Leader Arnold L. Christian (a relative of Fletcher Christian of *Bounty* fame) after fighting against a persistent recurrence of an old illness. Christian, who had previously been an instructor at 13 Operational Training Unit (OTU) had very little luck with the weather during his first month as CO. On the night of 27/28 December a Blenheim flown by Squadron leader M. L. C. McColm of 21 Squadron was shot down by light flak at Gilze-Rijen. The observer and gunner were killed but McColm survived and became a prisoner in the infamous Colditz Castle. On the last day of the month a Blenheim of 114 Squadron flown by Sergeant Leslie Young was also downed by light flak at Gilze-Rijen and exploded on impact at De Moer, killing all three crew.

The Blenheim squadrons continued flying night operations during the bitterly cold days of January and February 1941. On 10/11 February the largest raid yet mounted by 2 Group took place when 222 bombers, including thirty-four Blenheims of 18, 21, 105, 107 and 110 Squadrons, took off to attack U-boat factories at Hannover. Flight Lieutenant Peter Simmons DFC of 107 Squadron became completely lost when his wireless transmitter (W/T) failed after flying for six hours and he had to crash land. Meanwhile German intruders were active over eastern England. Squadron Leader J. S. Sabine, for example, was coming in to land, his mission completed, when he was attacked by an intruder and forced to crash land. At Bodney, Sergeant A. Chatterway was circling the aerodrome awaiting his turn to land when his aircraft was shot down, killing him, seriously wounding his observer, Pilot Officer Cherval and wounding his WOp/AG, Sergeant Burch in the leg.

Blenheims again figured in Bomber Command attacks on Germany on the night of 14/15 February when twenty-two (and twenty-two Wellingtons) were dispatched to Homberg. Only sixteen aircraft claimed to have bombed the target, an oil plant but there were no losses. Homburg was the target again the following night, 15/16 February, when thirty-seven Blenheims of 18, 101, 105 and 107 Squadrons in 2 Group (and thirty-three Hampdens) participated in the Main Force attacks. There were no losses. On 23/24 February seventeen Blenheims and thirty-five Wellingtons were despatched to Boulogne but the Blenheims were recalled early.

The next major raid involving Blenheims was on the night of 28 February/1 March, when seven aircraft of 139 Squadron carried out dusk raids on harbours in Holland and France and 116 Blenheims, Hampdens, Wellingtons and Whitleys tried to bomb the battleship *Tirpitz* in Wilhelmshaven harbour. Seventy-five crews claimed to have bombed Wilhelmshaven, but the *Tirpitz* was undamaged. Two of the 139 Squadron Blenheims collided on their return but both aircraft landed safely at Horsham St Faith. Sergeant Vivian, the pilot of one, was badly hurt and one of his crew later died of his injuries. Returning from Wilhelmshaven a Blenheim of 105 Squadron flown by Sergeant John S. H. Heape was shot down over Holland by a Bf 110 night fighter flown by *Oberfeldwebel* Paul Gildner of 4./NJG1 at Oosterhogeburg near Groningen. Heape survived to be taken PoW but his observer and WOp/AG were killed.[6]

At the beginning of March 'Dinty' Moore returned to Massingham after recuperation, having been declared fit for flying.

During my absence 18 Squadron had suffered from bad weather, which had limited them to twenty-nine operational sorties in January and forty in February (compared with the 127 we had flown the previous September). During March the situation was not much better, thirty-three sorties having been flown, with, sadly, the loss of one crew. Not being part of a crew, I felt very much the odd man out, even though there were a number of new faces. Then for some reason a WOp/AG in one of the crews was taken off operational flying and I was elected to take his place. I could not have been more fortunate because the pilot, Sergeant George Milsom, who hailed from Coningsby in Lincolnshire, had a natural flair for flying, coupled with courage and the ability to be decisive in combat. His observer, Sergeant Ron Millar, a New Zealander, turned out to be very competent and both of them were easy to get along with. They had joined the squadron shortly before I was admitted to hospital and had, so far, flown six night operational flights. We became known as 'The Three Ms' (Milson, Millar and Moore). I was now about to share in what, I believe, was the most exciting period in the life of the aircrews of 2 Group.

CHAPTER THREE

Ramrods and Circuses

The high sky was the amphitheatre, in the arena were the Blenheims;
all around them were the Gladiators – British and German fighters.

Eric Atkins DFC* KW* (Kryz Walecznych 'Cross of Valour')

On 6 March 1941 Churchill made a decision that was to have a far-reaching effect on the lives of the crews of the Blenheims based in the UK. The Battle of the Atlantic was causing a great deal of concern, with the U-boats taking a heavy toll of Allied shipping, so Bomber Command was now to concentrate on naval targets. The role of the Blenheims of 2 Group and the Beauforts, Lockheed Hudsons and Blenheims of Coastal Command was to harass, damage and as far as possible destroy communications between east and west by sea in daylight. Although naval patrol boats were out every night looking for enemy shipping, the navy could hardly undertake this task in daylight without running an excessive risk from aerial bombardment. German shipping habitually sailed close to the enemy coastline, where the *Luftwaffe* could readily bomb any ships or submarines that attacked its convoys, as they had already demonstrated.

The Air Officer Commanding (AOC) 2 Group, Air Vice-Marshal Donald F. Stevenson DSO OBE MC, was ordered to see that any enemy ship putting to sea between the Brittany peninsula and the coast of Norway should be sunk, irrespective of the cost. The cost proved to be considerable. The manner in which the campaign was to be carried out was to break down the whole length of the enemy coast into 'beats'. The formation of Blenheims would fly at wave-top height to the 'start line', which would be approximately 30

The only way a Blenheim crew could successfully attack a ship was to approach from wave-top height, lift to clear the masts, and either land the bomb on it or skim it along the surface of the sea to explode against its side. The attack would last for a matter of seconds but all too frequently with fatal results for the bomber crew. (*Wartime Watton Museum*)

41

miles from the coast, from where they would fly towards the coast at specified distances apart, depending on the weather conditions. On reaching a point 3 miles from the coastline they would turn at right angles and fly for three minutes parallel to the coast before turning for home. The order was to sink the first ship sighted, or indeed any ship in the 'beat' area.

The Blenheim had hardly been designed for this type of operation. The only way it could successfully attack a ship was to approach from wave-top height, lift to clear the masts of the ship and either land the bomb on it or skim it along the surface of the sea to explode against the vessel's side. Within weeks of the opening of this campaign, enemy convoys were always escorted by heavily armed motor patrol boats, so, with the combined AA armament of all the ships in the convoy, the bombers had to fly through an enormous concentration of fire. The attack would only last for a matter of seconds, but all too frequently had fatal results for the bomber crew.

Low-level flying is always a risky pastime, demanding absolute concentration on the part of the pilot, while over the sea this becomes even more hazardous in hazy conditions when it is very difficult to judge height above the water. Because low-level flying was to become a major feature of the life of Blenheim crews during that summer, over land it meant keeping as low as the contours of the ground would allow, having to lift over trees, telegraph wires, electricity pylons and so on.

These operations against shipping opened on 12 March 1941 when five Blenheims of 139 Squadron attacked a convoy of four ships, losing one aircraft. Two days later Wing Commander W. E. Cameron of 107 Squadron was more fortunate in bombing and sinking a 2,000 ton ship off Norway (Cameron and his crew were lost off the coast of Norway on 6 April). On the 23rd it was the turn of 82 Squadron. They found a convoy of five ships, including a destroyer, off the Ems estuary, which they attacked and claimed to have damaged. The squadron carried out its second shipping sweep the next day when, in attacking another convoy, it lost its first crew in this campaign. These sweeps continued daily. On the 29th, during an attack on a 5,000

A low-level attack by a Blenheim IV of 21 Squadron on a six-ship convoy in the Heligoland Bight on 30 July 1941 captured on film by the WOP/AG, 'Steve' Stephens, using a hand-held Leica camera. Operations against shipping opened on 12 March 1941 but the Blenheim had hardly been designed for anti-shipping strikes and losses on these operations were high. (*Wartime Watton Museum*)

ton tanker off Flushing, which was surrounded by six patrol boats, the Blenheim flown by Wing Commander George Bartlett DFC was very badly damaged. Showing great skill and determination Bartlett managed to bring the aircraft home on one engine. On 31 March the crews of 82 Squadron reported a very successful attack on a convoy of six ships off Le Havre, during which they left a 3,000 ton tanker ablaze.

At this stage a new operation, known as the 'fringe attack', was introduced. Fighters were given 'fringe targets' if no enemy aircraft came up. They were split roughly into three sections: 'Close Encounter', to protect the Blenheims, 'High Wave', to mass for attack at 20,000 ft and 'Withdrawal', to protect the Blenheims on return. Military targets could be found a few miles inland from the enemy coast, which was very convenient although they were also in the most heavily defended areas. It was now decreed that 'in order to cause alarm and to embarrass the enemy air defence system' transport columns, vehicles, troops, guns, searchlight emplacements and so on should be attacked from low level. These operations could be the objective or, having flown a shipping 'beat' and found nothing to attack, the crews would be directed to cross the coast to bomb any suitable target.

Flight Sergeant Freddie Thripp of 82 Squadron, who was by now fast approaching fifty operations, in a letter home on 19 March, described operations at this time.

We have been leading the attacks on those fire blitzes and what a time too! One night we got down low to miss the fighters, then we got a bit off course and found ourselves in the centre of Antwerp. Then a few hectic moments, a wide circuit. Then we found ourselves below the roofs of Brussels. After that Ghent, eventually coming out in the Channel, with somebody jamming our D/F station but we got back OK . . . We got back into camp yesterday and in the evening we were away again and as usual first on one of their northern ports and what a do. We have been there before, so we knew the easiest way in but after watching a nice, or a lucky, shot in amongst the buildings around the docks, one of their searchlights got us then about a dozen lit us, then hell was let loose and so were we. We were at 12,000 ft, then when the machine gun stuff started coming up. My driver just managed to find our altimeter and pulled out at about 4,000 ft and just about shook them off and was I glad. . . '[7]

On 31 March, in accordance with 2 Group's new 'beat' decree, Squadron Leader L. V. E. 'Atty' Atkinson DSO DFC led eight crews of 21 Squadron, having been briefed to attack ships off the Dutch Friesian Islands and to open the campaign against 'fringe targets'. He proved to be one of the most courageous and resourceful leaders in 2 Group. They certainly had beginners' luck for it proved to be a most successful foray over enemy territory. First of all they found two destroyers which they bombed, one being hit on the stem, whereupon a black column of smoke belched forth. Not content with this success, they flew on over the islands, skimming over the ground and disrupting a parade of German troops, which they sprayed with machine gun fire. Still they flew on, shooting up guns, more troops, pillboxes and a radio station, before Atkinson decided to lead his troops home. Their visit had not gone unnoticed, for their presence had attracted a great deal of flak, which, not too surprisingly, accounted for two of the Blenheims.

On 3 April Wing Commander C. G. Hill DFC took command of 18 Squadron in place of Wing Commander A. C. H. Sharpe (who took up a position at the Air Ministry) and moved it to Oulton, near the market town of Aylsham. Crew accommodation could not have been more different from that which they had enjoyed at Massingham, for they were now billeted in the beautiful Blickling Hall, the home of landed gentry since the time of the Domesday Book. 'Dinty' Moore recalled:

> One major improvement that had been carried out to the Blenheims during the winter was the removal of the single Vickers Gas Operated machine gun in the turret, which was replaced by two Browning .303 machine guns. These guns were fed not by pans of ammunition but by belts. My return to the squadron had coincided with a decision by Bomber Command that No 2 Group must adopt a much more aggressive role and there were to be no more night operations. On 10/11 April 1941 Blenheims of 105 Squadron flew the last 2 Group night operation, bombing targets at Cologne, Bremerhaven and Brest. Instead, we were to operate in daylight on tasks that came roughly under two headings. 1. Attacks at low level on enemy shipping close to the enemy coast, these shipping lanes from Norway to the Bay of Biscay being split into 'beats'. We would either be detailed to look exclusively for shipping or, on occasions, when no shipping was sighted, to cross the coast to look for and bomb suitable targets. 2. Low-level attacks on industrial or military targets on the Continent, sometimes using cloud for cover. Later (during May) we were allocated a further task, to operate in formation at heights of about 10,000 ft with fighter escort. These operations, known as *Circuses*, were to be flown with the primary objective of persuading the fighters of the *Luftwaffe* to attack us so that they could be engaged and destroyed by our escorting fighters. Similar operations, known as *Ramrods* were also to be flown where the target, rather than ourselves acting as the 'sacrificial lamb' was the primary objective.

The year 1941 would become known as 'the year of the Circus'. It was the aim to entice enemy fighters into the air and destroy them over France – perhaps with as

Blenheim *Q for Queenie* of 18 Squadron at Great Massingham early in 1941 Note the under bomb rack containing eight 250 lb bombs. *Q for Queenie*'s pilot was Sergeant Hawkins and the WOP/AG was Pilot Officer Charles C. Sherring. Jacky Crouch, a pre-war regular, was the original observer in the crew until he went on rest on 5 January 1941. Sherring became gunnery leader of 107 Squadron in July 1941. (*Mrs Vera Sherring*)

few as a 'box' of six Blenheims (the bait) and 103 British fighters from as many as nine squadrons (the hunters). The Blenheims were not only bait, as they also had a bombing target in the range of the fighter cover. The campaign actually began on 12 March, when one of the other squadrons in the group patrolling a shipping 'beat' along the Dutch coast sighted a ship of about 1,000 tons, which they bombed.

The Circus operation was not without some problems: it required a tight formation with no straggling, straight and level bombing on the leader, fighters and bombers being exactly at the right spot on the right time, and sorting out friendly fighters from enemy aircraft. Flying at 10,000 ft in broad daylight and attracting heavy flak, the Blenheims were wallowing around in the thinner air, far short of their best performance, wanting the enemy to come and attack but dependent on friendly fighters, which had limited range, to stop them.

By 12 April the Blenheims had flown 315 sorties and 121 ships had been attacked, of which six were believed sunk and eight damaged, with the loss of nine aircraft and their crews. On 15 April shipping strikes were flown against targets off France and the Friesian Islands and two ships were claimed sunk. Six Blenheims of 18 Squadron were attacked by Bf 109s off the coast of Holland and the Blenheim flown by Wing Commander C. G. Hill, 18 Squadron CO and his crew was lost without trace. On the afternoon of 18 April six Blenheims of 21 Squadron were dispatched on a shipping strike to Farsund, Norway, finding a well-defended convoy west of Stavanger escorted by Bf 110 *Zerstörers*. The Blenheims attacked and claimed to have set two vessels on fire. Pilot Officer H. K. Marshall was shot down by flak and crashed into the sea with the loss of all the crew. *Leutnant* Helmut Viedebannt of 8/ZG76 claimed Sergeant J. Dunning's Blenheim. A third Blenheim crash landed upon return. Six Blenheims of 107 Squadron were then despatched on a second anti-shipping strike, followed by four more from 114 Squadron. The 107 Squadron aircraft attacked at wave-top height into a wall of flak, which destroyed the Blenheims flown by Wing Commander Arthur M. A. Birch and Flight Sergeant Jack Hickingbotham and damaged a third flown by Sergeant Borwn, killing one of his crew. Wing Commander George R. A. Elsmie DFC led 114 Squadron in a dive-bombing attack on the convoy but *Leutnant* Helmut Viedebantt attacked and shot the Wing Commander's Blenheim down into the sea with both of its engines on fire. Viedebantt and *Leutnant* Tonne then shot down two Blenheims flown by Squadron Leader Augustine S. Q. Robins and Flight Lieutenant Thomas H. Myers RCAF.[8] One Bf 110 was claimed as 'probably destroyed' but the only German casualty was a Bf 109E flown by *Unteroffizier* H. Kind of I/JG77, who was killed by return fire from a Blenheim.

Forty per cent of the striking force had been lost and 82 Squadron were detached from 2 Group to help make up the losses, moving from Watton to Lossiemouth. On 19 April three crews of 18 Squadron, led by Squadron Leader H. J. N. Lindsaye, found a 7,000 ton freighter with a destroyer escort that was belching out what must have seemed to the attackers to be an impenetrable wall of flak. Undeterred, they ploughed in, delivering their attack from mast height and gaining hits on the freighter, which was soon listing and was firmly believed sunk.

Wing Commander G. C. O. Key took over command of 18 Squadron on 23 April. On the 24th a new and, if possible, even more dangerous tactic was introduced for the crews of 2 Group, known officially as 'Channel Stop', although those involved gave it a less complimentary title. The object of this particular exercise was to close the Straits of Dover to enemy shipping during daylight, leaving the motor torpedo boats of the Royal Navy to carry out the same exercise at night. The Blenheim squadrons would be based at RAF Manston; as soon as shipping was sighted they would take off and attack, accompanied by an escort of Spitfires or Hurricanes.

The first aircraft to be committed to this task was a flight from 101 Squadron, which waited at Manston for a report on shipping movements, supplied by fighters patrolling the Straits, which became known as 'Jim Crows'. On 28 April word came that there were some enemy trawlers off Calais and three of the Blenheims set off in pursuit with their escort. During the attack one of the Blenheims was shot down by the frightening firepower of the ship, though their escort drove off an enemy fighter that tried to intervene. The crews of 101 Squadron continued their role with varying degrees of success and casualties; for example, on 3 May, while attacking a small convoy off Boulogne, a 2,000 tonner was sunk off Ostend but two of the three crews were lost to flak. On 9 May, no doubt to the relief of those who had survived, the six surviving 101 Squadron crews flew their Blenheims back to their base at West Raynham to convert to Wellingtons in 3 Group. Meanwhile, 'Channel Stop' was postponed – but only for a while.

Not content with the variety of tasks to which the Blenheim squadrons had been committed, on 26 April six crews from 21 Squadron, led by the indomitable Squadron Leader 'Attie' Atkinson, flew out to Malta to study the feasibility of operating from that beleaguered island. The previous day was momentous for the crews of 18 Squadron, one of the crews finding a large merchant ship of at least 7,000 tons with an escort of motor patrol boats. A hit was scored on the ship, which caused an enormous explosion, while two of the escort vessels were bombed, a hit being claimed on one of them. 'Dinty' Moore takes up the story.

Having been involved in night operations, our squadron began a period of low-level flying exercises across the East Anglian countryside, preparing to make our contribution to this campaign. Flying low meant literally skimming over hedgerows, with telegraph and electrical wires proving to be quite a hazard, while flocks of birds were the cause of many accidents; collecting twigs and assorted greenery on the leading edges of the wings was commonplace. Compared with flying at medium or high level, when you were not conscious of the speed at which you were travelling, flying at low level was truly exciting and exhilarating, requiring total concentration by the pilot who could ill afford even to sneeze. Over the sea it was even more difficult, the sea and sky seeming to merge, especially if it was at all hazy. We also dropped practice bombs on the wreck of a ship lying just off the cliffs at Trimingham.

Our aircraft were now fitted with twin .303 Browning machine guns in the turret, fed by belts of ammunition. We WOp/AGs now felt we had something worthwhile to fight back with and we were to be given the opportunity to make full use of them. The black paint had been removed from the underside of the wings and replaced by a light blue to make us more difficult to find.

There were said to be five good reasons for us to fly at low level:

1. It was well nigh impossible for us to be picked up by German radar.
2. We presented a fast-moving target for German anti-aircraft gunners who would only have us in their sights for moments.
3. Enemy fighters could not attack us from below where we were most vulnerable.
4. Our camouflage was excellent, making it difficult for patrolling enemy fighters to see us from above.
5. We obviously had the opportunity to drop our bombs on the target with greater accuracy.

We were declared operational shortly after our move to Oulton and dispatched crews on the shipping patrols, though 'The Three Ms' had to wait. On 15 April our new CO, who had been with the squadron less than a month, with his crew, was shot down attacking one of the first convoys sighted. Flying at 200 m.p.h., skimming the waves, there was little hope of survival if the aircraft or the pilot was hit by flak. The casualties among the senior officers in the Group were to prove to be exorbitantly high.

On 25 April, a very pleasant spring day, we caught the flight truck up to the airstrip as usual but this was to be a day different from any that had gone before. We were called to the briefing room where we were briefed for a solo 'fringe beat' off the Dutch coast near Flushing. If we failed to sight any shipping, we could fly inland to search for a suitable target on which to unload our four 250 lb bombs, which had been fitted with eleven-second delay fuses. Once again there was that same mixture of excitement and apprehension I had experienced on the occasion of my very first operation in August 1940.

The minutes seemed to stand still as we waited our time for take-off. But finally it arrived and we taxied out and took off at 1848 hours, climbing to about 1,000 ft before setting course for the Norfolk coast. As soon as we were over the sea George brought the aircraft down to nought feet, our slipstream making a wake in the sea behind us. We flew on alone until the flat Dutch coast came into view, then turned north and flew parallel to the coast, searching in vain for any sign of enemy shipping. At the end of our area of search George turned the

Blenheim IV GB-X of 105 Squadron. Anti-shipping 'beats' during March-May 1941 continued to show scant reward for the high losses suffered. (*RAF*)

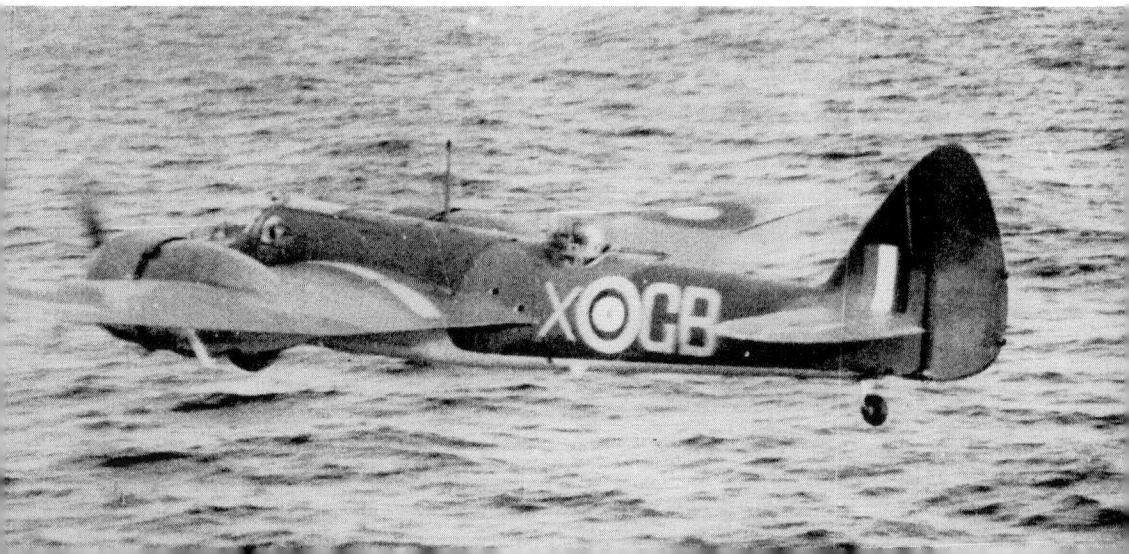

aircraft and headed for the land, where I felt the aircraft lift as we went over the sea wall like a steeplechaser. The countryside was very flat, not unlike parts of East Anglia and an old man on his bicycle looked up and gave us a cheery wave. We flew on undisturbed until we found ourselves on the outskirts of Flushing. Having found no other suitable target my colleagues decided to drop our bombs on the docks but just as Ron was pressing the bomb switch, George had to lift a wing to miss a derrick and the bombs fell on the railway line. This aggressive act was the signal for German anti-aircraft gunners to open fire with great enthusiasm to indicate their disapproval of our disturbing their evening schnapps or whatever.

They must have been pretty accurate, as they managed to knock two sizeable holes in our tail unit. George responded by 'putting his foot down', still keeping at nought feet and dropping down over a sea wall into an estuary that led to the sea. At one stage, as we were flying along the estuary, I was actually looking up at a German gun emplacement, which must have been infuriating for the gunners, who couldn't depress their guns sufficiently to fire at us whereas I was able to fire at them.

We headed out to sea expecting, but not receiving, the attention of the *Luftwaffe*, landing at Oulton after a flight lasting two hours twenty minutes feeling very pleased with ourselves. It had been a fairly exhilarating experience in which thrill had taken the place of fear – certainly an operation I will never forget. As well as being able to see what we were actually bombing and, in the case of the gun emplacement, to see the face of the enemy, gave a whole new meaning to the task in which we were engaged. It was such a marvellous contrast to the night operations on which we had flown the previous autumn and winter.

The following day, 26 April, six crews of 21 Squadron flew to Ameland, six of 110 Squadron went to Texel and twelve Blenheims of 82 Squadron operated off southern Norway. Between Schiermonnikoog and Vlieland 21 Squadron found a convoy of three 4,000 tonners, eight smaller ships and three flak ships. They put up a murderous hail of flak which shot down Wing Commander George A. Bartlett DFC, the CO, who was leading the attack, and the Blenheim flown by Sergeant Cyril Spouge, with the loss of all crews. North of Texel the 110 Squadron Blenheim piloted by Flight Lieutenant George Lings DFC was shot down by *Leutnant* Otto Vinzent of 3./JG54 with the loss of all three crew. The Blenheims of 82 Squadron attacked three cargo ships, while other crews were flying 'fringe beats' with varying degrees of success. Pilot Officer Ralph E. Tallis and his crew bombed and machine-gunned five Bf 110s on an airfield west of Sand, destroying one and damaging the others. He was joined by Sergeant Ted Inman and his crew and together they successfully survived a sixteen-minute battle with three 109s before escaping with only minor damage. (Flight Lieutenant Tallis DFC and his crew were lost on 29 April when 82 Squadron dispatched fifteen aircraft in a sweep off Sola, Norway. Pilot Officer D. White also failed to return. Sergeant Inman was KIA operating from Malta on 27 May 1941.)

'Dinty' Moore continued:

On the morning of 27 April we flew south to Chivenor in North Devon to refuel and to patrol a shipping beat off the French coast. At 1320 hours we took off again with five other Blenheims heading south until we reached a point 30 miles from the enemy coast, where we split up into three pairs to sweep a larger area. Our partner and we flew on until we were close to the coast, when we saw the telltale smoke of a small convoy of two merchant ships escorted by a patrol boat. There was no hesitation as we headed for our target, each aircraft heading for a different ship, George jinking our kite to present a more difficult target. We remained at nought feet until at the last moment George hauled us up just over the masts of our target while Ron dropped our bombs. As we hurtled over the top of the mast I found that I was looking up at the belly of the other Blenheim that had just bombed but fortunately we did not collide. We returned to nought feet immediately and I was able to fire several bursts at the unfortunate seamen who, together with the patrol boat, had sent up a terrific concentration of flak, through which we had to pass, without managing to hit us. As we flew away, looking back, I'm afraid I was unable to report any dramatic hits on our targets, though it must be remembered that the fuses on our bombs had an eleven-second delay. We called in at Chivenor to refuel, after a flight that had taken three hours fifty minutes, stopping about an hour before flying back to Oulton.

During the month one particularly successful shipping strike was carried out by the Commander of 'B' Flight, Squadron Leader Lindsaye, who found and attacked a 7,000 ton enemy vessel, gaining a direct hit and leaving it with a 35-degree list. Sadly, a few days later, on the 30th, he was flying a Blenheim locally on a test flight when the aircraft crashed, killing him and Flying Officer Frank Holmes. While we were saddened by the losses on operations, the impact was even greater when they died as the result of an accident.

On 3 May 18 Squadron moved, temporarily, to a new airstrip at Portreath near Redruth on the north coast of Cornwall. On the 7th 'Dinty' Moore's crew carried out a shipping patrol, within sight of the French coast, without seeing signs of any shipping. However, at the same time, in an attack on an enemy convoy, Squadron Leader Robert Bramston 'Binks' Barker (who had replaced Lindsaye) was shot down and killed. His observer, Sergeant Norman H. Meanwell, was a very good friend of 'Dinty', who had taken him to his home at Great Yarmouth to meet his wife Margaret and their baby daughter.

On 8 May six Blenheims of 105 Squadron, operating in pairs and carrying four 250 lb bombs each, set out to search for enemy shipping off Stavanger, Norway. Four Blenheim crews saw no shipping and returned to base but the first pair, flown by Wing Commander Arnold L. Christian and Pilot Officer Jack Buckley, found twenty ships forming up at the entrance to Hafrsfiord west of Stavanger. They made low-level dives on two merchantmen, one of which was an 800 ton flak ship, and raked the vessels with machine-gun fire from the front and rear guns. When last seen the first merchant vessel was down by the stern, billowing smoke high into the air. Christian's Blenheim was hit by flak and he was last seen 2 miles off the Norwegian coast with the port engine burning furiously. He crashed into the sea south of the entrance to Hardangerfjorden north of Stavanger. Christian, Flight Sergeant Harold

Squadron Leader Robert Bramston 'Binks' Barker, pilot of R3741 WV-X of 18 Squadron, which was shot down on 7 May 1941 after an attack on a cargo vessel. Barker, Sergeant Norman H. Meanwell, observer, and Sergeant V. Hughes, WOP/AG, were killed. (*Mrs Vera Sherring*)

F. 'Andy' Hancock, observer, and Sergeant G. Wade, WOp/AG, all perished. Buckley returned to Lossiemouth safely. The loss of Christian, with his skill, sense of fun, dry humour and superb airmanship, was a huge blow to the squadron that he had rapidly transformed to efficient daylight low-level operations. Just two days later, 26-year-old Wing Commander Hughie Idwal Edwards, an Australian of Welsh ancestry from Freemantle and CO of 139 Squadron, replaced him. At Horsham St Faith Wing Commander Edmund Nelson, on taking command of 139 Squadron with no experience of operational flying, found that the squadron had suffered from the losses of aircrew and had few experienced crews. However, there was one sergeant pilot who had almost completed his operational tour, so it was from this lowly officer that Nelson obtained most of his knowledge for his new command.

On 9 May 'Dinty' Moore's crew was more successful.

Patrolling off Brest we saw smoke on the horizon and as we approached we found a small convoy with the usual escorting patrol boat. We flew straight into the attack, following the same pattern as before, George doing his best to drop our bombs down the funnels of the merchantman. Quickly returning to sea level after the attack, I was again able to machine gun the decks of this ship and the patrol boat. Sadly we were unable to claim any direct hits, though we didn't hang around to find out. The concentration of flak was just as impressive but 'lady luck' was with us and we emerged unscathed. On our way back to Portreath, where we landed after a flight lasting three hours thirty-five minutes, we flew over the Scilly Isles, which, as we had climbed to a reasonable height, looked very small indeed.

The same afternoon, in attacking another convoy we lost one of the original pilots of the squadron, who had been a member at the outbreak of the war, Squadron Leader R. Langebear and his crew, Flight Sergeant A. K. Newberry and Sergeant I. R. Stone.

Wing Commander Hughie Idwal Edwards DSO* DFC, an Australian of Welsh ancestry from Freemantle, who assumed command of 105 Squadron on 10 May 1941 after the loss of Wing Commander Arnold L. Christian during a shipping strike off Norway two days earlier. (*RAAF Point Cook*)

[Langebear's Blenheim was last seen low over the sea with one engine on fire.] On the 12th those of us who had an aircraft that had not been damaged in the raid by the *Luftwaffe* flew away from sunny Cornwall to the grey skies of Oulton and the comfort of Blickling Hall.

The following day, in company with other members of the squadron, we took off to fly another shipping 'beat' but finding the weather most unfriendly we were back on the ground within one and a quarter hours. We were quickly refuelled and back in the air in a quarter of an hour to complete the patrol, without sighting any shipping, on a flight that lasted three and a half hours. On the 17th we took off at 1010 hours to fly another shipping 'beat', being in the air for three and a half-hours, doing our best to find a target but without success.

On 11 May 107 Squadron, commanded by Wing Commander Laurence V. E. Petley, a square-jawed, pensive and unassuming man known as 'Petters', arrived at Great Massingham from Leuchars, Scotland, where they had been based temporarily since March, attached to Coastal Command and flying shipping sorties. Although they had attacked two U-boats during April and had distinguished themselves in several shipping strikes and convoy escorts, the squadron had lost two COs, Wing Commanders J. W. Duggan on 21 January 1941 and W. E. Cameron, on 6 April.

No sooner had the Blenheim crews touched down and found their billets, in houses and country homes in the village, than they were on their way again, this time on a shipping strike off Heligoland on 13 May. Twelve aircraft were detailed to attack and they flew across the North Sea in line abreast, led superbly by leading navigator Sergeant J. C. 'Polly' Wilson RNZAF. Two Blenheims returned early with mechanical problems but the remaining aircraft went in at 200–400 ft and dropped almost 4 tons of bombs smack on the target. The attack was achieved with complete surprise and the Blenheims were safely away before the *Luftwaffe* could intervene. A congratulatory telegram arrived the same day from the AOC: 'Well done 107 Squadron - Stevenson'.

On 15 May twenty Blenheims flew anti-shipping sorties, attacking two convoys and claiming the sinking of two ships. Eight Blenheims on a shipping strike off Texel were bounced by Bf 109s of I./JG52. *Leutnant* Franz Bernhard attacked Pilot Officer J. F. T. Ogilvie's Blenheim and failed to pull out, both the bomber and the Messerschmitt crashed into the sea. *Unteroffizier* Strätling was credited with the destruction of a Blenheim but Squadron Leader Atkinson force landed at Copplestone, Exeter, without any injuries to his crew.

On 21 May 107 Squadron once more went after shipping at Heligoland. The Blenheims roared in at 50 ft, the prevailing good visibility unfortunately ensuring that there could be no element of surprise. As the formation drew level with the coast the gunners opened up in an attempt to swamp the enemy defences but they were immediately enveloped by bursts of heavy flak. Flight Sergeant Kenneth Wolstenholme's Blenheim was hit and he left the scene as fast as he could with one engine on fire and 'Polly' Wilson dead at his position. Another Blenheim was forced to ditch and would almost certainly have been picked up by the Germans if it were not for the actions of Sergeant J. R. G. 'Roy' Ralston. He turned back, climbed to 1,500 ft and sent out a distress signal in plain language, giving the position of the ditched crew who by now had taken to their dinghy. Air Sea Rescue (ASR) rescued everyone except Flight Sergeant D. J. R. Craig, who drowned. Ralston was awarded the DFM for his action.[9] Wolstenholme (who became famous after the war as a BBC sports commentator) made it back to Massingham, where 'Polly' Wilson was laid to rest in the lovely country churchyard close by the airfield.

Shipping sweeps continued on 22 May but 105 Squadron made only one attack, in poor visibility on a 1,000 tonner without result. On 24 May ten Blenheims of 110 Squadron were despatched to hunt for German shipping along the Friesians. After an attack on a convoy off Borkum Bf 109s of I./JG52 intercepted the bombers and *Leutnant* Karl Rung of 2./JG52 shot down Pilot Officer Michael A. Scott's Blenheim 72 miles north-west of Texel. A 21 Squadron Blenheim was damaged by flak while *Oberleutnant* Carganico of I./JG77 shot down a 114 Squadron Blenheim piloted by Sergeant J. McWilliam off Norway. 'Dinty' Moore of 18 Squadron, commented:

On each shipping patrol, you took off with your desire to find a convoy to attack, which you knew would be defended by a murderous curtain of flak, fighting with your natural desire to stay alive. You would fly alone or in company mile after mile over an empty cruel-looking sea searching continuously for an elusive target. If your search was successful, or unsuccessful, dependent on your point of view, the whole action would be over in a matter of moments. I submit that the manner in which this campaign was carried out in aircraft ill suited for the task showed a high degree of courage and determination on the part of the crews involved. Cannon-firing fighters later made such attacks and Beaufighter strike wings, some carrying torpedoes and others fitted with cannon, both of which were extremely successful.

On 25 May, a beautiful Sunday afternoon, we were briefed to carry out a low-level attack on a seaplane base on the island of Nordeney in the Friesian Islands off the north-west coast of Germany. The raid was to be carried out by eight Blenheims, five from our squadron and three from another [105 Squadron] in the Group. The raid was to be led by Squadron Leader Johnny Munro, a man for whom we had the highest regard. On the ground he had a slight speech impediment, whereas in the air he was articulate, decisive and a born leader. The plan was to fly to a point north of Nordeney and to approach the target from that direction with the intention of confusing the defenders.

We taxied out and took off at 1355 hours, one behind the other, forming up into three Vic formations with ourselves as No.2 to Munro. We crossed the Norfolk coast before coming down to sea level, settling down on to a course that would take us to the point where we would turn for our run into the island. It was a beautiful sunny day with excellent visibility and one couldn't help wondering what the folk at home would be doing on this Sunday afternoon. We knew it was to be a long flight, during which we would be constantly on the alert, searching for any sign of either ships or enemy aircraft. During operational flights we were required to keep radio silence so as not to give our position away to the enemy. So when we changed course to head for Nordeney, we could only make frantic signals to our leader to indicate that I had seen the smoke of a convoy on the horizon. On this occasion the land target was our main priority so, although there was the risk of an alert wireless operator on the convoy notifying the defenders on Nordeney of our approach, there was little choice but to carry on. Finally the island came into view, with a heavily armoured German patrol boat directly in our path, which we could have avoided. However, as if that wasn't enough, patrolling over the island were five Me 109F fighters [of I./JG52] who were obviously a welcoming committee we could have done without.

It is stating the obvious to say that 'our cover was blown' so our fears of an alert wireless operator reporting our approach were justified. Whatever Munro might have decided as to whether or not to carry on with the raid, the matter was decided for him as the three aircraft from the other squadron turned inside us and headed west with the rest of us in hot pursuit. We kept close together for our joint protection, jettisoning the bombs, giving the engines full boost and keeping as low as possible. The fighters wasted no time in mounting an attack and the sea bubbled and foamed as bullets and cannon shells churned up the water. There was no time for fear as we fought back, firing as the fighters came into range. There was the stench of cordite from my guns, then a perspex panel in my turret blew out so I felt as if I was sitting in a hurricane. I could see that the WOp/AG in the aircraft next to us had been hit and there was blood all over the back of his turret. One of our formation, obviously hit, crashed into the sea and disintegrated but this success did not satisfy the enemy, who still came in to attack, though one of the fighters, obviously damaged, with its undercarriage hanging down, finally withdrew. After what had seemed like an eternity, the others flew off, either due to lack of ammunition or fuel. I found I had no ammunition left for one gun and only ten rounds for the other.

At the conclusion of the engagement one Blenheim piloted by 'Tich' Thorne, who had joined the squadron with me had been very badly damaged to such an extent that I doubted if he would make it back to base. We were unable to stay with him, as we had to limp home with damage to both wings and the tail. We landed at our parent 'drome, Horsham St Faith after an operation that had lasted four hours. We had not been on the ground for many minutes when we saw another Blenheim, which was obviously in some difficulties, coming in to land. The pilot successfully landed and as the aircraft taxied towards us we could see that it was so badly damaged it looked like a sieve. Miraculously it was 'Tich' Thorne and his crew, none of whom, despite the enormity of the damage had received a scratch. We now made enquiries to find out 'who had got the chop'. We were told that they were Flight Sergeant David Keane, pilot, Sergeant George 'Jock' Duffus, observer, and Sergeant Ian Gow, WOp/AG.[10] The dead WOp/AG was Sergeant Eric Lloyd, who had flown with Pilot Officer P. G. C. Wilson and Pilot Officer Ernest K. Aires, observer.[11] This had been a bad day for the squadron as 'B' Flight had lost another Blenheim crew that morning in attacking a convoy off Denmark.[12] It is difficult to describe one's feelings after the loss of so many friends, for while we mourned their loss, we could not suppress a sense of elation at having survived. The only way you could carry on and retain your sanity was no matter what, you believed that you would be the one to get back.

Also that day in Beats 8 and 9 two small forces of Blenheims of 105 and 139

Squadrons respectively had been sent to patrol Ameland and Texel. Three of 105 Squadron's Blenheims attacked two 6,000 ton and one 4,000 ton merchant ships and hits were observed on all three. Twenty miles away and only three minutes later, another 4,000 tonner was attacked by another crew but without visible result. Intense light flak was met during all attacks and Messerschmitt Bf 109Es attacked 105 and 139 Squadrons. North of Texel 19-year-old Pilot Officer George E. J. Rushbrooke's Blenheim was shot down by *Unteroffizier* Bodo Nette of 1./JG1, probably from Bergen, and the stricken Blenheim was last seen flying toward Ameland. Rushbrooke, who the previous year had scored a century for Harrow against Eton at Lord's, Sergeant Eric Green, observer and Sergeant S. Parr, WOp/AG, all perished. During an attack on a convoy west of Texel Sergeant George A. Bye's Blenheim in 139 Squadron was hit by flak and he crashed into *Sperrbrecher Silvia*, which burned out and sank. The Canadian pilot and his two crew died in the wreckage.

Despite the continual losses June 1941 would see the continuation of the search for shipping, 'fringe attacks' and Circuses, and deeper penetration of enemy territory using cloud cover when it was available. On Thursday, 6 June, undoubtedly because of the recent high loss rate, Prime Minister Winston Churchill visited West Raynham to deliver a morale boosting speech to crews in 2 Group. Addressing them in the manner of a commander-in-chief before Agincourt or in the Crimea, his words were akin to 'once more unto the breach' although he gave reasons for their sacrifice. 'Winnie', as he was popularly known, aware that the offensive had to be maintained despite the cost, wanted to inspire them for the battles that lay ahead, as Jim 'Dinty' Moore, now a flight sergeant, recalled.

Aircraft were lined up for inspection by the great man and two crews of each of the squadrons in the Group arrived to take part in this special occasion. In addition to the Bristol Blenheims there were Short Stirling, Handley Page Halifax and Flying Fortress I aircraft and the twin-engined Avro Manchester. These aircraft, with wing spans of nearly 100 ft, looked enormous beside the Blenheim with its wing span a mere 56 ft. 'Winnie' appeared, accompanied by members of the Government and sundry senior officers. He mounted some steps used for the inspection of aircraft engines and invited us to gather round him. We did with alacrity. During his speech he referred to 2 Group as his 'light cavalry'. In his address he began by reminding us that 43,000 civilians had been killed in air raids on Britain in the previous twelve months and that his promise that the RAF would retaliate by day and by night had not yet been fulfilled. He had come personally, he said, to explain the importance of the special tasks we would be undertaking in the next few weeks, when our operations were likely to have a major impact on the course of the war. He then gave us some more unpalatable facts. German intervention in the Middle East was turning the war against us in that theatre. 'Germany must be forced to move her fighters westwards,' he told us. So, escorted by large numbers of fighters, we would attack targets in the West that Germany would have to defend. Our purpose was to relieve pressure on other fronts and to ease the stranglehold on our lifelines. 'I am relying on you,' were his closing words. There is little doubt that the personal visit of this determined individual with his magnetic personality was greatly appreciated by all of us who were present. He made us feel that the

Prime Minister Winston Churchill flanked by Air Vice Marshal Sir Richard Peirse, C-in-C Bomber Command (right) and Group Captain Paddy Bandon, station commander (left) visits West Raynham on 6 June 1941. AOC 2 Group, Air Vice Marshal Donald F. Stevenson DSO OBE MC is second from left, while behind Churchill (left to right) are Air Chief Marshal Sir Charles Portal, Professor Lindemann and Clement Atlee, Deputy Prime Minister. (*Mrs Vera Sherring*)

operations in which we were involved were well worthwhile. The great man made a second visit to the Group shortly after Germany attacked Russia on 22 June. On this occasion he reiterated his determination to carry the war to our enemy in every possible way in order to assist our new Allies.

In reality the *Luftwaffe* had no need to return fighter units to western Europe because the 250 fighters of *Jagdeschwader* (JG) 2 and *Jagdeschwader* 26 already in France and Belgium were considered adequate for operations in the west. Churchill's visit however, was a morale boost, which crews badly needed. Losses had become so bad that the mood among them, while determined, became grim – so much so that at Massingham one evening Flying Officer Ewels observed that after a particularly hazardous operation 'the Wing Commander and other 107 Squadron pilots in the mess sat for a long time in silence and then quietly got out notepaper and wrote out their wills. Not long afterwards all were gone.' Flight Lieutenant Anthony Richardson put it into words very succinctly when he penned 'Address to the Mother of a Dead Observer':

> *'Madam, this war is scarcely of my making – Why pick on me?*
> *I'm sorry about Jack.*
> *There was a gunner and a pilot, too, Who won't come back. . .'*

CHAPTER FOUR

Churchill's Light Cavalry

And you who trod the clouds – Oh! great of heart! –
And you who laughed beneath the shadow of death –
And you who toiled that other men might live –
Oh! getting on in years and short of breath!
'Recompense 'by Flight Lieutenant Anthony Richardson RAFVR

June 1941 began badly, with four frustrating missions, none of which were completed owing to the weather, and the Met officer bore the brunt of the crews' frustrations. On 7 June Blenheims of 2 Group flew twenty-two sorties searching for shipping from the Frisians to Norway. Nine crews in 107 Squadron were briefed to take part in a raid on a heavily defended convoy *en route* from Hamburg to Rotterdam. One was captained by Pilot Officer Bill Edrich, the famous England and Middlesex cricketer, who had joined the squadron on 31 May along with his observer, Vic Phipps and his WOP/AG, Ernie Hope. Squadron Leader Peter Simmons DFC, who was flying the last operation of his second tour, led the formation off and they formed up in the usual three vics of three aircraft, flying low over the sea. Shortly after leaving the Norfolk coast they flew into dense fog which was right down to sea level, making it almost impossible to judge the height of the aircraft above the sea or to see the next aircraft in formation. Simmons flew on with Edrich sticking as close to him as possible until, after what must have seemed an eternity, the fog thinned, then dispersed. Unfortunately there was no sign of the other aircraft in their vic of three. Sergeant Harry F. Fordham, Simmons's No.2, had hit the sea and was lost without trace, highlighting the dangers of low-level flying over the sea in such conditions. Fordham's, another flown by 20-year-old Sergeant Francis S. B. Knox from Northern Ireland, and one of 105 Squadron piloted by 28-year-old Pilot Officer Leslie S. Clayton, were claimed by *Oberfeldwebel* Oskar Wunder, *Unteroffizier* Karl Hammerl and *Feldwebel* Friedrich Karl Bachmann of JG52 piloting Messerschmitt Bf 109s. (Five days earlier Hammerl, Wunder and *Feldwebel* Walter Jahnke had shot down the Blenheim flown by Sergeant Frank Boroski RCAF of 139 Squadron during a shipping sweep off north-west Germany. There were no survivors.) The six other Blenheims had abandoned the operation and returned to England.

The convoy – about a dozen ships – eventually came into view 2 miles away. Simmons climbed to 250 ft, followed by Edrich, putting on full boost before diving towards their quarry, Simmons aiming for a large merchantman in the centre, while Edrich aimed for another. They were met with a terrific barrage of flak, the two pilots skidding and jinking their aircraft to present a difficult target to the gunners. In the turret Ernie Hope fired at the nearest flak ship, Edrich joining in with his front gun as they drew closer. As they closed onto their targets, just clearing the masts, the two observers released their four 250 lb armour-piercing bombs. As they flew off, keeping as low as possible, they were delighted to see one merchantman wreathed in flames and the other listing. During the attack a great deal of the rudder on Edrich's aircraft had been shot away, yet they both returned safely to base. Simmons was awarded a well-deserved bar to his DFC. The same afternoon Edrich played cricket for the squadron against a local village team – quite a contrast, although typical of the strange existence of all operational aircrew, one minute in the thick of battle then back to the comforts of their base with a trip to the local or whatever took the individual's fancy.

On 9 June 2 Group despatched eighteen Blenheims to look for shipping off the Dutch and German coasts. Six Blenheims of 18 Squadron flew to the area of Ameland where two of the bombers were shot down by Bf 109Fs with the loss of all six crewmembers. Twenty-four-year-old Flight Sergeant Ian A. 'Tubby' Bullivant's Blenheim was claimed shot down north of Schiermonnikoog by *Feldwebel* Heinrich Wilhelm Ahnert of 3./JG52 after the aircraft had been damaged by flak. (Ahnert, a fighter *experten* with fifty-seven victories and awarded the *Ritterkreuz* was KIA on the Russian Front, 23.8.42.) The Blenheim flown by 28-year-old Sergeant Leslie B. Box disappeared in a fog bank west of Texel and was never seen again. On 11 June twenty-five Blenheims were despatched to Bremerhaven and towns and villages in north-west Germany but nineteen turned back with full bombloads because of lack of cloud cover.

Insufficient cloud cover interfered with an operation to Brest by twelve Blenheims on 12 June. That afternoon three Blenheims of 110 Squadron escorted by the Biggin Hill Spitfires flew a *Roadstead*. Halfway to Holland Bf 109s of I./JG52 attacked and Squadron Leader Rankin leading 92 Squadron shot down one of the enemy. Squadron Leader Spencer's Blenheim was hit badly by flak but he managed to return and crash land at Manston without injury to the crew. On 13 June four Blenheims sent to Norway were recalled. On the morning of the 14th cloud obscured the primary target and the twelve crews of 105 and 110 Squadrons on Circus No.12 led by Wing Commander Peter Sutcliffe with fighter cover from Tangmere, bombed the Fort Rouge aerodrome at St Omer from 10,000 ft instead. In the afternoon a second raid by eighteen Blenheims on a Hipper-class cruiser berthed at Brest was called off again because of insufficient cloud cover. Then, on 15 June Wing Commander Hughie Edwards, CO of 105 Squadron, led a formation of three Blenheims on Beat 10 off the Mouth of Schelde and found a convoy of eight merchant ships off The Hague. Edwards carried out a successful attack on a 4,000 ton merchantman, Sergeant W. H. A. Jackson bombing a 6/8,000 tonner and Flying Officer M. M. Lambert making an abortive starboard beam attack on a 3,000 tonner. (On 1 July Edwards was awarded the DFC for this daring low-level operation.)

A second section of three Blenheims of 105 Squadron led by Squadron Leader

Bennett, and two from 110 Squadron, was intercepted by Bf 109s of 3./JG1. The almost tour-expired Sergeant Arthur E. Guesford in 110 Squadron was shot down west of Alkmaar. The 23-year-old, who had been married for just over a year, was killed, as were his two crew. (*Unteroffizier* Barein of I./JG1 in a Bf 109F claimed his destruction off Bergen-am-Zee.) A squadron of ten E-boats was seen off Kijkduin in Holland and was avoided by most of the formation. However, Sergeant D. O. Beacham and Flying Officer Peter H. Watts, the latter on his first operation with 105 Squadron, mistook the heavily armed and manoeuvrable craft for merchant shipping and went in low to carry out their attacks. Beacham hit one of them and incredibly was not blasted to oblivion by the fusillades of AA fire that peppered the sky in their wake. Watts, who attacked the leading E-boat, was not as fortunate in his exit from the hellish scene. His Blenheim was hit in the starboard petrol tank and disappeared into the sea in flames. There were no survivors from the crew who had only just arrived on the squadron from 17 OTU Upwood on the 9th. (Five days later, on 20 June, Beacham and his crew and two

Sergeant E. A. Rex Leavers DFM (right) with Sergeant Mike Cleary DFM pictured during an earlier detachment to Malta (*Wartime Watton Museum*)

On 16 June 1941, Beats 7, 9 and 10 resulted in the loss of more Blenheims. During an attack on a 'squealer' off Borkum in Beat 7 Sergeant E. A. Rex Leavers DFM of 21 Squadron went in so low that his Blenheim (V6034 YH-D) hit the ship's mast and he cartwheeled into the sea. Leavers (24), Sergeant Ian Overheu DFM RNZAF (23), observer, and Sergeant Joseph W. H. Phelps WOP/AG, who were on the last operation of their first tour were killed. (*via Theo Boiten*)

groundcrew died when the Blenheim he was flying crashed on take-off from Swanton Morley.)

On 16 June, Beats 7, 9 and 10 resulted in the loss of more Blenheims. During an attack on a 'squealer' off Borkum in Beat 7 Flight Sergeant E. A. Rex Leavers DFM of 21 Squadron went in so low that his Blenheim hit the ship's mast and he cartwheeled into the sea. Six Blenheims of 139 Squadron and one from 18 Squadron, piloted by Pilot Officer Ian Watson, sighted a German convoy off the Hook of Holland in Beat 10 to Texel. Bf 109Fs of I./JG52 attacked and shot down Watson's aircraft. The Scotsman from Edinburgh and his observer, Pilot Officer Ernest K. Aires, who had cheated death on 25 May and WOP/AG Sergeant Tom Dean were all killed. In Beat 9 in the Texel area two Blenheims of 139 Squadron piloted by Flight Lieutenant Ralph Langley DFC and Flying Officer Kenneth Laird RCAF were attacked by Bf 109Fs of 1./JG52 flown by *Leutnant* Karl Weber and *Feldwebel* Robert Portz who claimed to have shot down Langley's and Laird's Blenheims. Langley and his crew were lost although Laird managed to get his badly shot-up Blenheim back to Norfolk. The 24-year-old Canadian and his observer, Sergeant Leslie J. G. Wakefield, however, died in the crash landing at Rackheath airfield not far from Horsham St Faith.

'Dinty' Moore describes another June raid:

On 17 June we flew over to Horsham St Faith for a briefing for a raid that we would never forget. We found that we were to take part in a Circus attack on the Kuhlmann Chemical Works at Chocques near Bethune in northern France, accompanied by a large fighter escort. We were to fly in one large formation of twenty-four aircraft in eight Vics of three stacked up one slightly below and behind the other. We also discovered that we had drawn the 'short straw' in our position, as we would be the last aircraft in this large and unwieldy formation.[13] Later in the war, no matter how many bombers took part in a raid, we never flew in boxes of more than six aircraft, which could manoeuvre sufficiently to carry out evasive action in response to attack by flak or fighters.

At 1745 hours we taxied out, with my excitement having some difficulty overcoming my fear and took off, the last in the queue, gaining height and getting into formation. Flying down to our rendezvous with our escort, looking forward I could see this enormous formation of Blenheims, while looking back over the tail there was an empty sky. Whenever I see a flock of birds I am always reminded of that moment. Our escort of Hurricanes, who were our close escort, closed in around us while the Spitfires flew high above forming a protective umbrella. Most certainly they were a comforting sight.

We droned on towards the French coast, having climbed to our operational height of about 10,000 ft before being met by a heavy barrage of flak. We carried on towards the target, by which time our Vic was lagging behind the main formation and we attracted the unwelcome attention of a number of German fighters who had managed to avoid our escort, which itself was also under attack. The sky was full of fighters whirling around in combat while we were under constant attack. One determined character actually flew between us and the No 2 in our formation. Although I was surprised, I was astounded to find that I immediately reacted and managed to fire a burst as he went past. My instant reaction must have been due to the training I had received.

The fighters were armed with cannon, so on occasions they could stay off out of range of our machine guns and take pot shots at us. Doing this they hit us in both wings and put our port engine out of commission. If that was the bad news, the good news was that the starboard engine, which supplied the power for the landing gear and the turret, thankfully, was undamaged. Losing power on the port engine initially made our kite swing to the left, although George somehow managed to manoeuvre underneath our colleagues for mutual protection. Sadly, they gradually pulled away from us, leaving us an unfriendly and persistent Messerschmitt for company and a heavy flak barrage to speed us, if that is appropriate in this instance, on our way as we crossed the coast at Cap Gris Nez. Fortunately one of our escorting Hurricanes came to our aid and we heard later that he had shot down our 'German friend' near the English coast.

The Blenheim was not noted for its ability to fly on one engine and George had to fight with the controls to keep us in the air and on course. Apart from sending a message back to base notifying them of our problems, there was little I could do but cross my fingers. We could have landed at any aerodrome once we crossed the coast but George was determined to get us back to Horsham St Faith, which he not only did but also brought us in for a perfect landing. It was, by any standard, an example of marvellous flying, so there was no wonder that Ron and I were happy with our pilot. The flight actually lasted for three hours ten minutes, although it seemed a great deal longer.

Between 3 and 30 June twenty-two Blenheims from 2 Group were lost with fifty-six aircrew killed and six taken prisoner, mainly on anti-shipping strikes off the

A Blenheim of 21 Squadron returned from an operation. Flight Lieutenant H. Waples DFC (KIA 23.6.41) in flying kit; acting squadron CO, Squadron Leader Doug Cooper, with a plaster on his face; Group Captain Laurie F. Sinclair, station commander, RAF Watton, with hands in pockets, back to camera; and Flying Officer Tonks, intelligence officer, without a cap beside the aircraft, next to Flying Officer Duncan, 21 Squadron medical officer and Squadron Leader Buckler facing camera. Note the single VGO .303 in machine gun which was replaced by a twin Browning .303 in machine gun installation in the turret in the winter of 1941. (*Wartime Watton Museum*)

Dutch coast, the Friesian Islands and the Heligoland Bight. On 21 June the Blenheim flown by Sergeant P. Brown of 21 Squadron was shot down by *Oberstleutnant* Adolf Galland in his Bf 109E of Stab./JG26 as his 68th victory.[14] Two days later two 107 Squadron Blenheims were lost. On Thursday, 27 June ten crews from 107 Squadron were ordered to fly to Swanton Morley for a special briefing. They and ten crews from 105 were told that they would carry out a low-level attack in daylight on the docks at Bremen the following day. This meant flying over the German mainland for 105 miles, far beyond the range of fighter protection. The formation was to be led by Wing Commander Laurence Petley but when it was time for take-off, at 0430, he was unable to start his starboard engine. The remaining nineteen aircraft took off on time, so it fell to the lot of Pilot Officer Bill Edrich, flying his eleventh operation, to take over the lead.

They had been flying for some time when Petley, having persuaded his faulty engine to start, caught up with them and took over the lead, much to the relief of Edrich. When they reached a point opposite Cuxhaven they saw a large enemy convoy, which opened up on them, so the essential element of surprise had been lost. Reluctantly, therefore, Petley turned round and brought the formation back home. Hughie Edwards, at the head of the 105 formation, said afterwards that having got so far he thought they might have gone on. Command thought so too, as Bill Edrich explained.

> After landing back at Massingham we went straight over to the cottage that housed our tiny ops room and headquarters and there the adjutant, Tony Richardson, was standing with the telephone in his hand. He called out to

No. 107 Squadron pilots and observers May–June 1941. Back row, Flying Officer Youalls; Flying Officer Leach; Flying Officer Bryce; Flying Officer M. V. Redfern-Smith; Flying Officer Dudenay; Pilot Officer Sammels; Pilot Officer Bill Edrich. Front row: Flight Lieutenant R. A. Bailey DFC (KIA 4.7.41, Bremen); Squadron Leader Clayton; Squadron Leader Peter Simmons; Wing Commander L. V. F. Petley CO (KIA 4.7.41, Bremen); Flight Lieutenant Zeke Murray RNZAF; Flight Lieutenant Anthony Richardson, adjutant; Flight Lieutenant E. Wellburn (PoW 4.7.41). (*Mrs Vera Sherring collection*)

'Petters', 'Sir, the AOC's on the line.' We were all feeling pretty glum and the chatter that normally succeeds an operation was absent. All eyes were watching 'Petters' as he took the receiver. We saw his face blanch and tauten with anger and humiliation as he listened to the voice that we ourselves couldn't hear. In the silent ops room we were watching our leader being accused of cowardice and we knew that in Stevenson's mind we were all tainted with it. Watching 'Petters' and remembering how nearly the leadership had fallen to me, I wondered again what I would have done and I saw myself, like 'Petters', arraigned before the entire squadron by a contemptuous AOC.

'If that's what you think,' we heard 'Petters' say, 'We'll do the whole bloody show again this afternoon.'

We didn't doubt that he meant it. And we didn't doubt that Stevenson was capable of sending us. The political pressures he was being subjected to, six days after Hitler's attack on Russia, most have been enormous. We hung around to hear our fate but when it came through it was an anti-climax. We were to fly up to Driffield, a bomber station in Yorkshire, that afternoon and await orders.

Petley led nine crews to Driffield but was ordered not to fly on the subsequent operation. No. 107 Squadron was informed that six Halifax bombers, the first ever to operate, were to bomb Kiel the following morning as a diversion, while the Blenheims were to mount a low-level raid on the *Luftwaffe* base at Westerland on the island of Sylt. The news was received in silence for Sylt was renowned for its formidable defences. The station commander at Driffield did his best to boost morale, claiming that it was no accident that the raid was timed for midday on Sunday, 'when the German fighter pilots, creatures of habit, will be enjoying a pre-lunch lager'. This inspired planning was invalidated when the operation was delayed for twenty-four hours, until 1000 hours on Monday 30 June.

Seven Blenheims, led by a New Zealander, Squadron Leader Zeke Murray, took off and headed out over the North Sea. Eventually the island came into view and the crews soon experienced the intensity of flak for which the island was famed. In describing it, Edrich said: 'I have seen paintings of naval battles, with gun flashes illuminating the scene and the water being thrown up on all sides by shell bursts but never have I seen such an inferno of fire power as was directed at us in the next few minutes.' Despite the intense opposition the formation flew on towards their target, though one of the Blenheims had been shot down and three others were missing by the time the survivors arrived over the airfield, where they dropped their bombs with understandable haste before turning for home. The survivors held close together but, about 100 miles from Sylt and feeling reasonably safe, they were attacked by four Bf 109s. Murray's WOP/AG took over fire control over the radio, giving directions for evasive action and directing the fire of his colleagues. The battle continued with fire being exchanged, the Blenheims soaking up a lot of damage, one cannon shell hitting Murray's port engine, holing his petrol tank, though he was still able to stay in the air. Soon the guns on the Blenheims stopped, either because they had jammed or because they had run out of ammunition, though fortunately the same fate had befallen the Germans, who broke off the engagement.

Finally they reached Driffield, where Murray and one other pilot crash landed, the remaining aircraft being so badly damaged that they were found to be unfit to fly. Shortly after they had landed another Blenheim, obviously in trouble, came into the circuit and landed. It was piloted by Sergeant Levers who, flying through the concentration of flak over Sylt, had collided with one of the missing Blenheims, his flaps and ailerons on one side being chewed up. Somehow he had managed to regain control and quite remarkably had managed to guide the aircraft, using limited cloud cover, back across the North Sea to Driffield, keeping it level by holding the aileron control in the vertical instead of the horizontal position. When it had become too much of a strain he had borrowed a leather belt from his navigator and strapped up the controls. He received the immediate award of the DFM.

When, on the evening of 3 July crews in East Anglia went to bed, Bremen had already been scheduled as the target for the morrow. Operation *Wreckage*, as it was code-named, would be led by Wing Commander Hughie Edwards DFC who had followed behind Petley to the same target ten days earlier. As usual sleep was difficult, probably more so given the nature of the difficult and dangerous operation. Flight Lieutenant Tony Richardson RAFVR, 107 Squadron adjutant at Massingham, had already witnessed too many such days and nights at close hand. His was the painful duty to write to the bereaved relatives of his brother officers and men who never returned. He later dedicated a poem, 'Night Before Bremen', to his CO and the crews of 107 Squadron, who would fly the *Wreckage* operation.

At least one man relished the thought. Irishman Warrant Officer Samuel Joseph Magee, the legendary 107 Squadron armament officer, had persuaded Petley to let him go along as an extra gunner aboard one of the Blenheims. During low-level raids by German intruders at Wattisham, while everyone else took cover, Magee had calmly set up his .303 VGO with its wooden butt and special trigger and had blasted away at incoming Dorniers and Junkers 88. Off duty Magee ran a 180 h.p. Wolseley around the narrow country lanes at alarming speeds, on seemingly inexhaustible supplies of petrol.

On the morning of 4 July Magee joined Flight Lieutenant F. Wellburn, his observer, Sergeant D. A. Dupree, and Sergeant A. E. Routley, air gunner, as they boarded one of six 107 Squadron Blenheims taking part. Magee entered the almost dark compartment aft of the bomb well armed with his beloved VGO and several magazines containing 100% per cent tracer. He settled onto the uncomfortably small ledge behind the bomb well camera hatch so he could see through the small perspex panel in the centre of the door. He would remove the door just before the target and hurl a 40 lb GP bomb through it before blasting away with his VGO!

Edwards took off from Swanton Morley and led nine Blenheims into the clear blue Norfolk sky. It was his thirty-sixth operation of the war. His observer, Pilot Officer Alister S. Ramsay, and his gunner, Sergeant Gerry D. P. Quinn DFM, settled down to their tasks and the crew kept their eyes peeled for the six crews of 107 Squadron led by Petley, who would be joining them after take-off from Massingham. However, mist and fog, which were to dog the first 100 miles of the operation, shielded them from view as the formation droned low over the sea, maintaining radio silence. Edwards could see his two wingmen but little else. Meanwhile, diversions were in progress: Wing Commander R. G. Hurst was leading five crews of 226

Squadron to bomb gun emplacements on Nordeney and six Blenheims of 21 Squadron were flying a Circus with the customary fighter escort to the Chocques Chemical Works. Hurst's Blenheim, hit by flak literally blew up.

When the *Wreckage* Blenheims finally made landfall at the German coast, one sub-flight of three aircraft of 107 Squadron was no longer with them. Squadron Leader Zeke Murray and Flying Officer F. R. H. Charney[15] had returned to Massingham with mechanical problems while a third had aborted when Flight Lieutenant Jones, the pilot, became ill. The remaining twelve tightened up formation and pressed on. Just before 0730 hours a coastal convoy near Nordeney sighted the formation but Edwards pressed on. As the formation crossed into Germany a few miles south of Cuxhaven, people working in the fields, mistaking the low-level bombers for German aircraft, stopped and looked up to wave. Still at a height of between 50 and 100 ft, Edwards turned the formation south towards Bremen. The attack, timed for 0800 hours, was to be made in a 1 mile wide line-abreast formation, the aircraft spaced 100–200 yards apart and flying at treetop height. Edwards and his crews weaved between the barrage balloons hoisted to 50 ft above the port and braved the tremendous AA fire that greeted their arrival. As Edwards was to recall later: 'As we rightly assumed, the flak and balloons split up the formation and it became every man for himself. The flak was terrific and frightening. It was bursting all around me for ten minutes. There was a distinct smell of cordite in the air. I was flying so low that I flew through telephone and telegraph wires.'

About twenty shells found their mark on Edwards's Blenheim and Quinn was hit in the knee by shrapnel. Behind them two 105 Squadron machines were shot out of the sky. Sergeant W. A. MacKillop's aircraft was hit by flak and crashed onto a factory, Sergeants E. G. Nethercutt and G. F. Entwhistle dying with him. Flying Officer M. M. Lambert's aircraft was last seen by other crews heading away from Bremen, burning fiercely, later to crash, killing Lambert, Sergeant R. Copeland and Sergeant F. W. R. Charles. No. 107 Squadron also lost two Blenheims. Petley was shot down by flak in the target area; he, his observer, Flight Lieutenant R. A. Bailey DFC, and Sergeant W. M. Harris, air gunner, were all killed. Flight Lieutenant F. Wellburn was also shot down by flak and crashed in the target area. Sergeant D. A. Dupree, Sergeant A. E. Routley and Warrant Officer Magee, the latter no doubt firing to the end, died in the crash but Wellburn survived to be made a PoW. Dupree, Routley and Magee were buried on 7 July in the Hollefriedhot cemetery. In 1945 they were exhumed for reburial at Becklingen War Cemetery, Soltau, where all the other crews were buried after the raid.

Although four crews were lost, successful attacks had been made on the docks, factories, a timber yard and railways and great damage was caused to the tankers and transports that were loaded with vital supplies. All the aircraft were damaged. After the target Edwards proceeded to circle Bremen and strafed a stationary train that had opened up on them, before leading the formation out of Germany at low level. He recalled: 'I had great pleasure in using up the ammunition from my one front gun, which silenced the opposition.' Edwards, his aircraft minus part of the port wing, the port aileron badly damaged, a cannon shell in the radio rack and a length of telegraph wire wrapped round the tail wheel and trailing behind, headed for Bremerhaven and

Wilhelmshaven. More flak rose to greet them at Bremerhaven until finally the coastline at Heligoland came into view and the Blenheims dived down to sea level again. The battered formation flew north of the Friesians for a short time then headed westwards for Swanton Morley where Sergeant W. H. A. 'Bill' Jackson had to belly-land; his observer, J. A. Purves, and W. N. Williams, WOP/AG, were wounded. Edwards brought his ailing bomber home and put down safely at Swanton Morley where Gerry Quinn had to be lifted out of the aircraft with a Coles crane.

Operation *Wreckage* received considerable publicity. Congratulations were received from Air Chief Marshal Donald F. Stevenson DSO OBE MC, whose telegram read, 'This low-flying raid, so gallantly carried out, deep into Germany, without the support of fighters, will always rank high in the history of the Royal Air Force'. An immediate signal from the Commander-in-Chief of Bomber Command, Sir Richard Peirse, read, 'Your attack this morning has been a great contribution to the day offensive now being fought. It will remain an outstanding example of dash and initiative. I send you and your captains and crews my warmest congratulations and the admiration of the command.' The Chief of Air Staff, Sir Charles Portal wrote: I have just read the first account of the Bremen raid today. Convey to all units concerned my warmest congratulations on a splendid operation. I am sure that all squadrons realize that besides encouraging the Russians, every daylight attack rubs into the Germans, the superiority of our units. You are doing great work.' On the BBC Home Service 6 o'clock news on 7 July Bill Jackson broadcast his impressions of the raid.

On 21 July it was announced that Wing Commander Hughie Edwards DFC had been awarded the Victoria Cross for courage and leadership displayed on the Bremen operation. He thus became only the second Australian to receive this award (the first having been awarded to Lieutenant F. H. McNamara of the RFC during the First World War). Edwards assembled the squadron in the large hangar at Swanton Morley and told them that it was the squadron's VC and that he was simply the person presented with it. Several wits were heard to enquire when, in consequence, they would be permitted to wear their VC ribbons![16] Then the Australian, who had done more than most to restore Squadron morale and pride during the past few weeks, and his aircrew and NCO groundcrew decamped to a pub in Norwich for celebratory drinks.

On 28 July Pilot Officer Alister Ramsey was awarded the DFC, Sergeant Gerry Quinn a bar to his DFM and Sergeants Bill Jackson, Purves and Williams the DFM for their part in the raid. (By this time 105 Squadron was in Malta for operations in the Mediterranean, where on 1 August Alister Ramsey died as a result of wounds sustained in an attack on an Italian destroyer. At the end of the month Edwards was posted to Air HQ Malta and was replaced by Wing Commander

Blenheim IV V6028/D of 105 Squadron, flown by Wing Commander Hughie Edwards, CO 105 Squadron, on the Bremen raid on 4 July 1941, pictured after the return to Swanton Morley (*RAF*)

Don W. Scivier AFC RAAF of 107 Squadron. Scivier was in action on his first day but on 22 September his aircraft collided with another Blenheim and crashed into the sea after his tail fell off. Five days later the last sortie in the Mediterranean was flown and on 28 September the surviving 105 Squadron members sailed home in a cruiser.)

Meanwhile, amid all the bravura following the Bremen raid, at Massingham Adjutant Flight Lieutenant Anthony Richardson quietly sat down and penned letters of condolence to the relatives of the crews lost on the raid. He also penned 'Lines to A Widow', which began:

> *Lady in your faithlessness,*
> *Do you seek to make redress*
> *To the little one who's down,*
> *In his grave in Bremen town?*
> *. . . I served him once and served him well!*
> *I saw him pick his path to hell!*
> *I knew the very hour he died*
> *Over Bremen crucified!*

After the war the gifted Richardson wrote *Wingless Victory*, the story of Basil Embry, his CO when at Wattisham earlier in the war.

Bill Edrich, who returned from leave, had read the reports of the raid in the newspapers.

> When I got back to Little Massingham, the mess that had always been so full of life and personality was silent and empty. 'I'm afraid there's no one from the squadron here,' said the Mess Sergeant. 'We lost nearly all the officers on the Bremen raid. Those who are left have moved over to West Raynham.' He promised to lay on some transport and I went to my room to collect my things.

On 5 and 6 July small numbers of Blenheims carried out coastal sweeps off the Friesians and Holland losing two aircraft. On 7 July, twenty aircraft including six apiece from 105 and 139 Squadrons, were despatched on a shipping sweep off Holland again. They found a convoy between The Hague and Ijmuiden and attacked off Scheveningen. Sergeant Victor Farrow of 105 Squadron scored two hits on the *Delaware*, a 4,000 ton merchant vessel and Pilot Officer Ben Broadley hit another large vessel, which burst into flames and sank. Sergeant J. G. Bruce also scored hits on another ship. The Blenheim flown by Squadron Leader A. A. 'Tony' Scott was hit by a flak ship and set on fire. All three crew were lost. The Blenheims of 139 Squadron crippled a 4,000 tonner and two 2,000 tonners but 22-year-old Flight Lieutenant Horace Hilton's aircraft was hit by flak and burst into flames before hitting the sea and exploding. On the way home four Bf 109s jumped the five returning aircraft and Unteroffizier Fritz Metzler of 2./JG52 from Texel shot down 21-year-old Sergeant John Causton and his crew into the sea 60 miles west of The Hague. The successful but costly operation prompted AVM Donald F. Stevenson DSO OBE MC to declare:

> The group is filled with admiration by the determined attack carried out today by 105 and 139 squadrons, as a result of which an enemy convoy was practically

Blenheims on a shipping strike off the Dutch coast on 7 July when two hits were scored on the *Delaware*. Low-level flying was to become a major feature of the life of Blenheim crews during the summer of 1941. Always a risky pastime, demanding absolute concentration on the part of the pilot, it became even more hazardous while over the sea in hazy conditions when it was very difficult to judge height above the water. If during shipping 'beats' Blenheim crews found nothing to attack, they were expected to make 'fringe attacks' on military targets a few miles inland from the enemy coast 'in order to cause alarm and to embarrass the enemy air defence system'. (*RAF*)

annihilated, two ships only escaping from a convoy of eight. In tonnage, this is a loss to the enemy of some 18,000 to 19,000 tons that he can ill afford to spare. Well done. Please convey my personal congratulations to the crews who took part in this magnificent operation.[17]

No. 101 Squadron now converted to Wellingtons and transferred to 3 Group, and on 9 July 88 Squadron joined 2 Group at Swanton Morley (moving on 1 August to Attlebridge). At this time eight other Blenheim squadrons were thinly spread, operating from the UK and the Mediterranean: 110 Squadron was at Wattisham with 226 Squadron, which had joined 2 Group in May; 18 Squadron (which sent a detachment to Malta in October and saw out the rest of the war in the Mediterranean theatre) was at Oulton; 105 Squadron was detached to Lossiemouth as well as Malta; 21 Squadron was at Watton; 82 Squadron was at Bodney (which also sent a detachment to Malta); 139 Squadron was at Horsham St Faith, 107 Squadron was at Massingham and 114 Squadron was at Leuchars (attached to 18 Group Coastal Command).

Pilot Officer Charles Patterson was one of the pilots in 114 Squadron at this time.

I'd acquired quite a considerable degree of confidence in flying Blenheims at

OTU early in 1941. I was still frightened of night flying and instrument flying in cloud but just flying as such I enjoyed. My fear was that I would never be able to cope with being shot at and that I would fail, turn round and run away. The nearer it got the stronger the fear of failure became. Admittedly, Blenheims had had an easier time during the winter of 1940–41 because they had been put on night operations, especially quite a lot of bombing of barges at invasion ports. But by the time I was posted, at the end of April, to 114 Squadron, Blenheims had gone back on daylight again and they were being used on low-level shipping strikes. Blenheims were totally vulnerable once intercepted by fighters but I was incredibly fortunate. Instead of being thrown straight into the deep end by being posted to Norfolk to do standard, routine daylight bombing operations, I was posted to the one squadron in 2 Group that had been detached to Scotland to cover the North Sea and the Scandinavian coast. Opposition there was on a very much lower scale.

In the middle of July, the day of reckoning that I knew must come finally arrived. We had to leave Scotland and the comparative safety of the Norwegian coast and rejoin 2 Group in Norfolk for daylight bomber operations. Virtually every operation from now on meant being shot at in some way or other in broad daylight. We flew down to West Raynham in formation. Wing Commander George 'Bok' Hull DFC, our South African Squadron commander, a veteran from 1940 and the most marvellous CO, was absolutely thrilled that we were going back to 2 Group proper where he would be able to head his squadron into the thick of things. I could not help being caught up in the excitement, even though I was very nervous of what was to come. I was also, in a way, exhilarated. From the moment we landed the whole tempo became more highly charged. We arrived to find that our station commander was the famous, ineffable and unique Paddy Bandon, Group Captain the Earl of Bandon, whose personality and achievements were a legend. Behind his always cheerful and friendly exterior was a man of extraordinary sympathy, kindness and tolerance. His task was to maintain morale amongst very young, mostly inexperienced, raw and terrified crews during this period of appalling casualties. He was a teamwork leader, wonderful at getting people of conflicting personalities to work together. Also I had the unexpected and completely new experience of finding myself billeted in Weasenham Hall [about 2 miles from the airfield] which belonged to the Coke family[18] which had been turned into a mess for us. To my amazement I found myself a Flight Lieutenant overnight, having only done about twelve operations. A state of affairs had been reached where any officer pilot who completed about ten operations was virtually automatically a Flight Lieutenant. Anyone who could get through fifteen was a Squadron Leader. This situation most certainly never existed at any other time during the war.

'Bok' Hull was keen and ready to start operating. The very day after we arrived I had to move the whole of my flight to Bodney, a satellite airfield about eight miles away and have it ready for operations the next morning. It was a standard Circus, a formation of Blenheims going out with Fighter Command on a fighter sweep across the Channel at medium level, about 10,000 ft. Our target was a power station near Rouen. It was regarded as a fairly safe form of operation but it was made clear that there would inevitably be a great deal of heavy flak, which is what one encountered from 8,000 ft upwards. I had no idea what it would look like, although I was told there would be a lot of black puffs. The main thing that was impressed upon me was to keep formation and follow the Squadron commander in his evasive action, which would be gentle weaves and turns towards the target. I must follow him and keep them going straight and level when he said 'straight and level'. The moment bombs were gone the Squadron commander would swing away and resume evasive action.

I led a 'Vic' of three and formated under the Squadron commander's tail. It was a glorious, sunny day, necessary of course for a Circus – you could not do it with cloud. The whole thing was a sort of daze. I just did not know what would happen when the flak started. I genuinely had no confidence that I would be able to take it. On the other hand, the thing in my head was that it just had to be done. There was no way out. I suppose my training and instincts were subconsciously operating even though I was not aware of it.

We circled over Dungeness and out of the corner of my eye I saw a sight that raised my spirits to a remarkable degree. Down below, against a bank of cumulus cloud, I could see an enormous swarm of what looked like gnats, silhouetted against this cloud, racing across and climbing in a great upward sweep. This was 11 Group's Hurricanes coming up to provide our escort. They joined and took up close positions all around us; one could see the pilots in their cockpits. Of course, it gave a wonderful sense of security, although it was no security whatsoever against flak.

I felt quite good but crossing the enemy coast had a sinister connotation, then I seemed to just live from minute to minute, longing for the target to come up, dreading the flak. We carried on straight and level. Still nothing happened, then my navigator said, 'We must be getting to the target fairly soon.' Sure enough, the Squadron commander started gentle evasive action and then the dreaded moment arrived. There was a thud and the aircraft shook. My first sight of the famous black puffs produced an irresistible longing to just turn and run but I couldn't. I was in the middle of the box. I had my orders. I just had to carry on.

The puffs got nearer, the thuds got more severe. I actually saw the orange flash in the puffs of smoke but I didn't feel too bad while the Squadron commander was still doing this gentle evasive action, weaving slowly and gently to port or starboard with a climb or with a loss of height. Then we had to straighten up and go straight and level. I just sat there, frozen at the controls, waiting for the whole aeroplane to disappear into oblivion but we went on and on and still we were surviving. The longer it went on the more I thought with just a bit more to go that'll be when we get it. I don't know how but I carried on, on this long straight and narrow run, which never seemed to end. At last, the leading navigator gave the signal for 'Bombs gone!' In a Blenheim the bombs opened the doors with their own weight.

Every now and then some of the thuds were extremely close but we were still in one piece. Then to my unforgettable relief, Wing Commander Hull turned away and we were all able to swing away. I was so exhilarated that I had got through and done it that I really did not think much about the dangers that might occur on the way back. The fighters were all around us and we returned across the Channel. At the English coast the fighters fell away and we flew on at 8–10,000 ft back to Norfolk. Hull gave the order to break formation, then we all landed. I'd actually done it. I did a few more Circuses like that and managed to get through them but I still had not done a low-level daylight.

'Dinty' Moore flew one operation with 114 Squadron, having flown his last one with 18 Squadron on 5 July, another shipping patrol. 'My abiding memory of these operations was the seemingly endless sea, which looked both cold and cruel, rather than the three attacks we had made on enemy shipping.' (Having taken part in twenty operations, his crew's tour was complete and he was posted as an instructor to OTU, Bicester. The rest of his crew were posted to an OTU in the Middle East. He could not go with them because of his recent bout of pneumonia.) He had completed forty-nine operational sorties without a scratch, whereas between 12 March and 14 July that year 2 Group had lost sixty-eight Blenheims and their crews (fifteen from 18 Squadron). There were only twelve crews on a squadron and eight squadrons in the Group, so it represented a very heavy loss rate. Losses to the Blenheim detachments in Malta during 1941–2 were almost 100 per cent.

After *Wreckage* 107 Squadron needed to be re-formed before it could participate

Wing Commander F. A. 'Bunny' Harte DFC SAAF (centre), who took over command of 107 Squadron on 12 July 1941 from Wing Commander A. F. C. Booth, who lasted just six days before being KIA. (Harte himself was KIA on 9 October 1941 at Malta.) To his left is Pilot Officer Bloodworth and to his right is his gunner at Massingham, Pilot Officer Wewage-Smith, who had served in the French Foreign Legion, was a fighter pilot in the Bolivian War and had returned to Europe to fight in the Spanish Civil War as an air observer. When greeted by one of the squadron intelligence officers with, 'Well mercenary, what can I do for you?' his reply was, 'Mercenary I may be, but I'll have you know that I'm doing this at strictly cut prices for patriotic reasons.' (*Mrs Vera Sherring*)

Wing Commander Thomas N. Tim Partridge DFC, 26, CO of 18 Squadron, at Blickling Hall shortly before he was KIA on 16 July 1941 piloting one of four Blenheims that were shot down by flak during a low-level daylight raid on the docks at Rotterdam. (*Mrs Vera Sherring*)

in further raids. Bill Edrich, now with the rank of flight lieutenant (a double promotion only six weeks after first becoming operational), still had a serviceable plane and a full crew, so they were loaned to 21 Squadron, where in fact they stayed. Edrich was promoted to squadron leader (he had gone from pilot officer to squadron leader in nineteen days) and flew the rest of his operations with 21 Squadron. Meanwhile, at West Raynham, 107 Squadron took shape again after its mauling. On 6 July 32-year-old Wing Commander Arthur F. C. Booth took command. Previously he had been a squadron leader with 105 Squadron under Hughie Edwards. However, senior rank was certainly no protection. Within a week of his new posting, on 12 July, Booth was killed by flak during an anti-shipping strike on a convoy off Ijmuiden. Only his observer, Sergeant T. Scott, survived to be taken prisoner.

The new CO was Wing Commander F. A. 'Bunny' Harte DFC SAAF. Harte's gunner, Pilot Officer Wewage-Smith, was quite a character. He had served in the French Foreign Legion, was a fighter pilot in the Bolivian War and then returned to Europe to fight in the Spanish Civil War, as an air observer. When greeted by one of the squadron intelligence officers with, 'Well, mercenary, what can I do for you this morning?' his reply was: 'Well, mercenary I may be but I'll have you know that I'm doing this at strictly cut prices for patriotic reasons.'[19] ('Bunny' Harte was KIA 9.10.41 leading 107 Squadron in Malta.)

On 14 July Blenheim crews were put on stand-by with one hour's notice to form a strike force. The next day crews discovered that the reason for this was that 2 Group was going to carry out a low-level daylight raid on the docks at Rotterdam on 16 July. Wing Commander Peter Fitzgerald 'Tom' Webster DFC, the 21 Squadron CO, was selected as the leader of the operation. The first wave consisted of eighteen Blenheims of 21 and 226 Squadrons while Wing Commander Thomas Noel 'Tim' Partridge DFC, the CO of 18 Squadron, led the second wave of eighteen Blenheims of 18, 105 and 139 Squadrons. While 19 and 152 Squadrons from RAF Coltishall provided fighter cover, they would only give withdrawal support after the raid so on the way in the thirty-three Blenheims would have to fend for themselves. Just after 1500 hours the first aircraft of the second wave left Horsham St Faith and those of the first wave followed twenty minutes later from Watton. Flight Lieutenant Campbell-Rogers of 226 Squadron had to return with hydraulic problems. The formation crossed the North Sea at wave-top height and made landfall just to the south-east of Rotterdam.

At 1700 hours the first wave approached the target, followed a few minutes later by the second wave. Flak was fierce and accurate and the almost inevitable losses began. First to go down was the Blenheim flown by 19-year-old Sergeant James E. S. Bevan of 21 Squadron, which was hit by fire from a flak ship and smacked into a crane, losing a wing and exploding before swerving into the Waalhaven harbour. In the second wave Wing Commander Tim Partridge's aircraft was hit and he cartwheeled into the side of the Noordsingel Canal. Twenty-year-old Australian Sergeant Ronald J. B. Rost of 18 Squadron crashed near Ypenburg with the loss of all three crew. Squadron Leader Eric Sydney-Smith DFC of 139 Squadron, who had recently returned from a tour of duty in Malta, belly-landed his stricken Blenheim in the centre of Rotterdam. The former *Daily Express* reporter and his scratch crew from 18 Squadron survived to be made PoW.[20] Nineteen ships were claimed put out of action either permanently or for some time to come and five more vessels were believed to be severely damaged. Unfortunately, the majority of shipping that was hit had suffered only slight damage, probably as a result of the small-capacity 250 lb bombs carried by the Blenheims. Wing Commander Tom Webster, who received an immediate DSO for his leadership of the raid, was rested and replaced by Wing Commander John C. Kercher.

After Rotterdam the Blenheims continued flying coastal sweeps off the enemy coast. Off The Hague on 19 July Sergeant Victor Farrow of 105 Squadron, who twelve days earlier had scored two hits on the *Delaware*, successfully placed his four bombs all along the stern of a 4,000 ton merchant ship and the vessel exploded, sending debris high into the air. Flak shells peppered the sky around their fleeing Blenheim, which was thought to have clipped the ship's mast and the 19-year-old pilot, his Welsh observer, Flying Officer Oswald Robinson, and WOP/AG Sergeant Edwin Saunders, a Londoner, were all killed as their Blenheim crashed into the sea. A flak ship shot down his fellow squadron pilot, Pilot Officer Ronald W. Taylor and the New Zealander, his observer, Sergeant Reginald F. G. Withrington, and WOP/AG Sergeant Selwyn Sparkes, died.

On 23 July Blenheims of 18 and 139 Squadrons, led by 23-year-old Squadron Leader D. J. A. Roe DFC, the youngest officer of that rank in the RAF, whose father was a motor transport (MT) sergeant in his squadron, carried out a sweep off the Dutch coast without success. As they were turning for home, Bf 110s of 5./ZG76 appeared, damaging every Blenheim and shooting down Sergeants Peter D. Baker and William M. G. Dunham RCAF, who both fell victim to a combination of attacks by *Oberleutnant* Hotari Schmude, *Oberfeldwebel* Leschnik and *Feldwebel* Schmidt. A third Blenheim, piloted by Sergeant Wood of 18 Squadron, severely damaged in the attacks, limped back to Horsham St. Faith where Wood and Sergeant Johnson, his observer, were severely injured in the crash landing. Worse, six crews of 21 Squadron based at Manston attacked a 4,000 ton tanker escorted by four flak ships in the mouth of the Scheldt and four were shot down by fire from the flak ships.

On 24 July thirty-six Blenheims of 139, 18, 107, 226 and 114 Squadrons flew Circus operations to the docks at Cherbourg to cause a diversion for 100 bombers attempting to bomb the *Scharnhorst* and the *Gneisenau*. On 30 July twelve crews from 18 and 82 Squadrons, led by Squadron Leader (later Wing Commander) Roe, were briefed to attack shipping in the Kiel Canal, making use of cloud cover which, as so often happened, petered out before they reached the target. However, the operation was anything but uneventful, crews from 18 Squadron attacking a ship in convoy off Heligoland with the loss of Sergeant H. D. Cue and crew, who were taken prisoner. The 82 Squadron Blenheims seriously damaged three ships in another convoy with the loss of two aircraft. Off Texel 139 Squadron fared even worse, losing four Blenheims, including one piloted by 24-year-old American Sergeant George R. Menish an RCAF pilot from Salina, Kansas, to Bf 110s of II./ZG76. The four victories were claimed by *Oberleutnant* Wilhelm Herget and *Unteroffizier* Arngrimm from Leeuwarden and De Kooy, *Unteroffizier* Werner Dobreck and *Unteroffizier* Horst, a pilot and WOP/AG respectively in 5./ZG76.[21] So ended July, during which thirty-nine Blenheim crews failed to return.

One of the pilots on the shipping beat operations was Pilot Officer Charles Patterson of 114 Squadron.

On Blenheims we lived day to day, each governed by what the bomb load was, your fate designated on the notice board at Weasenham Hall. If you had instantaneous fuses in the bomb load, it meant that you were going on a Circus at medium level. If it was semi-armour-piercing (SAP) eleven-second delay, it meant a low-level shipping attack. Then you simply turned away from the notice board and assumed that your own death warrant had been signed. Ten days after I had arrived, on 2 August, I saw the dreaded SAP. There was nothing I could do about it. Then I got my first experience of flying across the North Sea, at low level, in formation. I was one of a 'vic' of three going to do a beat along the Friesian Islands. Apart from flying over to Norway, this was the first time I experienced the sensation of flying very low over the sea in broad daylight, little knowing that it was to be an experience that was to become so familiar over the years ahead. It is difficult to describe the sensation, really. You were literally racing across the surface of the sea. The concentration required to do this and formate at the same time kept the mind fully occupied but still at the back of one's mind was the dread of when one would have to turn on to the actual shipping beat and whether one would actually find a convoy.

We raced on and when we reached the Friesian Islands we turned to port and ran along the northern shores of Ameland towards Borkum. Suddenly, the leader said something on the TR9. Alan Griffith, my gunner, assured me on his intercom that it was a call of 'Snappers', which meant that fighters were coming to intercept us. I looked everywhere and couldn't see any. Suddenly, the leader climbed. Fortunately, there was a thin belt of cloud, enough in the leader's opinion to conceal us. He climbed and I tried to follow but I soon lost him in the cloud. Now the operation would have to be abandoned and we would drop down out of the cloud when out of range of the German fighters. I decided to take a peek below: on the port side from a thousand feet, as plain and as clear as anything, was Ameland. I just don't know what came over me but I was suddenly seized with the idea that to go home without dropping my bombs on anything was wrong. Against all the training and against all my own views and principles, I decided to use the thousand feet to get up speed, charge down and race across the island at full throttle in the hope of seeing something that might be worth bombing.

So, without consulting my crew, I just told them I was going to do it. I put the Blenheim into a dive, pulled the Plus 9 boost and went down to the sea in a fast shallow dive. I should think that the aeroplane was doing about 260 on the clock when I got down to sea level. The island raced toward me at an alarming speed and before I knew were I was, I was racing up over sand dunes. There in front of me were four enormous long barrels, 4.7mm AA guns, pointing to the sky, surrounded by a lot of sand bags and a lot of German soldiers. I pressed the tit and dropped the bombs. I saw a lot of steely blue flashes around the ground, which I realised, was machine-gun fire. Turning to starboard I raced down to the beach to get out to sea again. There were a lot of young naked men, presumably German soldiers, having a swim. Alan Griffith raked them left and right with machine-gun fire. As we raced out to sea he told me that there was a great deal of blood and so on. I thought he'd done very well. So did he. (I now look back on it with revulsion.) Then he called out that there were terrific flashes and a lot of smoke. Something had been hit. When I landed Group Captain Bandon was waiting to greet me. His face was wreathed in smiles. Apparently, the Squadron leader had seen me dive down and cross the coast and he saw, following my bombing, a tremendous flash and smoke up to 1,500 ft. It was evident that the detonation of these bombs had touched off their ammunition dump! Being very young and inexperienced this was the first time in my life I'd ever done anything that appeared to be individually rather successful.

Two days later, on 4 August, I was sent out on a shipping beat in the Heligoland Bight. I had to lead two Sergeants who'd never been on operations before. One was only nineteen and I don't think the other one was more than about twenty. My morale was lifted when we entered the cover of cloud. However, when we emerged, quite suddenly, there, two miles slap in front, was what looked like an 8,000 ton merchant ship, surrounded, to my horror, by twelve flak ships as escort. And we were racing toward it!

I got very low down on the sea and started to open the throttles. The two Sergeants, whose formation-keeping up to now was poor, weaved around, obviously panic-stricken by the sight of this convoy. One was at about 200 ft and the other at about 100 ft, one each side of me. The whole tactical essence of low-level attacks on ships was to keep right down on the sea so that the enemy did not see you until the last minute. If you were over 20 ft you could be seen over the horizon from the deck of the ships. To my final horror, a mile out the leading flak ship flashed an order signal for me to identify myself. There was a lot of cloud above and I made a sudden decision to lead the two Sergeants into it, try to drop out and attack again from about 800 ft.

When we came out all I could see was grey sea. We never found the convoy again. I set course for home, bombing a 'Squealer', a little vessel a few miles out to sea used as an observation post for anti-shipping Blenheims. I was crestfallen because although I could put a perfectly genuine tactical reason forward for having turned away, I knew in my own heart that I'd funked it. I was not so much worried about what the Group Captain and the AOC, 'Butcher' Stevenson, of whom we all lived in dread, would say; I was more worried by the fact that I knew the real reason. However, the explanation was accepted and I heard no more. Then I realised that I had got to try to live with it and cope next time. All my elation was gone. I went out again two days later, leading another shipping beat up the Dutch coast, low level but fortunately nothing was sighted.

Then something fundamentally changed my whole operational career and indeed my whole life. We got wind that there was a major operation to be laid on and as time went by the more alarming became the rumours. We understood that it was to be a major effort involving all the Blenheims in 2 Group. We did a lot of low-level formation practice. We had a new Squadron commander. Wing Commander James Nicol arrived with no previous operational experience to take over from Wing Commander Howe, who fell out of the first floor window of Weasenham Hall after a party and was in hospital in Cambridge – not a very gallant accident for such a gallant man. The operation was to be led by 114 Squadron and Nicol had never operated before. This seemed very strange to us but he had a wonderful navigator to go with him. Flight Lieutenant Tommy Baker DFM, Howe's navigator, was an ex-Halton boy who became a very great friend of mine and whom I admired tremendously.

Meanwhile, low-level practices went on. Then, on Friday 10 August Nicol and I were taken into the operations room. I was to be deputy leader and we were to look at the target and see what this operation was to be. It had been rumoured that it was to be a factory outside Paris, which, without fighter escort, sounded terrifying enough. I'll never forget the sight that met my eyes. On a table in the centre of the ops room a huge map had been laid out and there, leading

On 12 August 1941 fifty-six Blenheims, split into two forces, attacked the Quadratfortuna/Köln and Knapsack/Oldenburg power stations at Cologne. Four Blenheims of 139 Squadron, three of 18 and one each from 21, 82 and 114 plus two from 226 Squadron, which were used as fighter navigators for the Spitfire withdrawal support failed to return, as did four Spitfire IIAs. (*Wartime Watton Museum*)

absolutely straight, was a red tape from Orford Ness, across the North Sea, right through Holland and right down to Cologne. At first I just did not believe that this was the target. I assumed it referred to something else. Then I realised it did not. The truth, the reality, dawned on me. I was going to have to take part in a low-level daylight attack on Cologne – with no fighter escort – in Blenheims.

It was no use panicking so I listened to the briefing and the instructions I was given. The target was not Cologne itself but the Knapsack power station, which the Group Captain said, was the biggest in Europe. I was shown a photograph. It had eight chimneys on one side and four on the other (known in Germany as the 'twelve apostles'). We were to fly between these chimneys, then turn round and come back again. Of course I couldn't communicate what the target was to anybody else. I had to carry this secret about with me for two days. The chances of surviving an operation like this were negligible. How could I, a fundamental coward who'd managed to skate past it up to now, make myself do this operation? The next two days were spent wrestling with myself as to how I was to do it. The only thing to do was to stop worrying and to say to myself, 'You're not coming back. You've just got to go. You're caught in this situation.' The alternative was to funk it and not go at all. Of the two this seemed the more impossible, so I just resigned myself to the fact that I was not coming back. Curiously, this rid me of uncertainty and made it easier.

Then came the early morning of 12 August when we were to go. I had a pretty poor night's sleep the night before. When I woke at 6.30 I suddenly remembered that this was the Sunday morning when I was just not going to come back. I was still saying, well, it's got to be. In the operations room all the crews in the Squadron realised what the target was. Hardened though some of them were, there was the gasp of disbelief, even from the most hardened ones. Unlike me, they had not had the opportunity to prepare themselves. It was the only time that I saw some of my fellow aircrew, including my own gunner, who was a pretty imperturbable type, literally grey and shaking. Curiously enough, seeing all the others looking so alarmed rather bolstered me a bit.

One 21-year-old gunner later recorded:

We were keyed up when we went into the briefing room at 0645 and the Station Commander's opening remarks did nothing to lessen the tension. He started off by saying, 'You are going on the biggest and most ambitious operation ever undertaken by the RAF.' Then he told us what it was. Cologne, in daylight, 150-odd miles across Germany at treetop height and then – the powerhouse. Our orders were to destroy our objectives at all costs. We were given the course to follow, the rendezvous with other squadrons of bombers and the rendezvous with fighters. We were given the parting point for the fighters and the moment at which certain flights would peel off the formation for the attack on the second powerhouse and then – in formation across Germany. While pilots and observers were getting all they could from the weather man, we rear gunners gathered round the Signals Officer for identification signs, then hurried out to get ready. Someone said 'What a trip!' and got the answer, 'Yes but what a target!' Knapsack, we were told, was the biggest steam power plant in Europe,

Twelve Whirlwind I fighters of 263 Squadron at Martlesham Heath (six for Force I and six for Force II) with only enough fuel to escort the Blenheims a short distance inland from the Dutch coast, escorted the bombers as far as Doel, just inside the Belgian border on 12 August 1941. (*Westland*)

producing hundreds of thousands of kilowatts to supply a vital industrial area. If we got it, it would be as good as getting hold of a dozen large factories. One of the pilots on the raid was in civil life a mains engineer for the County of London Electricity Supply. He came away rubbing his hands and explained to us that, with turbines setting up about 3,000 revolutions a minute, blades were likely to fly off in all directions at astronomical speeds, smashing everything and everyone as they went.

Charles Patterson continued:

The operation was very comprehensively planned. Thirty-six aircraft were to attack Knapsack in six formations of six aircraft each. Everything was being done to mislead and divert the enemy fighter force, with diversionary bombing attacks in France and northern Germany. We took off at about 0800 and I formed up closely on Wing Commander Nicol, setting off for Orford Ness. We rendezvoused on time and came down to low level over the North Sea. Although we thought we were going to certain death, perhaps it was the scale, the element of the adventure, the actual flying but somehow one was not as panicky as expected. I had always wondered what enemy territory looked like. In fact, everything looked so normal that in some way it was actually reassuring.

Fifty-six Blenheim crews were to fly to Cologne, where they would split into two forces to make simultaneous attacks on the Quadratfortuna/Köln and Knapsack/Oldenburg power stations there. The huge Knapsack power station produced 600,000W and the Quadrath station 200,000W and their destruction would significantly affect war production. Six Whirlwind fighters of 263 Squadron with only enough fuel to escort them a short distance inland from the Dutch coast would escort each force as far as Doel, just inside the Belgian border. Three squadrons of Spitfires were to provide withdrawal support from Walsoorden onwards. The operation also involved four Fortress Is of 90 Squadron, two of which would make a high-level attack on Cologne, another De Kooy airfield and the fourth Emden. A 5 Group Circus involving six Hampdens of 106 Squadron and six of 44 Squadron and several squadrons of Spitfires and Hurricanes would make attacks on Gosnay power station and St Omer-Longuenesse aerodrome respectively.

At Watton the briefing was attended by the eighteen crews of Force 1 (twelve from 21 Squadron and six from 82 Squadron),

Wing Commander James L. Nicol, 27, a pre-war regular officer, pictured here hunting off duty from Upwood in July 1941, who was CO of 114 Squadron, was awarded the DSO for leading Force 2 on the attack on the Knapsack power station at Cologne on 12 August 1941. Seven days later he was KIA leading a shipping strike off Vlieland when his Blenheim was shot down by Bf 110s of II/ZG76. (*Pip Wray via Theo Boiten*)

none of whom had probably heard of Quadrath but they would certainly recognize on the map the city of Cologne nearby. Aircrew listened intently to their station commander, Group Captain Laurie F. Sinclair, who three months before had been awarded the GC for pulling a WOP/AG from a blazing Blenheim after two bombs on board had exploded. The aircraft were detailed to fly in three boxes of six aircraft (each split into two vics of three), led by Wing Commander John C. Kercher (lead box) with Bill Edrich (port box) and Squadron Leader H. J. 'Jack' Meakin of 82 Squadron (starboard box). At the same time thirty-eight crews of Force 2 (comprising 18, 107, 114 and 139 Squadrons), led by Wing Commander James L. 'Nick' Nicol, CO of 114 Squadron, were briefed for their attack on Knapsack. Being 12 August, grouse shooting could begin in Scotland that morning. There was a still sky with a hint of early autumn in the lingering mist. Would it be the Glorious 12th for the Blenheim crews?

Bill Edrich recalled that it had been hoped, by synchronizing the two attacks, to confuse the enemy.

> We had practised our attack many times over a power station at St Neots and now we prepared to put it into effect. With four 250 lb eleven-second-delay bombs each, we had to clear the target in fairly quick time. My box of six was going in last. At St Neots we had got everyone across the target in less than three seconds. Could we manage it now?

As one of the leaders of Force 1, Edrich flew low over a fairly choppy sea to the mouth of the Scheldt, following a series of dog-legs on the way to the target, hoping that the enemy would not guess their intentions. As they flew across Holland, pulling over trees and church spires, people everywhere waved them on. Crews looked down at fields planted out in the pattern of the Dutch flag. On the way in three Blenheims were lost. The aircraft flown by 18-year-old Pilot Officer Graham C. Rolland of 82 Squadron was hit by flak and crashed at Strijensas, near the Moerdijk Bridge at 1210 hours. Rolland and Pilot Officers Hugh M. Clark, observer, and Sergeant Ernest Bainbridge, WOP/AG, were all killed. Flying Officer G. H. Hill of 18 Squadron crashed at Diest, Belgium. All three crew survived and were taken prisoner. Pilot Officer Jim Langston of 21 Squadron was hit by a burst of flak, which knocked Sergeant Ken Attew, the 21-year-old rear gunner, out of his turret before the aircraft crashed at Potz, near the target. Langstone and Sergeant Dave Roberts, observer, survived and were taken prisoner. As the formation neared the German frontier crews noticed that people were no longer waving, they just watched. In Germany itself Germans looked skyward in stunned amazement, or so it seemed to the gunners, before scuttling off to their shelters. It was all so quick. Eventually, the twin spires of Cologne cathedral appeared on the skyline and they were there. Bill Edrich remembered:

> The tall chimneys of the power station stood out ominously, forcing us up to 400 ft and more. The three sections were stepped up slightly from front to rear. There was some light flak coming up from the target area but otherwise we were unopposed – we had achieved complete surprise. Kercher and Meakin flew their formations in like regiments, directly in front of us and slightly below. All we had to do was to keep our position. We were well past the target when the first

bombs went off. Rear-facing cameras in each Blenheim were recording our results. But we could see that the attack had been successful. The core of the power station was in flames when the first bombs went off.

All seventeen aircraft of Force 1 dropped their bombs within the target area. They all came off the target unscathed then drove off some Bf 109 fighters that approached them before, purely by chance, they crossed a *Luftwaffe* airfield near Antwerp. They machine gunned some Bf 109s on the ground and shot one down that was taking off. Still unopposed, they flew into a heavy thunderstorm near the Scheldt estuary, which broke up the formation and caused the loss of a Blenheim. On clearing the storm Edrich was joined by several other aircraft and together they sped across the shallows and mudflats of the estuary towards their rendezvous with the Spitfires. It was then that they experienced their most serious opposition, partly from intensive fire from coastal batteries and even more seriously from a huge flock of seagulls that they had disturbed.

Charles Patterson, who was in Force 1, recalled:

We had flown down the Schelde estuary, south of Woensdrecht airfield and into the heathland of Holland, all of it new to me. At any moment we expected enemy fighters. We went on, mile after mile, not a cloud in the sky and still no fighters.

I asked my navigator, 'How long?'

'Not long now,' he said.

On the R/T Nicol said, 'Turn to starboard.'

As I turned slightly, there, up on top of a long, long slope about three miles away was this enormous industrial complex. I realised that this was Knapsack. I thought, well, we've just got to go on now and there'll be a big bang.

We had to climb a bit to avoid the increasing maze of electricity pylons and cables. Then the chimneys came into view, until they were coming right at us. Wing Commander Nicol swung in between the chimneys and I followed him. I became enveloped in mist and steam. I was in it now. There was nothing I could do except concentrate on flying the aeroplane properly. We had been told not to release our bombs on the attractive-looking water coolers but to keep them for the actual powerhouse at the far end. We flew on down between these chimneys. As we did so I saw again a lot of blue flashes, which would be machine-gun fire but I was past caring about that now. At the far end I could see the great turbine house and the steam and the smoke and everything. I pressed the tit and let the bombs go. As I did so, Nicol, just ahead of me, swerved sharply to starboard and I did the same. I realised he was about to fly into a chimney, which he just missed.

In his rear turret the 21-year-old gunner did not know that they were over the target until he saw the power-house chimneys above: four on one side, eight on the other.

Then the observer called out 'Bomb gone!' and as I felt the doors swinging to, the pilot yelled 'Machine gun!' I burst in all I could as we turned away to starboard. Three miles off I had a good view of the place. We had used delayed-action bombs and banks of black smoke and scalding steam were gushing out. Debris was rocketing into the air and I thought of those turbine blades ricocheting around the building.

 Charles Patterson continued:

Then, out the other side, a lot more blue flashes and sparks and tracer. We dived down to the ground. Nicol was there. He'd survived. I formed up on him. We raced away across the cables again down past the other side of the power station. We started to turn to starboard to fly on the course for the Dutch coast, then to my amazement all the other five members of the formation emerged safely and formed up with us. We set off on the journey home.

Wing Commander James L. Nicol, leading Force 2, recalled flying below the level of the trees and, when they were only seven minutes away from their target, seeing the Blenheims of Force I crossing their path. It seemed to him that the air was alive with Blenheims. They had nearly reached the target when his WOP/AG called out over the intercom 'Tallyho – fighter to port' and he felt cannon shells hitting his port wing. He led his formation into evasive action when they ran into intensive flak. He could see the flak bursting among the Blenheims in front of him, so looked to see where it was coming from. Seeing flashes from a gun emplacement, he went straight for it, firing with his fixed front gun. Nichol went on:

You couldn't miss the target. There were twelve chimneys – a row of four and a parallel of eight – standing stark against the sky. There was smoke and flames coming from the plant, so we climbed to attack. The flames were fifty feet high and the smoke was too thick to let us bomb accurately from any lower. Inside the buildings we could see the sullen glow of explosions under the smoke. I flew straight between the chimneys when I heard my observer call 'Bombs gone!'

I did a steep turn over a belt of trees down into a sandstone quarry to get away from the flak. I should think we were about thirty feet below ground level. As we came up I heard my WOP/AG call 'Fighter again' and at the same moment a piece of my port wing fell away. I heard no more from my WOP/AG and it must have been then that he was wounded. I tried once more evasive action. A bullet came in behind my head and another smacked the armour plating at my back. My observer said that he could see a stream of bullets coming between his legs. I turned to the right to give the fighter a more difficult angle of fire and this seemed to work; he sprayed the air below us. While we twisted about I hit the top of a telegraph pole and clipped the airscrew, yet remarkably this didn't seem to affect our flying. There was, however, a film of oil over my perspex, which impeded my vision and we would have hit a church spire had my observer not warned me just in time. I banked sharply to avoid this obstruction, catching the tip of my wing on a tree. Once more we were lucky and managed to catch up to the others.

The worst of the attack was over but I have never known anything so welcome as the squadrons of Spitfires waiting for us, who warded off the attacks of even more Messerschmitts, then I had to think of my WOP/AG. I tried to call him up, then was passed a note that read, 'Please get here quickly. Bleeding badly.' I gave my observer a bandage and he crept through the bomb bay to give the gunner first aid. I flew on back in an interval between two storms and made straight for base. Our undercarriage had been damaged and would not go down. My observer held our WOP/AG as I made a belly-landing

Charles Patterson recalls:

I settled down in formation and another chap formated on me. The whole formation got together. On to Holland we went. No interception yet. Then we flew into a rainstorm and for a wonderful moment I thought we were going to get cloud cover but it was only a shower and we emerged shortly afterwards into the brilliant sun again and no cloud above us. On and on, past little villages and hamlets, occasionally an individual diving into a ditch beneath us. Just before we got to the Dutch border, we flew over a baronial German mansion. In the garden, beside a cedar tree, I just got a glimpse of a table with a large white table cloth, all laid out for lunch and a group of people standing around it. As we whizzed over the top my gunner let fly and it broke up the party. He felt that any rich Germans who were living like that while the war was on deserved it.

On across Holland, now it suddenly seemed to me that we were going to make it. Nothing was going to happen after all but it's always when that psychological moment comes that you're brought down to earth. Ahead of us, just as we were coming up to the Schelde estuary, black dots appeared. For a moment my navigator thought that they might be Spitfires that had come out to escort us home but of course they were not. They were not Whirlwinds either, which had escorted us out and were due to escort us back. Nicol called out 'Snappers!' Before I knew where I was, I was flying on straight into these Messerschmitts, which were circling around about a thousand feet above us.

Nicol told us to close in tight. He led us right down on to the water, sparkling in the sun, not more than ten, fifteen and occasionally perhaps twenty feet below. I got as tight into him as I could, with my wing tip practically inside his. I knew this was life or death. It took all the flying concentration and skill I possessed to do it, which drove out most of the fear of the fighters. The others closed in. Then Nicol handed over to the leading gunner, Pilot Officer Julian Morton, a very experienced second tour man. He directed the formation because the gunners, looking back, could all see the fighters coming into attack. He had to decide when it was the right moment to open fire and when to take evasive action.

Then I heard the rattle of machine-gun fire and realised that our guns were firing. Every now and then the water was ripped with white froth, which was of course the cannon shells of these 109s. On one turn, out of the corner of one eye, I caught a glimpse of a 109 right in front peeling off from the attack. It was so close that I could see the pilot in the cockpit, let alone the black crosses and the yellow nose of the 109. My reaction was simply one of interest in seeing a 109 so close. We all knew that the only safety was out to sea and out of range of these 109s. Would we make it? After each attack we just had to crouch down and prepare for the next. This carried on all the way up the Schelde. Yet we seemed to survive them.

Then, unbelievably, the islands to each side of us suddenly ceased and we were in the open sea. We'd hardly gone any distance when the leading gunner told us over the R/T that the fighters had broken off the attack. I suppose they were running out of ammunition. Still, we didn't feel it was all over yet. The first reaction of realising that one had survived was a sort of numbness. The leading Blenheim climbed gently to about 600 ft and I realised that we had survived. We'd made it. It was just marvellous, happy relief, sheer joy, flying back across the North Sea. Then the cliffs came up – England. We were back.

There was a general opinion that we'd all hit the target and reports came in that we'd got away with it but by the afternoon word got round that we had lost twelve of the 36 and that several others had been badly shot up and crash landed. Two Blenheims, which had navigated the Whirlwind fighters out to escort us home, had also been shot down. This was very tragic and a terrible waste.

Then, of course, the inevitable relaxation. We were all to go to Norwich, the whole group, for a party and a beat-up. We all met up and drank away. All great excitement, great fun. We felt very heroic and wonderful. We thought, 'This is it, we've done it.' We forgot there was any future. For the rest of my operational career I found that the way to make myself overcome my fear was to tell myself that I was not coming back and just accept the fact. That is the way I personally conquered fear. I don't think that all my fellow aircrew thought quite as I did. How we conquered our own individual fear was not a thing we ever talked about, however intimate or friendly we were.

Nicol was awarded an immediate DSO for leading the Knapsack raid. However, it had been taken for granted before we took off that if he got back he would get a VC. It caused a considerable disappointment. About a week later Wing Commander Nicol went out on his next trip and never came back.

On 19 August Nicol, Flight Sergeant Edward T. W. Jones, observer and Flying Officer Herbert J. Madden DFC were killed when their Blenheim was shot down by Bf 110s of II./ZG76 north-west of Vlieland during an attack on a convoy. Wing Commander Kercher also received the DSO for the Quadrath raid.

Force 1 had lost two Blenheims and Force 2 eight. Sergeant Harry Ingleby RCAF of 139 Squadron was shot down by flak over the target and his aircraft crashed at Berrenrath; all three crew were killed. A few moments later Sergeant G. Coast of the same squadron crashed at Hucheln. He had probably been hit by flak over the target. Coast and his observer, Pilot Officer K. J. Mackintosh, survived and were taken prisoner; Sergeant Dennis A. Wilson, the 19-year old WOP/AG from Kent was killed. Nearing the Dutch coast Pilot Officer Malcolm T. K. Walkden of 18 Squadron hit high-tension cables, which sheared off the tail and the aircraft crashed in the mouth of the Scheldt with no survivors. The aircraft flown by New Zealander Flight Lieutenant George A. Herbert of 139 Squadron was damaged by light flak over the target and also crashed into the mouth of the Scheldt, off Breskens, killing all three crew. Two minutes later Sergeant Douglas J. Wheatley of 114 Squadron was set upon by *Oberleutnant* Kurt Ruppert in a Bf 109 of III./JG26, who shot the Blenheim down in flames. It hit the sea off Flushing. There were no survivors.[22] *Oberleutnant* Baron Freiherr Hubertus von Holtey of Stab./JG26, in a Bf 109E, shot down Squadron Leader A. F. H. Mills RCAF, who ditched in the sea south of Flushing. All three crew took to their dinghy and were picked up a few minutes later by a small German vessel and taken prisoner. Among the withdrawal forces two Spitfires were shot down by the *Luftwaffe Flakabteilung* 43/XI. One pilot was killed and the pilot of the other belly-landed near Breskens and was taken to hospital. Two Blenheims from 226 Squadron, navigating as fighter leaders, were lost. Flight Lieutenant Gwilym I. Lewis was hit by flak and crashed at Berrenrath in Belgium, killing Lewis, Flight Sergeant Neville Cardell, observer, and Flight Sergeant Jack Woods, WOP/AG.

At Katwijk at 1245 hours the *Flakalarm* was sounded. Pilots of I./JG1 climbed into their Bf 109s and took off in the direction of Zeeuws-Vlaanderen, while at the same time Bf 109Es of JG26 took off from Wevelgem and Woensdrecht. As the returning aircraft approached, the flak guns opened up, only breaking off their barrage when *Unteroffizier* Siegfried Zick of I./JG1 dived his Bf 109E on to the tail of the Blenheim piloted by 20-year-old Flight Lieutenant Hugh S. Young, a Scot from Glasgow. Zick dispatched his quarry with a burst of gunfire, and it crashed at 1300 hours in the mouth of the Scheldt with no survivors. (Zick survived the war with seventy-six victories.)

On the way back Pilot Officer Jimmy Corfield of 21 Squadron, a day short of his twenty-fifth birthday, was lagging behind as one of his two engines had been damaged by AA fire. Off Texel, 12 miles west of Harmstede, *Oberstleutnant* Adolf Galland of Stab./JG26 at Audembert near Wissant in the Pas de Calais pounced at 1318 hours and easily despatched the ailing Blenheim for a simple seventy-eighth victory.[23] Galland watched as the Blenheim caught fire in the right engine and fuselage and hit the sea on its right side, his gun camera filming its last moments. No one baled out. A week before the raid Corfield's younger brother Bill, 'a hero-worshipping 17 year old schoolboy' had seen Jimmy on his last leave. He had told his older brother that if the war lasted long enough he would become a pilot like him. Jimmy quietly told Bill that he did not have the temperament and to get a ground job instead. Bill little realized at the time that he was trying to save his life. Jimmy Corfield was killed and Pilot Officers Arthur L. A. Williams and 32-year-old Maurice Williams, the WOP/AG, died with him. They were later buried in the Military cemetery at Den Burg on Texel Island off the Dutch coast where their bodies were washed up ten days and 118 miles later. Bill Corfield was shattered at the news of his brother's death and, determined to prove him wrong, he became a Lancaster pilot.

The twelve Blenheims that were lost represented 15.4 per cent of the force. This would have been acceptable had the damage to the power stations reported by the aircrews been confirmed by later reconnaissance but both were soon back in commission again. Charles Patterson concluded:

In the summer of 1941 the casualty rate on Blenheims in 2 Group was such that statistically you could not survive more than seven to ten ops but you had to do thirty. Anyone who did seven trips was promoted to Flight Lieutenant and on average anyone who'd done about fifteen was a Squadron Leader. Due to the fact that I'd survived for so long, I suddenly found myself made a Squadron Leader, when only six or seven weeks before I'd been a Pilot Officer and I had a flight to command. The tremendous privilege of commanding these men when I was only 21 seemed to me the most wonderful, worthwhile job in the world. The rest of my tour consisted of one or two shipping beats and a number of Circuses. To be taken off it, to be sent on a rest, on 10 October 1941, came as a terrible blow. It wasn't because I wanted to go on fighting. It was because I wanted to go on commanding the flight. After a course at Upavon, for the next ten months I was an instructor. Just before Christmas my spirits were suddenly lifted when I was told to my astonishment that a DFC had come through for me and a DFM for Alan Griffith. I've never been quite sure about whether I deserved the DFC except that I can always say anyone who got through a tour on Blenheims in 1941 could feel that he'd reasonably deserved it for surviving it.

Six days after the Cologne power stations raid, on 18 August, 88 Squadron received nineteen Blenheim Mk IVs from 105 Squadron for anti-shipping operations off the Dutch coast. Results were poor, however and they were little better on 21 August when cloud obscured the chemical works at Chocques; crews dropped their bombs on factories and railway junctions near St Omer instead. Shipping was again the target on 26 August when 21, 82 and 88 Squadrons all suffered losses attacking a convoy off the Dutch coast. Sergeant Alex S. Oman's Blenheim of 21 Squadron was shot down by a flak ship with the loss of all three crew. A 226 Squadron Blenheim flown by Sergeant Gilbert V. Smith crashed in the sea with its starboard engine on fire after being hit by flak during the attack on the convoy with no survivors. Worst hit was 82 Squadron, which lost four Blenheims to Bf 109s of 2. and 3./JG52. Nine crews of 88 Squadron attacked north of Borkum. Squadron Leader Alan Lynn, the CO[24] and Canadian Flight Lieutenant James O. Alexander attacked a 4,000 ton motor vessel travelling in convoy, scoring direct hits. The vessel was aflame and dead in the water as the Blenheims sped away. Pilot Officer George B. Dunn's aircraft was hit by flak and exploded as it hit the water. Dunn, his observer, Pilot Officer John Jones, and Flight Sergeant Basil Davies were killed. When Pilot Officer Tudor G. Edwards's Blenheim was attacked by two Bf 110s Flight Sergeant F. Tweedale the WOP/AG kept the *Luftwaffe* at bay while the Welshman jettisoned the bomb load and flew the aircraft home safely.

Also on 26 August Bill Edrich recalled a briefing when they were detailed to intercept a southbound convoy off the Dutch coast near Ijmuiden. He led the six Blenheims of 21 Squadron, flying low in two vics of three; 21-year-old Squadron Leader Richard A. 'Dick' Shuttleworth led the second, in what was for him his first shipping strike. The convoy came into sight and Edrich decided to make their approach from the direction of the Dutch coast and to attack the flak ships, opening the way for the second vic to attack the merchantmen. He gained height on his approach before diving over his target, just clearing the masts as he released his bombs and returned to nought feet. There had been no flak on the run in but as they pulled away the tracer overtook them, racing past like a blizzard. His No. 2 survived the attack but he saw his No. 3 plunging towards the sea with his port wing a blazing torch. Shuttleworth and the other two members of his vic attacked the merchantmen, scoring several hits without further loss.

The following day Edrich, who was then in charge of 21 Squadron, was informed that he was to supply six aircraft for a low-level strike on the docks at Rotterdam on 28 August. The order further specified that the aircraft were to be led by the inexperienced Shuttleworth. Edrich had a justifiable premonition that the Germans would be more than ready for such a raid following the successful operation that had taken place only six weeks earlier. He was so concerned that he requested to be allowed to lead the operation instead of Shuttleworth, a request that was turned down. Reconnaissance had shown that the Germans were once again assembling many ships in Rotterdam to carry war materials and food along the coasts of the occupied countries. It was therefore decided that the second raid, which went ahead on the 28th, was imperative. Crews must have been pleased to learn that they were to have Spitfire IIAs of 19 Squadron from Coltishall and 152 Squadron from Swanton Morley for fighter escort.

The first attempt, just after 1440 hours, was recalled at 1530 hours. At around 1720 hours eighteen crews – six from 21 Squadron at Watton, six from 88 Squadron at Attlebridge, three from 110 Squadron at Wattisham and three from 226 Squadron at Swanton Morley – were successful, though *F-Freddy* crashed on take-off at Attlebridge. The Spitfires were picked up and the formation flew to a point 4 miles south of Oostvoorm, where they would turn to their second point 5 miles south of Waalhaven. Where the three boxes of aircraft would come into line abreast and speed in at roof-top height. The formation made landfall at the Dutch coast but as soon as they reached the mouth of the Nieuwe Waterweg, the canal that links Rotterdam to the sea, destroyers and AA batteries threw up a terrific barrage of flak. As soon as they were clear of the flak they came under attack from enemy fighters but the seventeen Blenheims scraped through and flew on, hugging the ground all the way to the docks. Their arrival was greeted by a hail of light machine-gun and flak fire as they swept across Rotterdam at roof-top height in line abreast. The Spitfires, meanwhile, had climbed to 1,500 ft to provide top cover while the Blenheims hurled their bombs into shipping and construction yards.

No. 21 Squadron hit two large ships and dock buildings. *Leutnant* Hans Müller of 6./JG53, in a Bf 109F, shot down two of the squadron's Blenheims flown by Sergeant Kenneth Hayes and Pilot Officer W. L. MacDonald. None of Hayes's crew survived but MacDonald and his WOP/AG survived and were taken prisoner. (Müller too was taken prisoner on 25 March 1943. He had fifteen victories.) Pilot Officer Frank Orme RCAF and his crew were hit by flak from the ships in the harbour and crashed at Maassluis, exploding on impact. There were no survivors. The Blenheim flown by Dick Shuttleworth was also hit by flak and he crashed in Scheurpolder. The 21-year-old died of his wounds in the Wilhelmina Hospital in Amsterdam. Edrich's premonition had been fulfilled and he would have to break the news to his friend's wife Honor whom he had married only two weeks before. Two Blenheims of 226 Squadron joined three from 110 Squadron and made a run on shipping at just 20 ft. Pilot Officer F. M. V. Johnstone was hit by flak but he managed to belly land the crippled and flaming Blenheim at Kethel. Johnstone and his two crew survived and were made PoWs. Luck finally ran out for Pilot Officer Tudor Edwards and his crew of Fred A. Letchford and Flight Sergeant Frank Tweedale, who had returned after the brush with Bf 110s two days earlier. They too were shot down by flak and all were killed. So too were Flight Lieutenant James O. Alexander and crew, whose Blenheim crashed in a slaughterhouse at Schiedam.

Flight Lieutenant Mayer H. R. 'Dickie' Namias, a 19-year-old pilot in 88 Squadron spectacularly sank a 10,000 tonner when one of the Londoner's bombs bounced from the dockside and hit under the stem of the ship, which exploded and sank. Squadron Leader Alan Lynn caught a 5,000 ton vessel, while Flight Lieutenant

Stewart bombed a 4,000 ton ship, which he missed. Stewart then turned to the shipyards but was attacked by a trio of Bf 109s of 6./JG53. His gunner, Flight Sergeant Mills, was wounded and the aircraft was badly damaged. After the attack the Blenheims joined up with their escorts, now reinforced by a dozen Spitfires of 266 Squadron.

Obviously perturbed by the losses sustained in the operation Churchill wrote in a minute to the Chief of Air Staff on the 29th: 'The loss of seven Blenheims out of seventeen [and three Spitfires] in the daylight attack on merchant shipping and docks at Rotterdam is most severe. . . While I greatly admire the bravery of the pilots, I do not want them pressed too hard. Easier targets giving a high damage return compared to casualties may be more often selected.' The following day he drafted a message to the crews. 'The devotion and gallantry of the attacks on Rotterdam and other objectives are beyond all praise. The Charge of the Light Brigade is eclipsed in brightness by these almost daily deeds of fame.' The comparison with the unfortunate Charge of the Light Brigade may well have been appropriate but was hardly encouraging to those taking part. During August the loss rate was as high as 30 per cent. Of seventy-seven Blenheims that attacked shipping, twenty-three were lost, while of 480 sorties flown, thirty-six failed to return. Coupled with their losses in Malta, it was a very demanding and fateful period for 2 Group. The anti-shipping role and shipping 'beat' patrols of 2 Group Blenheims were coming to an end by September but not before they inflicted a terrible penalty on the crews taking part. On 6 September 88 Squadron moved on detachment to Manston in Kent to take part in Channel Stop operations. (Further detachments, to Long Kesh in January/February 1942, Abbotsinch in May and Ford in July 1942, were made before the whole Squadron moved from Attlebridge to Oulton, Norfolk, in September 1942.)

On 17 September ten Blenheims from 139 Squadron flew a Circus, their target being the Grand Quevilly power station near Rouen, on which they claimed three direct hits. They too came under attack from enemy fighters, one of the Blenheims being damaged, while the Spitfire escort claimed to have shot down four of the 109s for the loss of four of their own. In 82 Squadron meanwhile, Pilot Officer C. J. Harper and crew failed to return from an attack on Mazingarbe power station and chemical complex.

Three days later, on 20 September shipping 'beats' were flown off the Dutch coast by twenty-two Blenheims of 18, 139 and 226 Squadrons with Spitfires of 66 and 152 Squadrons flying escort. The search for a target by the crews of 139 Squadron proved fruitless. In an attempt to confuse the enemy defences Circuses were directed at three other targets. Three Blenheims of 18 Squadron went to the marshalling yards at Hazebrouck and nine from 82 and 114 Squadrons to the shipyards at Rouen, while Hampdens bombed Mazingarbe. Eight other crews of 18 Squadron found a 2,000 – 3,000 ton motor vessel and a tanker off the Dutch coast near Zandvoort, which they seriously damaged. Nineteen-year-old Sergeant John M. Nickleson RCAF and his crew of *F-Freddy* crashed into the sea with its starboard engine blazing. There were no survivors. (On 18 August this same crew had dropped Douglas Bader's artificial leg during a Circus over Gosnay in France.) Meanwhile, six crews of 226 Squadron led by the young Flight Lieutenant Mayer H. R. 'Dickie' Namias were on an early morning sweep off the Hook of Holland when they found a convoy of fourteen ships flying protective balloons. Namias led the Blenheims in to attack and they set fire to four of the ships and broke the back of the *Metz*, a 728 ton German merchant vessel. Sergeant J. C. V. Colmer's Blenheim was destroyed in one of the bomb bursts. Another aircraft, piloted by Flight Lieutenant A. Brian 'Digger' Wheeler, an incredibly tough New Zealander from Marton in the North Island who had been a sheep rancher in Argentina, was hit in one engine. Although he twice bounced off the sea, Wheeler somehow managed to bring his aircraft and his crew home safely. Following his attack, the aircraft flown by Dickie Namias was hit in the starboard engine. Canadian Flight Sergeant Bill O'Connell, assuming that he could not see that he was on fire, broke radio silence to tell his leader that his starboard engine was on fire but the 19-year-old Londoner did not reply. Namias hit the sea and his Blenheim disappeared in a great splash. All the crew died. (Next day after he had given a wireless interview on the BBC O'Connell visited Namias' parents at their palatial home in London and spoke to them. Mrs Namias was particularly distraught and wanted O'Connell only to tell her that her son would be home soon.[25]

On the 21st Circuses were flown by six Blenheims of 18 Squadron, whose target was the power station at Bethune and six of 139 Squadron, who unloaded their bombs on the power station at Gosnay. On the 27th 110, 226 and 114 Squadrons flew the last Circuses of the month, when the new Fw 190 was encountered for the first time. In October the last shipping 'beats' were flown by Blenheims in the UK, the Air Staff at last having concluded that the aircraft was just not suitable for this role. (Anti-shipping operations were taken over by Hurricane fighter-bombers of 402, 605 and 607 Squadrons.) On 12 October the most successful Circus flown took place. It was directed at the docks at Boulogne and involved twenty-four aircraft from 21, 110 and 226 Squadrons. Elsewhere on the same day three or four ships in a convoy off The Hague were hit and 82 Squadron found a convoy of seven merchantmen protected by three flak ships 8 miles off the Dutch coast between Ijmuiden and Scheveningen. Led by Squadron Leader H. J. Meakin, the aircraft swept into the attack, scoring a direct hit on a 5,000 ton tanker and leaving a freighter on fire. The flak was, as always, fierce. One severely damaged Blenheim ditched in the sea close to the convoy. Another plunged into the sea with the loss of all on board, while a third, more fortunate, having lost an airscrew somehow managed to stagger back to base.

Next day, 13 October, the Blenheims were out on another Circus, once more to the Mazingarbe ammonia production works. Pilot Sergeant Eric 'Tommy' Atkins, of 139 Squadron (whose second operation this was, his first having been a shipping attack on the Heligoland Bight on 11 October, when the squadron lost three of six Blenheims), viewed it philosophically.

The fact that the target had been pranged before on Circuses made it a less difficult 'second guessing' game for the Germans when they saw the formation approaching. They were well versed in retaliation methods. German radar in the Pas de Calais area had been vastly improved and this enabled their fighters to be high and waiting. They also knew that the Blenheim could do limited damage at 17,000 ft with only four 250 lb bombs and without the latest bombsights. Our own firepower against fighters was two Browning guns in the turret, one in the

Sergeant pilot Eric 'Tommy' Atkins of 139 Squadron at Oulton in September 1941. His first operation, a shipping attack in the Heligoland Bight on 11 October cost the squadron three of the six attacking Blenheims. (*Eric Atkins*)

port wing and another in the nose.

It was not a long trip as operations went: three hours, there and back. We took off from Horsham St Faith for West Raynham and quickly formated with one another in the box of six – two vics of three with the second vic slightly lower than the first to co-ordinate firepower. At the same time we climbed steadily and headed towards our first rendezvous point with our fighters. There was some ribald comment in the cockpit.

'Steer due south, Tommy, if No 1 gets lost;' said Jock Sullivan, my navigator.

'That'll take us to the Costa del Sol,' I replied.

'Can't see any of our fighters;' said Bill Harrison, the WOP/AG. 'Probably still having their breakfast.'

'Just don't shoot any of ours down, Bill,' I replied.

By this time, dressed in my altitude clothing, I was sweating from my exertions in keeping in the formation and still climbing. Still no sign of our fighters. We knew that they had limited fuel and range and we hoped that they were already in their positions, shadowing us in the clouds. Our leader had given up circling and set course for the target. As we climbed to 16,000 ft the earth looked strangely remote and unreal below, patchwork quilt in design. It was our first Circus and now that we were approaching the amphitheatre where the action would take place we felt vulnerable.

It wasn't easy to keep in formation in the thin atmosphere and the Blenheim wallowed on the controls. We were No. 2 in the front vic and Bill shouted out to me that the second vic had strayed and was line astern of us instead of stacked just below. 'Do they want their bloody heads shot off?' he said.

But there was constant movement of aircraft and vics and I wondered what would happen when we were attacked.

Suddenly heavy flak bursts surrounded us – subdued thuds and thick smoke, masking the deadly shrapnel flying about. I knew then why there were no fighters – both ours and the enemy's were keeping their distance and waiting for the flak to wilt before the air attack began. The flak was so heavy that it threatened to turn the Blenheims on their side. We were issued with a steel helmet to wear over our flying helmet when flying, as extra protection against flak but we preferred to sit on it – most of the flak comes upwards and not downwards! The bangs under the aircraft suggested that we had been hit but there was no visible large damage and the flying controls were not affected. The formation was being jostled about alarmingly in the air and we kept asking each other 'Are you OK?'

I said to Bill, 'Keep a good look out – after the flak will come the fighters.'

It was almost a clear sky with a winter sun and the scene was set for the next action. Our leader was losing height and we followed him to 14,000 ft, the bombing height, in between the light and heavy flak perimeters. Jock shouted, 'Target below and to port, Tommy!' I couldn't see it and I was too busy formating. The leader's bomb bay doors were open. Jock opened ours too. On the signal we let go our four 250 lb bombs. Jock and Bill sighted them down and reported bursts in the target area. We were too high to see what we had achieved. We were not allowed more than one run-up to the target, so we prepared to get the 'hell out of it'!

The leader headed home. The flak had ceased. Then Bill shouted, 'Enemy aircraft at eight o'clock!' It was on the port side of us but it turned out to be one of our close escort Hurricanes. There were others about but they were busy elsewhere. Jock saw a yellow-nosed fighter diving towards us but it veered away from the formation as a Spitfire engaged it. This was probably one of the new Fw 190s [one of which was caught on camera-gun film for the first time on this day by a 129 Squadron Spitfire], superior to our Spitfires in performance but not in pilot skill. We never saw it again.

The journey back was mostly uneventful, apart from a burst or two of light flak as we approached the coast. Our formation up to this point had been rather straggled but over the sea we closed up to prove that we could formate more effectively. At this point Spitfires appeared to cover our withdrawal.

On the ground back at Horsham St Faith we examined the aircraft. Five out of six aircraft, including our own, had flak damage. My steel helmet had a 'scar' on it adjacent to some flak damage to the airframe. It looked as though it had 'saved my bacon' or, more accurately, my 'privates'! Another piece of flak had pierced the perspex of the observer's compartment and must have just missed Jock's head. Bill was unscathed but frustrated because he had not had a real opportunity to fire at an enemy aircraft; however, he was mollified when he saw the flak holes peppering the outside of his turret! All the Blenheims got back safely.

We didn't like Circuses. They were for freaks and animals, not airmen! It didn't seem right that the Blenheim should be used as bait. Such tactics were far from being successful – the enemy often lacked presence. Better co-ordination was needed between our escort and ourselves. It wasn't easy for bombers under fire to give our fighters tactical co-operation.

Eric Atkins later flew Mosquitoes, Jock Sullivan was killed in action, while Bill Harrison survived the war but died of pneumonia soon after.

On 15 October Wing Commander V. S. Butler DFC led a formation of 226 Squadron Blenheims to Le Havre harbour. In a clear blue sky the CO began his bombing run 8 miles from the docks, making the aircraft an ideal target for the AA gunners, who not unnaturally responded not only with enthusiasm but also accuracy, literally shooting two of the bombers out of the sky. The escorting fighters, meanwhile, found themselves doing battle with Bf 109s. Butler led the remains of his formation down to low level and they made good their escape, though the aircrew undoubtedly could not forgive their leader for taking them on a ridiculously long bombing run.

Altogether 160 Blenheims and 480 airmen in 2 Group were lost between 24 March and 31 October 1941. This does not include aircraft that crashed on their return to the UK or the crippling losses by the squadrons detached to operate from Malta. Between 14 June and 31 December 1941 the RAF lost 411 fighters over the Channel and the Continent while the *Luftwaffe* lost only 103 Bf 109s and Fw 190s. On 17 December, Air Vice Marshal A. Lees replaced Air Vice Marshal Donald F. Stevenson DSO OBE MC at Group HQ; Stevenson was posted overseas and later commanded the RAF in Burma. On his departure, he said:

> Since February 17th I have watched with admiration the courage, determination and war efficiency displayed by squadron commanders, flight commanders, leaders and crews. These fulfilled the highest traditions of the service and were maintained throughout the vigorous day offensive against the enemy. Many hundreds of thousands of tons of Axis shipping, both here and in the Mediterranean, have been sunk and damaged, while such daylight raids as Bremen, Cologne and Rotterdam already have their place in the history of the air war. . .

CHAPTER FIVE

Boston Boys

We're flying binding Bostons
At 250 binding feet,
Doing night intruders
Just to see who we might meet.
And when the daylight dawns again
And when we can take a peek,
We find we've made our landfall
Up the Clacton binding Creek.

At the beginning of 1942 2 Group had just five bomber squadrons in East Anglia. On 5 January Wing Commander Alan Lynn DFC took over command of 107 Squadron at Great Massingham, while in Malta, Wing Commander Dunlevie RCAF and what was left of the squadron's Blenheims were waging war in the Mediterranean, where they would remain until the 12th. Training on the Blenheim continued until the first Boston III arrived at Massingham on 5 January. The new role for 107 Squadron (and 88 and 226, which also re-equipped with the Boston) was to be high-level, pinpoint bombing with a dozen or more aircraft. For two months 107 and 226 Squadrons converted together, using the range at Brancaster on the Wash for firing practice.

Meanwhile, crews in 105 Squadron, now commanded by Wing Commander Peter

Blenheim IV V550 intruder of 18 Squadron at Horsham St Faith, Norwich in the winter of 1942. In March of the year 82, 139 and 110 Squadrons were despatched to the Far East. The remaining Blenheims, of 18, 21 and 114 Squadrons, were employed in Night Intruder operations against enemy airfields, which was to last until the final Blenheim of 18 Squadron came in to land at Wattisham at 0145 on 18 August. (*Alan Ellender via Dr Theo Boiten*)

H. A. Simmons DFC (later killed flying a Turkish Air Force Mosquito) were kicking their heels at Swanton Morley. Sergeant Mike Carreck DFM was an observer in one of the newest Blenheim crews fresh from 17 OTU Upwood, 2 Group's finishing school. Pilot Officer Ronald Olney, first violinist in the London Philharmonic and his crew were one of the half dozen or so posted to 105 Squadron at Swanton Morley. Mike Carreck recalled:

> Waiting there for us were a very few survivors from 105's bloodbath in Malta where fourteen days was the lifetime of a Blenheim squadron. We rightly regarded these battle-scarred veterans with the deepest respect but they made us welcome. Life at Swanton Morley – a hellspot only fifteen miles from Norwich but which might well have been in deepest Siberia – began sedately enough. Now and then we did a Blenheim cross-country as I handled my pilot course, compass and ETAs. Sometimes we ventured as far away as Lincoln. We flew to the range and dropped teeny-weeny bombs and once, special treat and with much trepidation, a 250 pounder. Dullish days but nights were duller still, as for recreation, romance and merriment one had to rely on nearby East Dereham where mothers locked away their daughters after tea and every door slammed tight shut on the dot of 1800 hrs. Nothing to do but go shivering to our beds in our freezing Nissen huts. Excitement was somewhat lacking. Except for a nonsense of a rumour going the rounds that we were to be re-equipped with a fabulous new aircraft, the fastest in the world, a day bomber that could out-fly

The first Boston IIIs arrived at Great Massingham on 5 January 1942, as the new role for 107 Squadron (and 88 and 226, which also re-equipped with the Boston) was to be high-level, pinpoint bombing. These Boston IIIs were photographed at a press day an 8 April 1942. From right to left are: AL280/A, which was hit by flak at Vlissingen and ditched in the North Sea on 1 August 1942; W8373/R which served with several units including finally, 114 Squadron, where on 13 September 1945 it was taxied into a ditch at Gerbani No 3 LG (Sigonella) Sicily and the nosewheel collapsed; AL290/K, which was SOC 31 August 1944; W8387/D, which was hit by flak at Boulogne and ditched off Dover on 1 April 1942; AL284/B, which was damaged by Fw 190s and collided with Z2164 on 10 November 1942; W8355/C was hit by flak at Hazebrouck and ditched in the Channel on 12 April 1942; AL744/S, which was damaged by flak at Abbeville on 30 April 1942 and was SOC on its return; AL296/S, which joined 18 Squadron in Tunisia and on 25 April 1943, was damaged by a fighter and crashed at Medjez-el-Bab, Z2179/O, piloted by Pilot Officer Henry Collings, which was shot down by Lt Paul Galland of 8./JG26 during a raid on Pont-à-Vendin on 31 October 1942; and AL288/M was damaged by flak at Dunkirk on 4 June 1942 and was not repaired. (*Tony Carlisle via Nigel Buswell*)

any fighter and leave it wondering where we'd gone, that could fly 5 miles high into the stratosphere and had an incredible range of 1,200 miles. We shrugged our shoulders – we'd believe it when we saw it. Which we very soon did.

On 15 November it came suddenly out of nowhere inches above the hangars with a crackling thunderclap of twin Merlins. As we watched, bewitched, it was flung about the sky in a beyond belief display for a bomber that could out perform any fighter. Well-bred whisper of a touch down, a door opened and down the ladder came suede shoes, yellow socks and the rest of Geoffrey de Havilland. We pushed and shoved around this impossible dream of an aircraft. No other word for it, it was beautiful. An arrogant beauty, job to do, get out of my way, slim sleek fuselage, high cocked 'to-hell-with-you' tail, awesome power on the leash in those huge engines, eager on its undercarriage like a sprinter on the starting blocks, couldn't wait to leap up and away.

'Called a Mosquito,' they told us. Mosquito W4064 – it was to be shot down six months later on the squadron's first operation.[26] During those six months only seven more Mosquitoes joined W4064 so flights were few and far between; indeed we new boys had to wait weeks for our first. For us, back to Blenheims and Arctic nights, not counting a Station exercise when it was pretended that German paratroopers had landed and a batch of us were sent to guard the Sergeants' Mess. We stretched out on the carpet, blissfully warm at last until somebody came in to wake us with the astounding news that the Japanese had bombed Pearl Harbor. We turned over to sleep our best night ever, the war was won.

Another rumour now to scoff at, that the Squadron was going to move to a permanent station, central heating, two to a cosy room, hot baths at the turn of a tap. To our amazement this turned out to be pukka gen and on 10 December here we were, with all four of our Mosquitoes, at Horsham St Faith next door to all the joys of Norwich, mildly puzzled, one must admit, that a tremendously Top Secret aircraft had been put on display on an airfield bound by a busy road, spies galore clicking their cameras. Not for us to worry, warmth and comfort, Mosquitoes to fly and Norwich nearby – who could ask for more?

Three to a crew in a Blenheim, only two in a Mosquito so sadly some of our navs and WoPs were surplus to requirements. Sadder still they were posted to Blenheim squadrons flying in the Sea of Carnage, attacks on North Sea convoys whose escorting flak-ships didn't bother to aim, just fired splash into the sea, a curtain of exploding steel through which the doomed Blenheim crews flew with unmatchable courage. One afternoon one of our pilots had to hop the Station Tiger Moth over to one of these squadrons to deliver something bureaucratic. He went to the Crew Room to ask after an OTU friend. 'Jimmy so-and-so here?' 'There he is,' said someone, pointing to a photograph papered to the wall – a head over heels Blenheim somersaulting into the sea. Small wonder they called us 'Poor Bloody Two Group'.[27]

At Morley's grass airfield meanwhile 105 Squadron were replaced by 226 Squadron, commanded by Wing Commander V. S. Butler DFC. They arrived from Wattisham, where they had been flying Blenheims. Squadron Leader John Castle, a pilot in 226 Squadron, recalled:

Smiles on the faces of 114 Squadron aircrew at West Raynham on 12 February 1942 conceal the unsuccessful attempts to bomb the German warships in the 'Channel Dash'. Left to right are Kendrick; Squadron Leader John Newberry; 24-year-old Wing Commander John F. G. Jenkins DSO DFC, 114 Squadron CO, who led six Blenheims; King; 31-year-old Flying Officer Henry Paul Brancker DFC* and Flight Sergeant Charles H. Gray DFM. Jenkins, who received the DSO for leading thirteen Blenheims in a strafing raid on Herdls airfield, Norway on 27 December 1941 when British commandos stormed Vaagso Island, was killed on 27 March when his Blenheim, Z7276 N-Nuts, failed to return from a night intruder attack on Soesterberg airfield. Thirty year old Paul Brancker, observer (cousin of Air Vice Marshal Sir William Brancker, who lost his life in the R101 airship disaster in December 1930) and Gray died with him. An asthmatic, Brancker had initially been declared 'totally unfit for all types of service flying' by an RAF medical board shortly before the war. (*Mrs Vera Sherring*)

It's difficult to imagine now what a rowdy, rumbustuous squadron 226 was when it arrived at Swanton Morley on a grey 9 December 1941. We had come from all over the world: New Zealand, Canada, Australia, the USA, the Argentine, a Catholic from Northern Ireland and a Protestant from the South. The only officer left from the squadron that had been in France in 1940 was our CO, Bobbie Butler. The two flight commanders, MacLancy and I, were two of the five pilots surviving a tour of Malta with 110 on Blenheims; 105 came out from Swanton to take over from us. 226 had led the first low-level daylight raid on Cologne and had taken a fair pasting on shipping strikes.

Training in their new role took time and the Boston crews of 107 Squadron were not considered ready when Operation *Fuller* was mounted on 12 February. It was a vain attempt to prevent the 'Channel Dash' by the battle cruisers *Scharnhorst*, *Gneisenau* and *Prinz Eugen*, which were slipping through the English Channel from their French berths to Germany. Six of 226 Squadron's Bostons and four from 88 were involved (as were nine Blenheims of 118 Squadron, twelve of 82 and sixteen of 110). Only Flight Lieutenant Brian 'Digger' Wheeler and his crew in 226 Squadron found the German ships and they were beaten off by six of the escorting fighters. Wheeler landed at Swanton Morley with two holes in the fuselage and an unexploded 20 mm cannon shell in the starboard wing.

The first Boston operation took place on Sunday 8 March with three raids on targets in France. In the early afternoon six Bostons of 226 Squadron at Swanton Morley, led by Wing Commander V. S. Butler DFC in Z2209 and six from 88 Squadron at Attlebridge took off to make the first daylight bombing raid of the war on Paris. The target, the Ford motor works at Matford, near Poissy on the banks of the Seine, was turning out tanks and military vehicles for the Germans. Meanwhile, 107 Squadron provided six crews for a Circus operation to the Abbeville marshalling yards escorted by the Kenley and Biggin Hill Wings in 11 Group. Fighters of 10 Group flew a diversionary operation and six more Bostons, three each from 88 and 107 Squadrons, would attack the Comines power station. The Matford works were at the extreme limit of the Bostons' range, so 88 and 226 Squadrons had to use Thorney Island on the South Coast as a forward refuelling base. The Bostons would have to fly at very low level to and from the target without fighter escort, which did not have the range to accompany them.

One of the Bostons taking part, flying No. 2 in the 226 Squadron formation to the Matford works, was piloted by Pilot Officer W. J. 'Bill' O'Connell, a Canadian, with Pilot Officer Peter Saunders as navigator-observer and Flight Lieutenant Douglas 'Chappie' Chapman as WOP/AG. Peter Saunders recalled:

The first Boston Circus operations (C-112A & B) took place an 8 March when six aircraft of 107 Squadron attacked the Abbeville marshalling yards and three from 88 and three from 107 attacked the Comines power station. In the afternoon six from 226 and six from 88 Squadron carried out the first daylight bombing raid of the war on Paris with on attack from 400 ft on the Ford motor works at Matford, which is seen here burning after the raid. Wing Commander V. S. Butler DFC, CO 226 Squadron, who led the operation, was killed. (*RAF*)

We all felt unusually keyed-up at briefing. The target was an important 'first' that no one had attacked before. We did not know what to expect. We knew that split-second flying and navigation, map-reading and target-recognition would all be vital and we realised that if we failed to achieve swiftness and surprise we would be sitting ducks for the German ack-ack and fighters. The 'Wingco' had warned us to be prepared for 50 per cent losses.

After take-off we swept low in formation over the airfield and then settled on track for the French coast. The sea crossing was uneventful, save for the half-apprehensive, half-jubilant mood of expectancy that we always felt and always much more strongly because of the 'closeness' of everything when we were crossing at 'nought feet'. Everything below seemed to flash past at breakneck speed. Would

Peter Saunders, navigator-observer in Pilot Officer W. J. 'Bill' O'Connell's Boston crew of 226 Squadron (*Peter Saunders via Theo Boiten*)

we make the coast unobserved, as we hoped, or had they got word of our coming and were waiting, defences alert, to destroy us? The weather was good, the visibility was a little too good but enough haze was rising from the sea to help screen our approach and enough broken cloud above, if it should last, to give us some cover from the enemy fighters.

The cliffs of Cabourg on the skyline, we corrected five degrees to port.

'No ships around,' called Bill.

They were always a danger, these little coastal fishing smacks and trawlers, which saw you coming and often radioed word of your approach. 'Squealers' we used to dub them and, a regrettable necessity, shot them up or sank them if the need arose. This time none of them in sight, which was lucky for us as well as for them. The haze and the lowness and swiftness of our approach might get us to the coast before we were seen. We watched the cliffs come nearer and nearer. Not a shot, not a signal! We were up and over. Sea suddenly changed to land. Our engines sounded more vibrant. Startled heads on the ground jerked upwards, eyes incredulous and momentarily alarmed but we could detect only the onset of surprise as they flashed beneath us and we overhead.

The Wingco was turning the formation smoothly on to our new course. Next stop Paris, just 100 miles away to the south-east! We did not pause to dwell on our good luck, or the surprise we had so far achieved, for at low level something · happens every second and we were looking out in front. What a fast-moving kaleidoscope it was! Neat, chequered fields, trim, square-cut by green-rimmed ditches, came rushing towards and beneath us like a swift-moving film – so close, it seemed, that we could see the very structure of the soil and might have reached out and touched it. A small airfield in front of us, with a few low buildings: blister hangars and aircraft, all innocuous-looking beneath its expert camouflage. No time to line up for an attack on it – Paris was calling. Four sharp stabs of fire from the Wingco's nose and the rest of us followed suit, taking a target as it came through the sights, then it was past. The ground rose slightly ahead of us. We swept up the slope and as we breasted it a double-track railway line flashed beneath us. Maps and watches checked. Must be the line from Pont l'Eveque south to Lisieux. Ground speed OK. Twenty-four miles to Serquigny; six miles flying, nearer six and a quarter. Crossing a road, hedge-lined we had a split-second glimpse of two Hun soldiers diving headlong and panic-stricken towards a ditch. We hoped fervently that it was full and foul!

I looked out at the other Bostons on our port and thrilled at the sight. (Six Bostons of 226 Squadron had taken off from Thorney Island but one of the eight Bostons of 88 Squadron had become stuck fast in the mud and four more made a late take-off and never found the target.) They were flying along wingtip to wingtip and they looked like the arm of a gigantic flail sweeping across fields and skimming the hedgetops. Each man was taking his own hurdles. It might indeed have been the Grand National but with the jumps spaced unequally for each horse and with tremendously greater thrill and excitement. I felt the nose of our aircraft rise and looked around to see telephone wires straight in front. We leapt up and over a branch of a tree and then we were rushing down ploughed slopes into a miniature valley. A plump-faced girl in a yellow blouse and dark-brown skirt was standing in the garden of a whitewashed farmhouse. She swung round with a look of startled amazement and then she was lost to our view. We seemed to surge up the other side of the little valley. Over the top, a wide clean road and, right beneath us, like a cameo, a French family taking their Sunday stroll! What, I wondered, was racing through their minds as they stood gaping at us? The Dutch had a spirit. They had run, waved, given 'V for Victory' – one could almost see their eyes light up and their lips say, 'We won't give up!' But the French? Sometimes they waved. Further on, a stream, then a grey-stone cottage. I could see right in through a long, open window. An old man with a beard, wearing a light smock, dark trousers and a cap with a stick in his hand was sitting inside. He scrambled from his chair and hobbled to the window. As we shot overhead I had a momentary glimpse of him staring upwards, his old eyes alive with sudden interest.

Houses and spires on the port bow. Serquigny. We crossed a river. Flying Officer George Sayers, our squadron navigator in the Wingco's plane, is making a great job of the trip. I envy him his chance leading a show like this but I admire his skill and calmness. I can see him in the transparent glass nose of 'G-George' map in hand, placidly sucking his dry pipe, looking out at the ground to either side and ahead, coolly noting the landmarks, sizing them up, checking his map. No room for even a momentary slip-up on a trip like this. The Wingco is giving him every chance. His flying is superb and his leadership quick and decisive. He is putting everything he knows into this, his big bulk crouched behind the stick, his helmeted head looking small and oddly incongruous on huge shoulders and his big hands clamped on the control column, responding to every adjustment that his brain demands. He is flying terrifyingly low. The tips of his airscrews seem to crop the grass and as he pulls over trees in his path, the branches appear to bend and scrape along the underside of the Boston's fuselage. The Bostons were lovely machines, powerful-looking with their big, blunt engines, yet smooth-flying, sleek, graceful – and they were beautiful to watch, racing along side by side, fast and low, rising and falling to the contour of the ground like darting swallows. We were accustomed to low level but this was the very lowest that we had ever flown. As we stuck close to the Wingco's plane in formation, my heart jumped involuntarily from time to time as we swept over hedges and fields, as houses and trees slithered close past our wings and as we pulled ourselves precariously over the lip of gullies and embankments. It seemed at times recklessly and unnecessarily low but the whole success of our mission – and our survival too – hung upon the surprise that we must achieve. Flying low was the best method of ensuring that a gunner would have little time to draw a bead on us or an enemy fighter spot us.

Where were the Me 109s and Focke-Wulf 190s? Were their defences confused? Another flight of Bostons had been sent over as a decoy, flying some distance north of our track in the hope of attracting the German fighters away from us and then making homewards while we made straight and fast for the French capital. We passed Evreux, a mile to the south and altered course a few degrees to port. George had all the strings in his fingers and was pulling us confidently and surely to our target. In less than ten minutes we should be there. The Wingco had never let up for a moment and was still flying as brilliantly and confident as ever. His daisy-cutting was, if anything, getting better (or worse!). The pattern below us looked more ordered now and everything seemed to be running and pointing in one direction, as if to say, 'Paris, this way to Paris!' We shot over a large building with a huge sign reading, 'DUBO-DUBON-DUBONNET'. The words seemed to be shouting 'You must come to Paris – You must come to Paris!' 'Damn it!' I thought. I remembered I would be seeing the city only at a distance, for our target was Poissy. Bearing in mind the object of our mission, I hardly had a feeling of, 'Paris in the springtime!'

We came nearer and could see the Seine, highway to Paris. We crossed the railway line from Bueil to Mantes-Gassincourt in an instant and were flying alongside the great river, skirting its southern bank. It looked muddy and yellow but the sun glistened on its surface, conveying an air of somnolent majesty. Everything breathed peace. It seemed a cruel paradox that we were coming to shatter it.

Ahead of us, in the hollow of the river bank, stood a factory, its big brick buildings ugly and squat against the beauty of the river, its chimneys rising stark and impressive against the sky. The Wingco did not alter course. He climbed slightly, skimming the factory roof. We vaulted upwards and squeezed between the stacks. Our starboard wing seemed to cut one of them in two. I saw deep down into the black, cavernous mouth of another as it slid beneath us. This was the last lap. In just over two minutes from now we should be on target. Involuntarily, we seemed to have closed formation, tighter than before, as though each crew among us was afraid of being left behind or cheated out of our big moment. 'Bombs fused!' I called. Bill replied tersely (but I could detect the thrill in his voice), 'Yep. Check me on bomb doors.'

'Any moment now. A couple of miles in front?' I yelled back through the mike to Bill and 'Chappie'. Things were happening too fast. We were too tense with watchfulness and excitement to make conversation. There was no time. I had my target map in my hand but we were still flying too low to be able to see what lay ahead, beyond a fringe of trees. I felt a momentary panic lest we should miss the target and I prayed fervently that George might spot it. The trees were right in front. They rushed at us. Then the river. We were nearly across and – God, no island! Beyond a wooded island in the river lay Poissy. But George had spotted it and a moment later. So had I. We had come out slightly to the south. It was a couple of hundred yards up the river! The Wingco swung his Boston round and began to climb. We hung on his tail.

'Bomb doors open!' I bawled to Bill.

He yelled back, 'They're open!'

We were at bombing height – 400 ft – and levelling out. I had a momentary sight of Paris to the south-east but it was a glimpse only, as we turned. I felt a brief disappointment I could not see more but the Matford works lay ahead and the Wingco was running in. What a perfect target; a huge, long rectangular building lying close to the river bank and a tower nearby with the name 'MATFORD' on it. How obliging to mount it there, to help make doubly sure this was our target!

I saw the Wingco's bombs go winging down. As we were going in I saw them land, some smack in the middle of a concentration of lorries alongside the factory, the rest on the factory itself. We swept in behind him. Just as our bombs went down, his exploded. The terrific blast shook us and lifted us bodily upwards. Debris rose high in the air and dust swirled around. Some Flak was streaming up towards us from the ground. There was a sharp crunching against our starboard wing and the aircraft shuddered violently, then we were past. The other boys were coming in behind us. Chappie was looking out to watch our bombs burst. He yelled jubilantly, 'Plumb in the middle! Good work!' and we knew our bombs had hit.

Now we were losing height and turning on our course for home. Chappie was shouting out the score as he watched the others bomb. He was finding it hard to count. The Matford works was going up in smoke, which almost hid them from view. The Flak had been light. The Wingco's leadership had been superb, George's navigation perfect, the attack an obviously outstanding success.

We were down once more 'on the deck' in formation again, *en route* for home. We had a long way to go to get there but happy thoughts filled our minds. What a perfect day. What an experience; the target decidedly 'pranged'! What an achievement for Wingco and for George to have led this show; to have carried it off like this! What a thrill for them. What a feather in their caps. What ragging. What backslapping for them when we get back! They deserve it, they can be proud. . .

It was then that we saw that the Wingco was having trouble with his bomb doors, They were still hanging open. He was trying to close them, for we saw them come up, stick and then fall open again. He made two more attempts with no success. Had the Flak damaged them, or could it be the Wingco was hurt? He was still flying skilfully, holding the course, still terrifyingly low. A stretch of thickly wooded ground loomed ahead of us. We swept up and over it. The Wingco's props seemed to trail on the branches below.

Without warning it came. His port wing cleaved into a trunk. His aircraft lurched violently. We could not see him clearly but he was trying desperately to hold her up, trying to save George in the glass nose of the plane. It was no good. The Boston tottered, slipped heavily sideways and crashed into the trees. Still on its side, it went hurtling on. Trunks splintered and broke in its path. There was a blinding flash of white-blue flame and then the horror of the scene was cloaked in fierce red fire.

We could not stop. Our thoughts crowded in on each other. Chappie from his gunner's turret was the only one who could see. He said nothing. Neither could we. We sped homewards.

All six 226 Squadron Bostons placed their bombs on the factory, though only two crews in 88 Squadron bombed the target. Damage to the Matford works was later estimated at 35–40 million French Francs and it was out of commission for three months.[28]

Circus operations remained the order of the day and casualties were heavy. In April 107 Squadron alone lost seven aircraft from seventy-eight sorties dispatched and eleven aircrew were killed. On 17 April 88 and 107 Squadrons flew diversionary raids in support of Lancasters attacking Augsburg. Six Bostons from 88 Squadron bombed the Grand Quevilly power station near Rouen, while another six hit the shipyards nearby. Meanwhile, 107 Squadron attempted to bomb an artificial silk

On 16 April, in Ramrod 20 twelve Bostons of 226 Squadron led by Squadron Leader John Castle (who received the DFC for this raid) attacked the power station at Le Havre. The second box of six bombed from 14,500 ft, 500 ft above the leading box. Direct hits were scored on the power station, interrupting the electricity supply for 48 hours and gutting 75 ft of the northern end of the main building. A direct hit was also obtained on the bridge between the Bassin de la Barre and the Bassin Vaubin. All the Bostons returned safely, although eleven of the twelve received flak damage. (*RAF*)

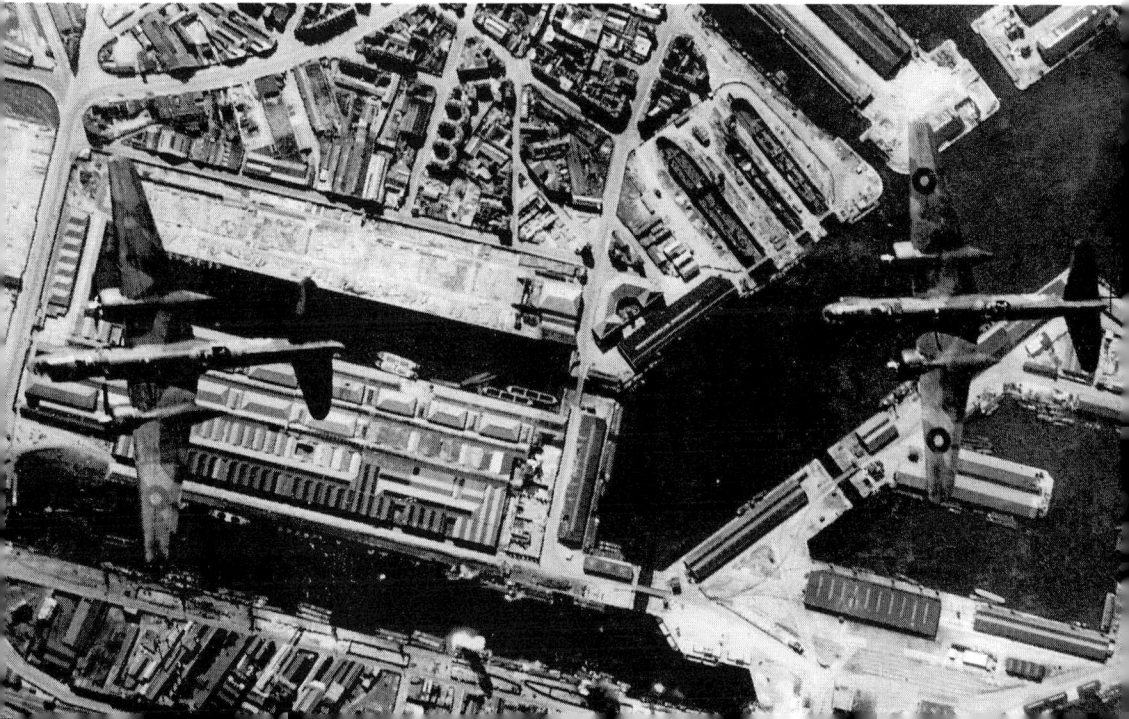

factory at Calais but their bombs were dropped on railway lines nearby and one of the Bostons (Z2255) was shot down into the sea by Bf 109s. On 25 April all three Boston squadrons operated in concert with one another with two operations against French ports: 88 Squadron attacked Le Havre, while 107 bombed Cherbourg and six Bostons from 226 bombed the dry docks at Dunkirk from 14,000 ft. Buildings on the northern end of the Citadel Quay were hit. On the second raid of the day Fw 190s attacked 107 Squadron's Bostons and they also came under a heavy flak barrage. One of the Bostons, badly damaged, nevertheless managed to make it home minus part of its tail.

May followed much the same pattern, except that on the 31st the first Mosquito bombers of 105 Squadron now entered the fray, five aircraft being dispatched to Cologne to photograph damage caused by the first 'thousand raid'. In June the second Mosquito squadron, 139, at Horsham St Faith, became operational. On their first operation on 2 July the CO, Wing Commander Alan 'Jesse' Oakeshott, and his navigator Flying Officer Vernon 'Titch' Treherne DFM were killed. Group Captain J. C. MacDonald DFC AFC, the station commander, and Flight Lieutenant Skelton became PoWs. On 7 May, meanwhile, six Bostons in 226 Squadron attacked a power station in Ostend. The German defenders put up a large flak barrage and Sergeant Goodman's Boston was hit and fell out of control. Sergeant Burt, the rear gunner, thought the aircraft was doomed and promptly baled out but Goodman wrested back control and crossed the North Sea safely; Burt was later reported to be a PoW. On 17 May twelve Bostons led by Wing Commander W. E. Surplice DFC raided the docks at Boulogne. Six of the aircraft were hit by flak and one pilot was wounded. A week later fourteen Bostons of 226 Squadron took a much-needed break from operations when they left for Thruxton for a week long army co-operation exercise.

In June 226 Squadron at Swanton Morley hosted the A-20 crews of the 15th Light Bombardment Squadron USAAF, who, being the only American unit in the UK at

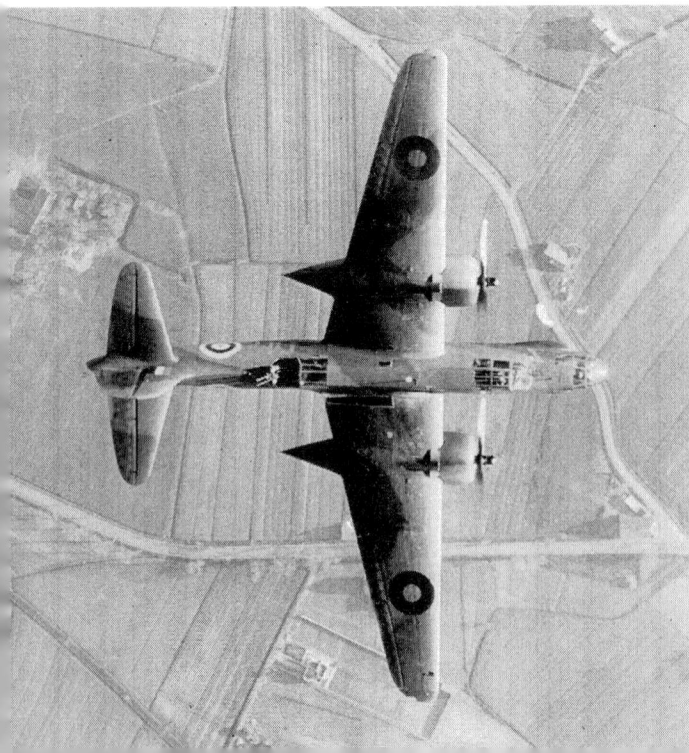

On 7 May 1942 six Boston IIIs of 226 Squadron led by Pilot Officer W. J. 'Bill' O'Connell attacked the power station at Ostend from 11,000 ft in Circus 164. No. 226 Squadron were bracketed by intense flak and the base of a shell lodged just behind the head of Sergeant Parsons, pilot of one of the Bostons; three gunners were also wounded and immediately after the bombing Sergeant Goodman broke formation, out of control, and his WOP/AG, Sergeant Burt, bailed out (he became a PoW). The photo shows the Boston (AL750 MG-Z) immediately after Burt had bailed out. Goodman regained control and flew back to make a safe landing at Swanton Morley. A report received later stated that, a bomb having hit a listening post, the local undertaker delivered twenty-two coffins to the Germans. AL750, which was built by Boeing and was flown on the 4 July 1942 raid by Captain Charles Kegelman USAAF and an American crew, was converted to Havoc II with a turbinlite but was lost with 307 FTU on 28 May 1943 when an engine cut on overshoot at Talbenny and it spun in at Little Haven, Pembrokeshire. (RAF)

Smiling sergeants of 226 Squadron gather around their maps for a photo call by *Illustrated* magazine after a briefing at Swanton Morley in April 1942. (*RAF*)

the time and with Independence Day looming, were needed for a flag-waving curtain-raiser to an American offensive in Europe. Both squadrons found that the other flew the Boston differently, even during take-off. While the RAF leader approached the end of the field still on the ground, the US pilot wingmen would be airborne and flying alongside with their wheels drawing up into the wheel-wells. The RAF mechanics were particularly grateful; damaged nose-gear wheels and struts had become a major headache for them. On 4 June the Americans sat in at a 107 Squadron briefing at West Raynham. The target was a 480 ft tower in the docks at Dunkirk. Captain Bill Odell, one of the American pilots, remembered the operation.

The route was almost direct using the tactics of sea-level flight to foil the radio aircraft detection system until about thirteen minutes from the coast. At that point a 1,000-foot climb was to begin, dropping four 500 lb bombs at 10,000 ft. All kinds of fighter protection were going over. Immediately after bombing we were to take pictures, make a steep diving turn to the right and continue down to sea level and come straight home. Twelve fighters would escort the return flight. I watched the RAF take-off procedure, which was much different from ours. Their engines were run from ten to twenty minutes on the ground before flight. The crews were all Blenheim trained, which may have accounted for such a procedure. The Bostons were kept on the ground with all three wheels until a bounce forced the pilot to fly it. One new pilot took off with upper cowl flaps open and reported back to the Squadron CO that he thought for a long while it was the bomb load causing the different flight characteristics. They attempted to take off in formation but didn't seem to hold it very well and did not become organized until after four-five minutes of flying. They had a much more open formation than we did.

Wing Commander Lynn kept a close check on the flight by checking his watch. As soon as they left the target we left the mess. Back at 'Ops' we learned very shortly that only five of the six that went on the run would be back. Pilot Officer ['Goolie'] Skinner and crew [who were on their first operation] had ditched their ship and were all in the dinghy. [Skinner and Sergeant Bernstein, WOp/AG, survived but Sergeant Paddy Poster, observer/navigator, died a month later of his wounds.] Shortly the five showed up over the field; one circled and shot a red flare to show he was in trouble.

On 5 June 24 Bostons bombed Morlaix airfield and power stations at Le Havre and Ostend. A direct hit was achieved at Ostend but bombing from 10,000 ft meant that German flak gunners had fairly easy targets at which to shoot and every Boston was hit by flak during their bomb runs. Still the losses mounted. On 11 June Pilot Officer T. B. Skinner and his crew in 107 Squadron failed to return after they were stalked by an Fw 190 five minutes from the English coast after a raid on Lannion airfield. Their Boston was raked by machine-gun fire from 800 yards; the tail fell off and they fell into the Channel. All the crew perished. Raids on French and Belgian ports, airfields and power stations continued. Then, on 25/26 June, when the second 'thousand bomber' raid took place, on Bremen, low-level bombing and strafing attacks were at dusk made on thirteen airfields in Germany. Taking part were sixteen Blenheims, twenty-seven Bostons of 88, 107 and 226 Squadrons (making their first Intruder sorties) and four Mosquitoes of 105 and 139 Squadrons, which attacked Stade. Extra bomb bay tanks were provided, carrying 100 gal.

Overall the raids were a success, though one flight in 226 Squadron bombed a dummy aerodrome. Six Bostons went to Leeuwarden and three more flew to Bergen-Alkmaar but it was darker than anticipated and four aircraft were unable to find their targets. The others attacked at 2230 hours with eleven-second and thirty-minute delayed-action 500 lb bombs and incendiaries. Flight Lieutenant A. F. 'Tony' Carlisle's aircraft was caught in the explosion of one of the bombs, which holed the tail of his Boston. His rear gunner had his guns blown overboard as the aircraft was overturned but Carlisle regained control and managed to return safely, his flying skill earning him a DFC. Light flak prevented Wing Commander Lynn and Pilot Officer Allen from attacking but Flight Lieutenant R. MacLachlan flew low at 75 ft and Pilot Officer Rushden dropped his bombs from 100 ft near a hangar. Both aircraft were damaged by ground fire but they returned to base safely. Wing Commander Lynn, meanwhile, was forced down over the coast.

On Monday, 29 June twelve Bostons of 226 Squadron, led by Squadron Leader J. Shaw Kennedy, a popular red-haired ace flyer, attacked the marshalling yards at Hazebrouck, escorted for the first time on a Circus raid by Hawker Typhoons. A US crew, captained by Captain Charles Kegelman, flew one of the Bostons, for the first ever US sortie from England. Bombing from between 12,500 and 13,000 ft, the formation recorded two hits on the railway lines at the eastern end of the yard and one or two were seen to burst on lines and sheds at the western end. The rest of the bombs fell on buildings to the south and north. No flak was encountered by the formation while over the target and all the aircraft returned. Not so fortunate were the escorting Spitfires, who encountered German fighters *en route* to the target, claiming three destroyed for the loss of five of their own.

On 4 July six American crews joined six crews from 226 Squadron for Independence Day attacks on De Kooy, Haamstede, Bergen-Alkmaar and Valkenburg airfields in Holland. General Dwight D. Eisenhower, newly arrived in England to command the US Forces in the European Theatre of Operations (ETO), was at Swanton Morley to see them off, at around 0710. When they returned it was immediately obvious that the raids had been less successful than the occasion had demanded. Three aircraft were missing, two of them crewed by Americans. At De Kooy Lieutenant F. A. 'Jack' Loehrl's Boston had been hit by flak and only Lieutenant Marshall Draper, the bombardier, survived to be made a PoW. After bombing Bergen aan Zee (Alkmaar) Lieutenant W. G. 'Stan' Lynn's Boston was also hit by flak; it broke up in mid-air, killing all on board. Unteroffiziers Erwin Grütz in Bf 190F-4 'White 6', Wrk Nr 7423 and Johannes Rathenow in his Fw 190A-3, both of IV./JG1, took off as their airfield at Bergen aan Zee was being bombed and sped after the Bostons. Grütz was shot down and killed by return fire and he crashed near the base. Rathenow caught up with Pilot Officer C. M. 'Hank' Henning and shot him down into the sea at 0830 hours, 12 miles west of Callantsoog. It was IV *Gruppe*'s first success.[29] The most amazing piece of flying was carried out by Captain Kegelman, whose Boston took a hit in the starboard engine; it burst into flames and the propeller flew off. Kegelman's right wing tip struck the ground and the fuselage actually bounced on the surface of the aerodrome, tearing a hole in the belly of the

Captain Charles Kegelman USAAF and an American crew piloted one of the twelve Bostons led by Squadron Leader J. S. Kennedy DFC that took part in a Circus (C-195) against the Hazebrouck marshalling yards on 29 June, the first time since 1918 that Americans had operated from England. Also on this operation Typhoons were used as high cover for the first time. Bombing was from 13,000 ft, no flak was encountered and hits were scored on the north-east edge of the yards, and on the railway embankment north-west of the town. (*RAF*)

The first 8th Air Force involvement in a mission to drop bombs on an enemy target was on 4 July 1942, Independence Day, when six of the twelve A-20 Bostons belonging to 226 Squadron RAF at Swanton Morley, Norfolk, carried American crews of the 15th Bomb Squadron (Light) in attacks on four airfields in Holland. The senior-ranking US officer was Captain Charles Kegelman (seen here second from left), who attacked De Kooy airfield in AL750/Z, crewed by Lieutenant R. M. Dorton, navigator, Sergeant Bennie Cunningham, rear gunner, and Technical Sergeant R.L. Goley, dorsal gunner. Kegelman's starboard engine took a direct hit and burst into flames, and the propeller flew off. The right wing tip struck the ground, and the fuselage actually bounced on the surface of De Kooy aerodrome, tearing a hole in the belly of the bomber. Lifting the Boston back into the air on one engine, Kegelman headed for the Channel. A flak tower on Den Helder airfield opened up, and the young captain returned fire with his nose guns. He lifted the Boston over the tower and headed for England with the right engine on fire. The fire went out over the Channel, and Kegelman continued home to Swanton Morley, hugging the waves across the North Sea. Charles Kegelman rose rapidly in promotion. From April to 8 November 1943 he was a lieutenant colonel in command of the 48th Fighter Group at William Northern Field, Tennessee. On 12 November he assumed command of the 337th Fighter Group at Sarasota, Florida, as a full colonel. On 16 November 1944 be assumed command of the 42nd Bomb Group at Sansapor, New Guinea, which by March 1945 was operating North American B-25 Mitchells from Moratai. On 10 March Kegelman's aircraft was involved in a mid-air collision with his wingman and he was killed. Kegelman airfield, near Cherokee, Oklahoma, is named in his memory. (*USAF*)

bomber. Kegelman nursed the Boston all the way back to Swanton, a feat that earned him the DSC. Flight Lieutenant R. A. 'Yogi' Yates-Earl and his observer, Pilot Officer Ken Houghton, were awarded the DFC and his gunner, Sergeant Ted Leaver, the DFM, for their part in the attack on Bergen-Alkmaar.

Crews had bombed and strafed the airfields but at Valkenburg Squadron Leader John Castle, the leader of the formation, found he was unable to open his bomb doors through an error in selection. On the run-in to a target Boston pilots normally had the bomb doors selected to 'neutral', then placed them to 'open' before dropping their bombs. Castle discovered too late that he was still selected to 'closed'; moving the door control had only placed the doors to 'neutral' and they failed to open. Captain Martin Crabtree and Lieutenant Leo Hawel, the two American pilots following, waited in vain for the leader's bomb doors to open as the signal to drop their own bombs. Instead, the formation used their machine guns on airfield buildings and three dispersed Bf 109s, setting one on fire. All three aircraft were forced to bring their bombs back. The experienced 226 crews were all of the same opinion – that the flak encountered was the worst they had ever experienced. At De Kooy the three Bostons led by Squadron Leader Shaw Kennedy were forced to fly through 3 miles of it, the worst he had encountered in over sixty operations and it prevented them from bombing. Kennedy machine-gunned anti-aircraft positions and personnel near the airfield and on the way home he attacked a 250 ft trawler with bombs and machine guns but his bombs overshot. He also attacked a second trawler with machine guns. Eisenhower and his fellow generals, gathered to fete the heroes' return, were confronted with the stark reality of Circus operations, something the RAF had long since come to accept as part of the game of war.

On Sunday 12 July a Circus of six Bostons of 226 Squadron led by John Castle and six American-crewed aircraft (in the last of sixteen sorties with the RAF) led by Captain Bill Odell and escorted by fighters, headed for Abbeville-Drucat airfield. There 150 fighters were reportedly dispersed in the woods just north of the runways. The crews bombed from 8,500 ft but owing to 4/10ths cloud over the aiming point the accuracy of the bombing could not be observed. Slight to inaccurate flak was encountered from both heavy and light anti-aircraft guns, with two aircraft receiving hits but all returned safely. (In September the 15th Bomb Squadron flew a few missions before transferring to the 12th Air Force, earmarked for North Africa.)

On 16 July 2 Group ordered the first of a series of low-level attacks by Bostons on power stations, marshalling yards and other industrial targets using cloud cover. Each squadron was to send ten aircraft a day when visibility and cloud cover permitted, escorted by fighters of 11 Group. Each squadron was given five targets, each target was to be bombed by a pair of Bostons. On Sunday, 19 July twenty Bostons of 88 and 226 Squadrons mounted raids in pairs on ten power stations in the Lille area, using low cloud as cover. Flight Sergeant Matthew G. Johnson of 226 Squadron nose-dived into the ground while making a bomb run on Mazingarbe

On 4 July 1942 Johannes Rathenow of IV *Gruppe* JGI returned victoriously to Bergen-op-Zoom airfield in his Fw 190A-3 White 12 (Wrk Nr 437) to be congratulated by his ground crew and fellow pilots after taking off during the attack by Bostons and pursuing Pilot Officer C. F. Henning's Boston (Z2213/U) for 20 miles out to sea before shooting it down. All the crew was lost. *Feldwebel* Johannes Rathenow was KIA on 3 November 1943 when he was shot down while flying Fw 190A-6 White 7 (550785) in combat with USAAF bombers and P-38s at Bad Zwischenahn. (*via Eric Mombeek*)

A photograph taken from the rear-mounted camera of the leading Boston (AL679/Y) flown by Flight Lieutenant R. A. 'Yogi' Yates-Earl of the attack by three aircraft on Bergen-Alkmaar airfield. The explosion is Boston AL741/V flown by Lieutenant Stan G. Lynn USAAF, which was hit by flak after bombing Bergen Alkmaar and crashed on the airfield, killing all on board. Of the four airfield targets, Bergen Alkmaar was the only one that was attacked successfully. A second American crew was lost when Lieutenant Jack Loehrl was hit by flak north of De Kooy airfield and he and his two gunners, Sergeants Wright and Whitham, were killed. Lieutenant Marshall Draper, bombardier, survived and became the first American airman to be taken prisoner. (*RAF*)

power station and his aircraft exploded in a wood east of Boulogne. Johnson, Pilot Officer Leonard S. Stewart, navigator and Sergeant Fred C. Thorogood, gunner, were given a military burial in the Cimetière de l'est at Boulogne. A second Boston, flown by Pilot Officer Aubrey K. G. Niner of 88 Squadron was also lost. Niner's aircraft and another Boston, flown by Sergeant G. W. 'Ginger' Attenborough, had made for the power station at Lille-Lomme but missed it, so they attacked the aerodrome at Lille-Nord instead. Niner's aircraft was hit in the starboard engine and he had to belly land on a football pitch in Lille. Niner, his WOp/AG, Sergeant George Lawman, and his navigator, Flight Sergeant Philip Jacobs, were made PoW.

During July the Bostons again intruded after dusk. On the night of 26/27th, when 403 RAF heavies attacked Hamburg, 226 and 107 intruded over night-fighter airfields at Jever, near Wilhelmshaven and Leeuwarden respectively. AL746/M of

Back at Swanton Morley on 4 July Captain Martin Crabtree of the 15th Bomb Squadron (right) asks why Squadron Leader John Castle failed to get his bombs away at Valkenburg. Castle, Crabtree and a third Boston piloted by Lieutenant Leo Hawel USAAF had to be content with strafing the airfield with machine guns. (*USAF*)

Squadron Leader J. C. Shaw Kennedy DFC leaving Boston Z2234/H on his return from De Kooy on 4 July 1942. Note the 'nose art' depicting an American Indian wearing a headdress and aiming a bomb – a suitable choice for this Independence Day! (RAF)

226 Squadron, piloted by Pilot Officer Victor N. Salmon RCAF, which had been flown by Captain Odell of the 15th Bomb Squadron on the Independence Day raid, was brought down by flak *en route* and crashed on the edge of Langeoog. All four crew were killed. Among them was Pilot Officer Harold F. Deck, the 29-year-old observer, whose two brothers also lost their lives flying with the RAF. (One died on 1 November 1941 in the first ever Typhoon crash, at Roudham, Norfolk and the other was killed flying a Tempest over Germany in April 1945). On 28/29 July eighteen Bostons of 88 and 107 Squadrons intruded over Dutch airfields at Alkmaar and De Kooy. Flight Lieutenant R. MacLachlan of 107 Squadron first eluded a night fighter and was then fired on by a flak ship but he and his crew made it home safely.

Early in August the Boston squadrons commenced army co-operation training to become proficient in smoke-laying from low level for the forthcoming Operation Jubilee, which would involve British and Canadian landings at Dieppe. Sixteen crews in 107 Squadron and those of 88 Squadron were dispatched to Ford while 226 Squadron crews were sent to Thruxton. On 19 August 107 Squadron carried out

On 19 July twenty Bostons of 88 and 226 Squadrons mounted raids in pairs on ten power stations in the Lille area using low cloud as cover. In progress is an attack by Bostons of 226 Squadron on the power station at Chocques. (*RAF*)

On 19 July Boston Z2236 flown by Pilot Officer Aubrey K. C. Niner of 88 Squadron was one of two aircraft given a power station at Lille-Lomme but the crew were unable to locate the target and so they bombed the airfield at Lille-Nord instead. Hits were scored on a hangar before Z2236 was hit in the starboard engine by flak and Niner had to belly land on a football pitch in Lille. (*Aubrey Niner*)

thirty-two sorties over Dieppe without loss but several aircraft were hit. At 0416 hours Wing Commander Alan Lynn and Flight Lieutenant MacLachlan joined four Boston intruders of 418 RCAF[30] and 605 'County of Warwick' Squadrons in trying to nullify coastal batteries as a prelude to the start of the Allied landings at 0500 hours. Light was poor, however, and results were unobserved. Fire was continuing from the Hitler battery, so 107 Squadron was ordered to send twelve Bostons in to silence it. Lynn led the formation in a bombing run west to east but ground haze reflecting back light from the sun made the target difficult to spot and all bombs overshot. Flak was heavy but none of the Bostons was hit.

The last Boston smoke screen action of the Dieppe operation involved four crews from 226 Squadron, led by Squadron Leader Graham 'Digger' Magill and one from 88 Squadron. They flew over the beachhead at 1414

Aubrey Niner is led away to captivity after his crash landing at Lille. The WOP/AG, Sergeant George Lawman and navigator, Flight Sergeant Philip Jacobs, were also made PoWs. (*Aubrey Niner*)

hours, being escorted by 66 Squadron, to conceal the few remaining ships still within gun range of the German batteries. Magill wrote:

'The trip was in answer to an urgent call for protection of the withdrawing naval forces, which were being severely harassed by fire from the shore. The idea was to put down a curtain of smoke from cliff to cliff either side of the town and

On 19 August the Bostons took part in Operation Jubilee, the Dieppe operation, 226 Squadron working from Thruxton and being engaged on smoke-laying, with 88 Squadron operating from Ford on bombing sorties. This photograph was taken by 226 Squadron while engaged in dropping smoke bombs to blind coastal batteries. Two Bostons of 226 Squadron did not return and of fourteen aircraft only three escaped damage. No. 88 Squadron completed thirty-two bombing sorties, losing one Boston. (*RAF*)

down to sea level. I think we can justly claim to have succeeded. It meant running in flat out from the east under the cliff, between the lighthouse and the beginning of the jetty, along the line of the beach and withdrawing under the western cliff. We had quite a view of the waterfront and the shambles on the beach. Unfortunately, we lost Flying Officer R. A. Marks AFM and crew in the process. I have little doubt that he collected the fire aimed at me. He was flying to seaward of me and a bit lower (to give depth to the screen) and should have been hidden to the enemy by the smoke from my aircraft. Hit as he was at nought feet, he had no chance.

Marks' observer-navigator Pilot Officer Kenneth A. I. Warwood recalled:

We were actually over the beach at Dieppe when hit by Flak and assorted ground fire. Within about twenty seconds we had lost the port engine and the tail and we landed in the Channel. Pilot Officer L. K. Brownson, WOp/AG, Marks and me, all very much alive, were picked up by a German E-Boat. I was not in very good shape and only semi-conscious. A Polish Air Force officer named Landsmann of 303 Squadron and two mechanics, part of the crew of an ASR craft blown up by an Fw190 and us were landed at Fécamp. Brownson, Marks and me were taken to Rouen, thence to Le Bourget aerodrome where we were interrogated by a high-ranking *Luftwaffe* officer who commented, 'We were expecting you six weeks ago' and later, 'You are a very old man to be flying' (I was 32). A train took us to Frankfurt-am-Main and from there to Oberussel, where we were put into solitary confinement for about a month. Early in October 1942 the three of us were taken by train to *Stalag Luft III* at Sagan, to the East Camp.

All three suffered the privations of prison camp and the forced march in the winter of 1944 when the whole camp was evacuated at very short notice. In 1946 Marks was killed at Farnborough while testing an experimental German aircraft.

A second Boston of 226 Squadron flown by Pilot Officer R. J. Corrigan, an American, failed to return from the day's operations. Corrigan and Flight Sergeant W. Osselton, gunner, were killed. Sergeant Moth, observer, although seriously wounded was rescued by a passing Royal Navy destroyer. Altogether, the Bostons made eleven runs in front of the cliffs from east to west. Squadron Leader Shaw

Kennedy's Boston in 88 Squadron was badly damaged by naval fire. Flight Lieutenant O. G. E. McWilliam, who was riding as a passenger, was killed by the blast from the cannon shell and Flying Officer G. A. Casey, air gunner, was wounded. Flying Officer Arthur Asker, observer, was uninjured. Kennedy crash landed the aircraft at Shoreham. Pilot Officer L. J. Waters, air gunner in Pilot Officer W. R. Gellatly's Boston, was also killed. Flying Officer Donald T. Smith received Flak hits that shattered his windscreen and embedded shards of Plexiglas in his right eye. Despite his injuries, Smith continued on and laid smoke. On the return flight his left eye filled with the powdered perspex which still filled the cockpit but he managed to land safely at Thruxton. Flight Sergeant J. C. Bicknell, air gunner, and Pilot Officer G. B. Tolputt, observer, were uninjured. Smith was awarded the DFC. Wing Commander W. B. Surplice DFC was awarded the DSO and Kennedy received a bar to his DFC. Asker, Casey and Flying Officers Rutherford and L. J. Longhurst were also awarded the DFC, as was Pilot Officer H. J. Archer of 88 Squadron. The Dieppe operation cost the RAF 108 aircraft; forty-eight German aircraft were lost and 4,000 army and navy personnel. Two Bostons of 226 Squadron, which flew 28 sorties between 0509 and 1500 hours, failed to return from the day's operations. No. 88 Squadron flew 32 bombing sorties, losing one Boston. The following message from AOC, HQ No 2 Group, was sent to the Boston stations in Norfolk: 'I cannot thank you enought for the whole hearted co-operation of your squadrons and hope you will convey my congratulations to them on a very fine performance.' Leigh-Mallory.

Returning to Great Massingham, 107 Squadron was again on bombing operations on 27 August when twelve aircraft attacked the airfield at Abbeville. The flak was heavy and accurate and Pilot Officer Allen was forced to ditch on the way home. He and two other crew survived but Flight Sergeant G. T. Relph, observer, was killed. Three Fw 190s also attacked the ASR launch that arrived on the scene while it was picking up the downed crew.

Pilot Officer Arthur Paget Eyton-Jones was a navigator in a Boston crew with Frank Swainson, WOp/AG,[31] captained by Pilot Officer R. M. 'Dick' Christie RCAF, which arrived at Swanton Morley to join 226 Squadron on 4 September. At this stage of the war a tour of daylight operations was counted as twenty. Eyton-Jones reflected: 'Nobody had done that many to my knowledge but a few lucky ones had got through fifteen and gone for a well-deserved rest.' Christie's crew had arrived on the squadron at a bad time. The previous week one of the crews had hit a telegraph pole on a low-level flight and damaged the nosewheel so that on landing it had collapsed and the navigator had been dragged along the ground on what was left of his legs. He died shortly afterwards. On 15 September Christie's crew carried out a sea-sweep. This was a very unpopular type of operation as it consisted of flying at wave-top height in formation out to a point very close to the enemy coast and then climbing to 500 ft to patrol a given area, keeping in line abreast about a half a mile apart. These trips were doubly unpopular, for they only counted as half an operation.[32]

On 13 September 105 and 139 Squadrons received orders to vacate Horsham St. Faith by 28 September, as the Americans were due to arrive to base medium bombers

Hits can be seen on the Finalens chemical works at Douvrin in this remarkable low-level photograph taken by Sergeant Savage's Boston of 88 Squadron, during his attack on 22 September. (*RAF*)

there. In November the 2nd Bomb Wing would assume control of the airfield for P-47 and later Liberator operations. The Mosquitoes were to move to RAF Marham, 9 miles south-east of King's Lynn, where they would replace 115 and 218 Squadrons of 3 Group. Amid the changeover, on 19 September, six crews in 105 Squadron attempted the first daylight Mosquito raid on Berlin. Two pilots – Sergeant Norman Booth[33] and Flight Sergeant K. L. Monaghan – were forced to return early. Flight Lieutenant Roy Ralston and his navigator Flying Officer Sydney Clayton, who had both been posted to the squadron in May 1942 after flying Blenheim IVs in 107 Squadron, bombed Hamburg after finding Berlin covered by cloud. Flight Lieutenant D. A. G. 'George' Parry and his navigator, Flight Lieutenant Victor G. Robson, were intercepted on two occasions by Fw 190s but managed to evade them. Parry jettisoned his bombs near Hamburg and turned for home, heading back across the north coast of Germany and into Holland. At 1,000 ft, just off the Dutch coast, two 109s attacked but although one of them scored hits, Parry dived down to sea level and soon outran them. Squadron Leader Norman Henry Edward Messervy DFC, an Australian from Point Cook, and his navigator, Pilot Officer Frank Holland, in *M-Mother* were shot down by an Fw 190 piloted by *Schwarmführer Oberfeldwebel* Anton-Rudolf 'Toni' Piffer of 2nd *Staffel*/JG1. The Mosquito crashed 14 miles north-north-west of Osnabrück with the loss of both crew. Messervy was a second-tour man, having flown Blenheims and PR Spitfires on sixty-eight operations. Only Warrant Officer Charles

On 6 September *Feldwebel* Erwin Roden of 12/JGI shot down Mosquito IV DK322/P of 105 Squadron crewed by Sergeant K. C. Pickett (PoW) and his observer, Sergeant Herbert Edmund Evans (KIA), which crashed at 1830 hours near Tourines-La Grosse, Belgium. Thirteen days later, on 19 September, *Schwarmfurhrer Oberfeldwebel* Anton-Rudolf 'Toni' Piffer (far left with *Oberfeldwebel* Worth (12th *Staffel* Adjutant) *Leutnant* Eberhard Burath and *Leutnant* Hans Munz) of 2nd *Staffel*/JGI shot down Mosquito DK326/M of 105 Squadron crewed by Squadron Leader Norman Henry Edward Messervy DFC RAAF and Pilot Officer Frank Holland (both KIA) of 105 Squadron. *Leutnant* Piffer was KIA by USAAF P-47 Thunderbolts on 17 June 1944. They shot down his Fw 190A-8 'White 3' near Argentan. Piffer was posthumously awarded the *Ritterkreuz* on 20 October 1944 for his twenty-six victories in the west. (*via Eric Mombeek*)

Mosquito B.Mk.IV Series II DK296 was first flown operationally on 11 July 1942. It was flown on the Oslo *Gestapo* HQ raid of 25 September 1942 by Squadron Leader D. A. G. 'George' Parry DFC and Flying Officer Victor Robson of 105 Squadron. It passed to Squadron Leader Bill Blessing DSO DFC RAAF, who crash landed it at Marham and broke its back. The aircraft was repaired and on 24 August 1943 was placed in store with 10 MU at Hullavington. In September 1943 it was issued to 305 Ferry Training Unit at Errol, Scotland where it was given Russian markings and trained Russian crews, who were convening to Albemarles. On 20 April 1944 it was ferried to the Soviet Union by a Russian crew, being officially accepted there on 31 August 1944 and subsequently going on to serve with the Red Air Force. (*via Graham M. Simons*)

On 11 October 1942 Mosquito IV DZ341/A of 105 Squadron flown by Pilot Officer Jim Lang and Flying Officer Robin F. Thomas, and DK317/K flown by Squadron Leader James Gerald Leslie Knowles and Pilot Officer Charles Douglas Alan Gartside of 139 Squadron failed to return from a raid on Hannover. They were shot down over the sea by Uffz Günther Kirchner (pictured) and Uffz Kolschek of 5th and 4th *Staffel* II./JG1 respectively. Lang and Thomas were captured and made PoW. Knowles and Gartside were KIA. A third Mosquito IV, DZ340, crashed at Marham on return. (via Eric Mombeek)

R. K. Bools MiD and Sergeant George Jackson[34] succeeded in bombing the 'Big City'.

Six days later on 25 September four Mosquitoes of 105 Squadron led by George Parry, now a squadron leader and flying from Leuchars in Scotland, bombed the *Gestapo* HQ in Oslo, Norway. Two Fw 190 pilots of 3./JG5 – 22-year-old *Unteroffizier* Rudolf 'Rudi' Fenten, who was on a training flight from Stavanger and who had landed at Fornebu and 24-year-old *Feldwebel* Erich Klein – received a report of the Mosquitoes' approach and took off to intercept the raiders. Fenten hit Flight Sergeant Gordon Carter and Sergeant William Young's aircraft in the starboard engine and set it on fire. Carter tried to crash land on a lake in a valley a few miles south-west of Oslo but hit a tree on the shores of the lake and crashed, killing both crew. Hundreds of Norwegian men women and children scattered flowers on the lake in their memory. Klein pursued the Mosquito flown by Pilot Officers Peter W. T. Rowland and Richard 'Dick' L. Reilly, but his wing clipped a tree and Rowland and Reilly escaped. A fourth Mosquito flown by Flying Officer Alec Bristow and Pilot Officer Bernard Marshall successfully evaded an attack by the Fw 190s.[35] At least four bombs entered the roof of the *Gestapo* HQ. One remained inside and failed to detonate and the three others crashed through the opposite wall before exploding. The AOC of Bomber Command described the raid as a 'first class show'. On the night of 26 September listeners to the BBC Home Service heard that a new aircraft, the Mosquito, had been revealed officially for the first time by the RAF and that four had made a daring roof top raid on Oslo.[36]

Throughout September and October pairs of Bostons from 88, 107 and 226 Squadrons continued low-level attacks on power stations in northern France. Twenty-year-old Sergeant (later Warrant Officer) Maurice 'Collie' Collins was a Boston pilot in 226 Squadron, much of whose time since joining the squadron at Swanton Morley was spent on formation flying, low level flying and gunnery practice. He recalled:

2 Group sent aircraft to look for pocket battleships and later to cover the landing at Dieppe but the only raids I went on were ten high-level Circuses and one low level against 'Squealers'. My original navigator, Sergeant 'Butch' Beaumont

suffered from claustrophobia and could not fly in a Boston (he had flown in the Blenheim with no problem) and Sergeant Arthur Grounds, my WOp/AG, fell downstairs at Bylaugh Hall and broke his leg. Beaumont and Grounds were replaced by Pilot Officer Harold Milford a 27-year old modern languages master from Wimbledon and Sergeant George Nicholls a 24-year old Londoner who had been a clerk in the General Accident Insurance Company respectively. Evenings were spent in Swanton Morley village, the 'King's Arms' in Dereham or the fleshpots of Norwich until the evening of 21 September 1942. We found ourselves on a battle order for a low-level raid on power stations. Early morning found us in the ops room. Eighteen Bostons would be going in nine pairs. We had Chocques in the Pas de Calais as our target. There was a delay in take-off time but at ten o'clock we started.

Shortly after passing Orford Ness the leader of my pair turned back. Off to North Foreland, two or three minutes and climbing to the clouds to cross between Calais and Dunkirk. Neither George nor I could see the other aircraft detailed to fly with us so we carried on alone. Harold managed to pinpoint our target, which was near Bethune. We hadn't gone far when we ran into a pretty thick rain patch and it was here that the trouble started. The rain obscured all forward vision and made it necessary to climb 200 ft or so to avoid hitting trees and houses. At this height we were an ideal target for the German light ack-ack gunners and they paid us most unwelcome attention. When we finally cleared the rain we were right over the centre of Bethune itself and we fell for some more light Flak. It was just as I was turning back to head for the target that the 20 mm and 37 mm cannon shells hit us right amidships. Poor old George was working overtime trying to shoot at the Germans whilst I was weaving like the devil. There was a horrible lurch and George shouted to me that a large chunk of the rudder had disappeared and that the starboard engine was on fire.

4th *Staffel* JG1 pilots relaxing in deckchairs at Woensdrecht in June 1942 beside an Fw 190A-3 of their *Staffel*. Note the *Tatzelwurm* 'emblem of II. *Gruppe*. (*via Eric Mombeek*)

Although it was a cold September day, I was in a sweat and to add to the general unhealthy atmosphere, the other engine began to cough. An oil or fuel line was hit and further flight was out of the question. The next few minutes seemed like years as we hastily jettisoned our bomb load on to a railway line and prepared to crash land. We hit some electricity cables, which caused blue flashes as we went by. Milford said, 'What about the trees?' I looked and saw thirty–forty foot high poplars. I went over them at right angles fortunately.

My guardian angel was certainly smiling on me that day because just ahead was a newly ploughed field and so I put the remains of '*K-King*' to rest as gently as possible. We ploughed along in the soft earth for quite a distance and finished up only six feet from a copse. One wheel was on fire and it rolled towards the trees but I didn't wait to watch the fire. I was scrambling to get out of the cockpit. Harold was the first out and I followed. We rushed round to the tail in time to see George making a hurried exit from the escape hatch. There was nothing more I could do to destroy the aircraft and so we three beat a hasty retreat over a road and into a corn stubble field. We found a ditch along by the hedge and dived in. We scampered along this ditch for about a quarter of a mile and then sat down to hold our first council of war. The first task was to make ourselves as much like civilians as possible and, to achieve this, we tucked our flying boot tops into our trousers and ripped our badges off our battle-dress blouses. George was loath to bury his flying jacket, claiming that the September nights were very cold. However, it was discarded and buried with our Mae Wests under a little bush. Next we had to decide how to travel, for obviously if we stayed in a group we would be captured in a short time. It was finally agreed that George and Harold should travel together and I should go alone. Some distance to the south of us was a small wood. We agreed to rendezvous there later that night. Near the bush under which we were hiding, the ditch forked and I took the right-hand turning. With handshakes and best wishes we took our separate ways.[37]

On 13 October 'Dinty' Moore, now a Pilot Officer gunner in 88 Squadron, was 'ready and raring to go' on his second tour in 2 Group but they were recalled after only twenty minutes in the air. 'Dinty' had already spent a frustrating time at Bicester, where he had made repeated requests for a posting. However, they continued to fall on deaf ears, so when Flight Lieutenant Johnny Reeve, who was in charge of the Gunnery Wing asked him to crew up with him and Pilot Officer Freddy Deeks, his navigator, for another tour of operations, he jumped at the chance.

Johnny was a rather complex character who I never really got to know, whereas Freddy, who had worked in Fleet Street, was most interesting and easy to get along with. Like myself, they had both completed one tour of operations on Blenheims, Freddy being one of the few who had survived a tour in Malta during the winter of 1941–1942 where the loss of aircraft and crews had been absolutely appalling. The air gunner who normally flew with us was an extremely likeable Newfoundlander called Johnny Legge. Losses in 2 Group, meanwhile, had fallen. It also meant living in Blickling Hall again, which for me was like going home, except that this time I lived in the Officers' Mess, with the

Leutnant Paul Galland of 8./JG26, who shot down Boston Z2179 of 107 Squadron piloted by Pilot Officer Henry Collings on 31 October at Ponte à Vendin near Houthulst, Belgium. It was Galland's seventeenth and last victory, for just five hours later he was shot down and killed by a Spitfire while returning from an escort mission for the bombers to Canterbury. (*via Nigel Buswell*)

services of a batman! Sadly, my memories of this tour, which was to last fourteen months, were of a squadron that, by comparison, was under employed. In the spring of 1943 our aircraft were needed in North Africa, so we spent some time converting from the Boston Mk III to the Mk IIIA. Second, it was a period of preparation for the invasion of Europe and the development of close links with the Army, to which the Group would provide close support. A third reason may have been the sobering experience of the very heavy losses we had experienced in 1941.

Only two Circuses were possible during October 1942. The first was on the 15th when three Bostons of 88 Squadron, eleven from 107 and nine from 226 led by Squadron Leader Magill DFC visited Le Havre. Their intention was to bomb a *Neumark* Class raider, which was reported to be still in dry dock undergoing repairs following damage sustained in an earlier raid. On arrival, however, the Boston crews discovered that the vessel had sailed, so they unloaded their bombs on a 5,000 ton motor vessel in the Bassin de Marée instead. Next day, 16 October, 'Dinty' Moore and his crew took off at 1155 hours as part of a formation of six Bostons in a Circus attack on the *Neumark* at Le Havre.

We flew down to Ford in the south-east, where we rendezvoused with our escort, climbing rapidly to our operational height after leaving the coast of Kent. The usual flak barrage was awaiting our arrival over the French coast, although it cannot have been too accurate as we flew on to bomb the target before returning home. The *Luftwaffe* stayed away from the party and we landed back, unscathed, at Oulton after a flight lasting two hours fifty minutes feeling on top of the world after completing our first mission. Our first flight in the Boston was a revelation, for here we had a fast, manoeuvrable aircraft, with a terrific rate of climb, capable of carrying a bomb load of 2,000 lb, twice the weight carried by a Blenheim. Unlike the Blenheim, the Boston could, with one propeller feathered, still climb without causing the pilot too many problems. Here we had a beautiful, highly manoeuvrable and powerful aircraft, so we were better equipped to carry the war to the enemy than we had been during the summer of 1941. Another factor that struck me was the manoeuvrability of a formation of six aircraft to evade flak or fighters, compared with the old unwieldy formation of twenty-four Blenheims.

In the late afternoon of 31 October seventeen Bostons of 88 and 107 Squadrons

Pilot Officer George Turner (2nd from left) pilot of Boston III *Est melior dare quam accipere* ('It is better to give than to receive') of 107 Squadron. Arthur Liddle, his navigator is to his right. George Murray, air gunner, and observer Ron Chatfield are on his left. (*via Nigel Buswell*)

headed for power stations in the area of Rijsel and Bethune. Four flew to Mazingarbe, four to Gosnay, six to Pont-à-Vendin and three to Comines. Of the four that had Mazingarbe as a target, only one reached its destination and dropped its bombs. The same happened to the ones at Gosnay: not one of the seven aircraft could find the target. Most of the them dropped their bombs on secondary targets and strafed them with their guns. Of the six aircraft of 107 Squadron *en route* to Pont-à-Vendin the aircraft of Flight Sergeant Grant had to return after experiencing problems with its guns. The other five continued in heavy rain and reduced visibility. Pilot Officer George Turner and Squadron Leader Philip Rex Barr DFC dropped their loads on Pont-à-Vendin while Flight Sergeant Nicols attacked Comines. In the two remaining aircraft Sergeant Simpson and Pilot Officer Henry Collings headed for Pont-à-Vendin. Simpson could not find his target so he dropped his bombs on an alternative. Collings did the same before, over Jonkershove, his Boston was picked up by two incoming Fw 190s of 8./JG26 from Wevelgem-Kortrijk. *Leutnant* Paul Galland (one of two younger brothers of Adolph) was flying the leading fighter and his wingman was probably *Oberfeldwebel* Johann Edman. They attacked as soon as the Boston came within range. Stanley Nash and Francis Pickering, the two air gunners, returned fire but shells from Galland's guns set the aircraft on fire. The other crew member was Ronald Tebbutt, the 32-year-old navigator. The Boston touched down, flipped over amongst some willow trees and carried on through a field before exploding. One of the crew members was still alive but he died shortly afterwards. The wreckage was spread for hundreds of yards. It was Paul Galland's seventeenth victory and his last. Five hours later he was killed when he was shot down into the sea by a Spitfire while returning from an escort mission for the bombers to

Francis 'Rex' Pickering, one of the air gunners of the Boston III flown by Pilot Officer Henry Collings on 31 October. All of Collings's crew were killed. (*via Nigel Buswell*)

Canterbury. Edman, who then dispatched the Spitfire, was himself shot down and killed on 21 March 1944, by which time he had five victories.

At the end of October 1942 the Battle of Alamein resulted in a victory for the Eighth Army over Rommel's *Afrika Korps* and then, on 8 November, Allied forces landed in North Africa. At last it seemed that the tide had turned in the Allies' favour. Better times were anticipated too, for 2 Group. The North American Mitchell II had begun to equip 98 Squadron (which had disbanded in Coastal Command in July 1941) and 180 Squadron, which had both re-formed at West Raynham in September, though the squadrons would not begin flying operations until after they moved to Foulsham on 15 October. Even then, problems with turrets, guns and other systems would delay them further. Also in October the Lockheed Vega Ventura entered the picture. Crews sardonically named it the 'Flying Pig' (a reference to its porcine fuselage). When asked what the Ventura could do that the Hudson could not, they answered, 'Consume more petrol!' Squadron Leader Ray Chance, CO of 'A' Flight in 21 Squadron (which had disbanded at Luqa, Malta on 14 March and re-formed at Bodney the same day) remembered:

> We spent the summer converting to Venturas - a larger version of the Hudson! In fact it was a Lodestar passenger aircraft, converted – its civil origins never deserted it. Venturas came in penny numbers, sometimes one a week, sometimes two. The manual came with it. As new crews came in (an upper gunner was needed), I taught the young pilots to take off and land and formate, etc. Squadron Leader Peter Shand did the same with 'B' Flight.

The Ventura carried a crew of four or five, could carry 2,500 lb of bombs and was armed with two .50 and six .303 inch machine guns. Two other Ventura squadrons, 487 RNZAF and 464 RAAF, were formed at Feltwell on 15 August and 9 September respectively, occupying dispersals recently vacated by 75 New Zealand Squadron Wellingtons. No. 487 was commanded by Wing Commander F. C. 'Frankie' Seavill, who came from a sheep-farming family at Waingaro and had left Hamilton, New Zealand, in 1930 for a career in the RAF. No. 21 Squadron remained at Bodney until October 1942, finally moving to nearby Methwold, where it would remain until April 1943.

Ventura operations began on 3 November 1942 when three crews from 21 Squadron, led by the CO, Wing Commander R. J. P. Pritchard AFC DFC, tried to raid a factory at Hengelo but had to bomb railway lines instead. Further sorties were flown on the 6th for the loss of three aircraft. Squadron Leader Ray Chance remembered:

> I lost two close friends on that foray. Flying Officer A. E. K. Perry was killed in action and Flying Officer Brown did not return but later we heard that he was a PoW. Another close friend was pilot Warrant Officer 2 V. R. 'Hank' Henry RCAF, a boy of twenty who had come all the way from Vancouver. He died on his first trip, on 7 November and is now buried at Flushing. My crew of S-Sugar on 7 November was Sergeant 'Steve' Stephens, WOp/AG, Sergeant 'Robbie' Robinson, navigator and Flight Sergeant Edinborough DFM, upper gunner. We took off around midday for Terneuzen to attack oil installations there. The flight over the North Sea at about 100–200 ft was uneventful. It was also called a

Ventura I operations began on 3 November 1942 when three crews from 21 Squadron led by the CO, Wing Commander R. J. P. Pritchard AFC, tried to raid a factory at Hengelo but had to bomb railway lines instead. The Ventura carried a crew of five and was armed with two fixed 0.50 calibre guns and two depressible 0.303 inch guns in the nose, two or four 0.303 in guns in a dorsal turret and two 0.303 inch guns in the ventral position firing aft. The bomb load was four 250 lb and three 500 lb bombs. (*Wartime Watton Museum*)

cloud-cover raid, the Met forecast being that there would be a front over the Dutch coast with cloud base at about 800 ft. We saw the Dutch coast approaching and flashed over the sand dunes at 50 ft, to keep below enemy radar. We had been going some while when Robbie called me up on the R/T and said, 'Sorry, sir but I'm lost.'

On 6 November 21 Squadron despatched four Venturas to attack enemy shipping at Maasluis in Holland and six more in pairs to Roosendaal, Ijmuiden and Den Helder. Bad visibility dogged operations and Wing Commander Werfield bombed a ship at Rotterdam and another hit barges at Maasluis while one aborted the raid and a fourth (YH-X) was lost. Two other Venturas (YH-V and YH-L), FTR, including AE784, which crashed at Waddenzee, 3 miles east of Den Helder, were downed by flak. (*Otto Keller collection*)

I said, 'OK, Robbie, stay on this course for a while and see what turns up. Silence and we skimmed along for another ten minutes when up pops Robbie again and says, 'Sorry, sir but I'm still lost.'

We were somewhere near the Dutch/Belgian border and could have been heading for Bruges or even Antwerp. As this was totally unsatisfactory I decided, rightly or wrongly, to pull up to 250–300 ft to see if I could pick up a pinpoint position. As soon as we reached that height without warning there was an enormous high-pitched explosion. A shell had gone through the fuselage about 3 ft behind my head and exploded in the fuselage. It should have blown my head off but I found later that I had one of the Venturas with a 2 in steel plate behind the seat. This saved me but unfortunately it caught my wireless operator. I kept a straight face and a straight course. I couldn't see behind me. Then Robbie came through from the navigation section in the nose and looked down the fuselage. In his slow, unemotional Lancashire voice, he said, 'Steve's been hit, sir.'

I said, 'Then bring him alongside me.'

The crew, including a Flying Officer who had 'come along for the ride', dragged him and laid him down at the side of me. He was covered in blood from head to foot. I later discovered that he had been blinded by phosphorus burns to the eyes, his elbow joint was smashed and he had thirty bits of small shrapnel in him. His lips were moving.

I said, 'What's he saying?'

'He wants to know if we're going back.'

Two of the crew said, 'He's bleeding to death. If you turn back now, sir, you might just save his life.'

This calls for very hard decisions when you have been in the same crew for six months. There is a deep personal friendship and bond that grows up quite regardless of rank. There lay poor Steve in an ever-widening pool of blood. I pulled the 'stick' back and shot up into the clouds at 800 ft, levelled off and let them give him such help as they could. Someone tried a morphine injection. They said again, 'He wants to know if we're going back.'

I shouted to them, 'Shout in his ear and say we've turned round and we're going back.'

We had not. We were going straight on.

After this I descended through the clouds to ground level again. I calculated that it would be ten more minutes to the target (and ten minutes back to at least this point), putting twenty minutes on to Steve's time. When the time was up on that course Robbie and I decided to do a square search of the area and if the oil installations could not be found I was permitted to look for a secondary target.

I decided to fly NNE, when we should come to the estuaries from the Rhine. Then Flight Sergeant Edinborough called me up from his top turret and said that firing was coming at us from behind. So up again into the clouds for blind flying, as one instrument had gone. After a few minutes I decided to come down again. As I broke cloud I saw to my left a broad estuary and three ships sailing out to the sea in line astern. I said, 'This is it.'

So we did a diving turn to the left and, pulling out above the masts of the rear ship, did an attack on all three from the rear. Having pressed the bomb button on the wheel, I immediately pulled up straight into the low cloud base and climbed to 800 ft in cloud. Steve wasn't taking any part in all this, though as we dived one way and then the other I saw blood run to one side of the cockpit, then the other.

After some time flying blind I felt sure we must be over the sea, so I put the nose down and broke cloud again quite low down. I was slap over a harbour. At once flak guns opened up, so yet again stick back and up into the clouds. This time we kept the course we had chosen for home. After fifteen minutes we ran out of cloud cover; we had passed through the front and were in clear blue sky at 800 ft. At once the worry was German fighters, so down to sea level and give it all it's got.

As we approached Great Yarmouth I pulled up to about 1,000 ft so that we could easily be seen and fire off the identification colours of the day. There were three Royal Navy ships parallel to the coast heading north but they were quite unimpressed by our activities and at once opened fire on us! I was just beginning to feel that it just was not my day!

Poor Steve was again thrown about the bloody cockpit floor. They didn't hit us but as I headed overland into Norfolk a low November mist had settled in the late afternoon. Finally we admitted that we were lost above this low fog, although there was a perfect blue sky above. We stooged around for over half an hour looking for something. At last by the grace of God I saw Swaffham church tower sticking up through the mist. A cheer went up. I knew where I was and the course to fly to Bodney and Methwold.

One of the crew must have worked the W/T set, for as I came in low over the hedge an ambulance and a fire engine were at the end of the runway and raced down the runway with us. The medics were wonderful. Before the great wheels had stopped they were inside with a stretcher and by the time I reached the perimeter track Steve was already on his way to RAF Hospital, Ely.

When I got to dispersal I walked slowly over to an elder tree, leaned against it wearily, then bent down and threw up. That evening I stole a gallon of petrol, put it in the Flight Truck and drove to Ely. Steve was propped up and was what is euphemistically called 'comfortable'. Matron told me of his injuries and the thirty little bits of shrapnel they'd got out of him. Thankfully he lived, regained his sight and later demanded to go back again to 21 Squadron and do some more. It is sad that they do not give medals to young men like Steve who showed such quiet but indomitable courage.

Losses in 2 Group generally were high. For instance, in November 107

Bombs dropped from 8,000 ft by 226 Squadron Bostons led by Wing Commander Surplice DSO DFC fall on Caen-Carpiquet aerodrome on 6 November (*RAF*)

Boston IIIs of 107 Squadron in formation. On 10 November 1942 during an abortive Circus operation against a *Neumark* class ship in Le Havre (the ship, which had been hit by twelve Bostons on 9 November, had been moved), AL284/B was damaged by Fw 190s, collided with Z2164/W and crashed into the sea. 107 Squadron continued operations with Bostons until 20 January 1944, after which it stood down to convert to the Mosquito FBVI. In spring 1943 Boston IIIs of 2 Group were replaced by Boston IIIAs and many surviving Mk IIIs found their way to 114 Squadron, which since November 1942 was based in Algeria flying Blenheims. Z2303 was one of these and it was lost on 23 April 1943 when it overshot landing at Victoria LG 23 in bad visibility and the nosewheel collapsed. Two of the other Bostons in the formation are AL719/O, which was destroyed by fire at Brindisi on 16 October 1943 and behind it, W8330, which was SOC on 31 August 1944. (*Aeroplane*)

Boston Squadron flew eleven sorties for the loss of four aircraft and sixteen aircrew killed – an almost 40 per cent loss rate! On a raid on the marshalling yards at Courtrai on 7 November Squadron Leader Philip Rex Barr DFC hit high-tension cables and crashed near Wevelgem; he and his observer, Flying Officer Walter Barfod DFC were killed. Two 107 Squadron Bostons collided near Le Havre on the 10th with no survivors. There was not even the consolation that the 'tip and run' raids by 2 Group on airfields, power stations and docks, flying low over the sea, so reminiscent of the shipping strikes, were accomplishing much material damage.

Flight Lieutenant George Turner DFC*, a pilot in 107 Squadron, recalled.

27 November 1942 was a typical November day with grey cloud sheer at about 1,000 ft and visibility of about 3 miles. It started out as a normal one for us Boston crews in 107 Squadron at Great Massingham, Norfolk. The officers had arrived from West Raynham in the crew bus at about 8.30 a.m. and the NCO aircrews had walked up from their billets in Massingham to the airfield. As usual we gathered round the stove in the crew room. Some played cards, some chatted and some read. By 9 o'clock normal training was under way. Some time during the morning, probably about eleven o'clock, the Flight Commander sent for Warrant Officer A. J. 'Tony' Reid and myself to tell me that we had been detailed for a low-level operation that I was to lead. (The squadron was only

sending out a pair of aircraft.) We were to tell our crews to have an early lunch and to report for briefing at 1 o'clock. I was a bit excited (low-level trips in Bostons were exciting) and rather flattered, as this was the first time we had been chosen to lead another aircraft on a raid. Tony Reid was not pleased. He was a much more experienced pilot than me (although his operational experience was about on a par with mine) who had spent nearly a year at Upwood flying observers under training in Ansons and had thus built up twice as many flying hours as I had. With this behind him he felt that he should be the leader and said so to me.

The Royal Dutch Steelworks at Ijmuiden lay behind and slightly to one side of the town and for some reason we were briefed to come in from the sea, cross the harbour and town, then attack the steelworks. In our ignorance this meant nothing to us (we were still very inexperienced as this was only our fourth low-level trip) but it certainly meant something to the Intelligence Officer, who came out to our aircraft as we were getting in and wished us luck. This was unusual – it had never happened before, nor did it ever happen subsequently!

We took off, flew to the coast at about 100 ft and set course for the target dropping down to sea level as we did so. The visibility was not very good and, being very conscious of Tony Reid's displeasure, I flew as low and as accurately as I could. We had no aids so accurate compass courses were essential. We had a full load of fuel and four 500 lb bombs fused for eleven-second delay. I was flying one of the few aircraft on the squadron (at that time) that incorporated an RAF modification to improve the Boston's range – a 140 gallon fuselage tank fitted over the bomb bay. The normal tankage was one inboard of the engine of 140 gallons and one outboard of 60 gallons, in each wing. For some reason I decided to use the outboard tanks first. I don't know why but it had a bearing on subsequent events.

We did not say much over the sea. We were never a chatty crew, so it was Arthur Liddle, my navigator, warning me that the enemy coast was five minutes ahead that broke the silence. I changed tanks to inners, went in to rich mixture, pushed the revs to 2,350 and the boost to 40 inches of mercury (flat out was 2,400 r.p.m. and 45 inches of mercury). As the speed built up to about 280 m.p.h. I re-trimmed the aircraft and gave a quick glance over my shoulder to see Tony Reid nicely in position a little to one side and behind. Visibility had improved as we neared the coast and we saw Ijmuiden from about 5 miles out. Impressions now get a little confused. I remember flying between two

Boston III OM-U of 107 Squadron banking over the Norfolk countryside (*via Nigel Buswell*)

breakwaters into the harbour and there was tracer flak from all directions criss-crossing in front, at the side and straight at me from ahead. I was flying as low as I could with the prop tips about a foot or so above the water and most of it seemed to be going over the top of us, then I heard four loud bangs and knew we had been hit. The engine instruments seemed OK although the starboard engine was a bit down on boost but the fuel gauge for the starboard inner tank and the fuselage tank gauge were sinking towards zero. At the time I conned myself that I was trying to check on the damage to the aircraft. I was probably suffering from shock because when I looked out again we were up about 300 ft and a target for every flak gun for miles around, which were having a field day. It seemed to take ages to register that I was the centre of all this attention. But it can only have been a second or two before I pushed the stick forward, shot down to ground level, pushed throttles and pitch levers against the stops and changed to the starboard outer tank, which still had a few gallons in it. I flew in a wide curve to port well behind the town and turned north for a couple of miles or so before taking up a north-westerly heading that Arthur gave me before passing out. In our sweep round I checked on the crew. The gunners were OK but Arthur said he had been hit. The starboard engine was making a horrible clanking noise and was down to about 30 inches boost but it was helping us along at about 270 m.p.h. so I kept it going.

We crossed some sand dunes and headed out to sea. Heavy guns opened up behind us and great spouts of water rose around but that did not last long, as the chances of us being hit were remote. Ron Chatfield, my WOP/AG, now reported a couple of Me 109s behind us, so I pulled up into cloud. After settling down there I switched off the starboard engine (it had done us proud but it did not sound at all well), transferred the remains of the fuel from the outer tank to the port inner and calculated that we had enough to reach England at our reduced airspeed. From time to time I tried to raise Arthur but with no success.

Just short of the English coast we came out of cloud and as we approached land I fired the colours of the day to identify ourselves. I had decided to land at the nearest airfield to get medical attention for Arthur as soon as possible. I pinpointed our position near Norwich and headed for Horsham St Faith, the nearest airfield. At that time the only R/T the Boston possessed was a set called a TR9 (the following year we were equipped with VHF radios), a very efficient apparatus with a theoretical range of 5 miles but which in practice rarely worked, so we tended to ignore it. Thus I just flew over the tower at about 800 ft, did a circuit and landed. As a Boston would taxi on one engine I switched off the starboard engine on touchdown.

At the end of our landing run we shot out of our cockpits, raced around to the front of the aircraft and started to get Arthur out. He and the nose were a mess. There was blood everywhere and great chunks of the perspex were missing. Arthur was covered in blood, unconscious and very cold. As we were doing this I looked towards the tower but nothing seemed to be happening, so Ron dashed off to wake them up while George and I finished getting Arthur out and laid him on the ground.

At an operational airfield a twin-engined aircraft landing on one engine would have had a fire tender alongside as it stopped and things would have happened fast. Unknown to us the RAF had left Horsham, leaving a care and maintenance party to hand over to the Americans, whose advanced party had just arrived, so things were very different.

Ron eventually turned up with a fire truck, having browbeaten the corporal in charge to take action. I went off with Arthur in the truck to SHQ [Station Headquarters] where I made a bit of a nuisance of myself because I thought they were so slow. In fairness to them, we had arrived unannounced and unexpectedly and they were short of men and vehicles. I was a bit overwrought and rather rude. Although it seemed ages it was probably less than ten minutes after landing that Arthur was rushed to the Norfolk & Norwich Hospital in the care of a medical orderly.

Having seen Arthur away I went back in a truck to the aircraft to pick up Ron and George. This time I had a good look at the machine, which was a sorry sight. All the shells that had hit her had come from ahead and the right. One had burst on the bombsight, flinging fragments of steel (and perspex) into Arthur's leg, arm and face. A second had entered the fuselage a foot or so behind my head and had burst in the fuselage tank. A third had smashed through the leading edge of the wing inboard of the starboard engine and holed the fuel tank there. The fourth had burst against the bottom two cylinders of the starboard engine, making a mess of the cylinder heads and rocker boxes. These were all 20 mm and probably came from one gun.

It was getting dark by now, so we collected up our flying gear and went to the control tower to report to base and arrange transport home. Eventually, an 8 cwt van with a WAAF driver came from Massingham to pick us up and we got back to our messes about ten o'clock. It had been rather a long day.

This operation illustrated the part that luck played in these things. We were lucky that the tanks that were hit were full, otherwise they would most likely have exploded and caught fire. Intelligence had given Ron a 16 mm cine camera to take a film of the target. He was using this, not his guns, when 140 gallons of 100 octane swished past his legs and out of the rear hatch. George told me that he was getting ready to fire back when he was soused in petrol and thought it unwise to do so. It was a miracle that we were untouched after bombing when I was stooging along at 300 ft; quite a lot of the stuff was coming from the harbour and town behind us and it was non-deflection shooting for them.

Conversely, it was our bad luck that our very experienced CO, Wing Commander Lynn, had been replaced by Wing Commander P. H. Dutton, who had come from India and had no experience of European operations. No experienced CO would, at that stage of the war, have allowed any of his crews to fly through a heavily defended harbour to attack a target behind it. I suspect that the instructions came from Group. Dutton, a regular officer, would not question it and the Intelligence Officer, who did know the score, was not senior enough to get it altered. Apart from the normal harbour defences, an E-boat squadron was stationed there and those not out on patrol would have joined in the fun. (107 Squadron attacked the steelworks again in 1943. Six aircraft under a very experienced CO, Wing Commander [Richard Grenville] 'Dickie' England, came in from the north and attacked the works, keeping the town between them and the harbour. Although a fighter shot down one aircraft, none were hit by flak.) I guess that our attack was to have an element of surprise – straight in from the sea was the shortest way to the target and it might have worked. We didn't surprise them but they certainly surprised us.

Tony Reid, who was behind us and theoretically in the more dangerous position, did not get a scratch. (The theory was that gunners aimed at the leading aircraft and did not allow enough deflection to hit the No. 2.) However, his luck ran out a week or so later and he was shot down on the Eindhoven operation, as was Wing Commander Dutton, both crews being lost. We were on this one too with a spare observer but were untouched.

Boston Z2234/H of 226 Squadron. Left to right: Jack Hayter, Tim Healey, G. R. Stewart, Mike Dillon. Z2234 finished its career with 114 Squadron and crashed on take off at Foggia, Italy on 17 January 1944. (*via Nigel Buswell*)

CHAPTER SIX

Operation Oyster

Kite mutunga – *'Through to the end'*
Motto of 487 Squadron RNZAF

R ain was falling in East Anglia on the morning of Sunday, 6 December 1942 but near the outskirts of Eindhoven, 60 miles from the coast of Holland, the weather was clear. Frits Philips and his wife, along with his brother-in-law van Riemsdijk and sister Jetty were visiting a niece who had christened a child. Philips was Director General of the Philips electrochemical factories in Eindhoven, a built up area of Holland only 50 miles from the Ruhr. It was the largest manufacturer of its type in Europe, thought to produce over one-third of the German supply of valves and certain radar equipment. Although some industrial processes had been dispersed to other sites, Eindhoven was still the main centre, especially for research into electronic countermeasures and radar. Production was centred in two factories, the Strijp Group main works and the Emmasingel valve and lamp factory, both in built-up areas within the town. Their destruction, which demanded precision bombing from a very low level to minimize the danger to the local people, was considered by London to be of vital importance. In Philips' opinion however, his factory produced only a tiny amount of material for the Germans, a view shared by the Philips family and staff in America. But, in order to satisfy the German commission from Berlin, Philips always prepared graphs showing that production totals were better than they were so that the Germans could return home satisfied. These graphs were seen by a number of employees, some of whom were members of the local resistance, but Philips' efforts to look less productive were not forwarded to the Allies so readily. After the church service Philips, his wife, brother-in-law and sister were drinking the usual cups of coffee, when suddenly they saw a formation of low-flying aircraft approaching in the distance. Their suspicion was that they were British aircraft. Philips' first reaction was, 'Are they going to bomb the Eindhoven railway station?' At the same moment they saw the first bombs being dropped and heard the crashing of the impact. With a feeling of deprivation they realized that their town was being bombed! As fast as they could Philips and his brother-in-law cycled to De Laak, where fortunately nobody was harmed. At some distance they saw the Demer, the most important shopping street in Eindhoven, which was already ablaze.

Only now did Frits Philips realize that it was his factories, that were the target of the bombardment. There was a momentary silence and he thought that the bombardment had finished, but while he was cycling to the Emmasingel factory yet another wave of bombers rushed in to the attack and he had to hurriedly seek shelter in a cycle-shop. Meanwhile, he noticed that the office building had been hit several times and was on fire. Despite this he wanted to rescue portraits of his father and uncle, which had been painted by Jan Veth in 1916 at the occasion of the 25th anniversary of the company. Fortunately all the other portraits and valuables had been stowed away safely long ago. The portraits were hanging in the commissioners' room at ground level. Frits climbed in through a window and was able to rescue a silver cigar-box from his desk. He distributed a box of good cigars which had been left by his father amongst the fire brigade who had joined him. He went into the commissioners' room, opened the door and at that same moment a large piece of ceiling came crashing down. The firemen would not let him enter the room and so, sadly, he had to leave the portraits to the fire. The building burned out completely.

Preparations for Operation *Oyster*, the most ambitious daylight raid conceived by 2 Group had been given the green light on 9 November 1942. Originally plans called for the Strijp Group main works to be bombed by twenty-four Venturas, twelve Mitchells and twelve Mosquitoes, while twelve Venturas and thirty-six Bostons would at the same time attack the Emmasingel lamp and valve works $1/2$ a mile to the east. The slower Venturas would lead the way at low level with HE and 30 lb incendiaries before surprise was lost. On 17 November a full-scale practice was held on a route similar to the one to be used, with the St Neots power station as the 'target'. Many basic lessons were learned, while other problems associated with a mixed force, such as the differences in bombing techniques and cruising speeds,

Wing Commander Hugh Pelly-Fry (centre), leader of the operation to Eindhoven on 6 December 1942 with fellow officers. Squadron Leader Dickie England is far left and T. H. J. 'Jock' Cairns DFM far right. (*via Jim Moore*)

were exposed. The Mitchells fared particularly badly on this first practice but even worse were the Venturas. Next day thirty of their crews tried again on their own on the same route and a vast improvement was recorded. All four aircraft types took part in the third practice, on 20 November.

Sergeant Stan C. Moss RAAF, a Ventura pilot in 464 Squadron was feeling a bit upset at not being chosen to participate in the first rehearsals. He consoled himself with the thought that his crew were recent arrivals at Feltwell and aged twenty, he was the second youngest on the Squadron.

Both my observer and wireless air gunner – Sergeants Reg A. Wagner and J. A. Wallis – were Londoners and we had teamed up through unusual circumstances. At OTU I had a 'million to one chance' accident and was sole survivor of a head-on collision with another Blenheim in smog-like conditions over the North Sea. I parachuted into the sea and floated around in a one-man dinghy for fifty hours before being picked up by a passing ship. It took me almost a week to get back to Bicester where my course mates at first greeted me with ghost-like awe. A Court of Enquiry, at which my actions were affirmed, inevitably followed and I was exhorted by the CO to get back to flying as soon as possible. I was given the option of accepting a staff job in Training Command to assuage the memory of those traumatic days. Eventually, I was introduced to another crew whose pilot had been held for further training. The fourth member, Sergeant F. C. Lindsay, an air gunner who hailed from South Australia, joined us at Feltwell. First, we had to become familiar with the Ventura. Vega was a subsidiary of the Lockheed Company, which produced the renowned Hudson to which the Ventura was similar but bigger. In fact, it was a military version of the Lockheed Lodestar, a short haul airliner. This accounted for its undesirable bulk as a warplane, its relatively slow response to the touch of control and its rather swanky interior appointments – automatic pilot was a dream. The best features of the Ventura were its powerful Pratt and Whitney engines and exceptionally strong all metal airframe.

Then came news of my posting to the Middle East. All was approved provided I would name my wireless air gunner. Transferring to the Middle Eastern theatre where Australian troops had long been operating had always been a priority for me but my English WOP/AG adamantly refused to go, understandably, because he was married. So the posting fell through and eight days later I was listed to fly as number two to the Flight Commander in what was to be the third and final rehearsal for the 'big do'. We flew east beyond the English coast then turned north, a tightly packed formation of Venturas at almost nought feet. But the 'tail-gating' effect meant we were flying in each other's slipstream and this caused ones's aircraft to twist and yaw with the fearsome danger of hitting the water or another aircraft. One sweated at the controls like a navvy. At Flamborough Head, where we turned inland to the supposed 'target' we became entangled with Bostons and Mosquitoes in a frightening shambles, exacerbated by a simulated attack by Spitfires which dived amongst us with amazing daring. Surprisingly, there were no collisions, even though more than 100 aircraft were involved. In the scattering of our formation, I managed to hang on to my number one until reaching base but jibbed at following him under high-tension wires!

Next day a frank post-mortem took place, which much relieved everyone's anxiety about the slipstream hazard. Then came the announcement: target Philips' radio factory at Eindhoven, The Netherlands. Bostons were to go in first and bomb from a medium height, followed by Venturas carrying a mixture of incendiaries and delayed action bombs and finally the Mosquitoes would sweep in to distract the fire fighters. To bluff enemy defences, our fighters would make three diversionary sweeps and there would be top cover for us as well. It all sounded foolproof.

The three simulated attacks revealed deficiencies that led to the two Mitchell squadrons, 98 and 180, being withdrawn from the starting line-up for the raid, scheduled for Wednesday 3 December. In any event, since converting to Mitchells both squadrons had been plagued by turret and gun, intercom and oxygen problems and were far from operational. It was also anticipated that smoke and fires from the Venturas' incendiaries would obscure the target for the succeeding waves, so they would have to go in last behind the Bostons and Mosquitoes. Consequently, the routes and timings differed between the aircraft, the fastest, the Mosquito, being followed by the Boston, then the slowest, the Ventura. Obviously, it was vital for each squadron to arrive over the targets separately, to avoid confusion, yet it was imperative that the whole attack be completed in the shortest possible time. Therefore it was finally decided that the Bostons would, after all, attack both plants and with eleven-second delayed action bombs. These would hopefully divert attention from the Venturas as they climbed to bombing height.

By 2 December preparations were complete. Jim 'Dinty' Moore recalled:

At 2030 hours at Oulton our presence was requested in the briefing room with eleven other crews from the squadron. There was a great deal of animated discussion. Various characters claiming to be 'in the know' told us what the target was going to be, followed by an expectant silence when our CO, Wing Commander Pelly-Fry [who would lead the operation] stepped on the dais, the cover being removed from the large target map. The operation would involve eighty-four aircraft from the Group. In addition, our withdrawal was to be covered by four fighter squadrons of Spitfires, Mustangs and Typhoons, who would meet us at the coast, while the Americans were to launch a high-level attack with [thirty-six] Flying Fortresses on Lille as a diversion. After the briefing we were confined to camp, the telephone was put out of bounds, so we settled down for a disturbed night. The following morning we climbed into the flight trucks and made our way up to the 'drome all keyed up for this special operation. We collected our parachutes with the usual comments from the packers such as, 'Bring it back if it doesn't work' and made our way out to the aircraft. It was then that the unforgivable happened and we were informed that the operation had been postponed [because of bad weather on the Continent]. It is difficult to describe your emotions at a time like that, for although you might feel a sense of relief you know that you will eventually fly on this operation so the overriding reaction is one of frustration. Having been briefed for the operation there was no way that the authorities were going to let us loose on the community in case word got out about our plans. They dreamed up a variety of service-type devices to keep us occupied, for which we displayed little enthusiasm.

Thankfully, the morning of Sunday 6 December dawned and we were told that it was on, so we were driven up to the 'drome with the predominant feeling being to get it over with. At 1115 hours we took off, forming up as No 3 to our 'Wingco' [James Pelly-Fry, who would open the attack, with Pilot Officer G. 'Jock' Campbell flying as his No 2] and setting off on a course that took us directly over Norwich on our way to the coast. The noise of this large force of low-flying aircraft brought many of the citizens to their doors to see what was going on. The instruction to fly at no more than 50 feet over the sea to avoid detection by German radar was strictly adhered to as we careered across the North Sea. The 'Wingco' had the good fortune to have an excellent navigator [T. H. J.] 'Jock' Cairns [DFM] who guided us to our correct landfall. It was a pleasant sunny day and as we skimmed over the flat countryside we saw some Dutch men and women bedecked in their Sunday best. Many of them gave us a friendly wave. Despite the occasion and the obvious risks, the sense of speed, flying at about 20 feet, was truly exhilarating. On our way to the target I saw a lone Fw 190 fighter, whose pilot must have had quite a shock on seeing the approaching aerial armada and sheered off.

Pilot Officer Jack Peppiatt, in 'B' Flight, behind Flight Lieutenant Johnny Reeve, had the same sense of excitement.

Flying on the deck was always thrilling and we watched each other from aircraft to aircraft. Crossing the coast was a bit tense for two reasons. One, you were anxiously looking to identify a landfall and, two, the ack-ack gunners had a

Boston III AL693 'U' flown by Flight Lieutenant Johnny Reeve and his crew on the Eindhoven raid. This photograph, taken during a practice flight just prior to the raid, shows WOP/AG Jim 'Dinty' Moore in the rear gun turret with Flying Officer 'Skeets' Kelly, who took photographs of the raid from this aircraft. AL693 flew thirty-one sorties in 88 Squadron between 23 March 1942 and 3 January 1943 before going to North Africa. It later served with 114 Squadron and was lost in a crash landing on 17 September 1943. (*IWM*)

head-on view of you; for this reason we came in firing our guns to make them keep their heads down.

Altogether, twelve Bostons of 88 Squadron, twelve of 226 Squadron at Swanton Morley and seventeen Venturas of 21 Squadron at Methwold were to bomb the Emmasingel valve factory. Another twelve Bostons of 107 Squadron at Great Massingham, fourteen Venturas of 464 RNZAF and sixteen of 487 RAAF Squadron at Feltwell (who were flying their first full-scale Ventura operation) were to attack the Strijp Group main works. The New Zealand Squadron would take off in two boxes of eight, one led by Seavill and the other by Flying Officer G. W. Brewer DFC from Papatoetoe, New Zealand. All the crews had been instructed to wear steel helmets to protect their heads from being knocked against the insides of the aircraft during evasive action and also to safeguard against flak splinters! Pilots and crews of 487 Squadron were concerned to learn that they were at the end of the bomber stream, behind and to the left of 464 Squadron. Squadron Leader Len Trent DFC, the 487 Squadron 'B' Flight commander, who hailed from Nelson in New Zealand, recalled:

I thought of the unfortunate troopers in the Charge of the Light Brigade as we prepared our maps and our aircraft were bombed up with heavy incendiary missiles capable of crashing through the factory walls before erupting into flames. We studied photographs of the target, a complex of huge buildings on the edge of the town. . . and the biggest building, which was to be my victim, was five storeys high – a bulls-eye impossible to miss.

As they were driven to their Venturas Sergeant John Bede Cusack RAAF, air gunner in a 464 Squadron Ventura flown by Pilot Officer P. C. Kerr RAAF heard someone say, "Well, it's something new but I hope those bloody Spits keep close to us. I don't want to tangle with any Focke Wulfs in this bloody crate." I looked at the faces of these young airmen who were about to be blooded. They were serious and generally quiet. As each crew got out the rest wished them luck.[38]

The American-built bombers would be joined by eight Mosquitoes of 105 Squadron, led by Wing Commander Hughie Edwards VC DFC, who had returned from Malta to take command of the squadron on 3 August 1942 and two of 139 Squadron. Squadron Leader Jack Houlston AFC DFC and Warrant Officer James Armitage DFC of 139 Squadron would take off at noon to carry out damage assessment. At Marham the briefings were carried out by Edwards, accompanied as usual by his white bulldog Sallie. If she was late Edwards would halt proceedings until she had settled down![39] Edwards and Flight Lieutenant Charles Patterson, who had a black spaniel by the name of Jamie, often took their dogs aloft in a Mosquito during practice flights. Patterson, who flew the Eindhoven operation with Flying Officer Mills ('armed' with a cine camera) in *O for Orange* and who had flown a tour on Blenheims in 114 Squadron, recalled:

Mosquito operations were far more ambitious than Blenheim ops but casualties were lower. For a period from about July–September 1942 the casualties were as high as the low-level daylights in Blenheims a year before. There was even talk of the Mosquito having to be written off after all. In some way we still had such enormous faith in this aeroplane so we just could not believe that it could not be made to operate successfully at an acceptable rate of casualties. Operationally, the Philips works from a Mosquito point of view was regarded as a comparatively straightforward target, nothing to get terribly frightened of. Something we would have taken in our stride as part of routine operations. I flew in the second formation of four Mosquitoes, No. 3 to Squadron Leader George Parry and one of our flight commanders, behind six led by Edwards. We were supposed to be so timed that we didn't get involved with either Venturas or Bostons. Our concern was that we would get tangled up with the Venturas or even the Bostons and have to reduce speed, which of course from a Mosquito point of view was very dangerous because we had no defensive armament. We were to fly to somewhere just south of Eindhoven and turn to port and then attack the target. The Mosquitoes were to go up to 1,500 ft just short of the target and shallow dive on to it because it was assumed that some Bostons would have gone over low level before us. We got across the Dutch coast flying at low level. Looking across my port wing-tip I saw 190s and 109s [of 4th and 6th *Staffeln* JG1] literally in line taking off from Woensdrecht to intercept us. They only looked about 200–300 yards away. It was actually about half a mile. They looked so normal, just like Spitfires taking off in England, that it was hard to realize they were coming up to kill you. We had to slow right down. We found ourselves getting involved with some Venturas. We were not far above stalling speed trying to get behind them.

B.IVs DZ353/E and DZ367/J of 105 Squadron in formation. DZ353 flew its first operation in 105 Squadron on 23 October 1942 and later served with 139 and 627 Squadrons in 8 Group (PFF) before failing to return from a raid on the marshalling yards at Rennes on 8 June 1944. Flight Lieutenant Bill Steere DFM and Flying Officer 'Windy' Gale DFC RAAF were killed. DZ367/J flew its first operation in 105 Squadron on 16 November 1942 and was one of the squadron's eight Mosquitoes that took part in the Eindhoven raid on 6 December 1942 when it was flown by Flight Lieutenant Bill Blessing and Sergeant J. Lawson. DZ367 failed to return from Berlin, 30 January 1943 when it was crewed by Squadron Leader D. F. W. Darling DFC and Flying Officer W. Wright (both KIA). (RAF Marham)

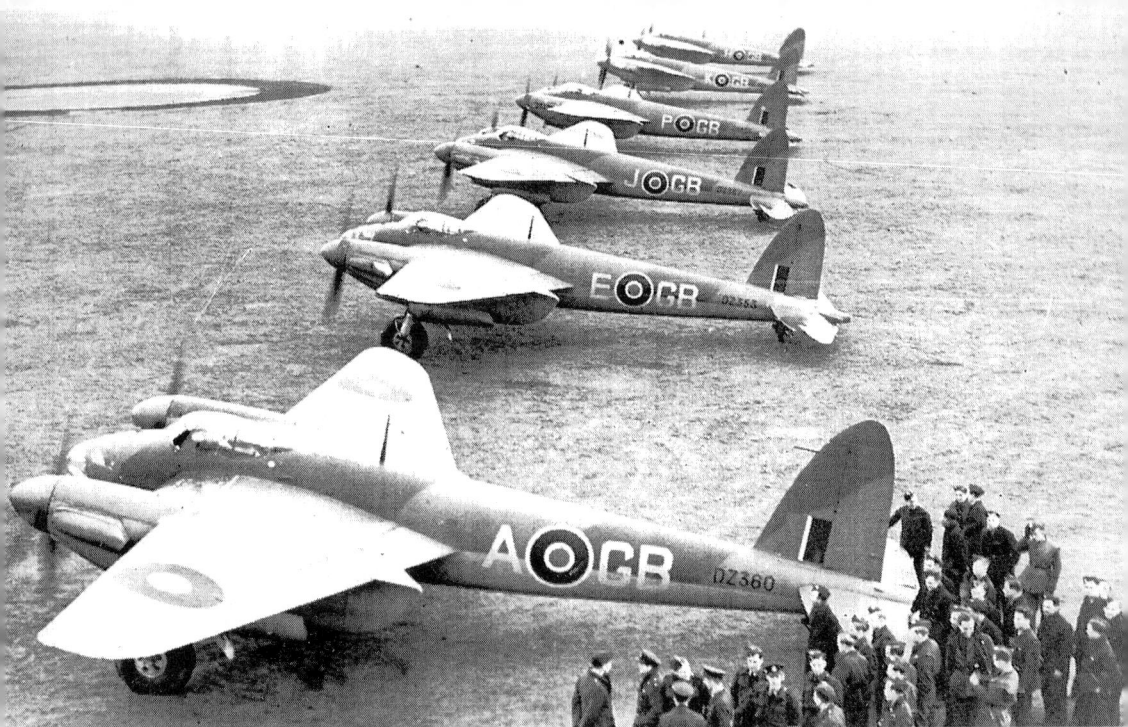

Mosquito B.IV Series IIs of 105 Squadron at Marham on 11 December 1942. DZ360/A flew its first operation in 105 Squadron on 13 November 1942 and was hit by flak while crossing the French coast near Dunkirk on a raid on the engine sheds at Termonde, East of Ghent on 22 December 1942. Flight Sergeant Joseph Edward Cloutier RCAF and Sergeant Albert Cecil Foxley were KIA when the Mosquito crashed at Axel just north of the Belgian border in the Netherlands. DZ353/F flew its first operation in 105 Squadron on 23 October 1942 and later served with 139 Squadron, becoming AZ-B of 627 Squadron but failed to return from Rennes on 8 June 1944 when Flight Lieutenant H. Steere DFM and Flying Officer K. W. 'Windy' Gale DFC RAAF were killed in action. DK336/P which flew its first operation in 105 Squadron on 16 September 1942, lost its starboard engine returning from a raid on Copenhagen on 27 January 1943, struck a balloon cable and a tree and crashed at Yaxham, Norfolk, killing Sergeant Richard Clare and Flying Officer Edward Doyle. DZ378/K, which flew its first operation in 105 Squadron on 14 December 1942, was damaged by flak and by bird strikes on the raid on a gasworks near Delmenhorst, Germany on 20 December 1942 after two sorties and relegated to Technical Training Command. DZ379/H, which flew its first operation in 105 Squadron on 8 December 1942 later joined 139 Squadron at Wyton and on 17 August 1943, the diversion for the Peenemünde raid. It was shot down by a night-fighter and crashed at Berge, Germany. Pilot Officer Cook, the American pilot from Wichita Falls, Texas and his navigator Sergeant D. A. H. Dixon were killed. (*via Phillip J. Birtles*)

With great coolness and decisiveness, Squadron Leader George Parry DSO DFC and his No.2, Flight Lieutenant W. C. S. 'Bill' Blessing, an Australian from New South Wales, broke away, at Turnhout, deliberately drawing the 190s on themselves, then let them go chasing as they opened the throttles to full speed. Parry was later able to rejoin the formation but Blessing and another Mosquito flown by Pilot Officers Jimmy Bruce DFM and Mike Carreck[40] were forced to return to Marham. Two Bostons had also aborted, while the Mosquito formation, which had departed the coast at Cromer and had flown further north of the main force, had unfortunately got ahead of schedule. Edwards and his navigator Flying Officer H. E. P. 'Bladder' Cairns successfully led the way through a 200 ft cloud base over the sea. The Mosquitoes were supposed to rendezvous with the rest of the formation at the target but they now made landfall with the Bostons and Venturas at the Scheldt Estuary. Edwards had to slow the Mosquitoes to just 150 m.p.h. and fly at 50 ft in order to stay behind the others when they should have been flying to the Strijp Works at 270 m.p.h., before climbing to 1,500 ft, diving and releasing their bombs from 500 ft.

John Bede Cusack in the Ventura formation continued:

It was a fine, windless day with a slight mist. As we streamed across the flat Norfolk countryside the field workers stopped to wave to the modern cavalcade that rose in the sky so close above their heads. The North Sea was grey and unruffled. We crossed it at zero feet. Our box was tail end of this bomber stream. A box consisted of six aircraft. No. 1 the leader had as his supports Nos. 2 and 3 on either side. No. 4 flew just below No. 1 to miss his slipstream and was supported on either side by Nos. 5 and 6. Thus No. 1 flew at approximately twenty feet so that No. 4, which was ourselves, to dodge slipstreams, was down to ten feet. Despite the nervous qualms at the pit of my stomach, I found this new experience exciting. The low-level approach was intended to spoof the enemy radar. The idea was that the island defences would be taken by surprise and we would be across them before they recovered. What someone had omitted to allow for was that the initial beating up by fighters and Mosquitoes who had gone in ten minutes ahead would have the Jerry gunners right on their toes. I heard Jack [Flying Officer B. J. E. Hannah RNZAF, navigator] say, 'Enemy coast coming up' and then the sea beneath us began to churn white as the enemy gunners extended their welcome. Overhead, black smudges lined with red appeared as if by magic. Luckily the heavies could not depress far enough to get our range but the concentration of Bofors, 20 mm and light flak was terrific.[41]

In the leading 464 Squadron Ventura flown by the CO, Wing Commander R. H. 'Bob' Young AFC navigator Flight Lieutenant E. F. 'Hawker' Hart observed that 'the whole formation of forty-eight Venturas looked a very impressive armada' as they flew just over the surface of the sea. Pilot Officer George M. 'Jock' Shinnie, a veteran of Blenheim operations and the WOP/AG was positioned at the astro hatch. Shinnie's first priority was to keep Young, a pre-war qualified flying instructor, who initially had given dual instruction to many of the young inexperienced pilots, commented on the overall state of the Ventura formations.

At times we reduced speed slightly to allow sections at the rear to catch up. Flying at tree top level and having to take evasive action individually to avoid trees, power pylons etc, made formation flying difficult at times but overall formation keeping was excellent. We were not very impressed by the size and shape of the Ventura. Neither were we impressed by its performance compared to the known performance of the Boston and Mosquito. To its credit it had two superb 2,000 hp Pratt & Whitney Double Wasp engines. The engineering staff adored them, as they were almost trouble free. So did the pilots but what a dreadful cumbersome airframe they had to drag around the air. Because of their power, large 'paddle' propellers were needed. These proved during formation flying to cause considerable turbulence to following aircraft within large formations. Again not a popular aspect particularly when flying at tree top level. My secondary role and the role of Pilot Officer J. M. Quinlan RAAF the other WOP/AG who was also positioned at the astro hatch, as there was no need for the lower rear firing guns to be manned at such low level, was scanning the sky for possible fighter attacks. We were fortunate as most of the fighters were elsewhere but we experienced considerable light flak from crossing the Dutch coast and *en route* to Eindhoven. After my Blenheim days of 1940–41 it was a new experience to me to have the flak coming from higher than we were flying.

Sergeant John Bede Cusack continued:

Two tremendous splashes that tossed water over our heads marked the passing of two crews.[42] Then we were over the defenders. A little to our right a plane plunged into the earth, skidded into a strongpoint and exploded in a burst of flame and debris. It suddenly struck me that in this sort of flying, parachutes were useless. If you went in there were no survivors. I sweated across those islands and anyone who says they were never afraid on ops is a bloody liar. Suddenly we were flying across the mainland. A few black smudges chased us but it looked as if we had passed the strongly defended coastal area. As we roared over the flat Dutch countryside the inhabitants out on their Sunday strolls waved frantically and jumped with joy. These Dutchies let it be known whose side they were on. Bill [Sergeant W. Kirk RAAF] had his head stuck out of the astrodome until the latter was blown away coming in over the coast, without giving him anything worse than a scare. He returned to the front of the kite. Suddenly Jack said, 'That's an aerodrome' and the next moment we were skipping across an excellently laid out 'drome. This was a costly blue on someone's part because two more planes ploughed in a smother of dust, flame and smoke. Probably this place had taken a beating earlier and was out for revenge. A cannon shell blew the perspex out on the starboard side of the cockpit, giving Bill his second fright but doing no damage. The gunners poured a fusillade back without much apparent effect. A little further on we passed another Ventura burning fiercely. Four figures scrambling awkwardly in their flying boots away from it showed they at least had escaped. As we swept over them they turned and gave a forlorn wave.[43]

Fellow Australian Sergeant Stan C. Moss RAAF and his 464 Squadron crew had been hit over Walcheren. Moss recalled:

Suddenly a muffled explosion sounded behind my seat. 'Sorry, Skip,' said the WOP/AG Sergeant J. A. Wallis, 'I mistakenly pushed the IFF button.' He must have known something, for shortly after a puff of black smoke appeared in the air directly ahead of us about 500 ft above the very flat shoreline some miles away. We had obviously been detected and our landfall was not an undefended shore somewhere up 'de Schelde' estuary as planned but directly over the coastline. As we were almost crossing the coast, the Squadron Leader's aircraft began to gently weave and I was about to follow suit when, like a flash of lightning, the right side cabin-window exploded almost noiselessly below the roar of the engines. Instantly and involuntarily I doubled up in my seat in reaction at being hit by pieces of exploding flak shell. My distress was immediate and my sudden movement had lifted the aircraft several hundred feet. One thought dominated my mind, namely, that I must get the machine on the deck before blacking out.

A Boston turns away after bombing the Emmasingel valve and lamp factory, about 1 mile south of the main works, and the target for 88 and 226 Boston Squadrons and 21 Ventura Squadron. The leading aircraft of 88 Squadron attacked at rooftop height with eleven-second delay bombs and the remaining aircraft bombed at 1,000–1,500 ft with HF and incendiary bombs. (*RAF*)

In a haze, I saw a tiny ploughed field to the left in a tree surrounded area and pulling back throttles and pitch, I pushed down undercarriage and flaps. As I came down over the treetops, making for the edge of the field, some interior prompting told me to lift the undercarriage lever. The plane touched down smoothly [at Vrouwenpolder] and sheared across the field at right angles to the furrow ending up about a cricket pitch length from a belt of trees. The observer, Sergeant Reg A. Wagner, sitting unharnessed on the bench seat next to me, was immediately thrown forward on impact into the bombing hatch, yet fortunately unhurt by the fall.

From some unrealized reserves of energy and determination, I forced myself out of the aircraft and collapsed to the ground about 10 yards away. Three of us had been wounded by shells bursting inside the cabin of the machine slightly above and behind my right shoulder. The observer received pieces of shrapnel into his left shoulder, narrowly missing his vertebrae and aorta, whilst the WOP/AG had perspex splinters in his face, upper chest, side, back, ribs and arm and I had also been well peppered by about a dozen smaller pieces. Bleeding profusely, a crewmember thoughtfully shot a capsule of morphine into me and a welcome calm descended. I remember looking up at the rolling cumulus clouds, which seemed so large and so near and thinking to myself, 'So this is how one dies'.

By contrast Flying Officer S. B. 'Rusty' Perryman a New Zealander from Christchurch flying a Ventura in 487 Squadron, saw three small children waving and waved back at them. Perryman would return from this operation but others in his squadron were not so lucky. He and the remainder of the formation headed inland where twenty-three Bostons and Venturas failed to avoid a huge flock of ducks that smashed windscreens, splattered the cockpits with blood and feathers and damaged wing surfaces. Over the Colijnsplaat two seagulls came through the nose of Flying Officer Philip Burley's aircraft injuring his navigator, Flying Officer Herbert L. Besford in the legs while at the same time the draught whisked his maps away. Besford directed his pilot from then on by memory. Twenty minutes later their Ventura was attacked by a Bf 109 when over Oost at 50 ft. The enemy fighter made four separate attacks from the stern but no strikes were scored and the Bf 109 was claimed as damaged by a five second burst from Flight Sergeant T. Smith, the rear gunner at 400 yards range.

Jack Peppiatt continues:

The journey cross-country was a Circus really. We slid about, keeping sight of our leader and watching to avoid airfields. The other hazard was overhead cables, etc, and the trick was to look out to the sides ahead so that you could spot the lines of pylons, which could reveal where the invisible cables might be. Although there was a lot of apprehension, there was also a great thrill in it. Talk over the intercom went on the whole time between the navigator and myself, discussing where we were, where the leader was going and did you see that railway or canal, etc? I saw the landscape flying by with brief flashes of recognition; a house, some people, vehicles and every now and then a blink as I thought we had gone too near an airfield. As we neared the turning point near

Pilot Officer Jack Peppiatt of 88 Squadron at his wedding to Fr[...] WAAF (*Jack & Freddie Peppiatt*)

Boston III AL749 *R-Robert* of 88 Squadron flown by Pilot Officer Jack Peppiatt of 'B' Flight behind Flight Lieutenant Johnny Reeve on the Eindhoven raid. AL749, a Boeing-built machine, had a chequered career, serving with 88 and 114 Squadrons and 155 MU before the undercarriage jammed up and the aircraft was belly landed at Sétif, Algeria on 24 October 1943 and damaged beyond repair. (*Jack Peppiatt*)

Eindhoven [at Oostmalle, south-south-west of Turnhout] it did get taut. We all knew that if the target were missed there would be no way of recovering. In front I had glimpses of the leading Bostons and we began to pack in as we saw the buildings of the factory way ahead. The first two went in low and we then sailed up to 1,500 ft, which felt very vulnerable! We seemed suddenly to stand still and hang about waiting to be shot at.

As the Venturas passed near to Woensdrecht the formation was bracketed by heavy flak. A 20 mm shell from the airfield flak defences hit the starboard engine of a 464 Squadron Ventura flown by Squadron Leader Tony Carlisle but he continued to the target. Sergeant Smock RCAF had more than 5 ft of his wing torn away when he hit a chimney. However, he was able to nurse the aircraft back to Norfolk safely. The Ventura flown by 32-year old Wing Commander Frankie C. Seavill RNZAF, 487 Squadron CO, was hit by flak and crashed at Schaapskooi on the airfield at Woensdrecht; all four crew were killed. Like almost everyone else in the Venturas, Seavill was flying his first operational sortie and he had refused a group captain post to stay with 487 Squadron (which was taken over by Wing Commander G. J. Grindell shortly afterwards). Squadron Leader Len Trent DFC pressed the firing button on his control column and sprayed a flak gun position with .50 and .303 machine-gun fire. At the Strijp target Trent climbed to 250 ft to clear the parapets and let loose his stick of two 250 lb GP bombs and forty 30 lb incendiaries on his high target building, holing it from basement to roof top. As his aircraft cleared the top of the flaming and smoking target he glimpsed on the left-hand corner of the building, a German machine

Smoke rises from several sections of the Philips Emmasingel valve and lamp factory. (*British Official*)

gunner stubbornly sticking to his post and pouring a steady stream of fire at him. None of the bullets damaged the Ventura but 'there,' said Trent, 'was in my book, a damn good soldier'.

A 21 Squadron Ventura flown by Pilot Officer H. T. Bichard was attacked by *Unteroffizier* Rudolf Rauhaus, one of the pilots in II./JG1 returning from combat with the American attacks in France and was shot down. Bichard belly-landed the Ventura at Rilland-Bath in Zeeland and he and two of his crew survived to be taken prisoner. Sergeant Roy Lamerton, the 30-year old navigator was killed.

'Dinty' Moore said:

Finally, I heard Freddy saying the target was straight ahead of us. Turning around I could see the factory towering above the surrounding houses. 88 Squadron approached the main site at the lamp and valve factory from the south side at rooftop height and immediately began climbing to 2,000 ft in order to make shallow dives on to the factory. The leading pair, whose bombs had eleven-second delay fuses, ploughed straight in at low level, while Johnny led the remainder of the formation up to our bombing height of 1,500 ft. By now the Germans had opened up with light flak from batteries around the town and one that was on the top of the factory itself. We dropped our bombs on the target, returning to nought feet without delay and looking back I could see heavy explosions in the building, so it was evident that the bombs had landed in the right place.

Pilot Officer Freddy J. Deeks added:

Over the target we found $^8/_{10}$ stratocumulus cloud base at 2,000 ft so we had to run up lower than intended. At 1230 hours we attacked the target. Wing Commander Pelly-Fry and his 'number two' attacking from low level, machine gunned as they went in, in order to cause a diversion, whilst the remainder of us bombed from 1,000–1,500 ft just outside blast range, diving back onto the deck afterwards. After the first element of surprise had passed away, the enemy flak positions on the factory itself and in the town got busy with heavy and light flak, thus more evasive action became necessary. The target was left in a cloud of smoke but some bombs overshot and exploded in the town itself. Wing Commander Pelly-Fry's machine was hit by light flak over the target, which caused him to hand the lead over to Pilot Officer 'Jock' Campbell.

The Stryp Group main works on fire as seen from a 487 Squadron Ventura (*via Peter Mallinson*)

Jack Peppiatt said:

By the time we were over the factory, it was all smoke and explosions, with Bostons all around at different angles and at that point there was a bang. R for Robert turned several degrees to port like a weather vane, while I heard Len Dellow, my air gunner, telling me that there was a big hole in the fin just above his head. But the aircraft seemed to handle all right and at that stage I was more concerned with where we were to go next.

Twelve Bostons of 107 Squadron dropped their loads on the Strijp Group main works. First over the target was Squadron Leader R. J. N. MacLachlan's crew. They encountered a flak gun on one of the factory buildings and one of his gunners opened fire on it, forcing the German crew to abandon their exposed gun position and flee into the factory building just as MacLachlan's bombs scored a direct hit and destroyed the structure. This feat would earn MacLachlan the DFC. Meanwhile, the Bostons of 226 Squadron, led by Squadron Leader J. S. Kennedy and Squadron Leader G. R. 'Digger' Magill, released their delayed-action bombs on the Emmasingel valve factory before the Mosquitoes came in behind at 1,000 ft with high-explosive and incendiary bombs.

Charles Patterson continued:

Ahead of me I saw the front formation of Mosquitoes in the distance already climbing up to 1,500 ft so I immediately took my formation up as fast as I could to 1,500 ft to catch Edwards' formation. We caught up about 2–3 miles south of Eindhoven. He banked over to port and started to dive down on the Philips works in the centre of the town. The moment I turned to port I could see this

A rear facing camera view of the destruction at Eindhoven (*RAF*)

factory standing out unmistakably, very prominently, right in the centre of Eindhoven. We all went down in this shallow dive, full throttle and at the appropriate moment, dropped the bombs. As I went across the Philips works the whole factory seemed to erupt in a cloud of smoke and flashes. It looked as though the whole thing was completely eliminated.

Squadron Leader George Parry and Flying Officer Victor 'Robbie' Robson, Canadian Flying Officers Spencer Kimmel and Harry Kirkland, Warrant Officer Ray Noseda DFC and Sergeant John Urquhart and Flight Sergeants K. L. Monaghan and A. W. Dean also bombed the target from 1,000 ft. Two Fw 190s intercepted Noseda and Urquhart on the return in the Overflakee area. Although damaged by cannon fire, they managed to return safely. Mosquito *A-Apple* of 139 Squadron flown by Canadian Flying Officer John 'Junior' O'Grady and Sergeant George Lewis was hit in the engine and, trailing smoke and flames pulled away to head back towards England. They made it only as far as 30 miles off Den Helder, where they crashed into the sea. Their bodies were never found.

Last in were the Venturas, flying four minutes behind the Bostons and carrying their incendiaries and delayed-action bombs. In the space of just seven minutes, four were shot down by flak. The 21 Squadron Ventura flown by Flight Lieutenant Kenneth S. Smith was hit by flak directly over the target. It ran in with a stream of flame from a punctured fuel tank, crashed into Nieuwe Dijk Street just north of the Emmasingel works and blew up on impact. All four crew including Flight Lieutenant Wallace Martin RAAF DFC, from Murrurundi, New South Wales, bombing leader of 464 Squadron, who had volunteered to navigate for 21 Squadron, were killed. The Ventura piloted by Flight Sergeant Beverly M. Harvey RCAF of 464 Squadron at the

Ventura AE692 YH-K of 21 Squadron, which was flown by Pilot Officer D. G. J. Smith on the Eindhoven raid. It was shot down on 21 April 1943. Flight Lieutenant J. E. Harrison and two of his crew were taken PoW. Twenty-year -old Sergeant. William J. Atkinson, WOP/AG, was killed. (*Wartime Watton Museum*)

rear of the formation was hit by flak and crashed with the loss of all the crew in the so-called 'Fitterij' on the Strijp complex. Another 464 Squadron machine, piloted by Flying Officer Maurice G. Moor, stalled and dived out of control before crashing into a square in Schoolstraat, north of the target, demolishing and setting fire to a row of houses. Pilot Officer 'Jock' Shinnie, WOP/AG in the leading 464 Squadron Ventura flown by Wing Commander 'Bob' Young, saw both Venturas crash.

It appeared that his [Harvey's] target was so obscured by smoke the pilot could not see the top of the building and tragically flew into it. Some minutes later I was shocked to see our number two aircraft [Moor] on our port side suddenly completely enveloped in flames. The aircraft dipped, flew into the side of a house and then appeared at the other side. It was all over in seconds. We successfully attacked our respective targets but the buildings appeared to be far taller than expected and they were well protected by flak batteries on the roofs. Although flying so low we did get over the buildings in our cumbersome Venturas, albeit with little room to spare.

Sergeant John Bede Cusack RAAF in the 464 Squadron Ventura flown by Pilot Officer Kerr, recalled:

In all the excitement I had completely forgotten about the target. Wilbur's voice, 'Target coming up' brought me back to reality. It would be hard to give my impression over the next minute for the area was a nightmare of burning buildings, smokestacks and high tension wires. Jerry gunners still manned their weapons on rooftops even though the windows belched smoke and flame. We went through so fast that it was hard to pick a target so I put my finger on the teat and sprayed the entire area. How we missed the stacks and wires I'll never know. I saw a Vent veer crazily and hit a smokestack plumb in the centre and plunge downward in a welter of dust, bricks and flame. Jack screamed 'Bombs Away' and we swung violently to the left. The clusters of incendiaries flew off at a tangent, travelling almost horizontally to smash into the front of the building in such a welter of explosion and fire that it really shook me. I knew why the place was so thoroughly alight. We straightened up and missed a set of high-tension wires by inches. I saw a burning Ventura [Moor] that had smashed into a row of tenement houses. The next moment we were doing a split-arse left turn as we went for home. It was only then that I noticed I still had my fingers on the teat and that neither gun was firing. Around us in the air dogfights were going on everywhere but enemy fighters appeared to have their hands full ...We came out along a canal about three-quarters of a mile wide. Guns placed on either side turned in and churned the water white below us. Bill who had gone to man the lower guns, had this third life when a shell hit both of them, curled them up in a 'V' but failed to explode. Miraculously, no direct hits were scored on this fleeing target. A mile astern we saw a plane, which turned out to be a Canadian 'Pete'[44] limping home. The German gunners concentrated on this inviting target but again, despite a hail of shell, the crew came through. We came out over a marshy flat area without a shot being fired which later prompted the thought, Why the hell didn't we go in that way?[45]

The Ventura flown by 26-year-old Flight Sergeant John L. Greening of 487 Squadron cleared the rooftops and was believed to have collided with another aircraft over the target area before crashing into the Veemgebouw on the Strijp complex. Both crews were killed.

After the bombing the aircraft streaked for home at low level, desperately avoiding high-tension cables, flak and flocks of birds again and fighters, before they reached the sanctuary of the open sea.

Jack Peppiatt remembered:

We headed after the gaggle of aircraft heading north-west, until both I and my navigator, Sergeant C. F. Kirk, began to wonder why they didn't turn west toward the coast. By now we were all down hugging the ground for comfort. We made a joint decision what to do and some of the aircraft made the turn; we went with them (they later proved to be 107 Squadron) but we were also joined and passed by Mosquitoes as time went on.

'Dinty' Moore continues:

We headed for home although the 'Wingco's' aircraft had been damaged by flak, so he was having difficulty in keeping it under control, which put us off course.[46] We were encouraged on our way to the coast by the efforts of German anti-aircraft gunners. The remainder of our formation reached the coast without the attention of any German fighters, which may have been due to the fact that we were not returning by our intended route. We must have been well off course for we saw no sign of the fighter escort with whom we should have rendezvoused at the coast. Other squadrons who did return by the planned route were less fortunate, not only being harried by flak, as we were, but also by the unwelcome attention of German fighters.

Fw 190s of 5./JG1, which had been summoned from Schiphol, now arrived on the scene. Jack Peppiatt's Boston was one of those singled out.

After a few minutes settling down it all went up with a bang as Fw 190s appeared. Without doubt the next twenty minutes or so were full of action and not a little confusion. Ten or twenty aircraft were screaming along, full throttle, in a loose mass; no one wanted to be at the back where the Focke-Wulfs were coming in to attack and wheeling away for another go. They had one problem, which I think was that, as they dived, they had to pull out early to avoid hitting the ground because we were all at zero feet. I distinctly saw cannon shells hitting ploughed fields in front of me and moving on ahead as the Focke-Wulf began to pull out. At one point a fighter slid past us and sat just to my right as he slowed – so close I could stare at the pilot and admire the yellow spinner. Meanwhile, Len was calling for me to jink and then shouted that he had got one. If he did I really don't know how he did it as I was sliding and diving constantly. The astonishing thing was that we didn't collide, as aircraft constantly criss-crossed in front of each other.

Over the Dutch islands the attacks petered out and we flew steadily just off the water until Len quietly told me that there was an aircraft sliding over us from the side, obviously unaware that we were under him. It all went dark as a big black shadow arrived and I sat rigid hoping that he wouldn't come lower, then throttled back gently to get behind him. If you know the height of a Boston fin you will know how we felt. Soon after this incident a Boston just exploded in front of us.[47] We flew through the debris; it was so completely destroyed that there was nothing big enough to hurt us. I may say that this occurrence really hit us. We looked down and back to see just the yellow stain of the marker from the dinghy, all that was left in just those few seconds. As we left the coast of Holland yet another Boston went in on our starboard side, possibly the pilot who had been wounded earlier [Warrant Officer Alan J. Reid of 107 Squadron, who crashed in the River Scheldt]. These two events perhaps weighed on us more than anything else did.

Another Boston, a 226 Squadron machine flown by Flying Officer Norman J. A. Paton DFM, crashed in the sea west of De Beer after being hit by Marine flak. The fourth Boston lost was flown by the CO of 107 Squadron, Wing Commander Peter H. Dutton, who was shot down into the sea 3¾ miles west of Katwijk aan Zee. *Oberfeldwebel* Ernst Heeson, *Unteroffiziers* Günther Kirchner[48] and Stellgeld and *Feldwebel* Reitshofen of 5./JG1 from Schiphol each claimed a Boston destroyed.

Just before they reached the Zuider Zee the Venturas were bracketed by flak. Sergeant A. V. Ricketts' Ventura in 21 Squadron, the ninth and last overall, ditched 7 miles off Bawdsey after a piece of flak severed a fuel pipe and he finally ran out of fuel. Their aircraft sank in about fifty seconds. ASR from Felixstowe rescued all four crew twenty minutes later. Another 21 Squadron survivor was Pilot Officer Arthur E. C. Wheeler who recounted that the raid was 'an exhilarating experience rather than a frightening one, seeing gunners on the flat roof of some of the buildings swivelling round as we flew over and dropped our incendiaries. We were at zero feet as I saw ahead of us a line of electrical pylons, which I knew we could not climb over. However, I breathed a sigh of relief when I realized that fortunately for us somebody had been there first and there were no power lines between them.' After debriefing, the operation was immediately hailed as a great success, although, from 21 Squadron's viewpoint it was tempered somewhat by the casualties they had suffered. The worrying statistic was that the three Ventura squadrons had suffered at least 20 per cent losses on the raid.

Pilot Officer Gordon A. Park of 487 Squadron put his failing Ventura down just outside Long Stratton village after oil pipes on the starboard engine were damaged by a bird strike. Others in his squadron also had lucky escapes. Flight Sergeant Ron W. Secord, WOP/AG, was grateful to his pilot, Flying Officer Brewer DFC, for ordering him to leave the astrodome and take up his gun position while flying over the coast, for when Secord returned later to his hatch he found the dome punctured by flak. In the same aircraft, Sergeant R. F. 'Bob' Edmonds, a Maori air gunner from Auckland, had his steel helmet knocked off his head by flak but was miraculously unharmed. The nose of the Ventura flown by Flight Sergeant Ian Baynton, also of Auckland, was broken when the Ventura struck a treetop but the aircraft returned safely. Boston *D-Donald* piloted by Flight Sergeant G. E. T. 'Nick' Nicholls of 107 Squadron crash landed at Great Massingham on one engine and with his wheels up, and overshot the airfield. The aircraft went through a gun position and a hedge and finally came to rest in a slit trench. *D-Donald* was written off but the crew escaped relatively unharmed; Nicholls was awarded the DFM for his exploits. Sergeant W. E.

Returning from Eindhoven Boston III AL754. It is piloted by Flight Sergeant G. E. T. 'Nick' Nicholls of 107 Squadron, and crash-landed at Great Massingham on one engine and with his wheels up it overshot the airfield. The aircraft went through a gun position and a hedge and finally came to rest in a slit trench. *D-Donald* was written off but the crew escaped relatively unharmed; Nicholls was awarded the DFM for his exploits. (Aeroplane)

Burns, meanwhile, put down at Ipswich. Sergeant Chas Tyler's Boston (Z2211) of 88 Squadron had been hit in the starboard engine and they had a very anxious flight across the North Sea, as Bob Gallup, the observer, recalled:

Shortly after we had released the bombs we were hit by flak in the starboard engine. We lost contact with the rest of the squadron as we began to slow down. We were unable to gain height and the prospect of covering the 150-mile North Sea return flight looked remote, so it was decided to force-land in Holland and give ourselves up. After turning back inland, however, we conferred once more and decided to 'have another go'. We turned for the Dutch coast once more and as we crossed out again every gun in Holland seemed to be firing at us. The tracers seemed to be like hailstones in reverse. Over the sea we tried to gain a little height but were unable to do so. After about fifty minutes we recognized Lowestoft ahead. We crossed the coast and force-landed immediately, finishing wheels-up in a ploughed field at Brewhouse farm, Carlton Colville. My feet were buried in soil and I had a problem getting out through the top escape hatch. As we hit the ground the strap of Chas Tyler's seat harness broke and he hit his head on the gun sight. Apart from that we were unhurt. Chas was taken to Lowestoft hospital while Stuart and I were taken home by the farmer for a lovely meal. After we had been to see Chas in hospital, we were taken to the local pub, where we were allowed to win every game of darts. We spent that night at the farm near the aircraft, with clean sheets and pillow. Life was great until next morning, when transport arrived to take us back to camp.

'Dinty' Moore remembered:

We landed back at Oulton after an exciting and memorable operation, which had taken us two hours and twenty minutes without a scratch, my only excuse to use my guns being to fire at some of the flak positions. The 'Wingco', in the meantime, found his way home with difficulty, having attracted the attentions of a German fighter; without hydraulic power he had to come in with his wheels up, making a safe if bumpy landing. The aircraft looked in a sad way but the crew walked out, though 'Jock' Cairns later found out that he had suffered a cracked vertebra.

As he approached Oulton Jack Peppiatt thought about the damage to his fin.

Len tried to assess what might happen as we landed, as he could see to some extent. I realized that the hole was through the pitot head and as a result I had no altimeter or ASI, which meant that I would be coming in faster than usual. When we reached the airfield and flew over I could see Pelly-Fry's aircraft belly-flopped on the grass in the middle of the longest run and I felt that I needed all the 1,100 yards for my performance, so it was off to Attlebridge where there was a long concrete runway. We plopped in with a sigh of relief and waited patiently for transport to Blickling, where we found that they had all gone to Swanton for a party, which we missed. The episode over Holland had resulted in me sweating profusely, so much so that my battle-dress tunic was saturated and my bar of chocolate had melted into the fabric.

Flying Officer Kerr's Ventura got back to Feltwell although many did not, as

Australian gunner John Bede Cusack recalled.

It was a badly mauled Squadron that limped home. Because of the absence of runways, planes all pleading various emergencies landed everywhere. The place was a shambles. Our petrol indicators showed empty 5 miles from the station and we landed, like everyone else, straight into the wind, with another plane on our tail and, while taxiing back on the tarmac, ground to a stop completely out of petrol. At interrogation I found the six bombers' gunners had come through, which was almost a miracle . . . A young gunner said, 'Well, that wasn't so bad.' 'Not bad,' said 'Hally' dryly. 'Another three ops like that and we will have completed our tour.' The young fellow looked at him open-mouthed and said, 'But it's thirty ops for a tour isn't it?' 'That's right,' said 'Art' patting him paternally on the head. 'Only we won't have to go that far.'[49]

For Sergeant Peter H. Mallinson, WOP/AG in the 487 Squadron Ventura piloted by Flight Sergeant Bill Lee, *Oyster* was his first operation and it had come no more than eight weeks after his eighteenth birthday. Shortly after he got back to Feltwell he wrote to his sister Connie:

. . . Now that it is all over England about our attack on the Philips Radio Works in Eindhoven, I can say more about my experiences. First of all, we had been on standby for this raid for many days but the weather was bad so it was cancelled each day until last Sunday. We were briefed for this raid about a week ago and were expecting to go the following day but, as I say, the weather was against us. Since that briefing (when we were told the target) we have been confined to camp. The telephones were locked and there was no outgoing mail. We were completely isolated from the outside world! However, the camp cinema had a new film showing each day, which helped. These precautions were, of course, so that there was no leakage of our intended target. Much to our relief, the secret was kept because on Sunday the weather improved and we had another hurried briefing, were issued with rations, escape kits etc and were in the air at about 11.40 on Sunday 6 December. We manoeuvred into our formations along with 464 (RAAF) Squadron who share our airfield.

Sergeant Ted Leaver DFM, Flight Lieutenant 'Yogi' Yates-Earl DFC and Pilot Officer Ken Houghton DFC of 226 Squadron, who crewed AL678/R on the Eindhoven raid ,examine a seagull's head that completely penetrated the leading edge of their Boston wing during the operation. (*George Casey*)

Before we reached our coast, we were joined by many other aircraft, I think there were about 100 in all. It was a very impressive sight, I can tell you. We were all flying very low over the sea, it seemed about 10 ft to me! It was not long before Burt [Sergeant W. Lowe] our navigator said, 'Dutch coast ahead'. No sooner had he said this, than we were greeted with a small amount of Ack-Ack, which increased, as we approached the coast. The first thing that struck me after crossing the coast were the sand-hills and pine forests which looked just like those at home – I soon found out the difference though, as these forests were full of machine-gun nests and the sky was filled with tracer. Little blobs of light were whizzing all around our plane, some very fast and others seemed to appear as a slow curve. Our pilot, Bill Lee, excelled himself with violent evasive action, which made it more difficult for the Germans to aim accurately. We were soon out of this area though and by dropping over the treetops, this made a screen, which gave us some protection behind.

You know Con, when I have read about other aircrew reporting people waving to them whilst flying over occupied countries, I found it hard to believe. I don't now! As we hopped over trees and roofs there were people waving like mad, handkerchiefs, even flags. I suppose, with the leading aircraft having already passed over, it gave more time for them to run out of their homes. After more Ack-Ack and machine-guns we at last reached the target area where we ran into a terrific barrage, again, as we were still so low it proved ineffective so far as we were concerned. Bill, the pilot, rose from about 20 ft to about 60 ft and I heard the navigator say 'Bomb doors open'. Then we flew into clouds of smoke and I heard 'Bombs gone'. I saw lots of flashes and sparks rise up as our bombs and incendiaries went into the centre of the target. What a blaze! As I looked back from my turret I saw two German machine-gunners still on the roof (this was confirmed later). I think it would have been impossible for them to get down and were most likely blown up by the other planes behind us. S/L 'Digger' Wheeler, our Flight Commander, was in front of us, so one by one we formated on him again, dived down low and belted as fast as we could for home but just before coming to the sea there was more flak which followed us right over the water. I then noticed big splashes of water in front and behind us – boy was I scared. I thought it was aircraft crashing but we later learned that it was German Ack-Ack shells bursting on the water in the hope of us running into one of these 'spouts'. It was about this time I saw a tugboat, towing a string of barges. I let go a few rounds at it but we were soon out of range. I'll bet the tug captain was as scared as I was because he was being shot at from both sides! Anyway, after using more violent evasive action we soon were over the open sea, heading as fast as we could for home.

I kept a good lookout, especially in the sun (we gunners were told time and time again 'Watch out for the Hun in the Sun!'). All this time we were very thankful not to be attacked by enemy fighters but we were told later that our own fighter escort was having a good time somewhere above us. We eventually sighted England and there were four loud cheers, one after the other, then altogether. Another 40 minutes and we were back at our dispersal, carefully examining our plane for damage. There wasn't a scratch. The only casualty was the remains of a stork, which was struck in the port engine air cooler. I only hope it wasn't carrying a baby cargo at the time. Birds are a menace when flying at low level and many of the other aircraft had broken perspex in the turrets and nose cones. I'm sorry I didn't manage to get you a genuine pair of Dutch clogs Con but we didn't stay very long!

My pal Pat Stokes and his crew[50] didn't return from this trip. We were so low, I doubt very much if they got away with it. They say that about 11 aircraft didn't return from this trip but if this is an overall estimate, then it's not too bad out of 100. Never worry about me Con, I will be OK and in any case, we won't be flying again for a few weeks as all the planes have to be inspected and repaired where necessary. In case you have forgotten, the planes (we call them kites!) we fly are called Venturas. The full name being Lockheed 'Vega' Ventura. On the side of our 'kite' is the painting of a Maori Tiki. His name is Kia-Ora. Well, that is my life story to date and an impression I have of the destruction of the Philips Radio and Valve works. I did not mention that there are two buildings separated by a playing field and according to how we were briefed some bombed one and some the other, joining up immediately after for the flight home. Much has been reported about this raid and on yesterday's 6 o'clock news a W/C from one of the other Squadrons with us gave his account of the raid – Did you hear it? The Germans say that we hit hospitals, houses etc. but that is all baloney as every bomb went right on the target. You could not miss it from that height! The Bostons went in four minutes before us with the H/E bombs; then we came in with the incendiaries and delayed action bombs. You should have seen the photos that were posted in the Mess of the Mess!! Write soon, love to Mum and Dad – Pete XX.

'Dinty' Moore concludes:

The following day the national newspapers carried the story of the raid with several photographs. The heading in the *Daily Mail* read 'Heaviest Day Bombing Raid of the War' – 'Big Dutch Radio Works Smashed'. It did much to raise the morale of the British people, who up to the end of 1942 had had little to cheer about. As for me, as soon as I had been debriefed I found a telephone to let Norma know all was well. She had been looking in vain for us to return over Norwich, so she was beginning to worry. Next day I met her during her lunch-break and proposed. She agreed to marry me, so she was easily persuaded to take the afternoon off work so we could go and buy our engagement rings. Pilot Officer 'Skeets' Kelly, who flew with us and Flight Lieutenant Charlie Peace took the film of the Eindhoven raid. I always remember sitting in a cinema when one of their productions was included in the newsreel and the audience applauded enthusiastically.

In Eindhoven meanwhile, it was a different story. Over 60 tons of bombs hit the factory buildings, which were devastated, essential supplies destroyed and the rail network disrupted. Fourteen aircraft – nine Venturas, one Mosquito and four Bostons – had been shot down. Photographs taken after the raid showed that both factories had been very badly damaged, fully justifying the decision to make the attack in

Pilot Officer 'Jack' Rutherford RNZAF, Squadron Leader J. S. Kennedy and Flight Sergeant Eric Lee of 226 Squadron who crewed Z2234/X on the Eindhoven raid.

daylight from low level. The Germans reported that 'Damage was caused to nearly all the work buildings'. The factory was in the middle of Eindhoven, so a considerable number of homes were also destroyed or damaged. Frits Philips recalled:

The destruction was enormous. The time of the bombardment, on a Sunday morning, was chosen because the factories were closed but the death toll was over one hundred civilians. The hospitals were crowded with injured people and part of Eindhoven was destroyed by fire. My wife and my sister Jetty visited the wounded. They told us that not one of them blamed the allies! There was one man who had lost his wife and three of his seven children. Still no complaints could be heard from him.[51] The morale of the population during that bombardment had been exemplary. Personally the bombardment caused very deep emotions. To see the factories that had been erected which such devotion and offered jobs to thousands of people going up in flames was a terrible reality of war, though I realized that this war against the Germans had to be fought hard if they were to be conquered. This thought reconciled me to this hellish scene.

The following morning I had visitors from The Hague. Our commissioner Mr Woltersom, Mr Hirschfeld and Dr Ringers, the government commissioner for reconstruction, came to see the results of the bombardment themselves. Ringers and myself were on good terms and it was his help we needed the most. He did not disappoint us. My immediate concern was to commence repairs of our factories on

Wing Commander R. J. P. Pritchard AFC of 21 Squadron, pictured beside his Ventura II, AFSS6 Z-Zebra, in which he led his squadron over Eindhoven. He received the DFC for his action, one of eight awarded to aircrew who took part on the operation. The cartoon duck is entitled 'Hell's a-poppin!' The Ventura II differed from the earlier model in having a larger capacity bomb bay and 2,000 hp Pratt & Whitney R-2800-31 engines in place of the earlier 1,850 hp Double Wasp S1A4-G. (via Wilf Clutton)

226 Squadron veterans of the Eindhoven operation, 6 December 1942. Left to right: Flight Sergeant W. H. C. 'Erby' Leavitt RCAF who flew W8287/F; Flying Officer L. P. Frizzle who flew Z2261; Flying Officer Bert Hoskins; and Flight Lieutenant Don T. Smith, who flew W8337. Leavitt was awarded the DFM for the Eindhoven raid. On 3 February 1943 Z2261 dived into the ground after take off from Swanton Morley probably because of incorrect trimming. W8287 served finally with 114 Squadron in North Africa and was lost on an operation at Battipaglia on 4 September 1943. W8337 also operated with 107 Squadron and 1482 Flight and 10 ADU. On 16 May 1943 its hydraulics failed and was belly landed at Gibraltar where it was destroyed by fire. (RAF)

short term, utilizing all our personnel to prevent them being deported to Germany. In the first months all the effort went into clearing away the debris. There was no way to make good the production capacity but it might have been worse. The heavy machinery could be repaired. Despite the never ending allied bombardment, the German war industry had suffered less then expected but the damage was substantial.

Wing Commanders Hughie Edwards VC DFC, James Pelly-Fry and R. H. Young AFC were awarded the DSO. Eight DFCs were also awarded. Recipients included Wing Commander R. J. P. Pritchard AFC of 21 Squadron, Pilot Officer J. M. Rankin of 107 Squadron, Flight Lieutenants 'Hawker' Hart and T. H. J. 'Jock' Cairns DFM and Flying Officer C. A. 'Buster' Evans DFM (Pelley-Fry's air gunner). Two DFMs, including one to Sergeant Pilot W. H. C. Leavitt RCAF of 226 Squadron, were also awarded.

What of the others who took part in the Eindhoven raid? Sergeant Stan Moss, who was peppered with pieces of shrapnel, had survived.

Other members of the crew were in state of shock and panic. Attempts to fire the aircraft failed and there was no real opportunity to escape. Glancing back across the field, I noticed how the four bombs had detached themselves from their racks and were lying forlornly on the surface of the field one after the other along the line of our crash path. Obviously, the retracting undercarriage had provided a cushioning effect. Whilst lying there, I heard a formation of low flying aircraft roaring back in the direction of England. Not many minutes later, some steel-helmeted German soldiers appeared running towards us from an adjacent field. When they reached us, they detached a wooden farm gate from its fittings and lifted me onto it. They carried me quite a distance but I don't remember any conversation. Still sedated and somewhat detached under the influence of the morphine, I was taken to a small wooden hut – a command post of some kind – and placed on soft material, maybe blankets. The other wounded crew members were seated and an officer at a desk rang for an ambulance.

As the effects of the morphine withdrew, I recall feeling terribly weak and sticky as the blood on my saturated jacket began to congeal on the skin of my right shoulder, chest and arm and the pain re-surged. When the ambulance arrived, the three of us, on stretchers, were slotted into it like sardines in a can. We had no clue as to where we were going but later ascertained that we were brought down on the island of Walcheren. At one point, we travelled very slowly across a causeway and, on reaching a town, were carried into a hospital and almost immediately out again, without explanation. We ended up at a German Army Hospital at Goes on Zuid-Beveland. Their X-ray equipment much impressed me and I was given a thorough examination. I soon gathered there was concern about internal bleeding, later confirmed when a group of immaculately uniformed medical officers came around my stretcher, talking earnestly to one another. There was a hush as one bent down to me with a pocket dictionary in one hand, questioning in guttural tones 'Belly gut? Belly gut?'

Taken immediately to the operating theatre, an electric clock on the wall indicated that it was 7 p.m., seven hours after being shot down. As I lay on the table, before proceedings commenced, several Dutch sisters came across surreptitiously encouraging by touching me and whispering, 'Englander gut'. Eventually the chloroform was dropped on to the mask and in a mind-blowing crescendo of screaming sound and flashing lights, I willingly went into oblivion, knowing that this was the only way to recovery. Feelings of regret in my misfortune at being captured came later with the return of health and strength. Subsequent passage of time has brought a wider realization of what could have happened to me and my abiding response remains - one of immense gratitude that the Providential Hand from above was overruling all things for good.

Others like Squadron Leader Jack Houlston AFC DFC of 139 Squadron, who with Armitage carried out two runs over Eindhoven and who survived the *Oyster* operation, went missing on subsequent operations over enemy territory. Though their Mosquito was attacked by two Bf 109s and was shot at by flak Houlston and Armitage got back to report that 'the Philips works was a mass of smoke and fire, explosions were still in progress and some buildings were completely gutted'. Both men were killed in action attacking railway targets in north-west Germany on 20 December. Warrant Officer Ray Noseda DFC and Sergeant John Urquhart of 105 Squadron were KIA on an operation to bomb rail sheds at Rouen on 9 January 1943. Sergeant W. E. Burns who had put down at Ipswich was KIA on 11 February 1943. Four of the pilots in 487 Squadron were killed on 3 May 1943. One of these was Pilot Officer Stanley Coshall of Auckland, who on the Eindhoven raid had flown so close to the Ventura piloted by Sergeant C. J. J. Baker a New Zealander from New Plymouth, that the wings of both aircraft had actually touched 'with a tearing sound'. However, as both had been flying at the same speed no damage was caused. Another was Flight Sergeant Andy E. Coutts of Whakatane, whose Ventura was hit on the Eindhoven raid by an explosive cannon shell which set a Verey light on fire, filling the aircraft with smoke. It was finally subdued by Sergeant W. D. L. Goodfellow an air gunner from Takapuna, with the aid of a fire extinguisher (Goodfellow was killed flying with Coutts on 3 May). Pilot Officer 'Rusty' Perryman and Flight Sergeant T. J. Baynton were the other two pilots who died on 3 May while Flight Sergeant T. L. B. 'Terry' Taylor, who reached the Strijp target but was unable to release his bombs, also failed to return that day.

To the vanquished, death or glory – to the victor the spoils. Hughie Edwards was later promoted to group captain and he finished the war as Senior Air Staff Officer, Air Command Far East Asia. Pelly-Fry, who when his crews were billeted at Blickling Hall was nicknamed 'Baron Fry of Blickling', was surprised to be appointed Air Equerry to HM King George VI in 1943 — the first RAF officer to be so honored. Several months later he managed to arrange a discreet move from Buckingham Palace and, now a group captain, took command of Holme on Spalding Moor, a Halifax bomber station. In 1945 he was posted to Australia to take command of RAF Camden, near Sydney. He retired from the RAF in 1958 and acted as civil air attaché for Australia and New Zealand until 1962.

CHAPTER SEVEN

Victors and the Vanquished

*Theirs was the most exhilarating and exacting flying job in the Air
Force. To fizz in tight formation across the frontiers of Europe called
for brilliant airmanship and faultless navigation: wavetop to the
enemy coast; up and over the cliffs, often through a hail of light flak;
and on . . . First, the fairer suburbs, the Eshers and Surbitons of the
enemy. Then the broadening railway tracks, the sooty suburbs. The
Maldens, the Clapham Junctions of the Continent. Now, the tall
smoky chimneys, grimy signposts pointing the way through the
swirling industrial haze to the target for today . . . And there it is. A
building a peacetime tourist will pass without a glance. But for the
two men, elbow to elbow in the tiny cockpit like spectators at the
Cup Final, this is the goal. Behind those smutty brick walls men and
women are passing out precision instruments which will help U-boat
commanders to drown British seamen and sink British supplies. . .*

> *Contemporary account of the raid by Mosquitoes on the Burmeister and
> Wain factory, 27 January 1943*

Early in January 1943 Jim 'Dinty' Moore returned to Norfolk with his fiancée
Norma from leave 'to get on with the war'. No. 2 Group was now
commanded, since 29 December 1942, by Air Vice Marshal J. H. d'Albiac.
Operations continued much the same, as 'Dinty' recalled:

B.Mk.IV Series II DZ379/H flew its first operation in 105 Squadron on 8 December 1942 before being
transferred to 139 Squadron. (*Temple Press*)

During January we were briefed to take part in four Circus operations with varying degrees of success due to the weather. It should not be forgotten that a method of identifying a target through cloud had not, so far, been fitted to our aircraft, although there would be a system known as Gee H brought into service within the next twelve months. On 9 January our target was Abbeville, so we took off 'into the wild blue yonder', everything going according to plan, meeting our escorting fighters on schedule and crossing the French coast, where we were met with the usual hostile reception. We flew on until we were only 40 miles from the target, only to find a thick layer of cloud that made it impossible for us to complete our mission. The risks were exactly the same as if we had actually bombed, so I'll make no comment as to our feelings as we landed after a trip lasting two hours twenty minutes.

On the 18th the story was exactly the same, the only difference being that our target was to be Cherbourg, which, of course was screened by cloud, our flight lasting two hours. On the 21st we had better luck, the Met man having got his forecast right. The target was the Dutch port of Flushing, which I had last visited on 25 April 1941 with George and Ron. On this occasion, however, we did not take off alone, nor were we to fly at low level. This was to be a Circus involving twelve Bostons, flying in two boxes of six aircraft accompanied by our usual fighter escort. It was a pleasant day with excellent visibility, so much so that I could see the Dutch coast long before we reached it.

We were obviously not welcome as large and menacing black balls of flak appeared in the sky ahead of us. The formation manoeuvred gently to avoid the threat, until we actually got on to the bomb run to the target, that anxious period when we flew straight and level. Finally, I felt the aircraft lift as our bombs left us on their way to the target. We now turned out to sea without any sign of the

Luftwaffe, leaving the flak behind us and returned to Oulton after a flight lasting just two hours. Flushing was of special significance to we members of 2 Group as one of our squadrons in a Circus attack there was attacked by an overwhelming number of German fighters, every one of our twelve being lost.

On 22 January six Mitchells of 98 Squadron, led by Wing Commander Lewer and six of 180 Squadron, led by Wing Commander C. C. Hodder AFC, flew their inaugural bombing operation, an attack on the Perfine oil tanks and the Sinclair oil refinery by the Ghent–Terneuzen canal in Belgium. The raid went ahead twenty-four hours late because the necessary bombs were not forthcoming on the 21st. Flying at wave-top height all the way, an unlikely hazard was encountered by Squadron Leader Slocombe in a 98 Squadron Mitchell, who was injured in the face when a seagull shattered his canopy. He had to abort the operation. Bombing was done from 1,500 ft amid heavy flak and fighter attack, which were responsible for the loss of a 98 Squadron Mitchell and two 180 Squadron aircraft, one of them flown by Wing Commander Hodder. Sergeant T. S. Martin's Mitchell of 180 Squadron endured six attacks by Fw 190s before Mustang Is of 169 Squadron drove off the German fighters, although two Mustangs were shot down. Two Venturas, part of a force of eighteen attacking an airfield in France, also failed to return, but there were no losses among the twenty-three Bostons despatched. On 25 January 226 Squadron returned to action with a raid on the docks at Flushing, when Flight Sergeant A. G. Wilson's aircraft was shot down by flak.

On 27 January Hughie Edwards VC DFC, with 'Bladder' Cairns as his navigator, led nine Mosquitoes of 105 and 139 Squadrons in a round trip of more than 1,200 miles to Copenhagen in occupied Denmark for a daring raid on the Burmeister and Wain diesel engine works. In war paint of dull silvery grey and green on the wings the Mosquitoes blended well with the cold, grey-green wave-tops and Danish countryside as they flew at low level in close formation to avoid attacks from enemy fighters. If it had been summer visibility would

In January 1943 Bostons of 2 Group, shortly to be reinforced by Mitchells and Ventura squadrons, carried the war to the Continent when weather permitted with Circus raids. 226 Squadron. 2nd from left; Flying Officer Jock Rutherford RNZAF; Squadron Leader Shaw Kennedy; Flying Officer Ken Houghton; Sergeant Eric Lee; Flight Lieutenant 'Yogi' Yates-Earl; Pilot Officer G. Tolputt; Sergeant Johnny Bicknell; Pilot Officer Don T.Smith; three unknowns; Flight Sergeant Doug Farquhar; unknown; Melhuish, unknown; Flight Sergeant Erby Leavitt DFM; Paddy McKee; unknown; Pilot Officer Bert Hoskins; three unknowns; Sergeant George Currah (KIA 29 January 1943); Pilot Officer Cliff Thomas (KIA 29 January 1943); Flying Officer 'Dickie' Bowyer (KIA 29 January 1943); plus Smithy's dogs Susie and Sally have been impaired by dust and squashed insects splattering their windscreens but Edwards' only concern was that they were too far south and fuel consumption was a vital consideration. Near the coast light flak from ships opened up on the formation and Flight Lieutenant John Gordon DFC and Flying Officer Ralph Gamble Hayes DFC thought their aircraft had been hit when the trailing edge of the starboard wing became enveloped in puffs of blue smoke. Thinking he had been hit by flak Gordon took evasive action but he had caught the port wing in telegraph wires and damaged the aileron. This, together with the fact that the rest of the formation had gained a considerable lead, caused Gordon to decide to abandon and he jettisoned his bombs at 1609 hours and headed home. Edwards and Cairns found the target only at the last moment, when they were on the point of returning, but bombed the target and then broke for the sea and home. Light flak at the target was intense and accurate and Edwards' Mosquito received two holes in the starboard nacelle.

Sergeant Pilot H. C. 'Gary' Herbert RAAF in 105 Squadron, whose navigator was Sergeant C. Jacques, wrote:

Quite a long trip. The leader got lost on the way out and led us around Denmark for over half an hour before we found the target. We went past a small coastal ship and it plastered us with tracer but didn't hit anybody. When we eventually found the target it was getting dark but we hit it good and proper. We attacked between two big chimneys and hit the machine shops and power station. Our bombs were delayed half-hour, three hours, six hours and 36 hours to disorganize the place for a while. Other kites had eleven second delay bombs as well as long delay. We got quite a lot of light flak as we left the target but kept on the housetops and nobody was hit. When we got well away it was pretty dark and one of the kites was hit and crashed in flames. The two sergeants in it [J. G. Dawson and R. H. Cox; it was hit by Flak and exploded on the ground at 1713 hours] were damn good chaps too. Petrol was getting short so we throttled back to 230 m.p.h. and as we passed the last island on the west of Denmark we went straight over a machine gun post at 200 ft. It threw up a lot of flak but I jinked and dodged it OK. We came back quietly and landed in the dark at 8 p.m.

One kite [DK336] ran out of juice and crashed about twenty miles away [killing Sergeant Richard Clare and Flying Officer Edward Doyle of 139 Squadron, who hit a balloon cable and tree at East Dereham after the starboard engine failed]. We flew number two to Wing Commander Edwards VC. Got a scare, on the way back we were struck by lightning twice and each time a ball of fire appeared on the wing and gradually died out. I looked at the wing but there wasn't a mark on it. Seems queer to me but the weather man said it had happened before so I couldn't have had the DTs. [Edwards landed with only fifteen gallons of fuel in his tanks; enough for about another 6½ miles]. Invited the Officers over to the mess in the evening to have a few drinks and fight the battle again. Nice evening. At the time for the bombs to go off we drank a toast to them. Wing Commander Edwards got his DSO for this trip. On Friday 30th some news came in from Sweden of our raid on Copenhagen. Apparently it was a huge success and the Diesel works were flattened. A sugar factory and another six-storey building burned to the ground. They thought our delay bombs were duds but they all went off OK on time.[52]

Three days later there was some trepidation among Mosquito crews at Marham who were due to raid Berlin to disrupt speeches in the main broadcasting station by Hermann Göring and Dr Joseph Göbbels, for 30 January was the tenth anniversary of Hitler's seizure of power. Most of the pilots and navigators could not face breakfast. An exception was Flying Officer A. T. 'Tony' Wickham, one of three pilots (with his navigator, Pilot Officer W. E. D. Makin) in 105 Squadron who, led by Squadron Leader 'Reggie' W. Reynolds and Pilot Officer E. B. 'Ted' Sismore, would bomb Berlin that morning. Wickham heartily drank three tins of orange juice and polished off half a dozen fried eggs. A month earlier, as a young pilot officer going on his first trip, a high-level dawn raid on cities in the Ruhr (when casualties were particularly heavy), his reaction during a gloomy five o'clock breakfast had been quite different. Wickham suddenly burst out and said, 'I suppose this is a death or glory effort?' Hughie Edwards leant forward, looked at him and said, 'There is no glory in it and that's what makes it so worthwhile.' Flight Lieutenant John Gordon DFC and Flying Officer Ralph G. Hayes DFC, who three days earlier had returned with a damaged port wing, completed the trio of aircraft due in Berlin for 'elevenses'.

The three Mosquitoes arrived over Berlin at exactly 1100 hours and the explosion of their bombs severely disrupted the *Reichsmarschall*'s speech. Listeners heard a few muffled words followed by a confusion of many voices, then another shout or bang, after which the microphone was apparently switched off and martial music played. It was then announced that Göring's speech would be delayed for a few moments – but after three-quarters of an hour, martial music was still being played!

In the afternoon, three Mosquitoes of 139 Squadron arrived over Berlin at the time Göbbels was due to speak. Squadron Leader D. F. W. Darling DFC and Flying Officer W. Wright, Flight Sergeant Peter John Dixon McGeehan and Flying Officer Reginald Charles Morris (both KIA 16.3.43) and Sergeants Massey and Fletcher dropped their bombs right on cue. However, the earlier raid alerted the defences and flak brought down the Mosquito flown by Darling and Wright. That night 'Tony' Wickham treated British listeners to the BBC's nine o'clock news to an account of the action. 'Lord Haw Haw', trying to sound convincing in a German broadcast to any who cared to listen, announced, 'Thanks to the U-boat campaign Britain is so starved of materials that she has been compelled to build her bombers of wood.' Reynolds was awarded the DSO while all the other officers received the DFC and the sergeants DFMs. (Gordon, was lucky on 26 April when his petrol tank was hit by a Bofors shell over Eindhoven but the shell failed to explode. Their luck finally ran out on 5 November when they were killed in a crash at Hempnall about 10 miles south of Norwich returning from an operation to Leverkusen on one engine).[53]

In France, meanwhile, the dislocation of the supply route to the Atlantic U-boat bases was uppermost in the minds of the War Cabinet and a directive issued for bombing operations in January-March 1943 called for round-the-clock attacks on U-boat bases on the west coast of France. This meant that while the heavies attacked at night, the mediums would support them with raids on railways and docks by day. One of the prime targets in the campaign was the railway viaduct at Morlaix on the north Brittany coast that carried the main railway line to the U-boat base at Brest. On 26 January twelve Venturas of 21 Squadron at RAF Feltwell, supported by fighters of 10 Group, set out to destroy the viaduct but the operation was aborted because cloud in the target area prevented accurate bombing.

Three days later thick cloud interfered with the operation to attack blast furnaces and steelworks at Ijmuiden by twelve Venturas of 21 Squadron and their fighter escort and only two were able to bomb. On 27 January crews in 2 Group were kept at fine pitch with a low-level exercise on the iron and steel works at Corby by eighty-nine aircraft from eight squadrons. Two days later twelve Bostons of 88 Squadron led by Squadron Leader Gunning DFM took off at 1353 hours on a Circus operation to attack the locomotive works at St Omer but they were recalled at 1400 hours. Nine-tenths cloud also prevented all except two Venturas of 21 Squadron from bombing the cocking ovens at Zeebrugge.

On 29 January meanwhile, a force of twelve Bostons from 226 Squadron led by Flight Lieutenant Don T. Smith was dispatched to bomb the Morlaix railway viaduct. Its destruction would force the Germans to re-route supplies via Lorient and this would add an additional 60 miles to the journey. The Bostons began taking off from Swanton Morley at midday. At 1320 hours they rendezvoused with thirty-five Spitfire Vbs of 310, 312 and 313 Squadrons of the Czech Wing over Exeter at 500 ft and the formation set course at 1330 hours. The trip across the Channel passed without incident. As the bombers approached the viaduct at their usual height of 10,000 ft Pilot Officer Arthur Eyton-Jones, navigator of the Boston flown by Pilot Officer R. M. 'Dick' Christie RCAF, noticed that at either end of the viaduct that there were some 'very pretty little houses'. The viaduct was a masonry structure more than 900 ft long and over 200 ft high set in a heavily built-up area. Its destruction therefore called for pinpoint accuracy because of the risk to the French population. The Bostons dived to bomb the target from 8,000 ft. The bombs from the first box fell in a built-up area to the north-east of and adjacent to the viaduct, with one or two hits on the railway line between the viaduct and a cutting to the east. Being very keen in those days, Arthur Eyton-Jones pressed his bomb release button a fraction of a second before the leader and watched the bombs closely all the way down until the first puffs of the explosions appeared. He observed that they were not white as they had been in the dock water of St Malo during an earlier operation, two days before Christmas 1942 but a 'horrible browny colour . . . They started right in the middle of the pretty little houses,

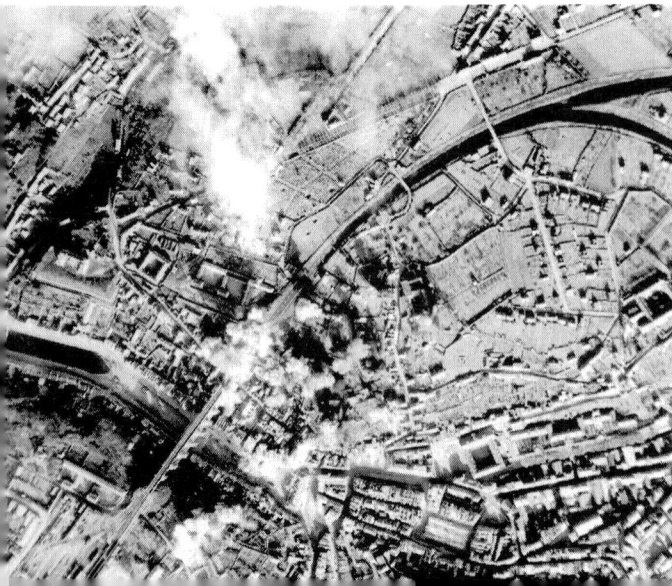

On 29 January 1943 eleven tons of bombs dropped from 8,000 ft by Bostons of 226 Squadron led by Flight Lieutenant Don T. Smith DFC rain down on the French town of Morlaix, the target being the viaduct, a masonry structure 958 ft long and 207 ft high, built in two tiers of nine and fourteen spans, on the main Paris-Brest railway line used to supply U-boat pens on the Atlantic coast. Stray bombs from the second box of Bostons hit a school, killing thirty-nine children and one teacher. (*RAF*)

crossed over the viaduct and finished right in the middle of the nice little houses on the other side.' It was a long time before Eyton-Jones got over where his bombs had landed.[54] Visibility was good, with little cloud, and the bomb-aimers had no difficulty seeing the target, though flak was heavy and accurate. Approximately 11 tons of high explosive was dropped in all. Several bombs from the second box fell on the railway line on the eastern edge of the viaduct. Stray bombs had also hit a school and thirty-nine children and one teacher lay dead in the rubble.

After leaving the target the Bostons turned for home, gradually losing height as they headed for the Brittany coast. As the second box was crossing the French coast just north of Lanmeur, Yellow Section of its close support broke and attacked a formation of about a dozen Fw 190s, in all probability of III./JG2, approaching from a mile away at 8,500 ft. One Fw 190 and one Spitfire were shot down. The Fw 190s continued their approach to the bombers, now 10 miles offshore, and tore into them from the south-west at 10,000 ft, making attacks and breaking away below and to the left. The close escort Spitfires turned back to help the flight escorting the second box and a Spitfire and an Fw 190 went down in flames. The Bostons had commenced a shallow dive before reaching the coast and were down to about 2,000 ft when the Fw 190s attacked. Flying Officer Bill Gray, pilot of *X-X-Ray*, No. 2 in the second box, recalled:

Attacks were made by enemy aircraft from starboard quarter and starboard beam. One Fw 190 stayed on the starboard quarter at a distance of 800–1,000 yards during the whole ten minutes the attack lasted and once made a mock attack without firing, giving the gunner the impression that it was acting as a decoy. Our aircraft sustained no damage but there were four stoppages due to belts hanging. As one enemy aircraft came in to attack on the starboard quarter, Pilot Officer Eric Lee, WOP/AG, got in a long burst and the enemy aircraft fell away, leaving a thin trail of smoke as it passed underneath.

Lee added:

All attacks were by Fw 190s. They pressed home their attacks with great determination and skill and I wouldn't be surprised if they were part of an 'elite' squadron. Apart from attacks from the rear and from starboard there was one spectacular dive right through our box when, very fortunately, no rounds were fired (possibly ammunition exhausted or fault in the firing mechanism). An attack from the rear, broken off at very close quarters (less than 50 feet) enabled me to get in a long burst (from twin .303 Browning machine guns) into his belly. He was so near that I could see my tracer entering his aircraft and knocking pieces off his fuselage and wing. He immediately turned back down towards the French coast trailing a plume of vapour (fuel?). Shortly after that the whole attack was broken off and it soon became obvious that Flying Officer Clifford Thomas's Boston was in difficulties with smoke pouring from his starboard engine and losing speed and height. [The 'probable' Lee claimed was most likely the one that hit Thomas's Boston.] He finally reached sea level and obviously attempted to ditch. Unfortunately, there was a high swell with choppy waves and a wing tip or other part of the aircraft hit the sea causing the aircraft to cartwheel and disintegrate.

Pilot Officer Cliff Thomas, pilot, 226 Squadron (KIA on 29 January 1943 on the Morlaix raid) pictured with his son Derek. (*Derek Thomas*)

Pilot Officer Gordon 'Major' Tolputt, Don Smith's WOP/AG, recalled:

Flying Officer Thomas had feathered the prop and was flying on one engine. He was very low over the sea. We slowed down and flew on a parallel course so we could escort him back to base. The next thing I saw was the port wing (good engine) rise quickly and the starboard wing hit the sea. The aircraft cartwheeled and sank in a cloud of spray. We circled sending 'Mayday' calls and the position. As no trace of wreckage was visible we sadly returned to base.

Cliff Thomas was thirty-three years old and had resigned from the Army in February 1942 to enlist in the RAFVR. The former captain had been posted to 226 Squadron in June 1942. Lost with him were Flying Officer the Honorable Richard L. G. Bowyer, 22-year-old son of the 1st Baron Denham and Lady Denham of Weston Underwood in Buckinghamshire, Sergeant Robert Morton aged twenty-two, and Sergeant George Currah. Flight Sergeant Leavitt's Boston limped back to England very badly damaged and was left at Exeter pending repairs. The remaining ten returned to Swanton Morley. The breaching of the Morlaix viaduct closed the main line used for naval supplies to Brest for almost two months but at a high price.

Bad weather during January and February curtailed much of 2 Group's operations but on 3 February Circus 258 by twelve Venturas of 21 Squadron from Methwold escorted by Spitfires of 64, 308 (Polish), 331, 332, 122 and 416 Squadrons of the Northolt and Hornchurch Wings went ahead. The bombers' target was Coutrai-Wevelghem aerodrome, which was used by Fw 190A-4 fighters of the Third *Gruppe*, JG26. At 0956 hours the Venturas of 21 Squadron took off led by Wing Commander R. H. S. King, formed up into two boxes and headed for the rendezvous point over Bradwell Bay where they formed up with the six escorting fighter squadrons. The formation crossed the Channel without incident and passed over the French coast at Furnes at 17,000 ft above $^{10}/_{10}$ cloud, which totally obscured the ground although it did not prevent heavy flak being encountered. The target was completely obscured by $^{9}/_{10}$ cloud at 2,000–4,000 ft and

Wing Commander King decided to abandon the raid. At 1045 hours 64 and 122 Squadrons left the formation. Two minutes later, with the Venturas heading to the coast between Calais and Gravelines in tight box down formation at 10,500 ft, the cry, 'Snappers' rang out as thirty Fw 190s were spotted 3,500 ft below in pairs about a mile away to starboard. (The Venturas were heading home on an unplanned route and five of the fighter squadrons continued on their original flight plan and returned to base without entering the action.) The enemy fighters (JG26) closed in from below to starboard to a range of about 800 yards but broke away without opening fire. Six of the close escort of 308 Polish Squadron Spitfire Vbs gave chase leaving about six fighters as close support to the bombers. The enemy tactics were considered a feint to draw away the fighters. A second attack developed between 1056 and 1059 hours when Fw 190s, still in pairs, climbed towards the formation and carried out a belly attack from head on. The leading pilot of one pair was *Hauptmann* Wilhelm-Ferdinand 'Wutz' Galland, CO of II./JG26, and younger brother of Adolph. Two Venturas of the first box were hit. The aircraft piloted by Sergeant Ronald P. Moodey started to smoke but he held formation until two more head on attacks by Galland forced him to crash into the sea 2 miles north of Calais at 1105 hours with the loss of all four crew. The victory was credited to 'Wutz' Galland, who later claimed it as a Hudson. It was his twenty-fifth victory of the war.[55]

A third attack was made when, 5 miles north of Calais Marck aerodrome at 1105 hours, climbing from below, the Fw 190s pulled up ahead to about 300 ft above the formation, maked a stall turn to starboard and attacked in a head-on dive. The first attacked the lead Ventura flown by Wing Commander King, passing above the formation, while the second attacked the No. 5 aircraft piloted by Sergeant Ionworth 'Ted' Bellis, dropping its starboard wing and passing beneath the formation leader's right wing. Both then broke away to starboard. The air gunner in King's Ventura opened fire on the Fw 190 at a range of 250–300 yards dead ahead and continued to fire to point-blank range. He saw his tracer bullets hitting the enemy aircraft, which turned over on its back and dived away vertically into cloud. The crew of the second Ventura saw the enemy aircraft on fire and the hood was jettisoned, while the air gunner of No. 4 Ventura of the second box saw it hit the ground. (A Spitfire of 416 Squadron shot down the only Fw 190 lost.) The second Fw 190 which attacked Bellis's Ventura was fired at by his turret gunner Flight Sergeant Denny Denton, who fired about 100 rounds from 300 yards, and the pilot of No. 4 who used both his .5 and .303s. It was hit with smoke seen coming from the engine, and was claimed as 'damaged'. Two more Venturas were claimed shot down, by *Hauptmann* Günther Kelch and *Oberfeldwebel* Heinz Kemethmüller of the 7th *Staffel*, JG26, but both made it back across the Channel to crash land in Kent.[56] Sergeant D. H. Lear came down west of Betteshanger Wood at Eythorn, north-west of Deal while Flight Sergeant J. L. H. Heagerty put down at Manston. One of the Polish Spitfire pilots was killed, two baled out and were captured and a fourth evaded capture and was in Gibraltar nine days later. The Ventura piloted by 'Ted' Bellis was the last to land back at Methwold at 1154 hours.

At Methwold the Venturas were refuelled and rearmed, crews ate a quick lunch and at 1448 hours a second formation of aircraft, again led by Wing Commander

King, took off on Circus 259 to attack the engine sheds and marshalling yards at Abbeville. Three Spitfire wings from 11 Group flew escort and one of these, the Northolt Wing, flew on ahead on an advance sweep. The Venturas rendezvoused with the fighter escort just before Beachy Head. Inland of the enemy coast heavy flak was encountered, especially by the second box, and cloud patches at the target area at 1553 hours made accurate bombing difficult, the 500 lb and 25 lb GP bombs undershooting and overshooting the aiming point. One Ventura, piloted by Squadron Leader L. N. Blome-Jones was slightly damaged by flak and was unable to bomb. The Second and Third *Gruppen* of JG26 attacked the Venturas after the target and north-west of Gravelines *Leutnant* Johann Aistleitner of the 8th *Staffel* tried to finish off the damaged Ventura. Although the German claimed it for his eleventh victory[57] Blome-Jones was able to make it back with his bombs still aboard. The Kenley Wing's 416 Squadron lost four Spitfires to JG26. The rest of the Ventura formation landed back at Methwold between 1700 and 1713 hours to end an eventful day.

On 11 February heavy cloud cover enabled low-level Circus raids to be made by pairs of Bostons on French targets. On the 13th five raids were mounted by 2 Group. No. 107 Squadron attempted to bomb the lock gates at St Malo but they missed and hit the docks instead. It would be two months before they would again operate Bostons on operations. On 15 February all three Boston squadrons, 88, 107 and 226, were stood down, most of their crews being dispatched to North Africa where the Blenheim V or 'Bisley' had suddenly been replaced by the Boston III. Blenheim losses had become untenable, especially after Wing Commander Hugh G. Malcolm of 18 Squadron had his formation virtually wiped out in a daylight raid on Chouigui aerodrome in Tunisia on 4 December 1942, an operation for which he won a posthumous VC. Daylight raids were then abandoned in favour of night raids but the Blenheim was outdated and lacked suitable defensive armament. All Boston IIIs were therefore ordered to the maintenance unit at Burtonwood to be prepared for modification for service by the light bomber squadrons in North Africa. All that now remained in 2 Group were the Mosquitoes of 105 and 139 Squadrons and the Venturas of 21, 464 and 487 Squadrons. There was further disruption in 2 Group at the end of the month when the Venturas, the Mitchells of 98 Squadron and a few 88 and 226 Squadron Boston crews participated in a large-scale tactical exercise aptly named Spartan. Thus for more than two weeks the Mosquitoes were the only aircraft operational in 2 Group.

On 18 February 'Dinty' Moore married Norma in the beautiful St Peter Mancroft Church in Norwich, with his brother Peter as best man. Peter had served at Oulton for a time as an electrician before being accepted for aircrew. When he returned to 218 Squadron at Waterbeach he found that his first crew had gone, having already been lost on operations and the second crew to which he was allocated had also failed to return from an operation. Friends to whom he spoke got the impression that he did not expect to survive his tour of operations. Sadly he was lost on 28 May when his Stirling was shot down off the Dutch coast. There were no survivors.[58] 'Dinty' Moore's return from honeymoon coincided with the beginning of a period of non-operational flying, which was spent mainly in adapting to the Boston IIIAs now being modified for gas-spraying and smoke-laying operations for frequent army co-operation exercises. 'During my absence from Oulton,' he said, '88 Squadron completed a number of operations but at this time our morale was pretty low as we had been declared non-operational. We still had a few Bostons left but until we received some more from the USA (which took until 28 June) we were to remain in the non-operational category.'

While the Boston squadrons were working up with new aircraft, much of the bombing burden fell on the Mosquito IV and Ventura squadrons. On the afternoon of 14 February, in what became known as the 'Great Tours Derby' six Mosquitoes of 139 Squadron attacked the engine sheds in the French city from low level. The following evening, twelve Mosquitoes of 105 Squadron attacked the goods depot from low level and on the 18th twelve made a shallow dive attack, two aborted and one aircraft failed to return. On 14 February Hughie Edwards, who had been promoted to group captain four days earlier, left 105 Squadron to take up a post at HQ Bomber Command prior to taking command of RAF Binbrook on the 18th. By the end of the year he had taken up an appointment in Air Command Far East Asia and held the rank of Senior Air Staff Officer (SASO) until the end of 1945. He remained in the post-war RAF and was awarded the OBE in 1947. In 1958 he was promoted to air commodore and finally retired from the service in 1963. He returned to Australia, was knighted, and in 1974 became Governor of Western Australia.

Edwards' successor, Wing Commander Geoffrey P. Longfield, was killed on 26 February leading an attack by twenty Mosquitoes of 105 and 139 Squadrons on the U-boat supply depot at Rennes. Ten aircraft were to go in at low level, led by Longfield, and ten Mosquitoes of 139 Squadron were to follow just behind, climb to 2,000 ft and dive bomb behind the first wave. Longfield's navigator Flight Lieutenant Ralph Millns lost his bearings on the final run up, which took the Mosquitoes to an airfield 6 miles south of the target. The defences sent up a hail of light flak as the Mosquitoes turned towards the target. Longfield, who had turned too far to the left, suddenly turned right again and collided with the aircraft crewed by Canadian Flying Officers Spencer Kimmel and Harry Kirkland, who were formating on him. Kimmel's airscrew chopped the leader's tail off just behind the wing and he went up into a loop and dived straight into the ground. Longfield, Millns, Kimmel and Kirkland, all died. Next day Pilot Officer G. W. 'Mac' McCormick and visiting Wing Commander John W. Deacon were killed on a training flight when they failed to pull out of a dive from 30,000 ft and crashed at Brick Kiln Plantation.

On Sunday 28 February six of 105 Squadron's Mosquitoes, led by Wing Commander Ralston, went to the John Cockerill Steel works at Liège. Four more led by Pilot Officer Onslow Thompson DFM RNZAF and Pilot Officer Wallace J. Horne DFC, went to the Stork diesel engine works at Hengelo, in what was the eighth raid on the Dutch town by Mosquitoes. At Liège they bombed at about 200 ft and results were 'good' but at Hengelo things were different. Teenager Henk F. van Baaren, whose father owned a shop in the Brinkstraat, saw at first hand the repeated bombing of his town, the first by RAF heavies on the night of 24 June 1940. This experience made a big impression on the young Dutchman. A single aircraft dropped bombs, which fell in the centre of town at the corner of the Brinkstraat, a street with shops whose shopkeepers, like his father, lived with their families on the first and second floors above. The bombs fell on a shoe shop and a pub, killing two adults and two children. Many of the inhabitants moved to the safety of the outskirts of town or in neighbouring villages The van Baarens moved to Enschede, 6 miles away and stayed there at night for six weeks with his grandparents, cycling back and forth to their shop during the day. Henk witnessed the first Mosquito raid on Hengelo, by 105 Squadron on 6 October 1942 and eleven more thereafter, including the one by 105 Squadron on 28 February.

Although there was a war going on the Dutch still had their football matches. Tubantia, one of the local clubs, were playing on their field between the Stork works and the Hazemeyer factory, which produced AA predictor and telecommunications equipment. After the match, at just after 1800 hours local time, when all the supporters had left the area, the formation attack began. Thompson and Horne bombed from 550 ft.[59] Then Flying Officer David Polglase RNZAF and Sergeant Leslie Lampen bombed from a height of only 150 ft. Afterwards they saw a column of smoke rising 300 ft into the air over the target. Another crew bombed from 100 ft. The debriefing reports suggested that the bombing had been accurate. However very little damage was done to the factories and some large houses opposite the football field were hit. Elsewhere in the town more houses were damaged. Ten people were killed, including seven members of one family. One crew bombed Borne, hitting several houses. Three people were killed and several were injured.[60]

On 3 March Wing Commander Peter Shand DFC led ten Mosquitoes of 139 Squadron to the molybdenum mines at Knaben in Southern Norway. Bomb bursts accompanied by orange flashes and a red glow were seen on and around the target, which resulted in the plant being enveloped in clouds of white and brown smoke and debris being blown to a height of 1,000 ft. Four Fw 190s intercepted the Mosquitoes on the homeward journey and Flying Officer A. N. Bulpitt and his navigator, Sergeant K. A. Amond, were last seen being pursued by two Fw 190s and crashing into the sea. Flying Officer J. H. Brown's aircraft was hit and badly damaged but he made a successful crash landing at Leuchars despite the loss of his hydraulics to operate the undercarriage and with no air speed indicator, rudder controls or elevator trim.[61] AOC Air Vice Marshal J. H. d'Albiac sent his congratulations for a 'well planned and splendidly executed attack . . . Mosquito stings judiciously placed are very painful.'

On 12 March twelve Mosquitoes of 105 and 139 Squadrons led by Squadron Leader Reggie Reynolds and Pilot Officer Ted Sismore were briefed to attack the John Cockerill steel and armament works in the centre of Liège. At briefing, which lasted two and half hours, the briefing officer stated that two crack fighter units had recently been moved to Woensdrecht, south of Rotterdam, and that they had recently been re-equipped with Fw 190s. (II./JG1 at Woensdrecht was equipped with thirty-five Fw 190A-4s of which twenty were serviceable). Allowing for several doglegs flight time to target was between two and two and a half hours. Attacks of this nature were normally planned for dusk or just before dark so that the Mosquitoes could return to England individually under the cover of half-light or darkness. Bombing had to be carried out very accurately indeed to keep losses to a minimum, and this task was given to the shallow dive section led by Squadron Leader John Bergrren of

139 Squadron, with his observer Peter Wright. Bergrren had by now completed almost sixty operations. In peacetime Wright was a 'serious-minded' schoolmaster.

At 1530 hours all twelve Mosquitoes taxied out onto Marham's huge expanse of grass and after warming up their engines took off ten minutes later. They headed south to Romney Marsh and Dungeness before flying across the Channel to France and up and over the cliffs to the west of Cap Gris Nez then on across the heavily defended Pas de Calais at nought feet. Finally, seldom flying at more than 100 ft and keeping echelon formation on the leader, they picked up the River Meuse which led straight in to the target. At around 5 miles from the target the Mosquitoes of 105 Squadron split from the rest of the formation and went straight in at low level to drop their four 500 lb eleven-second delayed action bombs. These burst in the target area as Bergrren and his six aircraft hurriedly climbed to 3,000 ft and then dived onto the target to release their four 500 lb bombs with instantaneous fuses. The Mosquitoes were buffeted by the concussion from the bombs and hit by flying debris, bricks and mortar, but every aircraft made it through. Turning away to the north the crews could see a huge mushroom of smoke building up over the main target area. Leaving the target the formation broke into individual aircraft and raced for the Scheldt Estuary at 280 m.p.h. in gathering dusk. They had to climb to 200 ft to avoid the hight-tension cables which criss-crossed Belgium and France. Bergrren and another 139 Squadron Mosquito, DZ373 XD-B, flown by Sergeant Robert McMurray Pace and Pilot Officer George Cook, overflew Woensdrecht and were fired on by AA guns. Bergrren evaded them by squeezing every last modicum of power from his Merlins by pushing the control into the fully forward position, opening the throttle fully and pulling the 'panic valve', a lever which when pulled produced full supercharger pressure on both Merlins. Bergrren glanced up and saw a flicker of flame emerge from the port engine of Pace and Cook's aircraft, which quickly became a flaming torch as the tanks in the port engine caught fire. In a long stream of bright light it crashed on the runway of Woensdrecht airfield and was smashed to smithereens on impact leaving a stream of burning debris in its wake.

Bergrren began counting the silhouettes of Fw 190s entering their circuit and was alarmed to see that there were twelve pairs. He went even lower to nought feet and exited the area at high speed with all the AA guns that could be brought to bear firing at him. He did not return the 'panic valve' to its normal position for several minutes and he did not really relax until they were over the North Sea![62]

On 15 March eleven Venturas of 21 Squadron bombed La Pleine airfield in Brittany in a 10 Group Circus. One was damaged by flak at St Brieuc and ditched in the sea 6 miles west of Guernsey. Next day sixteen Mosquitoes led by Squadron Leader John Bergrren made a low-level and shallow-dive attack on roundhouses and engine sheds at Paderborn. The aircraft flown by Flight Sergeant Peter J. D. McGeehan DFM and Flying Officer Reginald C. Morris DFC was lost. On 17 March Wing Commander John de L. Wooldridge DFC* DFM took command of 105 Squadron. He had joined the RAF in 1938 and flew two tours on heavy bombers prior to taking command of 105 Squadron, including thirty-two operations on Manchesters. (He survived the war only to die as a result of a car accident in 1958). On the 20th twelve Mosquitoes carried out low-level attacks on the engine sheds and repair shops at Louvain and another target at Malines in Belgium. The 139 Squadron leader was shot up by flak over Blankenburg and crashed at Martlesham Heath with the loss of both crew. On 23 March, timed to perfection as factory workers finished work, three Mosquitoes of 105 Squadron, led by Wing Commander Peter Shand DFC, and eight of 139 Squadron, led by Squadron Leader Bill Blessing DFC, attacked the St Joseph locomotive works at Nantes at low level. Next day, 24 March, three Mosquitoes of 105 Squadron were sent on a Rover operation to shallow dive-bomb trains and railway lines within specified areas in Germany. Sergeant H. C. 'Gary' Herbert RAAF in 105 Squadron had the line between Hamm and Bielefeld, a four-track section.

> We got a bit of light flak on the way in at the coast and also east of Osnabrück but we weren't hit. When I reached the line I found plenty of trains and stooged up and down the line dropping one bomb at a time. Stopped two trains – I don't know whether they were derailed or not and blew about half a dozen trucks of another off the line and down the embankment. We carried a vertical camera and also a cine camera in the nose. Made six runs altogether and then went down to the deck to get photos with the cine. On the way back we passed over a small village and all hell broke loose. Tracer came from all directions. I slammed everything wide open and jinxed all over the sky but they were good gunners and hit us, plenty with cannon shells. Tore a hole a foot across in my port engine fairing. The starboard engine began vibrating badly and I shut it off. I tried it again later and it was OK. At the coast again small cannon and Bofors gave us a hot reception and we had to jink plenty to dodge getting hit again. Got back to base and found that Squadron Leader Reynolds had done a belly landing on the flarepath, so I had to land at Swanton Morley. 'Groupie' [Group Captain Wallace H. 'Digger' Kyle DFC, later to become ACM Sir Wallace Kyle] was pleased with our effort.[63]

On 27 March 139 Squadron dispatched six aircraft on another low-level raid on the Stork diesel works at Hengelo. The results at debriefing were described as being uncertain, though photographs showed many near misses. On this occasion serious damage was done to the primary target, although nearby houses were hit once again. Henk F. van Baaren attended a funeral for the first time in his young life when a 17 year old boy from his school and a member of the same gymnastic club that he attended, was killed.[64] Targets in Holland remained the order of the day and on 28 March at Rotterdam-Wilton twenty-four Venturas of 464 and 487 Squadrons damaged six ships and scored direct hits on three more. Six Mosquitoes of 105 Squadron were dispatched to attack a railway yard near Liège but *Oberfeldwebel* Adolf 'Addi' Glunz of 4./JG26 shot down two Mosquitoes south of Lille and the four remaining aircraft bombed an alternative target. (Glunz finished the war with seventy-one confirmed victories). All three Ventura squadrons flew two Circus operations on the 29th. In the morning Squadron Leader Len Trent DFC RNZAF led a formation and followed an attack by 21 Squadron Venturas on warehouses at Dordrecht, and in the afternoon he led a large formation to bomb the docks at Rotterdam. On 30 March ten Mosquitoes bombed the Philips works at Eindhoven but could only hit the corner of the factory.

Next day, 1 April, six Mosquitoes of 105 Squadron led by Squadron Leader Roy Ralston and four of 139 Squadron led by Squadron Leader John V. Bergrren, bombed a power station and railway yards at Trier and engine sheds at Ehrang respectively from 50–400 ft. Bombs from the first formation were seen to fall in the middle of the railway workshops, throwing up large quantities of debris followed by showers of green sparks. Bomb bursts were also observed on the power station followed by a sheet of flame, which rose to a height of 100 ft. The attack by the second formation on Ehrang resulted in a huge explosion and a red flash from a coal container. One bomb was seen to bounce off railway tracks into a house, which was blown to pieces. On leaving the target area smoke was seen rising to about 1,500 ft. No aircraft were lost, although a Mosquito of 139 Squadron, which was hit by blast from bomb bursts and also by flak, returned on one engine with the gyro artificial-horizon and turn-and-bank indicator out of action, and landed safely at Manston. Another 139 Squadron Mosquito, which was hit by flak on crossing the enemy coast lost its hydraulics and was unable to open its bomb-bay doors to bomb and abandoned the strike.

Two days later, on 3 April, twelve Venturas bombed shipping at Brest and eight Mosquitoes carried out Rover attacks on railway targets in Belgium and France. One Mosquito of 139 Squadron was lost, shot down by *Oberfeldwebel* Wilhelm Mackenstedt of 6./JG26 $1^3/_4$ miles south of Beauvais for his sixth and final victory.[65]

At the end of March 320 (Dutch) Squadron, which had been formed in June 1940 from Dutch naval personnel, moved from Methwold to Attlebridge to await re-equipment with the Mitchell II. The 'Flying Dutchmen' had been operating a motley collection of Ansons and Hudsons, mainly on convoy protection and rescue duties from Northern Ireland, until they were transferred to 2 Group on 15 March. On 3 April 464 and 487 Squadrons moved to the grass airfield at Methwold, a satellite of Feltwell (which returned to 3 Group), replacing 21 Squadron's Venturas, which moved to Oulton. There they replaced 88 Squadron, which in turn moved to Swanton

At the end of March 1943 320 (Dutch) Squadron moved from Methwold to Attlebridge to await re-equipment with the Mitchell II. They had been operating a motley collection of Ansons and Hudsons, mainly on convoy protection and rescue duties from Northern Ireland, until they were transferred to 2 Group on 15 March. (*Jan P. Kloos*)

Morley, as 'Dinty' Moore recalled: 'During April the "powers that be" decided that we had had the privilege of living in the home of nobility long enough and moved us from Oulton and Blickling Hall to the purpose-built aerodrome at Swanton Morley. However, there was a marvellous chef in the officers' mess and the food was absolutely first class.'

On 4 April sixty Venturas were despatched to bomb targets on the other side of the Channel again. A formation of twenty-four was dispatched to bomb Caen/Carpiquet airfield. Another twenty-four flew a Circus to the shipyards at Rotterdam, escorted by five squadrons of Spitfires and one squadron of Typhoons, and twelve of 21 Squadron headed for Brest and St Brieuc, escorted by Spitfires of 10 Group. All the bombers attacking Rotterdam were hit by flak and Fw 190s finished off two ailing aircraft. Next day enemy fighters shot down three more on the Brest raid. Their luck then seemed to change for the better, for on the next four operations, aided by escorting fighters, they beat off fighter attacks to get their bombs on target.

On 11 April four Mosquitoes of 105 Squadron led by Squadron Leader Bill Blessing DFC and his navigator Flight Sergeant A. J. W. 'Jock' Heggie ventured to Hengelo to bomb the Stork works. This was the tenth and final low-level attack by 2 Group Mosquito IVs on the long-suffering town. Light was failing and visibility about 3 miles with $^{10}/_{10}$ cloud at 3,000 ft when the formation was intercepted by two formations of three Fw 190s before reaching the target. One section of the enemy fired a burst of two seconds and then they broke off to starboard to attack two of the Mosquitoes. Flying Officers Norman Hull RCAF and Sergeant Philip Brown, No. 3 in the formation, were intercepted by four 190s which came in from starboard and opened fire for about fifteen seconds at a range of 350 yards. The Mosquitoes carried out evasive action by turning into the attack, weaving and gaining and losing height between 150 and 200 ft and increasing speed. After making one attack, the enemy aircraft broke off and wheeled round to attack Z-Zebra flown by Flying Officer David Polglase RNZAF and his observer, Flight Sergeant Leslie Lampen. Z-Zebra was shot down by Unteroffizier Weigand of 2./JG1 and crashed in a wood near Bentheim, Germany, with the loss of both crew. Flying Officer 'Bud' Fisher and Flight Sergeant Les Hogan were unable to bomb the primary target and attacked a train in the area instead. Blessing pressed home his attack from 50 ft and he dropped his bomb load directly onto the Stork works, causing severe damage to the plant. The resistance seems to have signalled London that the Stork and Dikkers factories should no longer be considered targets as production of war machinery had stopped. (Mosquitoes of 140 Wing, 2nd TAF flew the eleventh and final RAF raid on Hengelo on 18 March 1944 when they bombed the Hazemeyer works.)

On the night of 20/21 April nine Mosquitoes of 105 Squadron and two from 139 Squadron led by Wing Commander Peter Shand DFC carried out a bombing attack on Berlin as a diversion for 339 heavy bombers attacking Stettin and eighty-six Stirlings bombing the Heinkel factory near Rostock. The Mosquito 'night nuisance' operations were also designed to 'celebrate' Hitler's birthday. Over the target it was cloudless with bright moonlight and bombs were dropped from 15,000–23,000 ft. Flak was moderate and quite accurate but the biggest danger proved to be night fighters. On the way home Shand and his navigator, Pilot Officer Christopher

B.Mk.IV Series II DK338 *O-Orange* flew its first operation in 105 Squadron on 16 September 1942 when six crews made dusk attacks on the chemical works at Wiesbaden at heights of 2,500–4,000 ft. On 1 May 1943 DK338 *O-Orange* took off for an operation to Eindhoven when an engine failed just after take off and the aircraft crashed about a mile west of Marham, killing Flying Officer Onslow Waldo Thompson DFM RNZAF and his observer Flying Officer Wallace James Horne DFC. The aircraft had completed twenty-three successful sorties, including one on 20 November 1942 by Squadron Leader Patterson and Flight Sergeant Jimmy Hill of the RAF Film Unit to take low-level reconnaissance photographs of the Ooster Schelde estuary from Noord Beveland as far as Woensdrecht airfield to assist in planning for the Eindhoven operation. (*RAF*)

Handley DFM, died when they were shot down over the Dutch coast by *Oberleutnant* Lothar Linke of IV./NJG1, to crash in the Zuider Zee.

On 21 April, however, when Venturas of 21 Squadron headed for the marshalling yards at Abbeville their frailties were exposed once again. One aircraft that taxied out failed to take off after getting into the slipstream of another aircraft ahead. The remaining eleven headed for France in two boxes, led by 28-year-old Flight Lieutenant David F. Dennis DFC.[66] *Generalfeldmarschall* Hugo Sperrle was inspecting pilots of II./JG26 at their base at Vitry when the Venturas were detected approaching the Somme Estuary at 9,000 ft. Immediately the pilots led by *Kommandeur Oberleutnant* Wilhelm-Ferdinand 'Wutz' Galland broke ranks and ran to their aircraft. They sighted the Ventura formation north of Abbeville. While Galland and some of his fighters took on the bombers in a ferocious assault, the remainder kept the Spitfire escort occupied. They attacked from head on, only breaking off at about 50 yards. Flight Sergeant Wilf J. Clutton, WOP/AG in Sergeant Ionworth 'Ted' Bellis's Ventura, No. 3 on the Squadron Leader in the first box of six, recalled:

Flight Sergeant Wilf Clutton, WOP/AG, who survived the operation to Abbeville on 21 April 1943 when three Venturas in 21 Squadron were shot down (*Wilf Clutton*)

173

As we crossed the French coast the leader's aircraft shouted, 'Bandits!' I got into the astrodome to look around. Our Spitfire escort immediately engaged the fighters and a ding-dong air-fight began. We weaved all over the sky but kept on course. Before we reached the target another attack on our box was made and our No 6, Sergeant R. H. Wells was shot down. Our bombing run commenced at the same time as another attack. Naturally it was 'steady, steady' all the way until 'Bombs away!' Cannon shells hit Flying Officer G. L. Hicks, our No. 4 and his aircraft's nose burst into flame. It was a nerve-racking period made more so by the fact that No. 4 did not go down immediately but remained in formation, a flying torch and still bombed up. However, down she went as we let the bombs go. It was a direct hit. We made for home being attacked all the way to the coast. In the last attack Flying Officer G. B. 'Chippy' Chippendale, our No. 2, had his tail shot away and went down. I had gone down to the guns but there was nothing I could do. I went back to the astrodome and looked around. There were only three of us left. At interrogation it appeared obvious that all the attacks were directed at the leading six; the second box got away scot-free. There was no doubt that but for the leadership of Flight Lieutenant Dennis DFC, it might have been a lot worse and we did get through to the target and hit it.[67]

Sergeant Ionworth 'Ted' Bellis, pilot, 21 Squadron (*Wilf Clutton*)

To encourage the Dutch resistance to resist German pressure in Holland and to aid Dutch workmen in organizing disobedience, on 2 May Venturas of 464 Squadron escorted by Spitfire Vbs of 118 Squadron from RAF Coltishall attacked the Royal Dutch steel works at Ijmuiden. Moderate flak greeted them and on the return Fw 190s intercepted them 40 miles from the coast. Two of the Venturas were damaged and four Spitfires of 331 and 332 (Norwegian) Squadrons were lost. Spitfires claimed two Focke Wulfs shot down. *Unteroffizier* Andreas Banz of 2./JG1 and *Oberfeldwebel* Peter Eberhardt of 5./JG1, a Legion Condor veteran, were KIA near Schiphol and in the North Sea respectively. The Fw 190

On 21 April 1943 the Venturas of 21 Squadron were attacked by II./JG26 led by *Kommandeur Oberleutnant* Wilhelm-Ferdinand 'Wutz' Galland (right), younger brother of Adolph. They shot down three of the Venturas and a Spitfire escort without loss. 'Wutz' was the second Galland brother to die (Paul having died on 31 October 1942), when he was KIA on 17 August in combat with 56th Fighter Group P-47s during the disastrous 8th Air Force raid on Schweinfurt. (*Bundesarchiv*)

flown by *Hauptmann* Dietrich Wickop, *Gruppenkommandeur*, II./JG1 was hit in the left wing, undercarriage and cockpit by return fire from the Spitfires and he was slightly wounded in the left arm by splinters from his canopy. Damage was caused to the coke factory, sulphate plant and numerous storehouses, and in the harbour nearby, three ships were hit – two of which sank – but the Steel works was undamaged.

Next day, when *Ramrod 16* went ahead, the Steel works was the target again on which six Boston IIIAs of 107 Squadron made a low-level attack. (No. 107 Squadron had resumed operations on 1 May under Wing Commander Dickie England, who had taken over the squadron on 10 April.) Twelve Venturas of 487 Squadron, led by 28-year-old Squadron Leader Leonard Trent DFC RNZAF, 'B' Flight commander, meanwhile were sent on a diversionary Circus to bomb the Amsterdam power station. Trent won the right to lead this Ramrod ahead of Squadron Leader Jack Meakin, 'A' Flight commander, on the toss of a coin. Before their departure from Methwold Trent told his deputy, Flight Lieutenant A. V. Duffill, that whatever happened he was going over the target. Pilot Officer Monty Shapiro, 30-year-old observer who like his pilot, Pilot Officer T. L. B. 'Terry' Taylor and their two gunners, was a veteran of the crew's Eindhoven raid, said of Trent: 'He was an outstanding leader in air combat. He really cared for his crews and was a brilliant leader of formation flying. He was the complete antithesis of what you'd expect of an outstanding combat flier. He didn't take part in any drinking parties. Every evening he went home to his wife. But he was an exceptional squadron leader.'

Two formations of three Bostons set out from Coltishall and then flew at their customary low level across the North Sea. The first vic scored good hits on the switch and transformer stations at Ijmuiden but again the Royal Dutch Steel works

No. 487 RNZAF Squadron at Feltwell in early 1943. Squadron Leader Leonard Trent is seated off centre (hands crossed without gloves) next to Wing Commander G. J. Grindell, CO. On Grindell's left after the adjutant is Squadron Leader 'Digger' Wheeler. Flying Officer Rusty Perryman (KIA 3.5.43) is second from left, while Gordon Park is first right. (*via Peter Mallinson*)

escaped damage. Shortly after leaving the Dutch coast the Bostons were intercepted by Bf 109s and Fw 190s but they escaped without loss. The second vic of Bostons scored direct hits on the works and on turning back out to sea they too were attacked by enemy fighters. The Boston flown by Flight Sergeant Frank S. Harrop crashed into the sea in flames with the loss of all the crew. The two other Bostons escaped but *en route* home they saw a Ventura plunge into the sea without any sign of survivors. They had in fact witnessed part of an unfolding tragedy.

At 1643 hours the twelve Venturas were airborne from Methwold and they flew to Coltishall where, at 1700 hours, they rendezvoused with their Spitfire Vb escorts of 118, 167 and 504 Squadrons led by Wing Commander Howard Peter 'Cowboy' Blatchford DFC RCAF, OC of Coltishall Wing. *En route* to Amsterdam the Ventura piloted by Sergeant A. G. Barker aborted after losing the escape hatch. Tragically for the rest of the Venturas, a mistimed 11 Group Rodeo 212 sweep by Spitfires to Flushing had already alerted the enemy defences. No. 487 Squadron and their escorting Spitfires ran headlong into a *Schwarm* of 2./JG27 and twenty-eight Fw 190A-4s of II./JG1 from Woensdrecht, led, despite his injuries sustained the day before, by *Gruppenkommandeur Hauptmann* Dietrich Wickop. While several pilots of all three *Staffeln* of JG1 kept the escorting Spitfires at bay, others went after the Venturas. Flight Lieutenant Viv Phillips, Trent's observer, yelled, 'Here's a whole shower of fighters coming down on us out of the sun; they may be Spits – 20, 30, 40...Hell's teeth, they're 109s and Fw 190s!' Wing Commander Blatchford desperately tried to recall the Venturas but by the time they responded to his calls it was too late. The Spitfires of 118 and 167 Squadrons had their hands full and 3 miles behind 504 Squadron entered the fight while still climbing from their transit height. They carried out a 360 degree turn in the hope of luring fighters away from the bombers but the enemy fighters were not fooled. 'Cowboy' Blatchford's Spitfire was hit by an Fw 190A-4 flown by *Hauptmann* Hans Ehlers, *Geschwaderadjutant* of II/JG1.[68] The popular Canadian from Alberta ditched 40 miles off Mundesley on the Norfolk coast at about 1815 hours. His body was never found. Over Holland Spitfires of 118 and 167 Squadrons claimed three enemy fighters but the Fw 190s and Bf 109s picked off the Venturas in just a matter of minutes. Among the first hit was Duffill's, which had its hydraulics put out of action and both engines set on fire. Both his gunners were seriously wounded and he turned for home trailing smoke. His navigator managed to get the bomb bay doors open and salvo the three bombs and the burning engines gradually extinguished, and Duffill landed safely back at Methwold at 1855 hours.

Flying Officer Stanley Coshall's observer, Flying Officer Rupert North, who was on his seventh sortie, recalled: 'Tracer bullets were whizzing around, enemy fighters were flashing past and our planes were going down in pieces or flames. It was plain that we would soon be hit and the tension and suspense were paralysing.' Two Fw 190s attacked at 11,000 ft and the air gunner, Sergeant D. H. Sparkes, was killed. A fierce fire was burning inside the fuselage. Coshall was last seen reaching for the cockpit escape hatch. This had the effect of sucking the flames into the cockpit and North jumped clear through this exit via the back of the pilot's seat. He managed to get one clip in place before opening his canopy and landing on his feet but was quickly captured. He spent three months in hospital recovering from multiple burns. The WOP/AG, Sergeant W. Stannard, who was on his twenty-first sortie, lost his parachute in the blaze. He saw North jump clear and was trying to reach his burning parachute pack when the flames drove him back right into the tail-cone. An explosion then cleanly severed the tail unit and Stannard came down trapped inside, landing near the village of Bennebroek. He had a badly burned left hand and forehead, two flesh wounds in the leg where he had been hit by exploding .303 ammunition, slight concussion and a cut on the head, the latter two sustained in the actual descent.

A few seconds and a few miles away, *O-Orange*, Taylor's Ventura, shuddered from the shock of deadly accurate cannon fire. The first thing Monty Shapiro was aware of 'was cannon fire passing through the front of the aircraft and the order to bale out. I thought it was the end. We appeared to be falling to earth with no engines. The rear gunner was dead. I had no idea what was happening to the others.' Shapiro had been wounded in the arm by the same burst of fire that had killed Sergeant L. J. Littlewood, the gunner, and wounded the WOP/AG, Sergeant T. S. Tattam. Inside the cockpit the badly burned pilot had decided to make a quick end to his suffering but incredibly, as the Ventura dived earthwards at 350 m.p.h., the fire diminished and he was able to gain some measure of control, enough to attempt a crash landing. He managed to belly land *O-Orange* with his bombs and two wounded crew members still aboard. The aircraft hit the ground at 250 m.p.h., leapt into the air and crashed down again, eventually coming to rest in marshland near the village of Vijthuizen on the outskirts of Haarlem, 5 miles from Amsterdam. After clambering out of the wreckage Taylor was surprised to hear cries for help from the rear of the aircraft. 'He had no idea that we were still aboard,' explained Shapiro. 'He thought we'd all baled out!'

Eight Venturas had been shot down before they reached the power station and Flying Officer S. B. 'Rusty' Perryman, who on the low-level Eindhoven raid the previous December had waved to three small children, went down at 1753 hours. Only Trent and Flying Officer Ian Baynton remained. As Trent saw his bombs overshoot the power station Baynton was shot down with the loss of the entire crew, all of whom had flown the Eindhoven raid. Then Trent too came under intense fire from both flak and fighters. *Hauptmann* Wickop (his eleventh victory) and his wingman, *Unteroffizier* Rudolf Rauhaus (his third victory) both claimed a Ventura and five more were credited to II./JG1 including one by *Unteroffizier* Hans Meissner, *Rottenführer* in 6th *Staffel*.[69] Finally, Trent's Ventura went into a spin and broke up. Flying Officer R. D. C. Thomas, WOP/AG, and Sergeant G. W. Trenery, air gunner, died trapped inside but Trent and Viv Phillips were hurled out to survive and become PoWs. (In March 1944 Trent, who was incarcerated in *Stalag Luft III*, was about to join the exodus of RAF PoWs escaping from the camp when the tunnel was discovered by the German guards.) It was only after they were repatriated that the full story became known and on 1 March 1946 Trent was awarded the VC for his leadership and gallantry.

Replacement crews arrived at Methwold shortly after the Ijmuiden fiasco. One of the navigators was an Australian, Sergeant Dudley Hemmings, who in 1941 had thought that 'Empire Day 24 May seemed a good day to join the RAAF' and had trained on Venturas at No. 34 OTU Penfield Ridge, Nova Scotia.

In Canada our RAF instructors gave us the 'gen' of the air war in Europe. Training was good under difficult flying weather but we were kitted out in good warm Canadian winter clothing. We crewed up – an Aussie pilot and wireless operator, a New Zealander gunner and me – all sergeants. A number of aircraft and crews went missing on training exercises in the icy waters off Yarmouth, Nova Scotia. We did night and day cross country flights, low level flying, bombing and target shooting. It was a good introduction to No. 2 Group RAF later but we didn't know that at the time. I spent Christmas 1942 in hospital in New Brunswick with the 'flu. Leave in New York for seven days followed. I got some newspaper publicity at the Stage Door Canteen in New York when my picture appeared with actresses in the Sydney newspapers later. My mother was thrilled! Soon it was goodbye to New York and our small group joined hundreds of RCAF aircrew on the *Queen Elizabeth* which steamed full speed across the U-boat infested Atlantic to Greenock, Scotland. It was a long train trip to Bournemouth where we saw green grass, buttercups and daisies, a welcome sight after months of snow in Canada. Bournemouth was pleasant in the spring of 1943 but we got our first taste of WAR. One Sunday at 1 p.m. three Focke-Wulf 190s flew low over the city bombing and strafing. A number of people were killed in the parks and a full hotel got a direct hit killing and injuring about 200. One of our group got into an open fireplace and the strength of the brickwork saved him. In May we were posted to 464 Squadron commanded by Wing Commander Jack Meakin, at Methwold near Thetford Forest, Norfolk. The other squadrons in 140 Wing were 487 RNZAF and 21 RAF – all on Venturas. Danny Walsh said, 'It's rough and ready but it will do me' meaning there were no morning parades, no strict discipline between ranks and easy to get a leave pass to a nearby village or town. The Wing had been engaged in medium to low level strikes on targets in Northern France and Holland with light losses. However, a few days before our arrival 487 Squadron had sent out eleven aircraft to a target in Holland where they were jumped by a flight of Focke-Wulfs and lost ten crews. This put an end to further Ventura operations for the time being so we began a lot of day and night flying training.

Our four-man crew got on well and flew all round England and Wales and out over the North Sea. On one three hour cross country exercise the weather was foul all the way – didn't see the ground at any turning point and arrived back at what we hoped was base all on Dead Reckoning Navigation with cloud base down to 500 ft. No Methwold flare path could be seen. I asked the wireless operator for a QDM (radio bearing) but he said his wireless had packed up due to the storm. So where were we? Lost at night, clouds low, not good. Back to lessons I learned in Canada. 'Fly around and search for a red flashing beacon – circle it with navigation lights on for two to three minutes'. Ground Observer Corps should see us and open up their searchlights and beam them up and down in the direction of an airfield. This we did and down the searchlight beams we flew. To our relief up came a flare path – great! Harvey our pilot prepared to land with wheels and flaps down but on the final approach at 300 ft I saw nine red lights at the beginning of the flare path. It was a dummy airfield meant to catch German night fliers out to shoot up an airfield. 'Pull up, pull up,' I shouted to Harvey. We searched for another red flashing beacon and finally landed at 1 a.m. at Duxford, an American base. We got beds and a meal from the Yanks.

In between ops we had leave of course and I had kind friends in Warwick – Vera, a lady of some means offered hospitality to many Australian aircrew in her large house and at the Wheatsheaf pub in Warwick. We played tennis with the ladies at the Warwick Boat Club Tennis Courts in the shadow of Warwick Castle, a lovely area near the River Avon. We toured England by car and visited many beautiful and famous places in the UK. London of course was a favourite leave venue. My commission came through.

On 11 May the Mitchells of 180 Squadron resumed operations when railway communications at Boulogne were the target of six aircraft, but bad weather prevented bombing and one aircraft was lost. Next day Mitchells of 98 Squadron bombed the target successfully. On 15 and 16 May 98 Squadron bombed Caen airfield and 180 Squadron flew their first Circus operation on the 16th when Triqueville was attacked. By now 107 was the only squadron still using Bostons on Circus operations. Meanwhile 88 and 226 Squadrons were flying almost daily exercises. On 15 May twelve Bostons of 107 Squadron led by Wing Commander Dickie England flew a Circus to Abbeville-Drucat airfield. They were met in strength by Bf 109Gs and Fw 190s of JG54 *Grunherz* ('Greenhearts'), which made repeated attacks on the formation between Poix and Le Touquet. Flight Sergeant Kindell, England's air gunner damaged two fighters while the escorting Spitfires shot down two. *Oberleutnant* Horst Hannig, who had thirty victories, was killed when his parachute failed to open. None of the Bostons was lost although Flight Sergeant Noble had to crash land at Detling and Flight Sergeant Truxler force landed in a Kent hop field near East Peckham. On 21 May twelve Mitchells *en route* to bomb Abbeville airfield were recalled. Meanwhile, four Mosquitoes bombed the locomotive sheds at Orleans. Squadron Leader Vernon R. G. Harcourt DFC and his South African navigator, Warrant Officer J. Friendly DFM were killed flying C-Charlie, which was shot down by flak over the French coast on the way home.

On 23 May 487 Squadron resumed operations with an attack on a power station and coking plant at Zeebrugge. They came through safely. Five days later it was the turn of 21 Squadron to attack Zeebrugge. Flying Officer David Pratt led the two boxes of six Venturas; Sergeant Bellis was his No. 3. Wilf Clutton, his WOP/AG, recalled:

> There was no flak and no fighters and we got our bombs away. Upon diving away from the target Davy Pratt's aircraft sideslipped into ours. His wing caught ours and immediately crumpled. His tail fins then hit us underneath. I shouted on the intercom 'Davy's hit us!' but Bellis could not hear me; the Ventura made a terrible row in the dive. He had not even felt the jolt. The last we saw of Pratt's aircraft was hitting the sea off Zeebrugge – an unforgettable memory.

Late on 27 May – 'a glorious, clear, hot but slightly misty, late May evening' – the final large-scale daylight raid by the Mosquito IVs of 2 Group took place when

HM King George VI and Queen Elizabeth visit 487 Squadron RNZAF at Methwold on 26 May 1943. (*John Robinson via Theo Boiten*)

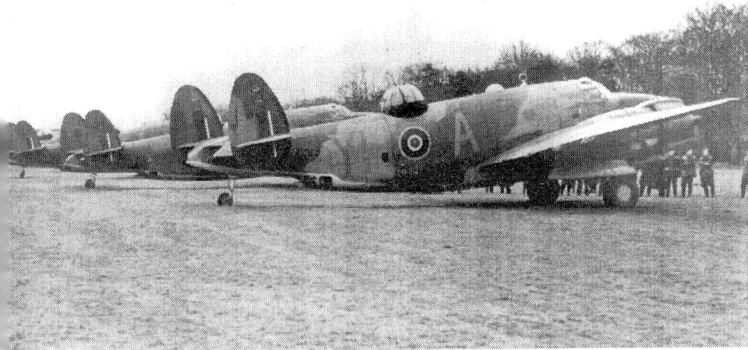

Venturas of 21 Squadron at Methwold. Note the Boulton Paul Type C Mk IV dorsal gun turret with two 0.303 in machine guns. Sixty-five Ventura Mk Is and 71 Mk IIs were delivered to 2 Group. Thirty-one Venturas failed to return from operations, nine were written off with severe battle damage and eight were lost in flying accidents. (*RAF Museum*)

fourteen Mosquitoes were given two targets deep in southern Germany. The briefing was very long and complicated. It meant flying at low level for well over three hours over enemy territory, of which a good two and a quarter would be in broad daylight. Six aircraft of 139 Squadron led by Wing Commander 'Reggie' W. Reynolds set out to attack the Schott glassworks at Jena. A few miles further on eight Mosquitoes of 105 Squadron led by Squadron Leader Bill Blessing DFC were to bomb the Zeiss optical factory, which at that time was almost entirely engaged on making periscopes for submarines. One of the 105 Squadron pilots taking part was Charles Patterson, with the Film Unit cameraman Flight Sergeant Leigh Howard as his navigator. Patterson recalled:

> We saw the red ribbon running longer than we'd ever considered, right down into SE Germany near Leipzig and the target, the Zeiss optical lens works at Jena. It gave a great sense of anticipation and excitement that such a tremendously long trip was going to be undertaken but not undue alarm because it was so deep into Germany, an area that had never seen daylight flying aircraft before. We rather assumed that by going deep down not only could we achieve a great deal of surprise but there might be much light AA fire round this factory and what there was the gunners would be inexperienced.

At seven o'clock all around the perimeter the engines started up and everybody taxied out. Forming up on these trips with a full muster of

Mosquitoes was quite a lengthy business, the leader circling slowly round and round the airfield for everybody to get airborne and catch up. The two formations swept across the hangars and the airfield at low level, an impressive sight and quite an exhilarating experience for the crews themselves. We settled down for the long flight right across to Jena in clear daylight as it was certainly a good two and a half hours before dusk. The Dutch coast was crossed with no difficulty but at the Zuider Zee we suddenly found ourselves flying slap into a vast fleet of little brown-sailed fishing vessels. In front of me the whole formation broke up and weaved in and around them, before we settled down again. On behind the Ruhr and down near Kassel we went, then on into the Thuringian Mountains where the Möhne and Eder dams are. Even then we were only two thirds of the way. You felt you were in a separate world, which has no end and will go on forever. On and on over the trees and the fields and the rising ground we went, mile after mile. Then suddenly, my navigator drew my attention to something. I looked across the starboard wingtip and I had a clear view of Münster cathedral quite a few miles away, the interesting thing being that I was looking up at the towers, not down on them!

We carried on past Kassel then suddenly we came across all the floods of the Möhne dam raid which had taken place only ten days before. For twenty minutes there was nothing but floods. It was fascinating and confirmed in our minds what an enormous success the raid must have been. We flew between the Möhne and Eder dams and suddenly came over a mountain ridge and there was a dam [Helminghausen] beneath us. On the far side the front formation was just topping the far ridge when Flak opened up. It didn't look very serious. An enormous ball of flame rolled down the mountainside, obviously an aircraft but it wasn't long after that I learnt that it was two Mosquitoes, which had collided. Whether one was hit by Flak or whether it caused one of the pilots to take his eye off what he was doing and fly into the Mosquito next to him, nobody will ever know. But two had gone.[70]

We flew on over this mountainous country, over ridges and down long valleys

The final large-scale daylight raid by 105 and 139 Mosquito Squadrons in 2 Group was on 27 May 1943, to the Zeiss optical factory and the Schott glass works at Jena. Mosquito DZ467/P of 105 Squadron failed to return. Pilot Officer Ronald Massie and Sergeant George P. Lister were killed. Only three of the eight Mosquitoes despatched by 105 Squadron bombed the target, while three out of six 139 Squadron aircraft attacked the Schott glass works as part of the same raid. (*RAF Marham*)

with houses on both sides. On my starboard wingtip we saw a man open his front door and look out to see these Mosquitoes flashing past. We saw the door slam in a flash of whipping past. Suddenly, the weather began to deteriorate and this had not been forecast. I think everybody was assuming that we'd soon fly out of it but it got worse and we were over mountains. We now began to fly right into clouds. Flying in formation in cloud and knowing you're right in the centre of Germany gives you a rather lonely feeling. Blessing put on his navigation lights to try and enable us to keep formation. Everybody put on navigation lights. I was very nervous flying on instruments in cloud and although I did my best to keep the next aircraft in view, I lost him.[71]

H. C. 'Gary' Herbert in the 105 Squadron formation added:

A bit further on another 139 kite [*B-Beer* flown by Reynolds and Flying Officer Ted Sismore] feathered his port airscrew [after it took a hit and part of the aircrew entered then cockpit injuring Reynolds in the left hand and knee] and turned back. He got home OK. Just before we turned to make the last run up the valley to the target the clouds came right down to the deck and the formation had to break up. When the clouds broke I found the formation OK but three other kites were gone.[72] So six kites out of the formation went on to attack.

Visibility was extremely bad and as we approached the target at nought feet we suddenly saw balloons over it. Then the fiercest cross fire of light flak I have ever seen opened up. I was last in the formation by this time. Free to go in how l liked and I broke away and climbed up the mountain at the side of the town hoping to fox the gunners and dodge the balloons, which I expected would be spread across the valley.

I didn't do either. As we went up the mountain they poured light flak down at us and we dived down the other side. The only thing to do was to weave straight in dodging the flak and praying not to hit a cable. We did that and as we screamed down the flak poured past us and splattered all over the town. They put a light flak barrage over the target hoping we would rim into it but somehow we dodged it and put our bombs fairly in the glass grinding section – a sixteen storey building. We were hit in several places on the way out.

The heavy cross fire they put up over the glass grinding building (my target) was not directed at us but obviously to deter us from going through it. They don't know how close they were to succeeding! I was absolutely terrified and did not think anybody could get through that and survive and was sorely tempted to turn away and bomb an alternative target. The only thing that made me go through was the thought that I couldn't face men like Hughie Edwards, Roy Ralston, Reg Reynolds and say, 'I lost my guts and turned away'. I now know that heroes are really cowards whose conscience would not let them hold their heads high in the presence of real brave men. Subsequent reports confirmed that I was not the only one who was tempted to turn away.

However, we managed to get away OK and only ran into one lot of flak on the homeward journey. We dodged it OK. When we got back we found that our hydraulics were out of action and had to put our wheels and flaps down by hand. The throttles wouldn't close and I had to cut the switches to get in. Made it OK.

Two other kites crashed when they got back and both crews were killed.[73] Another kite was missing, making five crews lost – our heaviest loss. It was certainly my stickiest operation and everybody else reckoned it was the stickiest too. There were so many aircraft pranged on the flarepath when we got back that we were ordered to go to an alternative aerodrome – Swanton Morley I think. We came back by car which took many hours in the blackout. By that time all the Bigwigs from Headquarters who were there to decide whether we should continue as a low level squadron or be switched to PFF work had left.[74]

On 4 June the Mosquito crews learned of a change in their role. They would do no more daylight operations, instead joining 8 (PFF) Group, where 105 Squadron became the second Oboe squadron and 139 Squadron high-level 'nuisance' raiders, flying B.IX Mosquitoes.[75] On 27 May Air Vice Marshal Basil Embry had replaced Air Vice Marshal J. H. d'Albiac at 2 Group HQ, Bylaugh Hall, five days before its transfer to 2nd Tactical Air Force. Embry's task was to prepare 2 Group for low-level day and night operations to support Operation Overlord – the invasion of France – planned for mid–1944. Embry had lost none of his fire and determination, which he now brought to bear on all echelons of his new command. He flew all the aircraft in 2 Group – Douglas Bostons, North American B-25 Mitchells and Lockheed Venturas – and decided that the slow and poorly armed Venturas were totally unsuitable. After dismissing suggestions that 2 Group should re-equip with Vultee Vengeance dive-bombers, he decided to replace the Venturas in 21, 464 RAAF and 487 RNZAF squadrons with Mosquito fighter-bombers. The Mk VI was fast and armed with four machine guns and four 20 mm cannon in the nose and could carry in various forms four 500 lb bombs, flares and long range fuel tanks. However, they were in short supply so re-equipment of the three Ventura squadrons would have to wait until August-September 1943. Boston aircraft were also slow to arrive, so 88 and 226 Squadrons re-equipped with the North American Mitchell II and III, while 107 Squadron was on gas-spray and ASR duties. On 1 June 2 Group was transferred first to Fighter Command then, when this divided to form Air Defence of Great Britain (ADGB), into 2nd Tactical Air Force.

No. 342 (Lorraine) Squadron was working up on the Boston IIIA at Sculthorpe. The Free French squadron, which re-formed at West Raynham, Norfolk on 1 April was commanded by Wing Commander A. C. P. Carver with Wing Commander Henri de Rancourt as French commandant. 'A' Flight was known as Metz Flight and 'B' Flight was called Nancy Flight. Boston IIIAs were in short supply so training was carried out on early Bostons and some Havoc Is and us. The need to lay concrete runways at West

On 27 May 1943 Air Vice Marshal Basil Embry (later Air Chief Marshal Sir Basil Embry GCB KBE DSO*** DFC AFC) assumed command of 2 Group at Bylaugh Hall with the task of preparing the Group for invasion support in the run-up to Operation Overlord. (*via Paul McCue*)

Raynham in May led to the French having to move to Sculthorpe. The squadron flew its first Boston operation on 12 June with an attack on the power station at Rouen.

Meanwhile, 98 and 180 Mitchell Squadrons at Foulsham, Norfolk, had finally cured their turret, gun, oxygen and intercom problems but participation in Circuses and Ramrods was limited. On 10 June six Mitchell IIs of 98 Squadron took part in an operation against a electricity plant to the north of Ghent in Belgium. For close escort they had the Spitfires of 167 and 485 Squadrons. They took off at 1755 hours but Flying Officer Fee was forced to abort with mechanical problems and put down at Manston. The rest continued across the North Sea to the enemy coast where they were fired on by AA batteries but there were no losses. In the region of Eeklo-Zelzate between Bruges and Ghent twenty-eight Fw 190s of II./JG1 met the formation. *Feldwebel* Kurt Niedereicholz in the *Stab* (Staff) Flight led by *Hauptmann* Robert Olejnik reported:

We engaged a mixed formation of enemy, between 20–30 aircraft. I identified five aircraft as being Mitchell B-25Cs. As they were flying in a south-easterly direction, *Hptm* Olejnik turned us on the left flank of the enemy and gave the order to attack. I turned towards them out of the sun and attacked the B-25 in the rear of the formation. I then observed hits on both engines, as well as a trail of white smoke. At this moment, I was brutally surprised by two Spitfires diving on me from above. In order to get rid of them I dived and returned to base at low level. I could not therefore observe the fate of the Mitchell. I landed at 1934 hours without any hits and *Oberfeldwebel* Ehlers was able to confirm my account.[76]

As if to emphasize the urgent need to replace the Ventura, on 22 June Wing Commander R. H. S. King, CO of 21 Squadron, was killed when his Ventura was hit by flak on a raid on a gun position near Abbeville-Drucat airfield in France. Group Captain W. V. L. Spendlove DSO, who had only taken over as the new station commander at Swanton Morley on the 13th, Pilot Officer Henry Gatticker, navigator, Flight Sergeant J. Koller, Pilot Officer Kinglake and King's bull-terrier,

No. 180 Squadron Mitchell IIs at Foulsham, Norfolk, in June 1943. The nearest aircraft is FL684/S, which operated with the squadron from 19 June until 20 March 1944. Behind is FL707/Z, which served with the squadron from 3 October 1942 and was shot down on 26 November 1943 during a raid on Martinvast. Nos. 180 and 98 Squadrons flew their first operation on 22 January 1943 when six from each squadron bombed oil targets in Belgium. FL684 was SOC on 17 December 1946. (*John Smith-Covington via Theo Boiten*)

On 22 June 1943 Ventura AE910 of 21 Squadron flown by Wing Commander R. H. S. King, CO, was shot down by flak north-east of Abbeville-Drucat. King, Pilot Officer Henry Gattiker, Flight Sergeant J. Keller and Pilot Officer Kinglake, plus Group Captain W. V. L. Spendlove DSO, station commander of Swanton Morley for just two weeks, were killed. King's faithful bull terrier 'Fiddle' also perished. (*RAF*)

'Fiddle', who always flew with his master, were lost. Flight Sergeant Wilf Clutton, WOP/AG in Sergeant 'Ted' Bellis's Ventura, in the second box of six, recalled:

One of the crew said the Wing Commander had gone down. We'd only had one burst of flak. We had also been hit. Ted Bellis said, 'I can't hold it!' I looked at him. He had both feet on the steering column. The trim tab wires had been snapped by a piece of flak and he was having trouble keeping the aircraft level. He said we might have to jump. Denny Denton, the top turret gunner and I got down and saw that the wire was hanging loose.

'What do we do now, Ted?' we asked.

He said, 'Pull on it!'

We pulled. I don't know how but we levelled out. By now we were alone. The rest of the formation had gone. Then we sighted two fighters. They were Spitfires! One came up on the right side, the other on our left and escorted us home. We had a long, low run into it and Ted landed perfectly.

Sergeant Eric Bateson's Ventura was severely damaged by flak but he managed to get it back as far as Lympne, where he attempted to lower the undercarriage but found that the starboard wheel would not lock down. Bateson proceeded to fly around the airfield for one and a half hours trying to get the wheel locked down, with the crew even using urine to top up the hydraulic tank, but this was to no avail and he was forced to make a belly-landing. On inspection the aircraft had twenty-one flak holes in the fuselage.

On 20/21 July 464 RAAF and 487 RNZAF Squadrons discarded their Venturas and left Methwold for Sculthorpe, an isolated airfield near Fakenham, Norfolk where they began training on Mosquito FBVIs in August. No. 21 Squadron at Hartford Bridge continued Ventura operations on a few occasions until September, when they joined the others at Sculthorpe, also to commence training on the Mosquito, although in June it had been rumoured that the squadron was to convert to Mitchells. Two Mitchells arrived and all crews made at least one flight. All members of a Canadian crew except for the rear gunner were killed on take-off in one of the B-25s when it crashed into a Ventura at dispersal.

Flight Sergeant Mike Henry, the gunnery leader, who had completed two tours on

Blenheims as a WOP/AG, was, with the other members of his crew, posted to 487 Squadron in July. He recalled:

A souped up version of the Hudson the Ventura wasn't very popular with the operational squadrons who had recently inherited them. Whatever merits it had as a piece of airborne machinery, pilots weren't impressed. 'Fine aeroplane,' I heard one pilot comment, 'for carrying mail but as an operational aircraft I don't rate it.' the Douglas Boston was far superior . . . [No. 487] Squadron was equipped with Venturas in which, we were told the squadron would not operate unless something 'big' was called for by Group. Large sighs of relief from [Flight Lieutenant] Court [pilot] and Henry and our navigator. It was also stated that the squadron and its sister squadron 464 RAAF would shortly be converting to Mosquitoes. Grins from Court and navigator, scowl from Henry for the Mossie carried a crew of two only; gunners were on the way out. Nevertheless, I did over forty hours flying in the Ventura, all peaceable flights covering every aspect of training. We survived the initial stages of circuits and bumps, by day and by night, local flying to graduate to a quick whip round Spalding/Goole/Leicester/Winchester/Reading/Cambridge in two hours forty minute. . . The crews of both squadrons were a mixed bag. I remember getting involved in many poker games in the mess and my inexperienced 'poker ears' were assailed by a variety of accents yelling 'Ante-up, sport', 'You lousy bum'. 'Get your thievin' hends off, cobber – my kitty' and so on. I always lost.

On 20 July we moved to a new base at RAF Sculthorpe, an isolated site a few miles from Fakenham. Entering the Nissen-hut mess that evening, we made for the bar. Standing by it was our new Station Commander, Group Captain Pickard and his grizzled Old-English sheepdog, Ming. Smoking his pipe, he nodded his acknowledgement to our 'Good evening, sir.' He watched us in silent amusement as we ordered 'Three large bitters, please.'

'Sorry, sir, bitter hasn't arrived yet.'

'Oh, well, what's it to be chaps? Scotch or gin?'

'Sorry, sir, no spirits in yet.'

'Christ, this bar matches the camp, empty and uninteresting.'

The Group Captain butted in at that stage, 'I'm afraid that we have caught the staff unawares. The Free French left here a few days ago and left us nothing but a hogshead of red biddy. We'll have to make the best of it until supplies arrive.'

'Thank you, sir,' Court answered. The mess steward then added, 'I can get you a carafe of wine very cheap.'

'How much?' we all said together.

'Two shillings.'

'Bring it on,' was the sharp cry.

With the Group Captain still watching us, we poured ourselves a glass of the 'stuff' and took a swig. The reaction from all of us was immediate and identical – 'Ugh . . . bloody hell.' It was so astringent that I spent the rest of the evening trying to untie my tongue.

'Perhaps a little sugar and warm water would help?' suggested the steward, trying to be helpful.

'Perhaps some decent British hootch would help,' replied my pilot, his face contorted like a ten-year-old prune. But we were landed with that ghastly potion which I was again to experience when catching up with the French squadron.

The Group Captain had enjoyed that lively little scene for he too had obviously suffered. What a grand chap he was. He had fought his way through red tape, which had banned him from operating again in Bomber Command (he had completed ninety-nine operations on heavies). They had given him the newly forming Mosquito Wing in order to keep him quiet. I had seen the film *Target for Tonight* in Malta and had enjoyed watching the locals bounce the energy out of their seat springs when the Wellington 'F for Freddie' flown by Pickard unleashed its load on the target below.'[77]

In early September Mike Henry was posted to 107 Squadron for the third time in the war as a gunner on Boston IIIAs.

Meanwhile, the former Ventura pilots and navigators in the three squadrons in 140 Wing got to grips with the Mosquito. Dudley Hemmings of 464 Squadron recalled:

Back on ops late in 1943 and now moved to Sculthorpe near Sandringham, we did more attacks on VI sites with varied success. In January 1944 we relocated to Hunsdon just north of London. I had a new pilot named Gerry who had already done half a tour of ops, some on Venturas. Gerry was an Englishman with a wife and child living in Gillingham. We did some Intruder patrols over German fighter aerodromes to keep them on the ground during raids by Bomber Command. We would circle a fighter aerodrome at about 2,000 ft for half an hour or as detailed and then make a low pass and bomb [all lights on the ground would be out] and head off back to base. Other Mosquitoes would then take over the patrol. On one of these trips over Juvincourt east of Paris we were caught by many searchlights and experienced the most intense flak ever. The cockpit was filled with searing brightness so Gerry put his head down, weaved, dived, corkscrewed and slung the Mosquito around. We escaped with just a few holes in the wooden fuselage.

In July 2 Group operated on eighteen days of the month, sending mainly pairs of Bostons to bomb rail targets in France. On 12 July 88 Squadron was assigned power stations at Gwent, Grand Quevilly, Langerbrugge and Yainville. 'Dinty' Moore recalled:

Johnny Reeve not being on the Battle Order, I volunteered to

Flying Officer 'Dinty' Moore (far right) with the rest of his crew in 88 Squadron: Flying Officer Freddie Deeks, observer (who was responsible for painting the *Excreta Thermo* design on the nose of their Boston), Flight Lieutenant Johnny Reeve, pilot, and Newfoundlander Sergeant Johnny Legge, air gunner. (*via Jim Moore*)

fly with Flying Officer Jack Peppiatt. We attended the briefing to find that we were detailed to attack a power station at Ghent, using cloud cover, with a number of other Bostons. We took off at 1015 hours, soon finding ourselves belting across the North Sea, skipping over the waves. The weather was not really suitable and as they came into the coast Jack Peppiatt and others had to judge how much cover there was. Peppiatt remembers that it was very much a guess as we were at sea level but clearly there was nowhere near the ⁷/₁₀ we were told to look for. In another aircraft was a friend of mine. He chose to go in and was the only one to do so. His photographs showed he had bombed a civilian target in error and he was removed from the squadron overnight.

On 23 July Johnny Reeve was back on the Battle Order. We were detailed to carry out a nine-aircraft attack from low level on a target at Alost. On this occasion we were briefed not to rely on cloud cover. We taxied out, taking off at 1040 hours, the remainder of the formation following us, as we were to lead the attack. We headed off, yet again, across the North Sea, meeting the usual enthusiastic reception as we crossed the coast. The pilots had become experts at flying low level so it was the usual exhilarating experience of madly dashing along hopping over telegraph lines and so on. Navigating at low level at the speed at which we flew was an extremely difficult task, giving the observer little time to identify landmarks. During any operation my feelings were a strange mixture of fear and excitement although on low levels there was always the exhilaration of our speed in relation to the ground. During attacks by enemy fighters there was no time for fear, as you were fully occupied in fighting back in order to survive. However, the worst moments were on Circuses when there was no sense of speed, no fighter attack but anti-aircraft shells bursting around you about which you could do nothing but pray. You felt terribly vulnerable. We were all tearing along, as the estimated time for the target to come into view arrived, when Freddy saw that we were slightly to the west of Alost. He pointed this out to Johnny, expecting him to lead the formation around to make the attack for which we had been briefed. However, Johnny in his wisdom decided not to, leading our formation back to Swanton Morley. Having risked our necks in a flight lasting two hours, we were less than pleased to land back at base still carrying our bombs. It is always easy to stand in judgement but whatever decision Johnny made, it had to be instant, so it may well be that his was the right one, for the defenders in Alost must surely have been more than ready for our arrival.

Two days later Johnny was not on the Battle Order so I volunteered to fly with Flying Officer Johnny Wilson, a New Zealander. During the briefing I suddenly had the very real premonition that this was going to be an operation from which I was not to return. It was a strange sensation. I seemed to be a spectator of all that was going an around me, having no control over the events. I automatically put on my flying gear, collected my parachute and walked out to the aircraft, climbing in and getting ready for take-off. The engines had been started and we were preparing to taxi out when a message came to say that the operation had been cancelled. It was just like waking up from a nightmare. It was as if I had been mesmerized, barely aware of what had been said in the briefing, almost as

During a Circus to the *Luftwaffe* base at Courtrai on 26 July 1943 Flying Officer Johnny Wilson's Boston from 88 Squadron was shot down by *Hauptmann* Johannes 'Hans' Naumann, *Staffelkapitan*, 11/JG26 from Lille-Nord airfield, home of 6./JG26 for his eighteenth victory. Wilson belly landed BZ399 on the airfield perimeter, as this photograph, with Naumann perched on the fuselage shows. Wilson, his observer, Pilot Officer 'Jack' McDonald, WOP/AG and squadron gunnery leader Flight Lieutenant Francis J. G. Partridge and Sergeant T. T. Terry' Hunt, a Pathe-Gazette cameraman, all scrambled out alive. *Hauptmann* Naumann scored twenty-eight victories in JG26. On 23 June 1944 his Fw 190 was badly hit by British flak during a dogfight with Mustangs of 414 Squadron RCAF and he hit both legs on the tail of his fighter when he baled out, injuring them severely. After hospitalization he transferred to II/JG6 in August 1944. (*via Eric Mombeek*)

if I was under the control of same strange force. The following day, 26 July Johnny was back on the Battle Order so another WOP/AG [the squadron gunnery leader, Flight Lieutenant Francis I. G. Partridge] took my place in Wilson's crew. At our briefing we were informed that our aircraft were to carry out a Circus attack on the *Luftwaffe* base at Courtrai.[78] We took off at 0940 hours, forming up, as had become our normal practice in two formations, setting course for our rendezvous with our fighter escort. On crossing the English coast we climbed rapidly to our normal operational height of about 12,000 ft. It was obvious on our arrival over the French coast that the Germans were determined to make life difficult for us, the flak barrage being even heavier than usual. As if this wasn't enough we were attacked by a number of determined Focke-Wulf 190 fighters, which had broken through our escort so battle was joined in earnest. Whenever the enemy fighters came within range we fired at them with some success for we WOP/AGs claimed to have damaged three of them between us. One of our aircraft was obviously in difficulties and eventually crashed, the pilot being Flying Officer Wilson. He managed to release his canopy so he and the navigator, Pilot Officer 'Jock' McDonald, Flight Lieutenant Partridge, my replacement and Sergeant T. T. 'Terry' Hunt of the RAF Film Production Unit [a Pathe-Gazette cameraman] were able to get out. We were very relieved to hear that they had survived though they had become PoWs. It would seem that my premonition had same substance. It really had been one of our more hectic operations, actually lasting for three hours, though I imagine it seemed a lot longer.

Hauptmann Johannes 'Hans' Naumann *Staffelkapitän* of II./JG26, flying an Fw 190A shot down Wilson's Boston. Naumann had fought during the Battle of Britain and was one of the pilots who had defended the German battle cruisers against Swordfish attacks on 12 February 1942. His fighters made contact with the Bostons north of Lille at 20,000 ft, immediately climbing above them until they reached the height of the escorts and reversed course. With their considerable height advantage the enemy fighters ignored the escorts and attacked the Bostons immediately. At first Naumann was unable to get a Boston in the rear vic in his sights because of his high speed but he managed to fire a short burst at Wilson's Boston in the right of the lead vic, which hit the fuselage and port engine. As he broke away Naumann saw the Boston drop out of formation. When he saw it again it was limping away on one engine towards his base at Vendeville. Wilson belly landed the ailing Boston almost in front of Naumann's own dispersal area. The German landed and examined the Boston for damage. He saw that none of the four crew was injured. Partridge was very much alive because when it became apparent that Naumann was the victorious pilot, the gunner 'protested strenuously', convinced that he had shot his attacker down! After examining Naumann's untouched Fw 190 he quietened down again. Naumann and the Boston crew continued their conversation in the command post over a cognac. They told him that they had completed their tour of thirty operations but had agreed to fly one more op after their CO had persuaded them over a bottle of whisky.

Naumann served with distinction in the home defence for the rest of the war. He claimed thirty-four victories and was awarded the Ritterkreuz. Forty-seven years after shooting the Boston down he met Wilson and McDonald and asked the New Zealander why he had not tried to reach England. Wilson replied that Naumann's attack had not only destroyed the port engine but had also damaged the controls to the starboard motor, and it would not give full power.[79]

During August 2 Group continued low-level daylight raids on targets in France. On 8 August fourteen Bostons from 107 Squadron, led by Dickie

On 8 August 1943 thirty-eight Bostons of 88, 107 and 342 Squadrons carried out a low-level raid on the naval stores depot at Rennes. The first six aircraft of 107 Squadron, led by the CO, Wing Commander Richard Geoffrey 'Dickie' England DSO DFC attacked from 50 ft and the remainder from 1,200–1,500 ft, dropping 5,800 lb of bombs. The target was well hit and the main section was set on fire. Intense flak brought down Pilot Officer W. P. Angus of 88 Squadron, and Squadron Leader Spencer of 107 Squadron was forced to crash-land at Hurn. England was KIA 22.10.43 (*RAF*)

The Denain steel and armament works under attack by twelve Bostons of 88 Squadron, led by Squadron Leader Cunningham, on 16 August 1943 (*RAF*)

England, twelve from 342 (Lorraine) Squadron and, bringing up the rear, twelve from 88 Squadron, carried out a low-level raid on the naval stores depot at Rennes. The target was well hit and the main section was set on fire. There were no fighters and later it was learned that they had been up in strength 40 miles to the rear. However, intense flak over the target area brought down Pilot Officer W. P. Angus of 88 Squadron, and Squadron Leader I. J. Spencer of 107 Squadron was forced to crash land at Hurn after receiving a shell burst on the nose of his aircraft. Pilot Officer Allison had flown so low near the target that he had left behind his pitot tube hanging on a high-tension cable and Dickie England returned with 5 yards of cable trapped in his bomb doors. He was heard later to remark that he had always wanted a towrope for his car!

On 16 August the Bostons tried a repeat of their success at Rennes, with a raid on the armament and steel works at Denain, a target not previously attacked. Dickie England again led, with thirteen Bostons, followed by twelve each from 342 (Lorraine) and 88 Squadrons. Take-off was made in the late afternoon and the Bostons flew in loose units of six abreast at low level to Pevensey Bay, where they headed across the Channel. On arrival over France they were joined by Typhoons for their escort 50 miles inland. 'Dinty' Moore wrote: 'The attack was very successful. However, the withdrawal was another matter, made worse by a multitude of flies smearing the perspex.' The first Boston to crash did so immediately after the attack and as they passed close to Douai another collided with high-tension cables and crashed in flames. By the time they reached Tournai, despite meeting their fighter escort, enemy fighters attacked them. Six Bostons were shot down on the raid, four of them from 88 Squadron. Flight Lieutenants Brinn and Arthur 'Rufus' Riseley evaded the fighters and eventually returned to England.

On 18/19 August 98 and 180 Mitchell Squadrons at Foulsham moved to Dunsfold in Surrey.[80] On the 19th 88 Squadron left Swanton Morley and flew to a new aerodrome at Hartford Bridge near Camberley. They were joined there the following day by 107 Squadron from Great Massingham and shortly after by 342 (Lorraine) Squadron to form 137 Wing, 226 Squadron making its debut using Mitchells on 17 August when an abortive attack was made on the marshalling yards at Dunkirk. No. 2 Group was now something of a 'United Nations force' with 464 RAAF and 487 RNZAF Squadrons, 320 (Dutch) Squadron (which in August moved from Attlebridge to Lasham) and 305 Polish Squadron. The Poles had suffered appalling casualties on Wellingtons and on 5 September they began to re-equip on the Mitchell II. 'Dinty' Moore remembered 342 Squadron:

> They were a lively crowd, easily identified by their navy blue uniforms. They had one fault, which was when they were airborne they would persist in using their radios to chatter to one another despite repeated warnings to comply with radio discipline. They could also boast the only female Intelligence Officer in the Air Force, the attractive Section Officer Massias. Our arrival at Hartford Bridge sparked off many rumours and a great deal of speculation, our aircraft being painted with new markings to indicate that we were part of the Allied Air Force, so we became convinced that the invasion of Europe was about to take place.
>
> The beginning of September was an opportunity for us to put into practice the time we had spent in laying down smoke screens for the Army. In this case though it was to be the Navy, which was carrying out mine-sweeping operations to within 7 miles of Boulogne, where they were threatened by batteries of heavy coastal artillery. Canisters were loaded into our bomb bay and we took off, flying low over the sea in pairs until we sighted the minesweeping flotilla, which

Douglas Boston IV (A-20J) BZ452 OA-E of 342 (Lorraine) Squadron with Lorraine motif on the forward fuselage taking off from Hartford Bridge in 1944. Note the frameless Plexiglas nose to accommodate the bomb aimer. (*IWM*)

Boston IIIAs of 88 Squadron in formation in September 1943 with 'U' nearest the camera. Behind is BZ210/A 'Excreta Thermo' piloted by Squadron Leader Johnny Reeve and behind him 'E' and 'Q'. (*IWM*)

was chugging its way towards the French coast. We flew between the ships and the coast laying down a smoke screen that was then extended by our partner. The next pair of aircraft from the squadron of course replaced the screen. It was a very satisfactory feeling to lay a smoke screen 'for real' after the number of times we had done it in practice.

On 4 September we led one of the formations of six Bostons in a Circus attack on the marshalling yards at Amiens and the next day we were part of a force of twenty-three Bostons detailed to carry out a Ramrod attack on the *Luftwaffe* base at Woensdrecht. The flak barrage was particularly heavy over the coast and the target though the *Luftwaffe* once again declined to get airborne. Despite the attentions of the anti-aircraft gunners we were able to bomb the target and return to Hartford Bridge. The climax to these combined operations, known as *Starkey*, which was obviously a rehearsal for the invasion, came on the 9th when we laid down another smoke screen for a naval flotilla 8 miles off Boulogne. Johnny was then promoted to the rank of Squadron Leader and we were posted to 107 Squadron on the other side of the aerodrome.

One of the other new arrivals in 107 Squadron was a crew composed of Flying Officer George Bernard 'Johnny' Slip, pilot, Frank Thomas, navigator and Pilot Officer John Bateman, the WOP/AG, who had 'crewed up' at 13 OTU Bicester that summer. John Bateman recalled:

We felt privileged to join the famous 107 Squadron, which was commanded by the equally famous Dickie England DFC. He was about twenty-seven years old and a born leader. It was a very happy squadron with a terrific feeling of 'esprit de corps' due principally to Dickie's superb qualities and personality and that of his two Flight Commanders, Squadron Leaders W. 'Paddy' Maher and H. G. Britten who welcomed us with great enthusiasm. Not once were we referred to or made to feel like 'new boys'.

On Sunday 3 October operations were flown against a series of transformer stations between Paris and Brittany. Every squadron in 2 Group was involved, each being allocated one in the series, which were to be attacked from low level. For the first time the Mosquitoes of 464 and 487 Squadrons at Sculthorpe took part, the latter being led by the station commander, Group Captain Percy Pickard, the former by Wing Commander H. J. Meakin. Their targets were power stations at Pont Château and Mur de Bretange and to reach them the two squadrons flew to Exeter before setting out across the Channel. Meanwhile, soon after midday Wing Commander I. J. Spencer led the Bostons of 88 Squadron off to attack the Distre transformer station while Dickie England led 107 Squadron's Bostons to another transformer station at Chaingy, on the outskirts of Orleans.

It was 'Dinty' Moore's sixty-ninth operation:

It was a beautiful sunny day as the engines of the thirty-six Bostons of the three squadrons were being warmed up prior to take-off. At 1240 hours we were airborne, forming up on Wing Commander Dickie England and setting course over the south of England, coming down as usual to nought feet as soon as we were over the sea. I felt a sense of occasion, as if we were taking part in something special, my excitement easily overcoming my fear. We made a perfect landfall, crossing the coast without opposition and speeding low across the French countryside towards Paris. Finally the outskirts of the capital city came into view with the Eiffel Tower dominant on the skyline. We had still not been challenged as we changed course for Orleans, although we saw first a Do 217 flying overhead and later a tiny Fiesler *Storch* spotter aircraft, which were both too far away for us to engage. Indeed, our camouflage was so good that I doubt if the crews of either aircraft were aware of our presence. On our arrival at the target the two leading aircraft with delayed-action fuses on the bombs remained at low level while we led the rest of the formation up to 1,500 ft as we had done on the raid on Eindhoven. Every one of the twelve aircraft dropped its bomb load and as we turned away I could see the bombs exploding, completely destroying the transformer station. During the attack there was no enemy interference from any source, which was a pleasant change. On the return journey the only target that presented itself to me was a railway goods train, peacefully plodding its way across the countryside. I fired a few rounds at it as we flashed past. As we crossed the coast on our way home the Germans opened up with some light flak, one of our aircraft being slightly damaged, the first and only aggressive act we encountered during our flight, which lasted for three hours.

This was one of those occasions which must have been the answer to a planner's dream – effective navigation, avoidance of flak concentrations and the finding and bombing of an undefended target that was destroyed, the whole operation passing without a single hiccup. It was later established that this series of attacks had caused maximum disruption to the French electrical system and the railways, which were electrified, from Paris to Brittany.[81] On this occasion one of the pilots of a Mosquito attacking another transformer station was Air Vice Marshal Embry, using his pseudonym 'Wing Commander Smith', who simply had to be involved.

If this operation had been a planner's dream, that on 22 October, by three squadrons of Bostons, was his nightmare. Pilot Officer John Bateman, WOP/AG in Flying Officer Johnny Slip's crew in 107 Squadron, whose first operation this was, explained:

On the evening of 21 October we looked at the notice board after dinner and saw that we were on the Battle Order for ops the following day. At last the moment had arrived after months and months of training and I suddenly found that I had acquired a colony of butterflies, which happily soon dispersed. As briefing was scheduled for quite early the next morning, we decided to forgo our usual after-dinner drinking and go back to our quarters, which was a small Nissen hut shared with John Brice and Dougie George. Sleep at first was elusive and we chatted on quite late into the night with much speculation as to what the target was to be but that would be revealed at the briefing. We arranged for an early call and after bathing and shaving I got dressed and filled the cigarette case that my father had given me, making sure my lighter was filled with petrol. The lighter and cigarette case filling became a routine before each op as I had a dread of not having a cigarette in the event of being shot down! We then walked over to the Mess for the traditional breakfast of bacon and eggs, then on to the briefing room in the back of an uncomfortable Bedford truck. The briefing room was a large Nissen hut with a platform at the far end, behind which was a map board nearly the whole width of the platform. The furniture consisted of hard wooden folding chairs, which would seat 130 bods. This morning it was full as the three squadrons were participating in a 'maximum effort' – 38 aircraft. As was usual, the Station Commander opened the proceedings with a 'Good Morning gentlemen' to the crews of 107, 342 (Lorraine), led by Wing Commander Henri de Rancourt and 88 led by Wing Commander (later Air Vice Marshal) I. J. Spencer. The destination was an aircraft and aero engine repair works at Courcelles in Belgium, a target of sufficient importance to warrant a maximum effort.

The briefing was then handed over to Dickie England, who was to lead the op. He described the target and surrounding pin-points in some detail; the route chosen would take us away from known flak positions and near Kolijnsplatt on the island of Walcheren off the Dutch coast and at some point we would turn south for Courcelles. Our bomb load was 250 lb HE with eleven-second delay fuses that would give us adequate time to clear the target. We would fly six abreast with approximately twenty seconds between flights and on the approach to the target we would fly in as tight a formation as possible. After bombing we would head for Knocke-sur-Mer on the Belgian coast and *en route* would be met by a Typhoon fighter escort. Under no conditions were bombs to be dropped other than on the target. If it was not located they were to be brought home or ditched in the sea if individual captains thought this action necessary for any reason. Dickie England was a highly professional officer who carried out the briefing in a quiet and authoritative voice, all the while pointing to the map and occasionally indicating possible hazards. After he had finished the Met Officer gave his forecast of the wind, cloud and weather conditions we were likely to encounter. Dickie then detailed off the pilots to their individual briefing, the navigators to theirs and the gunners to theirs, then wished us all 'Good Hunting'.

At the aircraft I climbed into the gunner's cockpit. I closed the hatch that formed the centre part of the floor and stowed my 'chute in the rack on the starboard side together with a spare packet of Martins cigarettes; as a non-smoker Frank always carried a bar of chocolate and a can of orange juice. I then set the radio transmitter to the allocated frequency and what a super little radio it was compared with the antediluvian 1083/1084 on the Blenheim. As I had synchronized my guns only the day before I knew that they were OK, as were the ammo belts to each gun. Meanwhile Johnny was walking round the aircraft with the rigger, visually checking all the moving surfaces and making sure that the pitot head cover had been removed. By this time Frank had settled himself at his little table with the maps, instruments and the rest of the paraphernalia that all navigators seemed to carry, which was a complete mystery to me. Eventually Johnny climbed up on to the port wing on his way to the cockpit, just pausing for a few seconds to have a quick word with me and we wished each other good luck. I put on my helmet with the mike hanging loose to one side and plugged into the intercom socket. After a while, 'Pilot to navigator – do you hear me?'

Frank's reply: 'Navigator to pilot, I hear you OK.'

Then, 'Pilot to gunner. Do you hear me?'

'Gunner to pilot. Hear you OK.'

Johnny then signalled to the fitter on the trolley-acc raising his left hand and started the port engine, similarly with the starboard engine, then ran them up gently. In a few minutes Dickie England moved away from his dispersal towards the perimeter track, followed by the rest of 'A' Flight, then 'B' Flight. Take-off time was scheduled at 1345 and at the precise moment the first two Bostons took off in echelon. Dickie led the procession in 'A-Apple', which beneath the cockpit had the inscription 'ENGLAND EXPECTS', followed by Flying Officer John Brice, Flight Sergeant Teddy Hoeg, Flight Lieutenant R. C. McCullough, ourselves and Flight Lieutenant H. G. 'Brit' Brittain. These six aircraft comprised 'A' Flight of 107, plus six more, who were to lead the operation. The remaining aircraft took off in pairs, the last two taking off at 1349. When all aircraft were airborne and at about 1,000 ft, they formed up into six flights of six aircraft abreast with about 150 yards separating each flight.

Our three ground crew – fitter, armourer and rigger – stood at the edge of the dispersal point and waved the 'thumbs up' sign. Like all ground crews, they were the backbone of all aircrews, who without their expertise would have been absolutely useless. They worked all hours and in all weathers and very rarely grumbled and on the odd occasions they did we fully sympathized with them. The 'Chiefy' was an older man with years of service and was always helpful and encouraging to his lads. One evening each week we would take them to the local pub at Yateley. I think they appreciated our gesture and we certainly appreciated their interest and what one could almost call devotion to what they considered *their* aircraft.

Having reached the runway the two leading aircraft formed up in echelon, then the next pair, then us. With the brakes full on the engines were run up and at the 'green' from Flying Control the first pair rolled down the runway followed by the rest of us, until all thirty-six aircraft were airborne. When we had gained sufficient height we formed up in a line abreast and circled the airfield until all three squadrons were formed up at about 1,000 ft, then set course for Orfordness where we were to cross the coast. When we were somewhere near Stowmarket, 'Gunner to pilot, Brit's broken off and heading for home – must have a problem.' Brit had aborted with what we found later to be an engine malfunction (he was replaced by Warrant Officer T. V. Glynn).

After a while, 'Pilot to navigator, coast coming up. Are we on course?'

As we passed over Orford Ness, 'Navigator to pilot - on course.'

We were always formal in our communications with one another over the intercom, which was really a matter of discipline and eliminated idle nattering – very rarely did we use Christian names.

We had descended a bit and crossed the coast at something under 500 ft. 'Pilot to gunner. Test guns.'

'Gunner to pilot. Testing.'

I swung the guns over the side and fired a short burst. 'Gunner to pilot – guns OK.'

At this time we were flying at about 50 ft above the water on a beautiful, clear autumn day that made it so much easier to scan the skies for possible bandits – no cloud cover for them. 'This is a piece of cake,' I thought. 'Just like an exercise.'

'Navigator to pilot - we appear to be about five degrees off course.'

'Pilot to navigator. Check again.'

Two minutes later, 'Navigator to pilot - confirm, five degrees off planned course.'

'Pilot to navigator, either Dickie has changed the plan or you have boobed. In any case, we follow the leader.'

As strict W/T silence was to be observed, as we had been told at briefing, it wasn't broken now but if we had really been off course we felt that a more senior crew would have broken silence, so we assumed we were OK.

'Pilot to navigator. Enemy coast ahead.'

'Navigator to pilot. OK but I'm convinced we are still off course, miles off course.'

'Pilot to gunner. Keep you eyes skinned. It's possible we're making a duff landfall.'

Within a minute we were over the Dutch coast flying over flat silt land when all hell was suddenly let loose. 'Without warning the whole flak battery must have opened up and the sky around us was full of flak bursts. They had got our altitude absolutely spot on. It was just like going through a wall and how we escaped must remain one of life's mysteries.

As Brit had gone home we were on the right of our flight and as the flak continued to come up I saw the four aircraft on our left take the full punishment. Dickie's plane took a direct hit in the starboard engine, which fell from the nacelle and rolled along the ground like a gigantic ball of fire. His aircraft pitched sideways, cartwheeling into the ground at 280 mph. The other three must have been hit almost instantaneously and all hit the ground in a complete shambles of fire, smoke and scattered pieces of metal. I couldn't see exactly where the flak was coming from and just fired my guns in the general direction without taking any sort of aim. Johnny had his finger on the button and exhausted nearly all his ammo. What seemed like an eternity probably lasted only a couple of minutes or so, then we were out of range. I could see the following aircraft getting a fairish dose but they were jinking all over the sky and not flying straight into the stuff as we had done. I saw only two of them go down. This was my first trip and it was the only time in all my operational experience that I had seen such a large formation broken up so completely.

Eventually, 'Pilot to navigator, any idea where we are?'

'Navigator to pilot, not a clue. Climb up a bit and I might be able to recognize something.'

'Pilot to navigator. Climbing up to 1,500 ft.'

But after a few moments Frank had to admit that he was unable to recognize anything and was quite lost. 'We could be anywhere,' he said. Johnny throttled back a bit and rocked the aircraft to indicate to anyone following that they should take the lead. Another plane came up alongside and we formated on him but it soon became evident that he was equally as lost as we were. Eventually some sort of leadership evolved and we pressed on towards Courcelles.

Now that the excitement was over I had a moment to take stock and to my astonishment found that I was almost ankle deep in empty cartridge cases, which I kicked away towards the tail of the aircraft. Although I was standing in an open cockpit I was quite amazed to find that 'I' was overheating, so I took off my battledress top and peeled off two pullovers before putting the top back on again. I would like to have thought that I was sweating through exertion but the awful feeling came to my mind that it must be fear, although throughout that short encounter I had been too busy to have had any thoughts about personal safety.

By this time we had got down on the deck again and I was keeping a sharp lookout for bandits, as the Hun flak boys must have radioed our course to the *Luftwaffe*. However, we pressed on weaving this way and that and eventually settled a course that Frank told us was in the direction of Courcelles. However, for one reason or another we failed to pinpoint the target and turned for home, meeting some more or less accurate flak.

Thirty miles off the coast, 'Navigator to pilot – unidentified fighters ahead and above.'

I craned my neck round as far as I could to see forward and about 1,000 ft above us was the welcome sight of our Typhoon escort. They turned and, still flying above and behind escorted us out of the coast. We were going home! Our chums kept a steady course with us and I then knew that there were no snappers about and could relax a little. As we crossed the water I could smell cigarette smoke, which could only have come from Johnny's cockpit, so I lit one, then another and another.

When we landed three hours and twenty minutes later and taxied to our dispersal, there was our faithful ground crew waiting for us and when we told them of our experiences their expressions had to be seen to be believed. But they just got on with their jobs in silence, which was unusual and when Frank opened the bomb doors they pushed the empty bomb trolleys under the fuselage to unload the bombs that should have been left behind at Courcelles.

Debriefing was a solemn affair. Several of the crews confirmed that they were five degrees off our planned course as we crossed the Dutch coast and we wondered why the more experienced crews had not broken W/T silence to query the change of course. I don't remember Frank expressing any satisfaction at being proved correct. It was later concluded that this disastrous navigational error could only be attributed to the fact that Dickie's compass was showing an error, though it had been swung only a day or two before by his navigator, Flying Officer P. Anderson. The crews of Flying Officer Brice, Flying Officer R. C. McCullough and Flight Sergeant Teddy Hoeg were the others lost. (Hoeg's commission had been promulgated that day.) Flying Officer Stolloff and Flight Sergeant Chappell and their crews in 342 (Lorraine) and 88 Squadrons respectively were also lost. Wing Commander England's award of the DSO was announced on the day after his death in the *London Gazette*.

Air Vice Marshal Basil Embry, a former commander of 107 Squadron, wrote of England, 'He was a great leader who commanded universal respect and admiration', a sentiment echoed by everyone who was privileged to have served with him.

Thus ended our first operation.

CHAPTER EIGHT

Hitting Back

Ii le fallait – *'It had to be done'*

On 5 November 1943 twenty-four Bostons of 88 Squadron (under a new squadron commander, Wing Commander Mike Pollard, a Canadian) and 107 Squadron, twenty-four Mitchells of 98 and 180 Squadrons, fourteen Mitchells of 226 with four of 305 and six of 320 squadrons, were scheduled to attack a secret German weapons site at Mimoycques. However, the proposed Circus attack was cancelled in the morning because of bad weather and another attempt in mid-afternoon only got as far as Guildford before Wing Commander Spencer decided that conditions were too bad and turned the formation round to return home. The operation finally went ahead on 8 November and follow-up Ramrod attacks were made on the 9th and 25th, while Typhoons of 2 Group hit a back-up site at Audignhen.

No. 320 (Dutch) Squadron crew members at Lasham in October 1943. Left to right: B. de Haan; C. J. den Tex-Bondt (KIA 20.6.44); A. Hamelink (KIA 29.11.44); Commander E. Bakker; Loeff; R. W. H. van Pelt; Breedveld. Bakker and van Pelt were KIA on 25 October 1943 when twenty-four Mitchells of 98 and 320 Squadrons bombed Brest-Lanvioc Poulmic airfield through heavy flak on the bomb run. Two 320 Squadron Mitchells were shot down and two more crash landed at Portreath and Exeter. Loeff's Mitchell was twice badly damaged by flak on a raid on shipping at Cherbourg on 28 October 1943 but he managed to fly the crippled aircraft home on one engine and crash-land at Tarrant Rushton. (*Jan P. Kloos*)

A few days after the 5 November abort Johnny Reeve's crew was greatly surprised to hear that they had been 'screened' and were sent on rest. 'Dinty' Moore recalled:

My feelings were completely different from those I had experienced at the end of my extended first tour. I had only taken part in eighteen operational sorties and we had been involved in so much training in preparation for the invasion that the news came as a sort of anti-climax.

John Bateman also found himself on the move.

After a further sixteen or so ops with 107 (motto '*Nous y serons*' – 'We shall be there'), some of them 'fairly hairy', I was posted to 98 Squadron (motto 'Never failing') at Dunsfold near Guildford. The CO of 98 was Wing Commander R. K. F. Bell-Irving, known to everyone as 'B.I.'. After a bit of a party the night before, Johnny [Slip] insisted on flying me to my new airfield.' [Slip stayed with 107 on conversion to Mosquitoes and was eventually posted to India, when he joined 84 Squadron. In December 1945, when the squadron was detached to help out the Dutch who were having trouble with the Indonesians, he was killed in Java.]

During January and February 1944 the Mitchells of 226 Squadron were used to make bombing strikes on flying-bomb sites in the Pas de Calais. On 1 February 107 Squadron moved to Lasham near Alton in Hampshire and re-equipped with the Mosquito VI. On the 14th 226 Squadron's Bostons flew from Swanton Morley for the last time, when they took off for Hartford Bridge to train for their role in the forthcoming invasion of France. The 2nd TAF would be tasked to destroy tactical rather than strategic targets as and when D-Day arrived, so to be near the invasion front, all squadrons were moved further south. On 15 October 1943 138 Wing at Lasham had begun conversion to Mosquito FBVIs when 613 'City of Manchester' Squadron traded in its Mustangs. The squadron flew its first Mosquito operation on 31 December 1943, an attack on a V1 site in northern France. No. 305 (*Ziemia*

Mosquito FBVI LR366 of 613 'City of Manchester' Squadron in 138 Wing, 2 Group, refuelling at RAF Swanton Morley, Norfolk, early in 1944 during night interdictor training at the 2 GSU base. No. 613 Squadron flew their first Mosquito operation on 31 December 1943, an attack on a V1 site in northern France. In 1944–45, as part of 2nd TAF, the squadron flew mainly night tactical operations against targets in France, as well as daylight precision raids on high security Nazi targets, the most notable of these being the attack on the *Gestapo* HQ at The Hague in April 1944 and the SS barracks at Egletons in August. The Squadron moved to Hartford Bridge in October and in November they moved again, to Cambrai-Epinoy, France, to harass German units. LR366 joined 107 Squadron and failed to return from the Arnhem operation on 17 September 1944 when the Mosquitoes of 138 Wing, 2nd TAF, bombed German barracks as part of Operation Market Garden. (*via Philip Birtles*)

Mosquito FBVIs of 464 Squadron at Thorney Island in mid-1944 (*A Thomas via S. Howe*)

Wielkopolska) Squadron converted to the Mitchell and on 18 November 1943 transferred from Swanton Morley to Lasham, joining 107 and 613 Squadrons to become part of 138 Wing. (In December 305 Squadron converted to Mosquito FBVIs after just five operations with Mitchells). It will be remembered that 88 and 342 (Lorraine) Boston Squadrons and 226 Mitchell Squadron in 137 Wing were at Hartford Bridge with 139 Wing, comprising 98, 180 and 320 Mitchell Squadrons, at Dunsfold. On 31 December 1943 21, 464 and 487 Squadrons of 140 Wing took off from Sculthorpe for the last time, bombed Le Ploy, France, then landed at their new base at Hunsdon. Early in 1944 2 Group HQ left Bylaugh Hall in Norfolk for Mongewell Park in Berkshire. Meanwhile, targets were nominally the V1 sites in the Pas de Calais. On 8 February nine Mitchells attacked targets at Pois de la Justice. Thirty miles inside France, Warrant Officer Storey's Mitchell took a flak hit in the port engine but he was able to recross the Channel and make an emergency landing at West Malling.

On 15 February George Murray and Harry Batt, Gordon Bell-Irving[82] and Bert Hott, and Flight Lieutenant J. L. 'Les' Bulmer, navigator, and his pilot Flight

Flight Lieutenant 'Les' Bulmer (back row, third from left) and his pilot, Flight Lieutenant Ed McQuarrie RCAF (front row, third from left), pictured at No. 3 Mosquito Course, 36 OTU, Greenwood, Nova Scotia, in 1943. Together with Flying Officer Harry Batt RCAF (back row far left), Flight Lieutenant George Murray DFC (front row far left) they joined 21 Squadron, 140 Wing, at Hunsdon on 15 February 1944. Pilot Officer Humblestone (back row 2nd from left) and Flight Lieutenant Evans RCAF (front row 2nd from left) survived one tour and Evans returned to Canada but Humblestone went missing on the first operation of his second tour with another pilot. Flying Officer Wakeman, an American who joined the RCAF before the USA came into the war (front row third from right) and Pilot Officer Holmes (behind him) joined 464 Squadron and were killed when they crashed into the Thames on take-off from Gravesend. Flying Officer Hole (front row second from right) and Sergeant West (behind him) were killed on a Gee-H course at Swanton Morley when the aircraft exploded in mid-air. Flying Officer Reeves (front row right) and Pilot Officer Prout (behind him) were posted to the Far East and were KIA. (*Les Bulmer*)

Lieutenant Ed McQuarrie RCAF joined 21 Squadron, 140 Wing at Hunsdon. This was a surprise to them for having completed the Night Intruder course at 60 OTU High Ercall they expected to join one of the three Intruder squadrons, 418, 605 (both in the UK) or 23 in Malta. Les Bulmer remembered the move.

When we joined 21 Squadron's principal occupation was attacking V1 (Noball) sites at low level. We had no experience of low-level navigation so we spent all of February practising low-level cross-country and formation flying. On 18 February we watched all three squadrons of the wing take off in a snowstorm for what we later discovered was the Amiens prison raid. The only time I saw the 140 Wing CO, Group Captain Charles Pickard, was in the mess the night before the raid. The whole squadron was sworn to secrecy when we heard he was missing in case he had got away but it was not long before we received news that he was dead.

Operation *Jericho*, as the raid was codenamed, went ahead after the French resistance informed London that over 100 loyal Frenchmen were being held in the jail, which was built in the shape of a cross and surrounded by a wall 20 ft high and 3 ft thick. Several attempts had been made by the Resistance to rescue them but had failed and they requested an urgent air strike to break open the prison walls. A dozen prisoners were due to be executed on 19 February. The prison wall was breached using eleven-second delay bombs dropped by five FBVIs of 464 RAAF led by Wing Commander R. W. 'Bob' Iredale and six of 487 RNZAF Squadron led by Wing Commander Irving S. 'Black' Smith. However, two Mosquitoes, including one flown by Group Captain Percy C. Pickard DSO DFC, the CO, and his navigator, Flight Lieutenant J. A. 'Peter' Broadley DSO DFC DFM, were lost. Group Captain Peter Wykeham-Barnes DSO DFC* became the new 140 Wing commander.[83]

Flight Lieutenants Les Bulmer and Ed McQuarrie RCAF flew their first 21 Squadron operation, a Night Intruder, to the airfield at Montdidier on 2 March.

Although we were new boys, because we'd been trained as Night Intruders we had more night-flying experience on Mosquitoes than the old hands. We took off at 1955 and returned at 2155. It was uneventful. I was not sure what to expect as we crossed the French coast but I rather imagined it would be flak and searchlight all the way in and all the way out. Instead there was just total darkness, with the odd glimmer of a light and nobody seemed to be interested in us at all – or was a night-fighter creeping up on us? I kept constant lookout rearwards. The night was very dark and Gee was jammed once we crossed the coast, so navigation had to be by dead reckoning.

We were somewhere in the area but could not locate the airfield and the Germans would not co-operate and put on the lights for us, so we returned home somewhat disappointed.

2 Group Mosquitoes tried various techniques in attacking *Noball* sites. The normal method was to go low level all the way but this had resulted in aircraft sustaining damage by 20 mm flak when crossing the coast. On 4 March we were one of four aircraft to attack two sites. Our target was near Esclavelles and we took off at 0810. Noball targets were far too small to get four aircraft over them within eleven seconds, which was the delay we had on the 500 lb bombs. The squadron CO, Wing Commander 'Daddy' Dale, led with 'A' Flight Commander Squadron Leader Joe Bodien as his No. 2. As a 'sprog' crew we were to stick with Flight Lieutenant Mike Benn, who was one of the squadron's most experienced pilots.[84]

We crossed the Channel at low level and climbed as we reached the coast to about 3,000 ft to avoid the flak. There we split into pairs for our respective targets and got down on the deck. Not long afterwards I noticed a red glow on the edge of a wood on the starboard side. This became several red balls that travelled rapidly towards us. It was then that I realized what flak looked like from the wrong end. The stream of 20 mm appeared to be heading along the wing and into the cockpit, so Mac and I instinctively ducked. Luckily it passed overhead and we went thankfully on our way.

At briefing we had arranged to fly beyond the target, turn and attack on the way out. We arrived at the turning point but nothing happened. There was strict radio silence so we couldn't ask Mike and his navigator, Flying Officer W. A. Roe what they were doing. We just had to stick with them and hope that they knew where they were. Eventually they did start to turn and all hell broke loose. In fact, Roe had missed the turning point and when he did eventually start to turn he led us into a real hornet's nest. Everything happened so fast but we suddenly found ourselves in a valley with a railway in the bottom and rows of huts up the valley sides. I don't know what the area was but they obviously objected to our presence and the sky erupted in 20 mm flak from all directions. Mike Benn started to climb out of harm's way and we followed behind but were surrounded by streams of tracer and we had an uncomfortable few seconds when flak intended for Mike was crossing in front of our nose, while that for us was crossing just behind the tail. Mac said, Sod this, I'm going down and shoved the stick forward. As he did so there was a loud bang. I checked to see if we were on fire or losing fuel but everything was normal.

By this time we had lost sight of Mike Benn and were somewhere south-east of the target. If we tried to make the target on our own we might arrive just as his bombs were due to explode, so we headed for a secondary target in a wood. We duly dropped our four 500-pounders on a hut in the wood and fled at high speed towards the coast. We flew low over a large chateau outside which German troops were milling around, then I told Ed to climb before we hit the coast. Unfortunately I left it too late and we were on top of the coast as we started to climb. Up came the flak, hosing around us and down went the nose as we sped out to sea, weaving like mad and followed by the now all too familiar tracer. Soon we were clear and heading for home, somewhat relieved to find ourselves still in one piece.

When we got back to Hunsdon we found that a 20 mm shell had come up underneath us from the port and entered the starboard nacelle. It blew a large hole in the inboard side of the nacelle and a smaller one in the outboard side. Shell splinters had knocked chunks out of the starboard flap and out of the fuselage side just about where I was sitting. I was thankful that a Mosquito had a thick skin; if it had been metal I would probably have had a sore bum. The shell struck in the only part of the nacelle where it couldn't do any damage – in the rear fairing. Any further forward and it would have smashed the undercarriage.

For another *Noball*, on 7 March, to near Les Essarts, our leader was Flight Lieutenant Duncan A. 'Buck' Taylor, with Squadron Leader Philippe Livry-Level as his navigator.[85] We decided to stay high after crossing the coast, identify the target, dive on it, then climb back up to 3,000-4,000 ft until clear of the coast on the way back. There was a flak position on the right of our approach to the target, so we arranged that we would both fire our cannons as we dived, hoping that this would make them keep their heads down until we were clear. Everything went according to plan and we arrived over the target and went into a steep dive, both of us firing cannons on the way down. There was no problem from the flak position but as we pulled out of the dive and released the bombs a burst of 20 mm shot up vertically in front of us. Buck was clear but we had no choice but to fly through it. As we climbed away I looked back to see the whole site erupt as 4,000 lb of high explosive went off. I must say that I've always had a grudging admiration for the guy who shot at us. To be blasted with eight cannons and yet have the nerve to jump up and let fly at us, presumably aware that he was about to get eight 500 lb bombs around his ear holes took some courage.

Flight Lieutenant D. A. 'Buck' Taylor and Squadron leader Philippe Livry-Level. One of the great RAF navigators in the Second World War, after fighting in the French 61st Regiment of Artillery in the First and at the beginning of the Second Livry-Level DSO DFC* CdG * DFC (USA) did at least four tours of operational flying in Coastal Command, on special duties and in 2 Group Mosquitoes. He could not be persuaded to have a break from operational flying. On 31 August 1944 'Buck' Taylor and his navigator, Flight Lieutenant Johnson were shot down on a Night Intruder to Strasbourg-Sarreborg when they attacked a train. Flak set fire to their port engine and the wing collapsed. They baled out and evaded capture, returning to England on 29 September 1944. Taylor rejoined 21 Squadron on 28 October after a spell in the RAF Hospital, Swindon. By January 1945 Squadron Leader Taylor DFC* Ld H CdG MiD had flown a total of forty-eight low level day and night bombing sorties. (*Les Bulmer via Colin Waugh Collection*)

Ed said, 'Check around. I think we've been hit.'

There was so much racket from the cannons as we dived that I hadn't heard any bang but I checked for fire and loss of fuel. The fuel gauges were reading normal, so we joined up with Buck for the return trip. We climbed to 4,000 ft and stayed there until clear of the coast, then dropped down to sea level over the Channel. Soon after we were clear of the French coast Buck's aircraft fired off a Very cartridge and he was obviously in trouble. I checked the list of the colours of the day but the one he'd used wasn't on it. We were puzzled and expected him to ditch at any moment but nothing happened. I tackled Philippe at debriefing and he explained that he had to have a smoke – he used a long cigarette holder – and since the designers of the Mosquito had forgotten to include an ashtray in the specification, he was forced to improvise. An empty Verey cartridge case would fill his requirements, so he emptied one! Smoking in or near an aircraft was strictly forbidden but Philippe was a law unto himself.

Ed had been right in thinking that we'd been hit – a 20 mm shell had exploded in the port spinner. It appeared that bits of it had gone rearwards through the engine, because the bottom cowling had a number of carbuncles that weren't there when we started. And yet the engine and propeller pitch mechanism had functioned perfectly, which gave me a great deal of confidence in the Merlin. I was beginning to think that if these sort of trips were the norm then sooner of later a shell would find a vital spot and our chances of completing a tour of ops looked none too promising. In the event these were the only times that we sustained damage although they weren't the only times the enemy took a dislike to us and let fly.

Our next two ops were also against V1 sites but employed a very different technique. Six aircraft, in two vics of three, joined up with two Pathfinder Mosquitoes fitted with Oboe, at the coast. We followed the lead Oboe aircraft up to 20,000 ft while the second Oboe aircraft tagged along behind in case of equipment failure in the lead aircraft. We had an escort of six Spits, which was some comfort. The idea was that we would maintain close formation on the Oboe aircraft. His four bombs were set to drop in a stick and the boffins had calculated that, by the time the third bomb appeared out of the bomb bay, we would have woken up and released our bombs also. So the leader's third bomb was supposed to be on target, with the first two undershooting and the last one overshooting. The only snag with this system was that Oboe required that we fly in tight formation, straight and level for ten minutes until bomb release. This was not exactly amusing, since the Germans were somewhat hostile and slung a lot of heavy flak at us as we approached the target east of Abbeville. It was a long ten minutes, sitting there at 20,000 ft, having to take everything that was thrown at us and not being able to take avoiding action. You just prayed that your name was not on any of the bits of metal that were being flung into the sky. The Spits, wisely, kept well clear of the formation at this time, as did the stand-in Oboe aircraft, who only closed in tight at the last minute.

With bombs gone we turned for home. From that height Dungeness looked so close. The rest of the formation had adopted a 'last man home's a sissy' attitude and were hell bent for the English coast. With wartime camouflage it was difficult to see an aircraft from above; it merged very effectively with the ground below. So suddenly Ed and I found ourselves all alone in the sky and, reckoning that we'd outstayed our welcome, stuck the nose down and went, hell for leather for Dungeness and safety. We were travelling so fast that even with the throttles right back and the undercarriage warning horn blowing continuously the ASI [air speed indicator] was indicating well over 300 m.p.h. And I was wondering at what speed the wings came off. Part way across the Channel we caught up with another Mosquito and tried to maintain some form of decorum by flying in formation with him. One of the Spit escort managed to catch us up in mid-Channel and stayed with us until we crossed the Kent coast when he did a victory roll and headed for his base, wherever that was. At debriefing the flight leader, Squadron Leader Ritchie issued a rocket. He said we'd behaved like naughty schoolboys who'd been breaking windows and then run away. I don't think we cared that much, as long as we'd broken the right windows. Sadly, we hadn't. The much-vaunted Oboe had caused us to drop our bombs several miles, I believe, from the target. So, as a penance for our sins, we had to go out next day and do it all over again and this time we did all come back together. For the rest of March and the first half of April our ops were all Night Intruders on airfields in Holland and France. We never spotted any aircraft but

Sergeant H. J. 'Appie' Otten, pilot; Jan P. Kloos, observer-bomb aimer; Wally Baumann, gunner, and Sergeant J. J. C. 'Jack' Lub, gunner of 320 Squadron. On 18 March 1944 after ditching in the sea following a raid on Gorenflos, Sergeant Jan Ot, Lub, Sergeant H. F. Gans and Corporal F. I. Posthumus were rescued by a Sea Otter, which taxied all the way across the Channel when it could not take off! Posthumus was KIA on 8 June 1944, but the others survived the war. Jack Lub, for instance, flew twenty-six operations on Hudsons and seventy-five more on Mitchells. (*Jan P. Kloos*)

we did bomb and strafe the runways and dispersals. At Evreux the Germans were most co-operative and switched the lights on for us. We made what we thought was a bombing attack – that is, until we got back to base and I got out to find a dark object hanging under each wing, which shouldn't have been there. Ed had forgotten to select the bombs.

The last raid on Hengelo by twelve Mosquitoes of 140 Wing, 2nd TAF took place on 18 March 1944. Although the Stork works were no longer on the target list there was still the important target of Hazemeyer. The low-level raid was led by Wing Commander R. W. 'Bob' Iredale DFC and involved four aircraft from each of 487 Squadron RNZAF, 464 Squadron RAAF and 21 Squadron RAF at Hunsdon. A Mosquito of 487 Squadron aborted its sortie 5 miles south-west of Lowestoft after an engine failure while another hit a tree when it took evasive action to avoid hitting another Mosquito. Three remaining aircrews bombed the target at 16.36 hours and very good results were claimed. The whole area was seen to have numerous fires. No. 464 Squadron bombed a minute ahead of 21 Squadron and crews succeeded in hitting the central part of the main building and setting it on fire. Fifteen-year-old Henk F. van Baaren was among those who took shelter in the cellar at the family shop in Hengelo. He recalled.

Some bombs fell in the town centre, one killing a German officer in the street. A couple of houses were damaged and two civilians were reported as having been killed. After the raid I saw two girls running away from the bombed centre area of the town. There was blood all over their faces and dresses but later I heard that they had been in a grocer's shop when the blast of the exploding bombs had blown debris from tomato juice and jam containers over them! Later when my father and I were talking together on the pavement in front of his shop window, there was a loud bang followed by the sound of broken glass. At that moment an ammunition train near the railway station exploded and the force of the huge blast blew out our shop window scattering glass all over us. Buildings in a large area around the station, including much of the main shopping centre, the main offices of the Stork Works and other factories nearby had all their windows shattered. Two German guards were killed and a number of soldiers were injured. The German AA gunners, having been in action on the roof couldn't leave their positions after the bombing as numerous fires surrounded them. The German fire brigade arrived to rescue them but when they connected the hoses to the fire hydrant they couldn't get any water. They were rather irate and angry and accused the local firemen who were called in from other factories nearby of sabotaging the supply! Peace was eventually restored between the two parties and the AA crews were rescued. The fire brigade report reads: 48 250 kg HE TD 11 bombs dropped of which forty were on target; twelve bombs hit the factory interior at 1636 hours after which the factory clocks stopped! It took until 3 a.m. to extinguish the last of the fires in the factory.[86]

464 Squadron had also bombed the primary target but the Mosquito flown by Squadron Leader W. R. G. 'Dick' Sugden and Flying Officer A. H. 'Bunny' Bridger was hit by flak in the starboard engine, which caught fire. The Australian crew crash landed in Albergen not far from the target area and were slightly injured. Luckily

Dutch farmers living nearby helped them out of the aircraft but they were disturbed to discover that there were still bombs on board. Some Germans, who quickly arrived on the scene, took Sugden and Bridger prisoner. They were taken to hospital for a check-up and three weeks later Sugden was sent by train to Amsterdam and from there with a group of American aircrew to Frankfurt. He ended up in *Stalag Luft I*, Barth, where he was reunited later with 'Bunny' and with his former commander, Squadron Leader Ian McRitchie DFC, who had been shot down on the Amiens prison raid in February which Sugden and Bridger had also flown. The Russians liberated all three airmen on 1 May 1945.

Moves were now afoot to prepare 2nd TAF squadrons for operations from French airfields, which, it was anticipated, would be largely derelict following a retreat by the *Luftwaffe* and the German army if the invasion went as planned. Pilot Officer John Bateman, a WOP/AG of 107 Squadron recalled:

In accordance with our role in support of the ground forces, we were supposed to be a mobile force capable of moving from airfield to airfield at a moment's notice. And when we moved out of the comparative comfort of our sleeping quarters at Stovolds Farm and into tents erected in a rise just beyond the perimeter of the airfield it was a bit of a shock to the system. But we soon adjusted and settled into our new way of life. We were fortunate in retaining the use of the mess and all the other amenities previously available. We also gained a slight financial advantage in that we were paid a 'hard living' allowance of a few bob a day. But in gaining this we lost the services of our batmen and batwomen who had previously made our beds, cleaned our shoes and buttons and provided us with early morning tea!

Fellow WOP/AG in107 Squadron, Mike Henry DFC, added:[87]

When we lived under canvas at Hartford Bridge Stan Adams [the navigator] and I shared a tent. The tent site, which had a large marquee for our messing, was a long walk across many muddy fields from the main camp. It was good fun in a novel way but it had its drawbacks. For one thing I ruined one of my best suitcases which had soaked up the moisture through the coconut matting on the grass floor of our tent. However, it wasn't for long and there was a good reason for preparing us in the event of a dire lack of accommodation when we moved across the Channel. As it happened we never saw a tent when moving to France.

Apart from the three Boston squadrons at Hartford Bridge, we had two Dutch squadrons using the airfield for a short time – 322 with Spitfires and 320 with Mitchells. Their crews were dressed in the uniform of the Royal Netherlands Navy. When we found out how much they were paid, we gasped. Apart from their set pay scale, which was higher than ours, they received extra money for every flying hour. We didn't see a lot of the Dutch chaps for they messed elsewhere but we often saw in our mess Queen Wilhelmina and Prince Bernhard.[87]

More discomfort followed in March and April. To simulate the type of tactical targets against which 2 Group would be employed in the run-up to D-Day, Boston, Mitchell and Mosquito crews arrived at 2 Group Support Unit (GSU) at Swanton Morley to take part in two-week training exercises in full field conditions. All crews

General Dwight D. Eisenhower, Supreme Allied Commander, flanked by Air Chief Marshal Sir Trafford Leigh-Mallory and Group Captain Larry Dunlap RCAF station commander, with Wing Commander Alan Lynn and AVM Basil Embry behind, during a visit to Dunsfold on 18 April 1944. (*via John Bateman*)

lived under canvas and life was distinctly uncomfortable, while night interdictor training (bombing and strafing the enemy's communications by night), bombing of illuminated targets and convoys and runs on a 'spoof' V1 rocket site and a four-gun flak battery installation were carried out.

During their sojourn at Swanton, on 11 April six FBVIs of 613 Squadron led by Wing Commander R. N. 'Bob' Bateson DFC attacked and completely destroyed the Huize Kleykamp a five-storey, 95 ft high white building on Carnegie Square in The Hague, which contained *Gestapo* records. An Air Ministry bulletin later described the raid as 'probably the most brilliant feat of low-level precision bombing of the war'. For his leadership of this operation Bateson was awarded the DSO and he received the Dutch Flying Cross from Prince Bernhard of the Netherlands. More pinpoint raids followed. On Bastille Day, 14 July 1944 a German barracks at Bonneuil Matours in the north-east part of Forét de Mouliere was attacked by eighteen Mosquitoes of 140 Wing led by Group Captain Peter Wykeham-Barnes DSO DFC*. Their target was a group of six buildings inside a rectangle just 170 ft by 100 ft, close to the village, which had to be avoided. The Mosquitoes dropped nine tons of bombs in shallow dives on the target. On 18 August fifteen FBVIs of 613 Squadron led by Squadron Leader Charles Newman carried out a daring low-level daylight attack on a school building at Egletons, 50 miles south-east of

General Eisenhower addressing 320 (Dutch) Squadron personnel in a hangar at Dunsfold on 18 April 1944. (*via John Bateman*)

Limoges, which it was believed was being used as an SS barracks. Fourteen of the Mosquitoes scored at least twenty direct hits to destroy the target.[88]

The main work for 138 and 140 Wings was *Day* and *Night Ranger* operations and Intruder sorties from England. On 12 April Flight Lieutenant J. L. 'Les' Bulmer and Flight Lieutenant Ed McQuarrie of 21 Squadron were intruding over the airfield at St Dizier when a searchlight was turned on them. Said Les Bulmer:

We took exception to that, so we flew right down the beam, firing our cannons as we went. That soon put it out. Didn't do our night vision a lot of good, though – we were almost blinded for a while. On our return journey we ran into searchlights near Abbeville and there were so many that we were in and out of them for about ten minutes. There was no sign of flak so I kept a sharp eye out for night fighters but didn't see any. I was beginning to wonder where I'd taken us, because a concentration of searchlights

Mitchell II FV914 VO-A of 98 Squadron dropping its bomb load over northern France on 19 April 1944. This aircraft was SOC on 5 June 1947. (*IWM*)

such as this was normally reserved for large cities and I was convinced that we were nowhere near a town, let alone a city.

All was revealed when we got back to debriefing. While we'd been away the flak map had been changed and where before there had been no flak position, there was now a large green area with '800' marked against it. This meant that we had just flown through a large defended area with 800 light AA guns in it. It seems that the Germans, in a bid to stop the destruction of their individual V1 sites, had concentrated a number of them into one large area heavily defended against low-level attack. I think someone might have told us before we took off.

For the second half of April Ed and I were on a Gee-H course at Swanton Morley. This was to be our precision blind-bombing aid. Although I got good results in practice raids on Boston Stump and the central tower of Ely Cathedral, on operations it – and sometimes I – was something of a failure, so this piece of equipment was not much used. In fact I only carried out three Gee-H sorties. On the first the equipment packed up. On the second we dropped our bombs from 20,000 ft on the Seine crossing at Duclair – at least that was where they were supposed to go. I have a feeling that they were nowhere near. The third and last

Mitchell IIs FV905/S for Stalingrad, FW130/A and FW128/H of 226 Squadron in May 1944. No. 226 Squadron became operational on Mitchells at the end of July 1943 and flew its first Mitchell sorties on 17 August 1943, when six aircraft set out for railway marshalling yards at Dunkirk but the leader's aircraft refused to climb and the operation was aborted. (*via A. S. Thomas*)

I put down in my log-book as Gee-H trouble but some unkind person came along afterwards, crossed out 'Gee-H' and inserted 'finger' and drew a small picture of Percy Prune's award of the highly Derogatory Order of the Irremovable Digit.

John Bateman returned from Swanton Morley to Dunsfold to find a pleasant surprise.

I suppose Wing Commander Bell-Irving must have felt a bit sorry for me, as he asked me if I would care to fly with him temporarily as a supernumerary crew as he already had a full crew. I was very happy with this offer and operated with him four times as a tail gunner and once as course winder, where I sat next to him in the jump seat and had an entirely new view of everything. Our targets were flying-bomb sites in northern France. On 8 May I was due to fly with 'B.I.' on ops but the night before Nick Carter asked me if I could take him to London as he had an appointment at the Air Ministry and couldn't get station transport. After dinner I asked 'B.I.' if this would be OK and he readily agreed. In any case I was only a spare bod. Nick and I duly went to London and returned late-ish in the evening, having stopped for a noggin at the 'Jolly Farmers' in Guildford and at the 'Three Compasses'. When we called in at the guardroom we were told that 'B.I.' had been shot down and was reported missing. In the morning he had led the squadron to Charleroi marshalling yards but $^{10}/_{10}$ cloud prevailed and the formation did not bomb. In the evening he had led the formation to attack a Noball at Bois Coquerel from a bombing height of 13,000 ft. Flak was extremely accurate and just after bombing 'B.I.'s' machine had received a direct hit in the nose. It broke away from the formation and went into a spin before crashing. No chutes had been seen to leave the aircraft. He was twenty-four and

Pilots of 107 'Jamaica' Squadron in 1944. Left to right: Wing Commander Mike Pollard, CO; Flying Officer De Rosier (USA): Flying Officer J. Ballachey (Canada); Flying Officer Sanderson (Canada); Flying Officer Karl Aiken (Jamaica); Flying Officer Taylor (Canada) and Flight Lieutenant McLure (Canada). (*J. Ballachey via Paul McCue*)

is buried at the cemetery at Abbeville. Flight Sergeant Winter, the navigator of Flight Sergeant Anstey's Mitchell, was hit in the head by shrapnel and died without regaining consciousness just after the Mitchell landed at Friston. The next morning a Mosquito flew into Dunsfold flown by Johnny Slip who knew that I was flying with

Applying black and white invasion stripes to a Mosquito of 2nd TAF just prior to D-Day. (*British Newspaper Pool*)

'B.I.' and heard that he had bought it and assumed that I had too. He had come to collect my belongings to take to my parents and just couldn't believe that it was me he saw in the mess. It was very touching of him to have bothered but just typical of him. We rather overdid the celebrating that evening, so he stayed

Boston IIIAs of 88 Squadron at Hartford Bridge fitted with smoke installation pipes below the fuselage for smoke-screening the beachheads on D-Day. (*IWM*)

the night at Dunsfold before flying back the next day. Nick, of course, joined the party and it was through him that I lived to enjoy another day. Then for the second time I was crew-less and a few days later I was posted to the Central Gunnery School at Catfoss to take a Gunnery Leaders course. After about a week I phoned Wing Commander Alan Lynn who had assumed temporary command of 98 Squadron to ask him if I could come back. But he would not let me and to cap it all I received a telegram from Keith Cudlipp with the message, 'Get some D-Day hours in!'

'Dinty' Moore was on an air gunnery instructors course at Manby, Lincolnshire, during which they were informed that Allied forces had, at long last, landed in France.

I sat back and thought that here I was in the safety of a classroom while my old friends were involved in a truly historic event for which we had worked so hard and risked so much. I also wished Peter and so many others I had known could have lived to see this day. I later learned how 2 Group's two remaining Boston squadrons, 88 and 342 (Lorraine), had, in addition to bombing the enemy, laid

A 320 (Dutch) Squadron crew at Dunsfold in the summer of 1944. Left to right: Almekinders, Fransen, Vos and de Groot. (*via Jan P. Kloos*)

smoke to screen the invasion force at one beachhead from the German coastal guns. Further, all the squadrons, Bostons, Mitchells and Mosquitoes, had been heavily engaged in bombing troop concentrations, railways, *Panzer* divisions, indeed any target requested by the Army, with considerable success.

All six of 2nd TAF's Mosquito fighter squadrons performed defensive operations (264 Squadron flew jamming patrols before they went looking for enemy fighters) over the invasion coast on 5/6 June. (In the spring of 1944 29, 264, 409, 410, 488 RNZAF and 604 Squadrons had formed in 85 Group and 219 joined 147 Wing on 26 August.) Fewer than fifty plots were made on 5/6 June and only Flying Officer Pearce of 409 Squadron claimed a kill. Then things hotted up. 604 Squadron alone destroyed ten aircraft on 7 and 8 June (on 6 August 604 became the first fighter squadron to move to France). On 7 June 456 Squadron destroyed four He 177s and three more on the 8th. (On 5 July 456 claimed three enemy aircraft to bring its score to thirty victories since 1 March.) Les Bulmer recalled:

When D-Day arrived, 21 Squadron was out whenever weather permitted patrolling behind the battlefront looking for anything that moved. The night of D-Day, the 6th, we were briefed to patrol the Caen–Lisieux–Boisney road to stop German reinforcements reaching the beachhead. We were told that there was a corridor across the Channel in which every aircraft must stay on outward and return flights. Our night fighters were patrolling on either side of the corridor and were likely to regard any plane that was found outside the designated area as hostile. As we left the English coast a hail of flak went up from a ship in mid-Channel right where we were headed. Pretty shortly down went an aircraft in flames – it looked like one of our four-engined bombers. It seemed that one of our own ships (the Royal Navy got the blame) had parked itself right on the path that every aircraft going to and from the Continent that night would be following. And, in true naval fashion, it let fly at everything that went over. We decided to risk the night-fighters rather than fly through that lot and did a wide detour.

In night operations on 7/8 June 1944 70 Mosquitoes of 107, 305 and 613 Squadrons operating to the west on rail targets at Argentan, Domfort and Lisieux, sealed approaches to the bridgehead. 'The scene over France,' continued Les Bulmer, 'had changed completely. Whereas before D-Day there had been almost total darkness, now there were lights everywhere and most of the Normandy towns burned for several nights. Navigation was much easier; you just flew from one fire to the next.'

On the night of 22/23 June Flight Lieutenant Mike Benn DFC was killed. He took off on his 31st Mosquito operation with his navigator, Flying Officer W. A. Roe, on a Night Ranger from Thorney Island in FBVI *G-George*. On becoming airborne he found that his ASI was not working and so he radioed Control that he had problems and was returning to base. Another Mosquito crew was able to formate with *G-George* and led them into the approach to ensure that they were at the right speed but Benn's approach was such that he touched down too far down the runway. He overran and the Mosquito went over the low sea wall at the airfield boundary and bounced on the shingle strip. The undercarriage and wheels were torn off as they hit the barbed wire fence entanglement beyond the shingle and the tail dropped when it hit the mud flat. The fuselage snapped completely off near the tail fin and the nose dropped and dug into the mud, bringing the aircraft to a halt about 30 yards from the sea wall. Bill Roe survived but the sudden stop caused the

Mitchell II VO-W of 98 Squadron flown by Flying Officer Nevin Philby RAAF operating from Dunsfold in June 1944. (*National Archives of Canada via Paul McCue*)

armour plate behind the pilot's seat to hurl itself forward and this broke Mike Benn's back. They were in shallow water and Roe managed to keep Benn's head above water and carried him some way back to the airfield before the ambulance finally found them. Benn died the following day in St Richard's hospital, Chichester. The Squadron records stated, 'Michael was a favourite of the Squadron and his death is a great shock to us all.' On 28 June Wing Commander 'Daddy' Dale and other squadron personnel attended his funeral. As soon as he heard the news William Wedgwood Benn, who was also in the RAF at that time with the Allied Control Commission in Italy, returned home. Mike's younger brother Anthony, who was training as a pilot in Rhodesia at the time, received a telegram reporting his brother's death. Tony Benn became a sub-lieutenant in the RNVR but the war ended before he could see action. Demobbed in 1946, he became Viscount Stansgate upon the death of his father but later renounced the title to become the well-known Labour politician.

(Left) The Honorable Michael J. Wedgewood-Benn DFC, at twenty-two, was the eldest of three sons of (right) William Wedgwood Benn DSO DFC Ld H and CdG, a First World War veteran pilot and prominent politician who was created Viscount Stansgate on 22 December 1940. (*Tony Benn*)

John Bateman returned to 98 Squadron in July.

On the 24th we bombed German troop concentrations in a wood 5 miles south-east of Caen and met some intense and accurate flak that severely damaged our aircraft. It was on this trip

Mosquito VI NS837 YH-C crewed by Flight Lieutenant Mike Benn DFC and Flying Officer W. A. Roe, which overshot the runway at Thorney Island on the night of 22/23 June 1944. The aircraft was led in to the approach by another Mosquito, but touched down too far along the runway and went through the sea wall. Benn died of his injuries. Roe, who was slightly injured, later crewed up with Flight Lieutenant Lloyd and they were shot down and taken prisoner on 7 August 1944. (*Les Bulmer via F. R. Lucas*)

The crew of Mitchell II 'O-Orange' of 98 Squadron. Left to right: John Bateman, Keith Cudlipp, Kees Vandenbergh, Wing Commander Alan Lynn and a sergeant cameraman who took photos on the trip. (*John Bateman*)

that Keith Lynch and I decided to change places in the top turret. I tugged at his trouser leg to indicate that he should come down and just after he came out a chunk of flak penetrated the seat, which would have caused him severe discomfort if he had still been in position, not to mention his marital chances. At 0600 the next morning we were off again to the same target and again we met with heavy opposition but no damage this time. We returned after two hours and later that day led another attack on a fuel dump near Châteaudun, again meeting opposition *en route*. We led two further trips on 26 July, again in two different aircraft. The first attack was on a fuel dump at Alençon and the second on another at Fontainebleau near Paris. On both occasions we ran into heavy opposition but at Fontainebleau it was extremely accurate and we lost one aircraft from our flight at Dreux. All these ops were carried out at about 16,000 ft but we did not see a single snapper.

Our navigator, Kees Vandenbergh, who had completed 100 ops, was a lieutenant in the Dutch Naval Air Service and had completed a tour of ops with 320 Squadron when Alan asked him to join his crew. He spoke excellent English with only a very faint accent. He was also a qualified pilot, which would have been useful if Alan had been incapacitated. As the Dutch were paid extra for each hour of non-operational flying and even more for operational flying, he would take the aircraft up at every opportunity for air tests and so forth.

One day in the late summer of 1944, with a new Flying Officer gunner who had just joined us, he did an air test in '*O-Orange*', which had a new engine fitted. Alan asked Keith and me if we wanted to go with them but we both declined as we wanted to listen to a radio serial that we had been following; Alan, too, stayed to listen to it as Kees took off. The air test should have taken about twenty minutes but after half an hour when they hadn't returned we all went up to Flying Control to see if they had any information but they had heard nothing since take-off. After another thirty minutes there was a telephone call from the police at Guildford to report that a Mitchell had crashed near Chidingford and as it was the only Mitchell airborne from Dunsfold it had to be Kees.

We were all a bit shattered but within a few days we were flying again, this time with Squadron Leader Bunny Reece the Wing Navigation Officer, as our navigator. On our first trip with Bunny we were heading for France at about 10,000 ft and had just crossed the coast and tested our guns when Keith and I looked up and saw a very large formation of Liberators of the USAAF about 15,000 ft above us. They were silver and looked very impressive against our

216

Mosquito FBVIs of 464 Squadron RAAF shuddering and shaking with vibration caused by high speed at low level zooming across the Channel to attack targets in France. (*Vic Hester*)

rather drab colours. While we were watching with admiration one of them burst into flames and within a minute or so we counted five or six parachutes heading for the drink. We never found out the cause but concluded that a gunner in the formation had put a burst into one of his chums while testing his guns. Bad show!

In July Squadron Leader David F. Dennis DSO DFC became the CO of 21 Squadron. He had rejoined it when the build-up to D-Day was in progress and on 29 July he flew his first night operational sortie of his third tour. Having carried out an interdiction sortie in southern Germany with his navigator, Flying Officer Grantham, his Mosquito was hit by flak, which put one engine out of action. The propeller refused to feather and only by maintaining full power on the other engine could he maintain flight, albeit in a slight descent. Arriving in darkness at the recently recaptured area around Caen in northern France he found an emergency landing strip and put the aircraft down without injury to himself or the navigator but the Mosquito was a write off. The next night he was back at Thorney Island carrying out night-flying training and at that time it was not unusual to carry out two-and-a-half-hour operational sorties in one night.

Les Bulmer wrote:

August was a very busy month for 21 Squadron. With the breakout from the beachhead things moved very swiftly and we harried the Germans in retreat. Sometimes it was sheer slaughter as we found roads jammed with enemy transport just waiting to be set on fire. Ed and I flew eighteen sorties that month, sometimes two in one night. On the 18th we took off at 0010 for our thirty-ninth op and were back at Thorney Island by 0145. We refuelled and rearmed and were off again at 0350, landing again at 0530. After debriefing and a meal, we snatched a few hours sleep before attending briefing for the next night's raids. We were off at 2310 that night and back at 0110 on the 19th. Once again we refuelled and rearmed and were off at 0415, returning at 0550. So in less than

Mosquito FBVI LX917 EG-E joined 487 Squadron RNZAF in July 1943 and was lost on 5 July 1944. (*RAF Swanton Morley*)

A Mitchell II of 180 Squadron taking off from Dunsfold in mid-1944 (*via Paul McCue*)

thirty hours we had carried out four operations. Coming back over the Channel on the last one I must have dozed off because I awoke with a start when the aircraft gave a violent lurch. Ed had also fallen asleep and woke just in time to stop us spiralling into the sea.

Mike Henry DFC in 107 Squadron recalled:

After D-Day, the radio in the mess did a roaring trade, especially with the French crews. We were all eager to know how the Allied front was moving although a few of us semi-privileged people could walk into the ops room and see the current situation chalked up in chinagraph on the talc-covered large-scale map. I shall, however, never forget the day when the liberation of Paris was so dramatically announced. I was standing by the radio looking out into the anteroom. There was a large circle of attentive faces: French, British, Canadian, Australian and New Zealand all agog for latest news. After the pips the announcer, in calm measured tones, said, 'It has just been announced that Paris was entered this morning by American troops. Paris is liberated. . . ' There was a momentary pause, during which a pin would have been heard if dropped, broken by the first strident but stirring notes of the *Marseillaise*. Looking round the sea of faces I saw many an unashamed tear. I, too, felt a lump welling in my throat. It was truly a wonderful moment'.[89]

On 26 August, the day after Paris was liberated, Les Bulmer and Ed McQuarrie had a change from beating up transport, as Bulmer explained.

The Army wanted the railway bridge at Rouen destroyed to impede the German retreat. It was too small a target for the heavies, so 21 Squadron was asked to have a go. It had to be a night attack because the enemy was bound to defend it

The air and ground crew of 'N-Nuts' 'Avt rvmpere avt stercvs facere' (the nearest that one of the squadron's Latin scholars could get to a well-known service expression) of 88 Squadron at Hartford Bridge in late 1944. Left to right: A. F. W. Valle-Jones; Mike Henry DFC, Wing Commander (later Air Vice Marshal) Ian J. Spencer (CB DFC) with Butch; and Flying Officer G. E. Ploughman. Below the Latin inscription are two rows of foaming beer mugs instead of the usual little yellow bombs denoting the number of sorties completed and above them is the fierce portrait of Butch with tin helmet and holding a bomb. (*Mike Henry via Roy Brookes*)

with everything he had. Four aircraft, working in pairs, were allotted the task. One of the pair would fly at around 3,000 ft and drop flares for the other one, which would be waiting underneath. After dropping his bombs the two would change places. Since we were carrying flares in the bomb bay, we could only carry two bombs each under the wings. Flight Lieutenant Swaine and another crew took off first. We, together with our partner Flight Lieutenant Winder, left at 2235, thirty minutes or so later. On the way over to France Swaine called up on the R/T to say that it was pretty hot in the target area, that he'd been hit and he recommended that we abort. Ed and Winder had a brief conversation and decided to give it a whirl – I was more than happy to call it a day but I wasn't consulted.

We had been selected to do the first flare drop, so went in at about 3,000 ft. The enemy took a dislike to us at Cap d'Antifer as we crossed the coast, then we settled down for a straight run in to Rouen. I had my head stuck in the Gee set following a Gee line that should take us over the bridge from the north-west. Ed was concentrating on following my instructions to stay on the line and waiting for me to give him the order to drop the flares. Thus neither of us was aware of what was going on around us. This was just as well, because afterwards Winder said that he could see exactly where we were above him because of the flak that was following us in. Ignorance is a wonderful thing at times. Our three flares went down right on target but by the time we had turned to watch Winder attack, two flares had gone out – presumably shot out – and another had its parachute damaged and fell to the ground on the east bank of the river. However, this remaining flare gave enough light for us to see Winder's bombs burst on the south-west end of the bridge. Ed stuck the nose down and we dived on the bridge before our one remaining flare expired. We let go the bombs just as the flare went out so I couldn't see the results, then called up Winder to tell him that he needn't bother to drop his flares. I think he was as relieved as we were to get the hell out of it. I don't suppose we did much damage to the bridge – if any. But at least we tried.

Falaise Gap in a speeding Mosquito on D-Day plus about 20 ft! (*Vic Hester*)

CHAPTER NINE

Rangers on the Rampage

Train-busting on a dark night was pretty much a cat's-eyes thing.
Sometimes a plume of steam might be just discernible,
sometimes the glow of a fire box moving along rails.

Les Bulmer

At Hunsdon in summer 1944 Pilot Officer Dudley Hemmings's pilot in 464 Squadron completed his tour with him and was rested. The young navigator met Squadron Leader Don Wellings DFC, 'a tall, unassuming man', who had completed a tour on Blenheims at a night-vision course. It was Wellings who on 13 August 1940 had gained an eleventh-hour reprieve when, taxiing out for the suicidal trip to Aalborg airfield in Denmark, he and his crew were recalled because their posting had just come through. Wellings was returning to ops on Mosquitoes with 107 Squadron and did not have a navigator so he asked Hemmings if he would fly with him. Hemmings readily agreed and his transfer to 138 Wing at Lasham was arranged. Wellings had a son named James and was married to Stella, who lived about 20 miles from Lasham. He often rode home on his motorbike on stand down nights to 'spend a night between the sheets' as he called it, as at Lasham they were living under canvas tents with blankets only, with a view to moving into France wherever airfields could be cleared. 'During the period June to October 1944', recalled Hemmings:

Don Wellings and I did thirty-five ops, thirty at night, five day low-level trips. We commenced our first ops on the V1 flying bomb sites in northern France. The targets were difficult to locate in the woods, the ramps not much longer than a cricket pitch. I must say I was scared on my first trip when we saw the heavily defended French coast ahead 50 ft over the sea. Low-level tight formation in Vics or Boxes was a must for the squadrons. This was difficult for some pilots to do continually. Wellings was a fearless man and could fly a perfect course from his navigator. During night attacks in Normandy with me he would press hard to destroy the target going as low as possible for accuracy – hence I would yell out to him altimeter readings fearing he was getting too low for my liking!

A typical night op. Take off Lasham 2300 hours. Sixteen minutes to Littlehampton on the coast, across the channel at 50 feet. When the French coast was coming up we climbed to 3,000 ft, crossed the coast in a weaving dive to escape any flak then down to about 1,500–2,000 ft and patrolled a given area in the battle zone. Eventually to find a moving train or transport column, climb a bit and drop a flare over the targets. It would burn on a parachute for about seven to ten minutes turning night into day. Bomb the train – engine if possible – the train would stop – rake the train with machine guns and cannon and set it on fire. Sometimes got flak and the cockpit filled with cordite smoke which nearly made me sick as I called out altimeter readings to Wellings in our dives. I would identify the location with a Gee fix if possible and when all armaments expended set course for the French coast and back to base. Then a debriefing – bacon and eggs – and on to our camp stretchers for sleep around 3 a.m.

Early in September Mosquitoes in 2 Group, 2nd TAF played their part in Operation *Market Garden,* which was aimed at cutting the German-occupied Netherlands almost in half and to prepare the way for the invasion of Germany that would bypass the northern flank of theWestwall fortifications (The Siegfried Line). The Allied plan was to capture bridges on the Rhine in Holland at Veghel, Grave, Nijmegen and Arnhem, using Britain's 1st and America's 82nd and 101st Airborne Divisions. They were to cut off the German army in the Belgian sector and save the bridges and the port of Antwerp for the American army units and British XXX Corps advancing north from the Dutch border.

Dudley Hemmings and Don Wellings, who in August had moved to 613 Squadron, were involved:

The attacks were scheduled to begin five minutes before midday Dutch time to soften the German defences ahead of the invading paratroopers. As was usual with all Mosquito daylight raids, low level flying and careful routeing into the targets to gain surprise was essential for success. Whilst by late 1944 the *Luftwaffe* had diminished in the air, enemy anti-aircraft guns were still heavy around German held positions. The task given the Section led by Squadron Leader Don Wellings DFC and I as his navigator, was to attack the barracks in the centre of Arnhem.

The thirty-two FBVI Mosquitoes of 107 and 613 Squadrons in 138 Wing were to attack two German barracks complexes in Arnhem, in shallow high-speed dives at between 800 and 1,500 ft. The barracks were in Willemskazerne in the centre of the town and the Saksen-Weimarkazerne in the northern outskirts. Fifteen Mosquitoes of 21 Squadron in 140 Wing were to bomb three school buildings in the centre of Nijmegen, which were being used by the German garrison. One of the crews who took part was Canadian Flight Lieutenant Ed McQuarrie RCAF and his navigator Flight Lieutenant 'Les' Bulmer, who were flying their last operation as a crew. Bulmer recalled:

It was to be quite an exciting finish to our tour together. Both raids were to eliminate the opposition before the airborne forces of Market Garden went in later that day. We were still based at Thorney Island, so we would have quite a way to go to reach the target. As a result we had to carry wing tanks, which meant that our bomb load was confined to two 500-pounders in the bomb bay. At briefing we had the usual 2 Group model of the town so that we could familiarize ourselves with the target and the run-in over the town. There would be fifteen aircraft in five sets of three in echelon starboard. Wing Commander

David F. Dennis DSO DFC DFM led with 'Jock' Murray as his No. 2. We led the third echelon with Flight Lieutenant Bert Willers as our No. 2. To ensure that all fifteen aircraft would be clear of the target before the bombs exploded the leading aircraft (the first ten) had 25-second fuses, whereas the rear echelons had the normal eleven-second delay. To stay clear of trouble we planned to fly across the Channel and up to the front line at high level. Once over enemy territory we would drop down to the deck and head for a road that ran north-west from Cleve into Nijmegen. The road would give us an accurate run-up to the target, which consisted of three large buildings forming a semi-circle facing the direction from which we planned to attack, so it would be easy to identify.

On 17 September 1,113 medium and heavy bombers escorted by 330 fighter aircraft carried out bombing attacks to eliminate the opposition before the airborne forces of *Market Garden* went in later that day. The first airlift alone involved 360 British and 1,174 American transport aircraft and 491 gliders, accompanied by 910 fighter escorts. During the course of the operation 20,190 parachutists, 13,781 glider-borne troops, 5,230 tons of equipment and stores, 1,927 vehicles and 568 pieces of artillery were landed behind the German lines. The bombing strikes included seventeen Mosquitoes of 107 Squadron and sixteen Mosquitoes of 613 Squadron at Lasham and sixteen Mosquitoes of 21 Squadron at Thorney Island. No. 107 Squadron finally began taking off at half-minute intervals at 1051 hours after a few last minute hiccups as Dudley Hemmings related:

We formed up in tight formation and set course for Southwold on the English coast for the 750 miles round trip. Across East Anglia we had a marvellous view of the sky filled with the great armada of some of the 2,000 transports and gliders *en route* to their drop zones several miles west of Arnhem. Crossing the English coast at Southwold we soon left the brave Red Berets behind and skimmed over the North Sea at 50 ft and 250 m.p.h. – IFF off and bombs switched to 'Fire'. As lead navigator I was map reading each pinpoint every two minutes to keep on track knowing there were seven crews behind relying on our lead. Our routeing into Arnhem was circuitous and required good timing, pinpoint map reading and the use of Gee over the 130 miles of sea to the Dutch coast. Midway over the North Sea we turned slightly to port at a DR position in order to cross the Dutch coast 1 mile south of Egmont, a position presumed undefended. Landfall without incident was made as planned and we swept across the lowlands of Holland, lifting up over some high-tension lines east of Alkmaar. At a headland on the Zuider Zee near Hoorn we turned south-east to cross 32 miles of the Zuider Zee, making for a checkpoint at Nijkerk where a railway ran 90 degrees to our track. We crossed the town of Nijkerk at house top level and looking behind us it was good to see the flight still in close formation.

We were now eight minutes to our time on target. About 10 miles west of Arnhem we turned on an easterly course and climbed rapidly to 3,000 ft, the others breaking the box formation to line astern. I had an oblique photo of a model made from aerial photographs and knew that a white gravel road led straight to the barracks. We flew in a shallow dive down this road. I pointed out the target to Don Wellings and we dropped our bombs from 1,000 ft. The

Mossies behind us did likewise. We carried instantaneous bombs on this trip and could not bomb at low level for fear of blowing up either the following aircraft or ourselves. When really low level bombing was done, eleven-second delay bombs were carried. Pilot aimed bombing became quite accurate after much practice by pilots on the bombing ranges back in England. Up came some flak and with the bomb doors open Wellings opened up with the firepower in the nose as our bombs were released. The Section followed us in. Until now the crews had maintained radio silence but soon after flattening out past the target I heard one of our crews over the radio call out 'We've got it!'

In 21 Squadron meanwhile Ed McQuarrie and Les Bulmer had taken off at 1045 hours for Nijmegen and the Mosquitoes formed up into tight formation. Bulmer recounted:

Somewhere short of the front line we shed our drop tanks – empty tanks could be lethal if hit by flak. Just after crossing the front line we came under heavy ack-ack fire near Weert. There was nothing we could do to avoid it, as this would have destroyed the formation. But this didn't stop No. 2 in the second echelon from trying to weave. He was a bigger menace than the flak. As far as I know nobody was hit, although a message came over the R/T calling someone by name – which we didn't catch – telling them that they were on fire. I think it probably came from some other formation because there were no signs of fire in ours. But I reckon it caused a mild panic among all our crews. On the deck it was hard work for the pilots trying to keep one eye on the ground and the other on the rest of the formation. Somewhere along the way there was a cry of 'Wires, wires!' and we had to climb to get over an electricity pylon. I was amazed to see that Willers on our right seemed to fly underneath! In fact, I found out afterwards that he'd taken advantage of the droop in the cables to stay low.

Our turning point on the Cleve–Nijmegen road came up, which we planned to follow into Nijmegen but we carried straight on, then circled starboard to come up on Cleve from the east. I had no idea what was going on. Every navigator in the formation, except the leader, must have been wondering what the hell was happening. I could hardly believe my eyes when the leading aircraft opened their bomb doors. Ed followed suit and I yelled at him that this wasn't the target and not to release our bombs. Poor Ed was totally confused and probably thought I had gone off my head since the leaders were obviously intent on bombing whatever was coming up. After what seemed ages but was probably only seconds the leader's bomb doors closed and I breathed a sigh of relief as we shot over Cleve. On the straight road, with houses on either side and a larger building, which could have been a church or chapel, people were standing watching us go over. I looked back to check that the rear echelons had noticed that bomb doors had been closed and saw to my dismay a large cloud of black smoke. Some of the rear six aircraft had let their bombs go. (According to later official reports three aircraft bombed a barrack square in Cleve and machine-gunned troops.)

Our turning point South-west of Cleve is the Reichwald, a large forest and we proceeded to career around this. By now there was not much formation left, just a gaggle of aircraft milling around waiting for someone to make a decision. Suddenly I saw two aircraft haring off in the right direction – one of them, I later discovered, was Jock Murray. I told Ed to follow and we chased after them, with everyone else tagging along behind or beside us. We were now fifteen aircraft all flying individually towards Nijmegen. And we had no means of knowing whether any of the leading planes were the ones with the short fuses.

We sped up the road to Nijmegen and I could see the bridge over on the right. Then we were over the town looking anxiously for the target. It seemed to be chaos, with Mosquitoes going in all directions, flak coming up and Mustangs milling around above us. I noticed one Mosquito climbing away to the north and wondered where the hell he was going. Then another Mosquito shot underneath us almost at right angles. I shall never know how he found room between the rooftops and us and I wondered why he was going in that particular direction. Then I realized that he'd seen the target and was heading straight for it. I yelled to Ed to pull round and pointed to the target, by now almost on our port wing tip. He put us into a tight turn but we couldn't make it in time. We shot over the town and I recall the railway station with crowds waiting on the platform and what appeared to be a green-coloured train alongside. In a flash we were clear and out over farmland where we dumped our bombs and fled. On the way in and on the way out the farmers and their families were standing in their doorways waving like mad – probably cheering on 'the brave RAF' while we were thinking, 'What the hell are we doing here, let's get the hell out of it.' The element of surprise is essential on low-level attacks and there is no going round again unless you have suicidal tendencies so we found a convenient wood and jettisoned our load. In the confusion we forgot to put the arming switches to 'OFF' so I just hoped that no one would be passing that way within the next twenty-five seconds. (We weren't the only ones to blow holes in the countryside. At the subsequent inquest there were several photographs taken by rearward-facing cameras showing jettisoned bombs exploding. There were a few caustic comments from the flight commanders about this. Fortunately we didn't have a camera on board so we managed to conceal our misdemeanour.) We found another Mosquito, which seemed to be going in the same direction as us, so we joined him for the journey home. This was uneventful; we didn't even get shot at over Weert this time. Maybe the Germans didn't consider two

Corporal Jan Pronk and Piet den Haajer of 320 (Dutch) Squadron arming Mitchell II 'Owe Jongens'. (Jan P. Kloos)

aircraft to be worth wasting ammunition on. And besides, we were heading for home.

We returned to Thorney Island (one crew was missing) where the full story of the confusion over the target route unfolded. Wing Commander Dennis had a bird hit his windscreen just before reaching the turning point. In retrospect it might have been wiser for him to pull out and hand over to Jock Murray immediately but he chose to carry on, not being able to see properly and hence the mess we finished up in. Only five aircraft claimed to have located and bombed the target. Most of the rest did as we did and dumped them in fields, apart from those who had already got rid of theirs over Cleve. I've always felt that it was a mistake to have fifteen planes in one formation. The usual formation on previous raids of this sort was groups of six in two vics of three. Because each of the following echelons had to be stepped down on the one in front to avoid slip-stream problems, it meant that the leader had to keep a reasonable height above the deck, otherwise the rear echelons would be ploughing a furrow across the countryside. In the event, it was impossible to avoid hitting slipstreams and we were being thrown all over the place and at treetop height this is not the healthiest of situations. It was only later that we learned that the German troops were not in their barracks anyway, so all we succeeded in doing was probably to kill a few innocent Dutchmen and some German civilians. Such is war. In wartime I suppose you can't very well admit to the world that you made a cock-up.

Hemmings concluded:

Safely back at Lasham after three hours in the air a debriefing, some discussion of the other Sections' experiences (two aircraft failed to return), a beer at The Swan in Alton nearby clouding the knowledge that tomorrow was another day, another 'op'. As to whose bombs hit the barracks or went astray I do not know. It is best not to know as a number of Dutch civilians were killed during the raid. For navigator and pilot on such missions it was purely a test of one's navigational and flying skills, a hope of survival under fire, a task completed as ordered and a mental isolation from the outcome on the ground. When my CO told me my operational tour was completed and to take Rest Leave Wellings said to me that the CO had told him the same. While he insisted I go Wellings stated that he would ask to stay on because he wanted to 'see out the war'. Sadly, when I was on leave he took a new navigator and went missing on 9 October 1944.

The Arnhem operation was the last one for Ed McQuarrie, and for Les Bulmer – or at least he thought so at the time.

Ed had done the requisite fifty trips and I'd managed fifty-two because Ed had an argument with a motor cycle early in our tour and finished up in hospital. While he was in there I did two trips with an Irishman, Flying Officer Smith. Ed and I went on two weeks' leave and I expected that we would be sent on rest to an OTU but I was in for an unpleasant surprise when I returned to pick up my kit and move on. While I was away 2 Group had moved the goal posts. A tour was now eighty-five ops with a month's leave around the halfway mark, 200 operational hours or twelve months on the squadron, whichever came first. I was told to take another fortnight's leave and come back for another thirty-five trips. It was rather like being given the death sentence. Having survived fifty-two ops I couldn't believe that my luck would last for another thirty-five. I never saw Ed McQuarrie again and it is only in recent years that I learned that the RCAF would not go along with the extended tour and Ed was shipped back to Canada.

On 18 September the Germans counter-attacked and forestalled an American attempt to capture the bridge at Nijmegen. *Market Garden* has been described in an official report as 'by far the biggest and most ambitious airborne operation ever carried out by any nation or nations'. Of over 10,200 British troops landed in the Arnhem area, 1,440 were killed or died of their wounds. 3,000 were wounded and taken prisoner and 400 medical personnel and chaplains remained behind with the wounded, and about 2,500 uninjured troops also became PoWs. There were also 225 prisoners from the 4th Battalion, the Dorsetshire Regiment. About 450 Dutch civilians were killed. The operation also cost 160 RAF and dominion aircrew, twenty-seven USAAF aircrew. Seventy-nine Royal Army Service Corps dispatchers were killed and 127 taken prisoner. A total of fifty-five Albemarle, Stirling, Halifax and Dakota aircraft of 38 and 46 Groups failed to return and a further 320 were damaged by flak and seven by fighters, while 105 Allied fighter aircraft were lost.

Altogether, nine Mosquito bomber squadrons now equipped 2nd TAF. In September 1944, following the outbreak from the Normandy beachhead, plans were in progress to move them to airfields in France. As part of the new offensive, Mosquito squadrons outside 2nd TAF also made daylight Rangers from France and intruder sorties over the Continent. On 31 October twenty-five Mosquito FBVIs of 21, 464 and 487 Squadrons, 140 Wing, escorted by eight Mustang IIIs of 315 (Polish) Squadron, 12 Group, made a daring low-level attack on the *Gestapo* HQ building at Aarhus, Denmark. Group Captain Peter Wykeham-Barnes DSO DFC* led the operation and Air Vice Marshal Basil Embry, AOC 2 Group, with his navigator Peter Clapham, flew the operation in a Mosquito of 2 GSU. Embry wore no medal ribbons and was known as Wing Commander Smith. The attack was carried out at such a low altitude that one Mosquito hit the roof of the building, losing its tail wheel and the port half of the tailplane but it limped back across the North Sea and managed to land safely. The university and its incriminating records were destroyed. Among the 110–175 Germans killed was SS *Obersturmbnannführer* Lonechun, Head of the Security Services.[90]

Pilot Officer Harry Randall-Cutler and Pilot Officer Hubert Cohen of 305 (Polish) Squadron beside FBVI LR303 A-Apple at Hartford Bridge in October 1944. No. 305 Squadron carried out night intruding over the continent from Hartford Bridge and Lasham that October before moving to Epinoy near Cambrai in November 1944. (Harry Randall-Cutler)

CHAPTER TEN

Swan Song of the Panzers

We are attacked all day and then the Mosquitoes
harass and bomb us at night.
We cannot em Schläfchen machen *or* eine Scheiesse
machen
We are caught with our pants down!

> Complaint of German prisoners to Flight Lieutenant
> Eric Atkins DFC* KW*

By November 1944 Nos 107, 305 (Polish) and 613 Squadrons of 138 Wing finally arrived in France, to be based at Epinoy, near Cambrai. No. 137 Wing, with the two Boston squadrons, 88 and 342 (Lorraine), 226 Squadron Mitchells and 107 Squadron Mosquitoes, was now stationed at Vitry-en-Artois between Douai and Arras in northern France. No. 139 Wing, comprising 98, 180 and 320 (Mitchell) Squadrons, was based at Brussels (Melsbroek). Mosquitoes of 21, 464 and 487 Squadrons remained behind at Thorney Island but in December 1944 the Australian and New Zealand squadrons both sent advance detachments to Rosières-en-Santerre, France, although 21 Squadron did not join them until February 1945.

On 17 November 'Dinty' Moore, now a flight lieutenant, should have flown to France to join 226 Squadron to begin his third tour.

I returned to Swanton Morley on 22 October 1944, ostensibly as Gunnery Leader of 'B' Flight, No. 2 GSU having persuaded the Group Gunnery Leader, Squadron Leader Jerry Levack that I wished to fly a third tour. It may seem crazy but I was terribly unsettled and I became determined to return to 2 Group to complete another tour. I believe the reason for this was threefold. First of all my second tour had been less than satisfying; then the loss of Peter and finally hearing the heavy bombers flying over us every night on their way to bomb targets in Germany. I was delighted to learn that I was to fly as fighter controller on a 226 Squadron Mitchell with Squadron Leader Jock Campbell, whom I had known and greatly respected when he was on 88 Squadron. I was due to leave for France in an Anson on 15 November but we were delayed when the weather closed in and it was not until 19 November that I was flown over to Vitry-en-Artois to join the crew. On the date of my arrival I met Jock and his crew but they had been briefed to take part in an attack on Venlo in support of the Army so there was little time for conversation. I waited until I saw them take off, thinking that I would have plenty to talk about with them when they got back. I then got on with the usual routine of settling into the mess and finding out the location of the squadron office and so on. While I was doing this Jock was leading his formation in their approach to the target when his aircraft received a direct hit from an anti-aircraft shell and broke up. He and his crew were killed. On the return of the remainder of the squadron I found it difficult to believe the tragic news they brought with them. I suppose, human nature being what it is, that my main reaction would be to thank my lucky stars that bad weather had postponed my arrival.

Vitry-en-Artois had been a *Luftwaffe* base and was very cleverly camouflaged. It was situated on the main road between Douai and Arras, an industrial area over which many of the battles of the Great War of 1914–18 had been fought. There were many reminders of that horrific conflict, with many memorials to the dead, the most impressive being the enormous Canadian Memorial on Vimy Ridge, which was in our circuit when we were taking off or landing. The officers' mess was, for a short while in hutted accommodation on the aerodrome. Then we moved into a rather grand chateau in the little village of Corbehm nearby. This building stood in its own grounds surrounded by a dry moat, the most recent occupants having been *Luftwaffe* officers. The walls of the dining room were completely covered with murals depicting the Battle of Britain. The City of London was being subjected to a bombing raid. Numerous German aircraft were flying over with Spitfires going down in flames. We were told that some of the local people who had supported the Germans were not too keen on our presence so we were instructed not to go out alone and always to carry a loaded revolver. By

Mosquito FBVIs 'B' and 'H' of 613 'City of Manchester' Squadron at A75/Cambrai-Epinoy France in late 1944. The squadron had moved here, together with 107 and 305 Squadrons of 138 Wing, in November 1944 to be closer to the frontline for harassing operations against German units retreating further eastwards. (Philip Beck)

contrast we received invitations and could not have been made more welcome.

This tour turned out to be completely different from my previous ones, for if the weather was fine it was a case of saying, 'What time is take-off?' and not 'Are we flying today?' as we had previously done. As I did not have a crew, being a gunnery leader, I was to fly as fighter controller with whichever pilot was leading a formation. We had no need of an escort. Operating at around 12,000 ft, generally in formations of twenty-four or thirty-six aircraft (flying in units of six aircraft), we had sufficient firepower to cope with any isolated fighter attacks. Our role was to act as a form of very long-range artillery in support of the Allied armies engaged in their battle with the *Wehrmacht*.

I did not have long to wait for my first operation for two days after my arrival I was detailed to fly with Squadron Leader Betts AFC on an attack on troop concentrations at Randerath. There were thirty-six aircraft, twenty-four Bostons and twelve Mitchells, taking part and once we were airborne it was an impressive sight to see six boxes of six aircraft all heading for the same target area. Every aircraft dropped their bombs, meeting little opposition from the enemy and we were all back on the ground after a flight lasting two hours twenty-five minutes. I couldn't help thinking that if this was what operations were like, this was going to be a 'piece of cake'. Bombing German troops was so impersonal. One just couldn't visualize what mayhem we were causing on the ground, though, as they were troops and not civilians one felt that it was thoroughly justified. Even though almost all our targets were on or immediately behind the German lines it was impossible to see any sign of the land battle that was taking place. On many occasions we could see the vapour trails of the American Fortresses and Liberators on their way to and from targets in Germany 20,000 ft above us. On one operation a German rocket on its way to London narrowly missed the aircraft in one of our formations as it sped upwards.

My next operation took place on 25 November when I was briefed to fly with Flying Officer Parsons, our target being the marshalling yards at Mönchengladbach, some distance behind the enemy lines. The operation called for maximum effort involving thirty-four Mitchells and twelve Bostons flying in the usual boxes of five or six aircraft. I chose to sit in the tail position where, though there were no guns fitted, I had an unimpeded view to direct the fire of all the gunners in our box in case of attack by enemy fighters. Our force looked a pretty impressive sight. Approaching the target I could see the menacing black balls of heavy flak bursting in the sky as the Germans tried to find our height. I had been leaning forward to get a clear view when something made me sit up straight. At the same instance a piece of shrapnel burst through the perspex cover of my tail position where my head had been and my face was cut by fragments of perspex. At that moment the Mitchell flying as our No. 3 piloted by Pilot Officer Sidney Moore received a direct hit on the port engine, which burst into flames. The aircraft plunged to the ground below with the loss of all on board. Despite this tragedy every one of our aircraft, ignoring the barrage, flew on and bombed the target, which was well clobbered. Apart from shooting one aircraft down the Germans damaged six others in addition to ours, which had twenty holes in the fuselage. On landing I went into debriefing not appreciating that my face was smeared with blood. News reached the officers' mess before I did that Moore had 'bought it' so it was assumed that it was me and not Pilot Officer Moore who had been shot down, so my arrival caused something of a surprise.

Next day my pilot was Squadron Leader Lyle DFC*, a very popular and well-known member of 2 Group We were briefed to bomb a bridge being used by the German army at Deventer. Our force on this occasion was eighteen Mitchells and eighteen Bostons, which would represent a total bomb load of 108,000 lb. Perhaps as a result of my last operation, I decided to control from the mid-upper turret, only to find that my view was restricted, so I never used it again. On our approach to the target the anti-aircraft barrage was very heavy and despite our evasive action it was beginning to find our height. It was then that the Mitchell flying as No. 5 in our second box of six aircraft received a direct hit amidships, breaking in two and hurtling towards the ground below with the loss of all on board. The pilot, I learned later, was Flying Officer Twining. Despite the unwelcome attentions of the anti-aircraft gunners once again every remaining aircraft bombed the target. The result of our efforts cannot have been particularly successful however, as this was a target we would visit several times, unless the Germans replaced the bridge after our call. The flight lasted two hours fifty minutes, which was rather longer than many in which we were involved. I had only been with the squadron for seven days, yet during that time we had lost three Mitchells and their crews, so any notion I had that this tour was going to be a 'piece of cake' had quickly been dispelled. I couldn't have blamed my colleagues if they had looked upon me as a 'Jonah' – you know someone who brings bad luck – although they never gave any such indication.

On the 29th I returned to Deventer flying with Flight Lieutenant Rimmell, occupying my tail position, as part of a force of twenty-four Bostons and eighteen Mitchells. The anti-aircraft barrage was again heavy though to our relief it was not concentrated on our formation. The following day, with the same pilot we bombed Dunkirk, which was still occupied by the Germans, having been by-passed by the advancing Allied armies. The town was completely surrounded but the garrison refused to surrender and was a target we bombed without deriving any satisfaction. They were probably low on ammunition for we found only a light and inaccurate barrage.

In 21 Squadron, meanwhile, Les Bulmer began the second half of his tour, flying with Flight Lieutenant Bert Willers.

It was comparatively quiet compared with the first half. The pace had slowed down quite a lot because of poor weather conditions. Our first sortie took place on 18 November and by now we were patrolling into Holland and Germany. We only managed three ops in November and just two in December. On 4 December, as there was not much doing, we were ordered to keep our hand in on low flying, so we did a cross-country over France, which by this time was

Flight Lieutenant Bert Willers (left) and Flight Lieutenant 'Les' Bulmer of 21 Squadron supposedly going over the route while their Mosquito VI is warmed up behind in this staged photo taken by James Jarche for *Illustrated* magazine. Les Bulmer recalled that he did not seem to appreciate that crews did not get into a Mosquito with the engines running and he also had to borrow a pair of flying boots because apparently he did not look the part of an intrepid aviator without them! (*via Les Bulmer*)

clear of Germans, apart from the Channel ports. We quite enjoyed ourselves, the French countryside being ideal for low-level flying, especially as we were no longer being shot at. Somewhere along the way we came across a large field that sloped up to a house standing on a ridge. This was just the place to practice a camera gun attack using the house as a target. We tore across the field, just about clipping the grass with our prop tips, then climbed to get over the house between the chimneys at either end of the building. As we did so there was a loud bang and a flash just in front of the windscreen. I thought we'd flown into some power cables that we hadn't seen or an aerial stretched between the chimneys.

We climbed to about 500 ft and turned to see what damage we'd done to the house. There was nothing we could see but several figures shot out of the house and gazed skywards. I don't know whether they were shaking their fists or not but at that moment Bert said, 'Oh Christ, look at that.' Sticking out of the top surface of the port wing was a large chunk of very solid-looking cable. It was buried into the leading edge right up to the main spar and just outboard of the engine. The rest of the cable trailed back under the wing and was whipping up and down just clear of the tailplane. We left the scene of the crime a bit sharpish and pondered, on the return journey, how we could explain the presence of 35 ft of cable dangling from the port wing when we got back to Thorney Island. Bert reckoned that we might be able to creep into dispersal without anyone noticing, then have a quiet word with 'Chiefy' Bishop to request a quick patch-up job and no one would be any the wiser. But it was not to be.

As we slowed to a halt after landing, the control tower called us to ask if we knew that there was something trailing from our port wing. We had to admit to them that we did. Back in dispersal we discovered that the bottom panels of both engine nacelles were dented and there was a chunk of wood missing from the nose just in front of the cockpit. We assumed that we had hit the wire fair and square and that the props had chopped it, flung one end over the nose causing the flash we saw, then throwing the whole lot into the port wing. I never discovered whether Bert Willers got a rocket for this episode, nor if the RAF ever got a bill from an irate French farmer for the unexpected removal of part of his property by a Mosquito. When 2 Group ordered low flying it was really low.

By this stage of the war the *Panzers* and other German troops deployed in the invasion area and beyond were given no respite in the daylight raids by Mitchells and Bostons and the nightly visits by Mosquitoes, all of 2nd TAF. Flight Lieutenant Eric Atkins DFC KW* (Krzyz Walecznych), a Mosquito pilot in 305 (Polish) Squadron at this time, recalled:

Prisoners captured complained, 'We are attacked all day and then the Mosquitoes harass and bomb us at night. We cannot *em Schläfchen machen* (take a nap) or *eine Scheiesse machen* (have a crap) – we are caught with our pants down!' Nowhere was this more apparent than when we attacked the *Panzer* billets on the night of 6/7 December 1944 in the village of Wassenberg, just south of Mönchengladbach, on the edge of the Ruhr itself. The attack on the billets would be my seventy-eighth operation, the twenty-sixth in my third tour. My navigator was Flight Lieutenant Jurek Majer, a Pole who spoke little

English. There was talk that I would be stood down after this operation and this made the raid even more significant. As all aircrew know, it can be a superstitious moment when you wonder whether you will 'get the chop' on the last one.

However, there was no time to worry about the consequences to me of the operation – there was much to do! The Met officer warned us that although the weather was set fair for the night, snow was on the way. (December's weather was the worst of an already bad three months. On some nights we operated when visibility at the base was less than 800 yards.) Our route to the target took us near Brussels. It was a very dark night but the radar kept us on the track. There seemed to be a lot of activity about. I was probably more finely tuned than normal on this trip and thought I saw enemy aircraft on our beam but Jurek just grunted and got on with his navigation. There was not normally a lot of conversation in our Mosquito – we both had our jobs to do and we reserved speech for when action was needed – no idle chatter!

Flight Lieutenant Eric Atkins DFC* KW* (centre) of 305 (Ziemia Wielkopolska) (Polish) Squadron in 1945 (*Eric Atkins*)

My thoughts drifted to three operations ago, 29 November, when we had attacked Hamm, in the east Ruhr area. The weather had been appalling and the flak over the target was heavy. After bombing, something had gone wrong with our aircraft, the electrics and hydraulics were amiss and I had to 'belly-flop' at night at our new base at Epinoy near Cambrai, France, a grass aerodrome on a slight hill. Without flaps we floated almost off the top of the hill before I forced it down. I hoped nothing like that would happen to us tonight!

Jurek said that we were approaching the German border and now we saw much more activity – searchlights and tracer fire. We were flying at about 3,000 ft.

'Look out for flares and a river,' said Jurek. We had HE and incendiary loads, flares, cannons and machine guns. We were not the only ones attacking this target and it should have been well lit up. However, we were among the first in. I came down much lower, soon picked up the Roer River and then saw the target. There were no flares at the time but there was a glow and Jurek confirmed that it was Wassenberg. We could see the fires starting as we did our first run. In the light of the flares we dropped we came round again and bombed and strafed the target. All hell seemed to be let loose below and heavy flak was coming up just south of us. There was some rain about and I remember thinking that it might put the fires out!

We did another run strafing with cannon fire. 'That's enough,' said Jurek. 'Save some for the others!'

A black shape zoomed up and passed our nose. 'What the hell's that?' I cried, then realized that it was probably another Mosquito going in to attack. We had overstayed our welcome. Flying straight and level in the darkness, heading for base, we checked our instruments, oil pressure and engine temperatures. I had flung the Mossie around rather a lot and sometimes engines overheat, then you have to shut one down. However, everything seemed all right and Jurek grunted the course back to base. It had been a very successful operation. The Panzers had been caught with their 'pants down'! After we had landed and been debriefed the station commander told me that it had been my last operation. They were standing me down on my seventy-eighth 'enough was enough'! I was very disappointed however, to lose Jurek. He had to carry on with another pilot to finish his second tour.

'Dinty' Moore's first four operations for December had been intended to be attacks on German troop concentrations in support of the army but on each occasion the target area was covered with cloud and as none of the aircraft were fitted with Gee-H they were unable to bomb.

With the approach of Christmas I was pleasantly surprised to be given a fourteen-day pass. On 22 December I was flown over to Hartford Bridge in a Mitchell, where I simply walked off the aerodrome on the main London to Southampton road and hitched a lift into London. There were no Customs & Excise officers or passport controls to trouble me. I spent a very pleasant Christmas in Norwich with my wife Norma and an equally good New Year in Hawes on a leave that neither of us had expected.

On Christmas Eve 1944 2nd TAF dispatched 139 Mosquitoes to targets in south-west Germany. No. 613 Squadron despatched thirty Mosquitoes; Warrant Officer Baird and his navigator Sergeant Whateley-Knight failed to return from a sortie to harass German movement behind the enemy thrust in the Ardennes. Also thirty-seven Mosquitoes of 2nd TAF patrolled the areas of Aachen, Arnhem and the Dutch Friesian Islands and flew close-support sorties over the front lines. None of these Mosquitoes was lost and they destroyed fifty vehicles and six trains. The *Luftwaffe* night fighters, deprived of fuel and experienced pilots, were nonetheless far from finished and in January 1945 attempted one last major air offensive against the Allied air forces on the ground at twenty-seven airfields in southern Holland, Belgium and northern France. Since 20 December 1944 many *Jagdgeschwader* had been transferred to airfields in the west for *Unternehmen* (Operation) *Bodenplatte*, which began at about 0900 hours on New Year's Day 1945 using 875 single-engined fighter aircraft, primarily in support of General von Rundstedt's Ardennes offensive. Total Allied aircraft losses during the four-hour operation amounted to 424 destroyed or heavily damaged but German losses – most of which were shot down by Allied AA guns – were catastrophic. Three hundred aircraft were lost, 235 pilots were killed and 65 pilots were taken prisoner. The big gamble had turned into a disastrous defeat.

'Dinty' Moore returned from his Christmas and New Year leave.

All good things come to an end so on 9 January I presented myself at the Group Support Unit, which had moved from Swanton Morley to Fersfield near the market town of Diss in Norfolk. I was flown back to the squadron in a Boston, carrying with me not only my luggage but also an extremely painful carbuncle on the back of my neck. I was admitted to the station sick quarters for a few days but missed no flying due to weather, which grounded all the aircraft. My incarceration coincided with the historic Battle of the Bulge when the Germans in a desperate attack broke out though the Allied lines in the Ardennes. My next three operations were with Flying Officer Conchie flying as a beam gunner. On each occasion thirty-six aircraft from our wing were involved. On the 21st the target was a wood at Wassenberg, in which units of the German army were concealed. The enemy threw up a heavy barrage although the gunners had an off day, for it was inaccurate. The following day our target was the same, as was the barrage though the gunners this time, having had some practice punished the box flying behind us but without shooting any of them down.

Sergeant John 'Ginger' Walsh, a Liverpudlian and a navigator in 487 Squadron and his pilot, Flying Officer John Patterson, flew their first operation, a three-hour round trip from Thorney Island to Arsbeck, on 21 January 1945. Walsh had trained at Greenwood, Nova Scotia, and training losses had been high, many of the Canadian-built Mosquitoes ending up in the Bay of Fundis. However, the 21-year-old was 'desperately keen' to fly the 'fast weapon'. Losses climaxed near the end of his training and he was one of only four to volunteer for Mosquitoes. Leeds-born 'Pat' Patterson had been an instructor in Canada, where he had met and married a delightful Canadian girl. Both men had teamed up at High Ercall. 'Ginger' Walsh recalled:

North-west Germany was divided into three, one for each Mossie wing, then into three again, one for each squadron. Spitfires and Mustangs from 2nd TAF, which attacked the German army on the ground during the day, returned with details of troop concentrations and targets, which we then bombed by night. Our main target was anything that moved, especially trains and transport but you were bloody lucky to find a moving target at night! Trains were a high priority but they were blacked out and we were lucky to see them. On the Arsbeck op we flew at about 1,000 ft through low cloud to the target. I navigated all the way using maps 'illuminated' by a tiny pin-prick of light from my torch filled with three layers of paper in the bottom to retain our night vision and prevent us from being seen from the air or the ground. (Gee could not be used too far into Germany before it got interfered with and 'railings' confused the two-three 'spikes'. I had to take the best signal, the best 'cut'.) Moonlight was a bastard. You could count the rivets. Over Germany on moonlit nights I felt that I had no clothes on. Our mates in the squadron had been to Arsbeck earlier and had started fires. We would bomb on the Gee-set co-ordinates. I selected the four bombs, fused them and 'Pat' pressed the 'tit' on his spectacle control column.

On the way home 'Pat' saw a train for what was the only time. The first I knew was that the Mosquito was suddenly standing on one wing! We had been told that if we saw a train we were to go straight in – no messing! 'Pat' circled (he was following his instincts) for the best position, then adopted a shallow dive and went in, all four .303 and four cannons blazing. By now I was 'climbing out of the roof'. The sky filled with 40 mm flak. I soon learned that German ack-ack gunners were mustard! In the cockpit cordite fumes and dust filled the air.

'Pat' broke off immediately and on my advice flew to the west! On reflection it had done us good. It was thought provoking.

It was a terrible night. Ron Batch, a fellow navigator I'd been with at navigational school and had known for eighteen months, who had already flown two ops, failed to return. He and his pilot had 'got the chop'. Forty-eight hours later Ron's father, a Metropolitan Police Inspector, came to see me. He wanted to know what area of Germany Ron had been flying over and any other details; Ron was his only child. I could tell him nothing. It really carved me up.

We got shot up ourselves one night. We got back and landed and the props had barely stopped when our two faithful groundcrew opened the door (we never bothered with the ladder). They asked if we'd hit anything. They were always so thrilled, so keen, that we should be successful. They asked, 'Were we fired at?'

I said, 'Yes, I think it was the British Army!'

'Were we hit?'

I said, 'No.'

Then they pointed to a hole beneath the wing! I looked and was thrilled. It was strangely exciting! However, next day they could see that the hole had been caused by oil dripping from the guns – our Mossie was a clapped-out machine and had flown many ops.

On 29 January Les Bulmer and his pilot, Bert Willers, were one of the crews in 21 Squadron who flew from Thorney Island to Fersfield for a secret briefing. They discovered that it was for an attack on the *Gestapo* HQ in Copenhagen to destroy their records of the Danish resistance movement.

We knew that some resistance members were held prisoner in the building and would probably die in the attack but the Danes feared that if the records were not destroyed the whole Danish resistance network would be at risk. We were presented with the usual model of the target area, together with photographs of the building and the approach path to be used in the attack. Some of the photographs had been taken by the Danes themselves and smuggled out. A Danish naval officer was also present. He had been brought out of Denmark to give us up-to-date information and had left his wife and family behind in Copenhagen. The next morning we arrived at the briefing room for final instructions and found that the weather had deteriorated and was unsuitable for low flying over the sea, so the operation was postponed for twenty-four hours. That evening some crews went into Norwich for a few jars and finished up in the local theatre where 'Jane' of *Daily Mirror* fame was performing. On 31 January the raid was postponed again for a further twenty-four hours and next morning, 1 February, Embry announced that he could not afford to have his aircraft hanging around doing nothing for any longer. The operation would have to take place at a later date and we were to return to Thorney Island that day. He warned us not to breathe a word to anyone and that when the raid did take place all crews present would be on it. He also added that he had arranged for extra copies of the *Daily Mirror* to be delivered to the mess at Thorney Island! On 2 February 'Daddy' Dale and Hackett, his navigator, went missing on a night patrol. Four days later the squadron transferred to Rosières-en-Santerre and shortly afterwards Wing Commander V. R. Oates took over command.[91]

On 2 February 'Dinty' Moore attended a briefing with Squadron Leader Kyle.

We found that our target was not, as was our usual practice, in immediate support of the army but an oil target, at Emmerich. We crossed the battlefront and found the target, in spite of the usual flak. The aircraft in the second box scored direct hits on the target, which made quite an impressive sight even from our height. I flew a further seven operations during February, when having one of the leading aircraft fitted with Gee-H proved to be invaluable. The Lancasters of the Bomber Command Pathfinder Force were using this electronic marvel. In our case, where cloud covered the target, the aircraft fitted with this equipment took over the lead, the observer transmitting to the rest of the formation, who dropped their bombs on his instructions. The recipients of our bombs were all German troop concentrations, the 8th at Kallenberg, the 9th at Rheinberg, the 10th at Xanton and the 11th at Sonsbeck. The German anti-aircraft gunners did their best, though their efforts were not helped by the presence of the cloud, with the result that they were not accurate. The next operation, on the 14th, was identical, other than the target being at Udem, which was notable in that any anti-aircraft fire did not disturb our progress at all.

I flew my last two operations on the same day, 14 February, first taking off at 0830 hours with Squadron Leader Lyle and at 1430 hours with Squadron Leader Edmondes. The morning attack was on German troop reinforcements at Udem and in the afternoon on Straaelen. We found no cloud on either occasion other than the threatening little black clouds of heavy flak that came up as an impressive barrage. All of these eight operations flown during February, ending on the 14th, lasted between two and two and a half hours without any damage to the aircraft in which I was flying. Thus, my operational career came to an end, leaving me with the satisfaction of making my final contribution, unlike the end of my second tour with Johnny Reeve. I had taken part in twenty-three missions on this tour, our aircraft being hit on three occasions, nearly being decapitated in one of them, yet had survived. The role of the wireless operators and air gunners on heavy bombers was still essential but with the sophisticated radio equipment and the Allied air forces having complete control of the skies over the battle front, our role in medium bombers was becoming almost unnecessary. We had been an essential part of the crew, using our skill as wireless operators to maintain a link with our base and to obtain bearings and fixes for the observer. Similarly, we had been our only real defence against attacks by enemy fighters. I felt, therefore, no sense of guilt when I was told that it was time to quit, being in a position to claim to have flown on operations in every year of the war, except 1939, with a total of ninety-two missions spread over, in effect, four operational tours. I had been extremely fortunate to survive. My only regret was that the same degree of luck had not been extended to Peter, so we could have been together to fulfil our plans after the war.

On 6 February 1945 21, 464 and 487 Squadrons of 140 Wing left southern England and moved to Amiens and Rosières-en-Santerre. Les Bulmer in 21 Squadron recalled:

Personnel were scattered around the airfield in villages. The admin types naturally picked the best chateau for themselves. 21 Squadron aircrew were billeted in a chateau in Warvillers. It served as the mess and sleeping quarters were in an orchard at the rear. These were wooden huts thoughtfully provided by the Germans. There was even a small dance hall suitably decorated with *Luftwaffe* murals. It wasn't the Ritz but at least it was better than the tents we'd had at Gravesend and Thorney Island and which we were led to believe we would have to use in France. Actually, we did cheat a little at Thorney Island. As winter developed, so came the gales and one night one of the senior officers lost his tent. Since there was a large empty mess on the other side of the airfield it seemed only logical to fill it. So we did, still sleeping on our camp beds so that we could continue to qualify for the 'hard living' allowance.

The arrival of the Mosquito squadrons at Amiens and Rosières-en-Santerre coincided with the first anniversary of the Amiens raid by 140 Wing Mosquitoes on 18 February 1944, when the walls of Jericho had come tumbling down. Pickard's widow was flown out especially from England to visit her husband's grave and for the mass in Amiens Cathedral. 'Ginger' Walsh was among the personnel who attended and afterwards he visited the wall, now patched, through which the French Resistance had escaped.

The bulk of our squadron was billeted in Amiens. At first I slept at Meharicourt, near the bomb dump in what had been the *Luftwaffe* hospital site at the airfield. *Wehrmacht* and *Luftwaffe* personnel too badly wounded to be evacuated were still there. Later the local village butcher adopted a friend Bob Belcher and me and we were billeted at his elderly mother's small chateau. Near our base was a huge First World War cemetery filled with thousands of white crosses. We buried Flying Officer Joe Coe and his fellow New Zealander Squadron Leader pilot there after they crashed on take-off one day and their bombs and fuel load exploded. Joe had already lost his fingers and been badly burned in a Wellington crash earlier in the war. At their funeral a group of French schoolchildren sang 'God Save the King'.

One of the crews in 305 Squadron at Epinoy at this time was pilot Flight Lieutenant Reg Everson, an ex-railway policeman and his navigator Flight Lieutenant Tony Rudd, a university graduate. They had crewed up at 2 Group GSU at Swanton Morley in September 1944. Everson recalled:

At Epinoy our enthusiasm was somewhat dampened when we found the airfield covered with 6 ft of snow and we spent most of the daylight hours using shovels to help clear the runways. Eventually flying was possible, taking off along runways with snow piled high on either side. It did, however, concentrate the mind and made the pilots even more careful than ever to avoid a swing on take-off. Night patrols were carried out most nights, incurring a number of casualties, attacking enemy road and rail transport when possible and bombing rail junctions on Gee when bad weather prevented visual sightings. One night we returned from patrol to find $^{10}/_{10}$ cloud at 200 ft over the base. As our Gee set had gone 'on the blink' I declined the offer of a diversion to Brussels (I learned better later) and received permission to land at base. This proved somewhat 'hairy' but landing was completed without damage. No operations were carried out for the next few nights, diverted aircraft having to return to base and the weather remained such that even the birds were walking. Normal service was resumed until 13 February when the squadron had a break from operations to practise for a daylight formation operation – *Clarion*. As it was to be a twelve-aircraft formation some crews (including us) were not involved. However, on the day of the operation, 22 February, it was decided to increase it to maximum effort and all crews and serviceable aircraft were to be involved. Without the benefit of practice we had an unenviable position, eighteenth in an eighteen-plane formation.

Wilf Jessop, a navigator in 418 Squadron recalled:

After testing the aircraft for night flying and with fine weather, we expected to do our usual night patrol. However, operations were cancelled and bad weather given as the excuse but navigators were instructed to report at 0630 hours the next morning with long-range maps. We were cautioned about security. AVM Basil Embry, Officer Commanding 2 Group appeared next morning and explained our part in Operation *Clarion*, which was to attack road junctions, railways, transport and buildings in North Western Germany aiming in twenty-four hours to decimate German ground transport. Nine thousand Allied aircraft were to take part in the operation.

Clarion was intended to be the *coup de grace* for the German transport system. It started at 1300 hours and full scale attacks were made on German communications, railway stations, crossroads, bridges, ships and barges on canals and rivers, railway trucks and engines, stores and other targets. No. 2 Group put up every available aircraft, flying 215 sorties, 176 from the Continent and the remainder from 136 Wing in England. It was to be the last time that the Mosquitoes operated in daylight in such numbers.

Les Bulmer of 21 Squadron commented:

We fielded sixteen aircraft, eight from each flight. The squadron was allocated an area between Bremen and Hannover in which any form of transport was to be attacked. This area was sub-divided between 'A' and 'B' Flights and these two areas in turn were divided again so that groups of four aircraft each had their own particular patch to cover. As by now we were one of the more experienced crews on the squadron, we were to lead four aircraft to the farthest areas just to the north of Hannover. The whole squadron took off at 1130 and formed up in two sections of eight, 'A' Flight leading. We flew north-east to the Zuider Zee, then turned east. Over the Dummer Zee 'A' Flight left us to fly north-east to their area. 'B' Flight continued east and shortly afterwards four aircraft turned away northwards, leaving us and our brood of three to carry on eastwards to our patch, which covered the area bounded by Nienburg, Schwarmstedt, Hannover and Wunsdorf. Over Schwarmstedt we found two engines and a freight train in the station, so we dived on them with cannons and bombs followed by our No. 2, Pilot Officer Bolton. The other two aircraft left us to find a train of their own to play with. We got cannon strikes on the engines and Bolton reported large clouds of steam as we pulled away. We continued around our area but saw nothing worth attacking, so set off westwards for home. Just south of the Dummer Zee we found another train at Lemforde and turned to attack it but they'd already seen us and sent up a hail of 20 mm flak, so we decided to give it a miss. Soon afterwards, a single-engined aircraft appeared heading in the opposite direction and above us. He apparently didn't see us and we didn't stop to identify.

Reg Everson and Tony Rudd in 305 Squadron meanwhile also braved flak. Wing Commander S. Grodzicki DFC led 305 Squadron and Squadron Leader P. Hanburg led the British flight. For half an hour the Mosquitoes of 305 Squadron wreaked havoc in the Bremen-Hamburg-Kiel region. The German ground defences were strong. Ten aircraft suffered damage and one with a British crew was lost; the pilot was killed and the navigator taken prisoner.

Reg Everson recalled:

We flew in close formation at 4,000 ft until we crossed the enemy lines when we encountered some light flak bursting at that height. We took evasive action and rejoined the formation as soon as we were clear of danger. When we arrived at the area Stade, River Elbe, we broke into 'pairs'. I was No. 2 to Warrant Officer Smith. Our main targets were barges and shipping, secondary targets being warehouses, trains and road transport. During our patrol we attacked railway trucks. The eighteen aircraft did considerable damage and eight of them were damaged by ground fire. We then set course for base, formating on Warrant Officer Smith at low level. Shortly after leaving the patrol area we passed over a machine gun post and Smith's aircraft was hit and caught fire; we saw it make a crash landing. Not being sure of our exact position and as we had used up all our machine gun ammunition and cannon shells, I climbed to a safer height of 4,000 ft, at which we could get an accurate Gee fix. We soon found out where we were! The guns of Bremerhaven opened up and the air was filled with black puffs of exploding shells. A sharp diving turn to port down to nought feet followed, for a reassessment of the situation. Bremen was to our south, so a course was set for Zwoller on the River Yssel, which was the 'Bomb Line' for the day. Once we felt safer from immediate danger we made a tentative climb to 4,000 ft to enable us to use Gee to keep away from further 'hot spots'. Shortly after reaching this height an American Mustang formated on our starboard wing. A cigar-chewing pilot waved a friendly greeting before peeling off to go about his own business. As we approached Zwoller I opened the throttles to maximum boost, put the nose down to get maximum speed and crossed the River Yssel as quickly as possible. The rest of the trip was uneventful.

P. D. Morris was the pilot of a Mosquito FBVI fighter-bomber in 613 (City of Manchester) Squadron at Epinoy near Cambrai, France, on 22 February recalled:

My navigator Ron Parfitt and I had flown together on every operation since arriving in France on 19 November 1944. Six days after arriving at Epinoy we did our first night operation – the first of forty. However, on 22 February we were briefed for our first Day Ranger sortie against the enemy. All the squadrons were to take part and the area given to Ron and me to patrol was the very north of Germany up in Schleswig Holstein near the Danish border. Our job was to patrol a large area and bomb, machine gun and cannon any enemy transport or personnel we spotted. After being able to cause a little havoc on various targets, the time came for us to make our way home. To do so, we were to go directly west until we reached the North Sea and to fly back to friendly territory before crossing to land back again. We were flying fairly low, roughly at about 10–15 ft, as it was safer. As we crossed over very low-lying fields that were separated by dykes, which were about the same height as that at which we were flying, I was looking well ahead when I suddenly saw a German soldier 300 yards ahead who was having the audacity to be firing from the top of the dyke directly at us. This I thought was not good enough so I armed first my four machine guns and then my four cannons. After that I took a very careful bead on this presumptuous fellow. When about one hundred yards from him I pulled both triggers but all that emerged from my guns was complete silence! However, I was determined at least to frighten him badly, so I passed over him a few feet over his head and saw him fall flat on his face. I feel after that he must have headed for the nearest Schnapps! When we got out over the sea I decided to try out the guns again, so having armed them, I pulled the two triggers and both guns fired perfectly. My aircraft was and until that moment not known as any particular friend of the Germans! This soldier, if still alive must be among the luckiest imaginable!

At 1117 hours Wilf Jessop and his pilot, Wing Commander Jack Wickett, led 418 Squadron's twenty aircraft in formation at a height of about 1,000 ft from Hartford Bridge to Aldburgh and then over the North Sea to Holland at 50 ft above the waves.

Whilst over the sea we sent three aircraft back home. One was hit by birds and damaged. Two collided due to ballooning drop tanks during the tricky and dangerous manoeuvre of skidding out of formation during the drop and skidding back in. We climbed just before reaching the Dutch coast then dropped down to 50 ft again to avoid German radar. When the formation reached the east coast of the Zuider Zee Wickett ordered the seventeen aircraft remaining to split up and go for their individual targets. We cruised along at 240 m.p.h., 50–100 ft above the ground. At about 1230 hours our aircraft was hit by light flak near the Dortmund–Ems canal south-east of Osnabrück before reaching our target. The aircraft was on fire and as the wheels and flaps were hanging our hydraulics had probably been damaged. My pilot broke radio silence to say we had been badly shot up and would try to land in a marshy area. I had given him a course of 270 degrees magnetic for home but he could not keep the aircraft in the air and made, in the circumstances, a marvellous landing alongside the canal. The whole of my side of the cockpit caved in and, with our cannon shells and machine gun bullets exploding, I got out rather sharpish, not having a parachute hanging on my backside to hinder me. My pilot, sitting on and fastened to his parachute, was having difficulty getting out.

I have a faint recollection of helping him, knowing we were sitting on top of two 500 lb bombs ready to explode. We both ran out like the clappers away from the aircraft – the direction did not matter! We got about 60 yards away when the bombs went off. We were glad of the eleven-second delay fuses on them. Armed Germans quickly picked us up and it was then that I found I had only one boot on. We were taken to a barge on the canal where my pilot was briefly questioned. Most of the Germans on the barge were quite young, about fifteen and manning an anti-aircraft gun. Towards late afternoon we were marched off in the direction of the remains of our aircraft and I had visions of us being disposed of near it. I mentioned this to my pilot but we decided to hang on a bit. We arrived at a factory, which was shut and our guards could not get in so they took us back to the barge. I think they thought they could hand us over to someone else. Some of them lost a bit of sleep that night guarding us. I found out much later that this operation turned out to be the costliest to date for 418 Squadron – four aircraft failed to return to base.

Les Bulmer, returning to base, noticed that all the way back to the Zuider Zee Pilot Officer Bolton was staying well back behind them.

We couldn't figure out why he didn't stay close. (At the debriefing he explained that we were being shot at at several points on the way out and he didn't really want to get involved. Fortunately for our peace of mind, Bert and I were totally unaware of this.) Just short of the Zuider Zee we spotted two trucks on the road north of Elspeet. We were almost over the top of them before we noticed them and did an imitation of a Stuka, with an almost vertical dive, to give them a blast of cannon. Several characters left them a bit sharpish. I only hope that they were Germans and not Dutch. From there we had an uneventful trip back to base, where we landed at 1450. No. 21 Squadron was one of the lucky ones that day. We lost only one aircraft, Fielding-Johnson and Harbord. No. 464 lost two and 487 took a hammering and lost five. I believe that this was principally because they chose to take the long route around the coast and got caught by flak and fighters as a result. No. 2 Group lost twenty-one Mosquitoes on *Clarion* with forty damaged. I think it taught the 'powers that be' a salutary lesson that the Mosquito was not, after all, invulnerable.

Hugh Henry Fielding-Johnson had joined 21 Squadron in March 1944 and he flew his first operation on 26 March with his navigator Flying Officer L. C. Harbord. Fielding-Johnson was known on the squadron as 'Fee-Gee' (or 'Fiji') and he sported a typical RAF moustache. He also wore a navigator's or an air gunner's brevet above his right breast pocket, perhaps out of respect for his illustrious father, Squadron Leader W. S. Fielding-Johnson who was also a pilot and a qualified air-gunner. At fifty-two Squadron Leader Fielding-Johnson was the oldest air gunner on operations in the RAF serving as gunnery leader of a 2nd TAF Mitchell squadron taking part in an attack at Venlo in Holland. His aircraft was severely hit by flak over the target. The captain gave orders to jump. Johnson climbed down from his upper turret and, at 8,000 ft, jumped. As he said later, 'This was the thing I have always wanted to do. As soon as I had pulled the cord I found the sensation quite splendid.'

 Bulmer continues:

Thankfully we returned to night patrols and did our twenty-third and last op together on 10 March. I had been on the squadron for thirteen months and had completed seventy-five ops. After acting as 'officers under instruction' at a court-martial in Lille, we returned to the squadron to find that we were posted to No.1 Ferry Unit at Pershore. Peter Kleboe had arrived to take over the squadron, Wing Commander V. R. Oates having failed to return from an op on 12 March. We left 21 Squadron on 18 March. As we climbed aboard the Anson to take us back to the UK the adjutant came out to see us off and whispered that the Shellhaus raid was on again and was due in the next few days. My feelings were mixed when I heard this. I'd missed out on all the much-vaunted 2 Group pinpoint raids except the attack on the barracks in Nijmegen at the beginning of Market Garden and that had ended in a complete fiasco. On the other hand, I would probably be pushing my luck to do just one more op. It was with sadness that I heard of Peter Kleboe's death three days later. I'd only known him for a few days but I liked him and reckoned he would be good for the squadron. With three COs lost in just over six weeks, 21 Squadron was going through a bad patch. But such is war.

Squadron Leader Malcolm Scott DFC, a Mitchell navigator in 180 Squadron recalled:

For more than a week during March 1945 the Mitchells and Bostons of 2 Group had been pounding targets in the Rhineland in close support of the 21st Army Group fighting its way to the great river barrier. Some 22,000 British, Canadian and American casualties had been suffered in clearing the area between the Maas and the Rhine. Xanten, one of 2 Group's earlier targets and more recently the recipient of a devastating night raid by Bomber Command, was now occupied by British and Canadian troops. The last strong bastion of the German troops on the west side had fallen and within a few days the rest of the territory was cleared and the Allied armies stood on the west bank looking at the remains of the Wesel bridge blown up by the retreating Germans. For the six squadrons of 137 and 139 Wings in 2 Group the targets now shifted to the east side of the Rhine. At least two, occasionally three, raids were made each day on marshalling yards, communication centres and bridges, oil dumps, billeting areas and barracks, artillery emplacements and troop concentrations. Some penetrations were deeper to important rail centres but mostly attacks were concentrated in the Weser-Emmerich-Munster area where Plunder, the code name for the overall operation covering the Rhine crossing, was to take place. Maximum effort had been ordered and quite often up to fifteen aircraft per squadron took part instead of the usual dozen aircraft in two boxes of six.

Montgomery's preparations for the Rhine crossing were, as always, massive and painstaking: troops being ferried to the rear echelons to practise 'boat drill' and the handling of small craft up and down the muddy banks of the River Maas at night in preparation for the real thing. There could be no misleading or attempted feints this time. Within a mile or two, the Germans could estimate where the Allied crossing would be made. As Kesselring wrote, 'The enemy's operations in a clearly limited area, bombing raids on headquarters and the smoke-screening and assembly of bridging materials, indicated their intention to attack between Emmerich and Dinslaken with the point of the main effort on either side of Rees.' The only questions facing the enemy was when and how? Always before, the Allies had launched a parachute and glider attack as a prelude to the full force of the main assault. Kesselring could but wait to see where the paras dropped, or so he thought. In the meantime, RAF medium bombers and Typhoons and the 9th AF Marauders and Thunderbolts carried on with their now familiar role of 'softening up' the area around the chosen points of the great river and the hinterland of the proposed bridgeheads on the east bank. One important road and rail junction town and troop-billeting area was Bocholt, which became the object of almost daily attacks and quickly gained a reputation for providing a very warm reception. On 18 March it was bombed and again two days later. We all got back but with our aircraft and a few aircrew heavily peppered by shrapnel.

The next morning, 21 March, Bocholt was again listed as the target. On the bombing run No. 1 in the box was badly damaged and an air gunner's leg was almost shot away but the pilot retained control and made an emergency landing at Eindhoven. No. 2 in the box received a direct hit as the bombs fell away and virtually disintegrated, taking down No. 3, an all-Australian crew, from which one parachute was seen to emerge. This belonged to an air gunner who although captured on landing was freed eight days later by advancing British troops. The pilot of No. 4 was severely injured, shrapnel smashing through his right thigh bone but he managed to retain consciousness long enough to get his aircraft back over friendly territory after bombing, before passing out. The mid-upper gunner then took over the controls and managed under the pilot's guidance to crash land at the first airfield *en route* without further casualties. The leading aircraft of the second box was seriously damaged by flak, wounding an air gunner but the pilot pressed on, bombed and led his formation back over the Rhine before breaking away to force land at Eindhoven. Bocholt deserved its thick red ring on the map as a place to be avoided if possible!

Of the twelve 180 Squadron Mitchells that had left Melsbroek earlier only seven returned to base, all with varying degrees of flak damage and some with wounded aboard. Only six aircraft took part in the afternoon show but the other two squadrons operated twenty-four. The next day they were joined by eleven aircraft from 180 Squadron, attacking an enemy strongpoint near Dingden in the morning and Isselburg in the afternoon. Notification was received of an immediate award of the DSO to the wounded pilot, Pilot Officer Perkins, a CGM to his air gunner, Flight Sergeant J. Hall who carried out the emergency landing and a DFC to the leading pilot of the second box, Flight Lieutenant G. Howard-Jones.

On 23 March the Mitchells and Bostons bombed strongpoints near Wesel in the morning. On return from a second visit to Isselburg in the late afternoon, we were told at debriefing that this was 'R-Day' and that British, Canadian and American troops would be crossing the Rhine that evening at various points on either side of Wesel and Rees. An early night was suggested and while we slept Bomber Command put in a heavy attack on Wesel. Long before dawn on the 24th, 'R-Day + 1', we were called to attend briefing at 0530. The target was set in the forest of Diersfordterwald, northwest of Hamminkein, where we would be making the final bombing raid before Operation *Varsity* the airborne assault, came in. Our bombload was six clusters of 20 lb APs. The bombing height was to be between 11,000 and 12,000 ft and the approximate heading on the bombing run 075, turning right off target after bombing.

By 0735 we were checking over our individual equipment in the aircraft and half an hour later we took off leading 'Grey' Box, while 'Brown' Box tucked in behind as we set course. We picked up our Spitfire escort as we set course for Xanten, where we contacted 'Cosycoat', the MRCP controller. Within minutes we crossed the Rhine but the flak was minimal and not particularly accurate. Bomb doors were opened as the pilots followed the instructions given by 'Cosycoat' on the run-in to the target and the six clusters dropped clumsily away from each bomber. Flak was now more accurate but, judged by earlier standards, only moderate. 'Cosycoat' signed us off and took control of another box running in. It all seemed very impersonal as the bombing details were entered in the log and the pilot was given the new course and it was not until we'd made our right turn off the target that I became aware of all the activity taking place below. Even during the Ardennes breakthrough in the snow of the previous December and January I saw nothing to match the scene below us.

On either side of the river we could see the ripple of flashes from gun batteries and tanks and the occasional puff of dust and smoke as a flurry of shells landed. The little boats (from our height) handled by the Navy were ploughing back and forth across the river and we could see the spans of the demolished bridges lying in the water; already pontoon bridges were being thrown across the great waterway looking like threads of cotton. We knew, although we couldn't see them, that the army and Marine Commandos alongside various infantry units were fighting around Rees and Wesel and our tanks were already in action on the east bank, having 'swum' across during the night and early morning. Smoke was still drifting about and we could see Tempests, Typhoons, Mustangs and Thunderbolts diving in to attack enemy positions. We learned afterwards that Churchill was there on a high vantage point with Alanbrooke, Eisenhower and Tedder but I don't think they got the marvellous view we did.

As we left the Rhine behind us we could see, coming in from the west, several thousand feet below, the vanguard of the Airborne Divisions. Dakotas, C-46 Commandos and C-47s loaded with paratroopers and their equipment occupied the first waves of the assault, heading three great columns stretching back as far as the eye could see. Following the paratroops came the gliders towed by Halifax, Stirling and Albermarle tugs and of course the ubiquitous Dakotas. Our south-westerly course was gradually taking us away from this awe-inspiring sight. We hoped our bombing had been of support and had reduced in some measure the opposition that the Airborne were bound to encounter. Our fighter escort left us over Goch and we were all back at base by 1010. There was the inevitable 'turn round' call; the bomb trolleys were waiting to fill the empty bellies of our aircraft as we taxied in. Another briefing was on at 1045 and the squadron was airborne again by 1250, attacking another strong point near Brunen. The great colonnade had gone. All that remained of it were masses of 'broken' gliders and splashes of discarded parachutes. Smoke and gunfire were still in evidence but it was not the same. The morning of 'R-Day + 1' was the only time that I really appreciated to the full our true role in tactical air support.

Reg Everson in 305 Squadron meanwhile still had a tour to finish.

After all the excitement of *Clarion*, night operations resumed and on 5 March, on return from patrol, we found the base covered with $^{10}/_{10}$ cloud. This time we took the offered diversion to Brussels, a wise move. Owing to the adverse weather conditions we had to stay in Brussels, enjoying an enforced 48-hour 'leave'. By this time our patrol areas were moving further into Germany, making a longer trip there and back, which cut down the time we could spend in the patrol areas, due to fuel capacity. On these operations we used 'drop tanks' and carried flares in the bomb bay instead of bombs. On sighting anything suspicious we would climb to 4,000 ft, drop a flare and circle below it to give Tony a chance to inspect the ground more thoroughly. We then attacked using machine guns and cannon.

On 8 April, for operation 436 (the squadron's, not mine), twelve aircraft were briefed to patrol and attack enemy movements on railways and roads in the Leipzig-Berlin-Magdeburg-Braunsweig region. My aircraft was u/s so I borrowed Duke Earle's. The weather was cloudless, visibility good. All aircraft completed sorties except 'U', which returned with a defect. We completed the patrol on the Berlin–Magdeburg road and made an attack under flares on enemy transport. Lights on the transport were extinguished and movement stopped but the flares went out so we could not assess fully the extent of the damage.

On the return flight, while flying at 4,000 ft indicated at about 0200, we were attacked by a night fighter. He fired a long burst of machine gun fire and I immediately took violent evasive action. However, the port engine caught fire. Tony operated the fire extinguisher and I feathered the engine. A further burst of machine gun fire and the starboard engine caught fire. I throttled back and operated the fire extinguisher but the fire did not go out so I ordered Tony to abandon the aircraft. He clipped on his parachute, jettisoned the door and successfully jumped clear. During this manoeuvre the aircraft was losing height rapidly. I struggled out of the seat, at the same time trying to keep the aircraft on an even keel. With some difficulty I reached the doorway and dived head first through the opening.

Reg Everson was captured and taken for interrogation later, at *Gestapo* HQ in Gummerbach, where his interrogator, a former insurance agent in the Purley area before the war, questioned him at length before having him sent to *Stalag VIG*, a PoW camp near Olpe. After a short stay the prisoners were marched under armed guard to another camp, at Enbach. During the forced march the prisoners were quite often attacked by American fighter-bombers, who thought they were German troop columns, but fortunately there were no casualties among the prisoners. Finally, on 12 April at 1400 hours, the 78th US Infantry Division liberated the camp. Reg was reunited with Tony Rudd and later they discovered that the aircraft that had shot them down on 8 April had been a P-61 Black Widow whose pilot had claimed a Ju 88 destroyed! (Black Widows of the 422nd NFS were by this time based at Strassfeldt, Germany and P-61s of the 425th NFS were stationed at Etain, France.)

When, on 21 April, 'Ginger' Walsh and 'Pat' Patterson of 487 Squadron in France flew an op to Emden, everything that could go wrong went wrong. Walsh remembered:

We took off and landed at Melsbroek first before we reached the Rhine. We had a funnel only about 2 miles wide. A Mossie that had aborted flew back past us at a closing speed of more than 600 m.p.h. and narrowly missed us! Crossing the Rhine we almost hit a barrage balloon that our boys were flying from a barge. We ended up at 1,000–1,500 ft in the middle of a German airfield. I compressed myself into a small space but nothing happened. We turned west and came back towards Hamburg. Finally, we dropped our bombs on a German town. 'Pat' threw the aircraft around but nothing happened. Back at Amiens our NZ Squadron Leader who was acting CO berated 'Pat' for bringing his ammo back.

'Pat' must have taken it to heart because four days later, on 25 April, when we were coming back from Emden, he lowered the nose and began firing. I told him three times that we were nearing our lines! His target could have been a haystack or it could have been Hitler. 'Pat' continued firing off our ammo. We got light flak; the tracer was utterly fascinating and missed us but I had to do something. I reached up and fired off the red and yellow colours of the day from the Verey pistol mounted in the roof of the cockpit. It did the trick! The cockpit filled with cordite and there was a big flash.

'Pat' said, 'What the – was that?'

I giggled and told him that I'd fired the Verey pistol. You never gave away the colours of the day but it was of no consequence to me! The firing stopped. I had visions of a German down below looking at his flimsy [his 'colours of the day', which could be easily destroyed when no longer needed].

It was on this operation that Flight Lieutenant Johnny Evans and his navigator, Flying Officer Ifor Jenkins, were lost. Johnny had lost two pilot brothers killed in the war. I'd spent time in Montreal with Ifor. They put out a Mayday call: 'I'm on fire and losing height!' They'd got him.

Another voice said, 'You'll be all right.' Evans replied caustically, 'It's all right for you.' That was it – they were dead.

During April the retreat by the *Wehrmacht* had left medium bombers far to the rear of the battlefront, so at the end of the month 138 Wing advanced to Achmer. Right up until the German surrender, Mosquitoes, Mitchells and Bostons of 2 Group continued operations against rail and road targets. On the night of 2 May, for instance, forty-two aircraft attacked troop transports with 500 lb bombs, flares and cannon and machine gun fire, leaving nine trains burning furiously. At 0800 hours on 8 May the cease-fire came into effect and VE Day was declared.

VE Day, 8 May 1945. AC1 Phillip Beck (on the nose of Mosquito FBVI 'U') and fellow ground crew of 613 (City of Manchester) Squadron at Epinoy celebrate. (*Phillip Beck*)

NOTES

[1] KIA 18.9.41 having scored 27 victories and awarded the *Ritterkreuz*.

[2] LAC C. 'Tich' Birch was KIA 16.2.40; LAC J. B. Johnny Ball was KIA 6.4.40; Paddy B (AC1 R. Charleton) died on 11.5.40 and LAC A. C. B. Butch Burgess was KIA on 12.5.40.

[3] A superb account of 2 Group Blenheim operations can be found in *Bristol Blenheim* by Theo Boiten, Crowood Avaition Series, 1998.

[4] Theo Boiten, *Blenheim Strike*, ARP, 1995

[5] On 9 August 1943 Squadron Leader Edgar Alfred Costello-Bowen AFC, Chief Flying Instructor at 1655 MTU was killed in a flying accident while a passenger in a Ventura. Squadron Leader Tommy Broom DFC** went on to complete fifty-eight operations on Mosquitoes in 8 Group. (See Martin W. Bowman: *The Men Who Flew The Mosquito,* Pen & Sword, 2003).

[6] On 26/27 March 1942 Gildner, now a *Oberleutnant* in II./NJG2, shot down over Holland a 114 Squadron Blenheim flown by Flight Sergeant Bill Popplestone RCAF. There were no survivors from the aircraft, which crashed into the Waddenzee north of Wieringen. On 24/25 February 1943 Gildner, who was awared the *Ritterkreuz* and had forty-four victories, forty-two of these at night, was KIA near Gilze Rijen. (See Theo Boiten: *Blenheim Strike*, ARP, 1995).

[7] Twenty-year-old Flight Sergeant Freddie Thripp survived fifty-five Blenheim operations in 82 and 110 Squadron (the latter as gunnery leader). He was KIA when Wing Commander Theo 'Joe' Hunt DFC, CO of 110 Squadron, and crew were shot down by a Fiat CR.42 Falco Biplane fighter off Tripoli on 18 July 1941.

[8] Viedebantt was KIA 1.5.45.

[9] Joseph Roy George Ralston, a 1930s 'Halton brat' who by 1938 was a sergeant pilot in 108 Squadron flying Hawker Hinds and Blenheims, came to be regarded by many, including Hughie Edwards VC, as the greatest bomber pilot of all time. He did two tours of daylight operations on Blenheims and another on night and then he went on to do another, very long operational tour on Mosquitoes at night, so he really did four tours. He and his navigator Syd Clayton were later awarded the DSO after completing 100 ops. Clayton, who later trained as a pilot, had a record of finding and hitting the target that was certainly unsurpassed. By March 1945 Wing Commander Ralston DSO* DFC DFM AFC was CO of 139 Squadron and still flew on operations. He was invalided out of the RAF in 1946 with tuberculosis.

[10] *Oberleutant* Karl-Heinz Leesmann and *Oberfeldwebel* Karl Munz of 1./JG52 claimed the 20-year-old Glaswegian's Blenheim.

[11] Wilson's Blenheim had been claimed shot down by Karl-Heinz Leesmann and Munz.

[12] Naval flak gunners shot down and killed Sergeants F. Wood, pilot, E. G. Baker, observer and C. N. Harris, WOp/AG.

[13] 105 Squadron, meanwhilte, would fly their first Circus operation with six aircraft making a high-level attack on shipping at Le Havre.

[14] Galland also shot down a Spitfire to take his score to sixty-nine.

[15] Squadron Leader F. R. H. Charney DFC was KIA flying on operations from Malta on 12 September 1941.

[16] Stuart R. Scott: *Battle-Axe Blenheims*: *No. 105 Squadron RAF at War 1940-1*, Sutton 1996.

[17] Stuart R. Scott: *Battle-Axe Blenheims*: *No. 105 Squadron RAF at War 1940-1*, Sutton 1996.

[18] Major the Honorable Richard Coke, fifth son of the second Earl of Leicester and his French wife known affectionately as 'Pheas'.

[19] Mike Henry DFC, *Air Gunner*, Foulis & Co, 1964.

[20] For an account in full of the Rotterdam raid see Theo Boiten: *Blenheim Strike*, ARP 1995, and Stuart R. Scott, *Battle-Axe Blenheims*: *No 105 Squadron RAF at War 1940-1*, Sutton 1996.

[21] Herget was a *Zerstorer* pilot with twelve victories during May–September 1940 including nine Hurricanes and Spitfires during the Battle of Britain. '*Der Kleine*' or 'The small one', as he was known because of his lack of height, ended the war as an Me 262 pilot having scored seventy-three victories, fifty-three of these at night including eight four-engined bombers in forty-five

minutes on 20/21 December 1943. He was awarded the *Ritterkreuz* with Oak Leaves. See Theo Boiten *Blenheim Strike*, ARP, 1995.

[22] *Hauptmann* Kurt Ruppert, *Staffelkapitän* of III./JG26 was KIA near Neumunster on 13 June 1943 when his Bf 109G-6 was hit by return fire from an 8th AF B-17. He baled out but he tried to open his parachute too early and the harness ripped, throwing Ruppert out of it to his death. He had twenty-one victories. (See Donald Caldwell, *The JG26 War Diary*, Vol 2 1943–45, Grub Street, 1998).

[23] Galland was also credited with a Spitfire 16 miles west of Vlissingen for his seventy-seventh victory. He scored eighty-four victories with JG26 between 14 June 1940 and 18 November 1941. In January 1945, when he was relieved of his position as *General der Jagdflieger*, he formed the jet fighter unit JV44. Galland finished the war with 104 victories. (See Donald Caldwell, *The JG26 War Diary*, Vol 2 1943–45, Grub Street, 1998).

[24] Squadron leader (later Wing Commander) Alan Lynn DFC, a South African, had joined the RAF just before the war on a short-service commission. In 1940 he had flown Fairey Battles in France but had taken a dislike to the single-engined machine and was sent home and put into training Command. However he somehow eventually persuaded his seniors to release him for operational duties on twin-engines. On 5 January 1942 Lynn took command of 107 Squadron and remained with it until 13 September 1942. By late 1944 he had completed at least 150 operations and had been awared the DSO and bar and DFC and bar, together with a Dutch gallantry medal.

[25] See Theo Boiten, *Blenheim Strike*, ARP 1995.

[26] W4064/C failed to return on 31 May 1942 when it was hit by flak on the operation to Cologne and was ditched 6 miles south-west of Antwerp, at Bazel on the bank of the Schelde. Pilot Officers William Deryck Kennard and Eric Raymond Johnson were killed.

[27] The Mossie, 36, September 2004.

[28] Squadron Leader John Castle took temporary charge of 226 Squadron until the appointment of Wing Commander W. E. Surplice DFC.

[29] Grütz was buried with full military honours. Feldwebel Johannes Rathenow was KIA on 3 November 1943 when he was shot down in combat with USAAF bombers and P-38s at Bad Zwischenahn.

[30] In March 1943 418 Squadron re-equipped with Mosquito FBVIs and in 1944 was adopted by the City of Edmonton. No 605 Squadron re-equipped with Mosquito FBVIs in February–March 1944.

[31] KIA during a low-level attack on Mazingarbe, 31.10.42.

[32] See Arthur Eyton-Jones, *Day Bomber*, Sutton Publishing Ltd, 1998.

[33] KIA 13.11.42.

[34] Both KIA 9.10.42 when they were shot down by *Feldwebel* Fritz Timm of 12./JG1 (See Eric Moubeek, *Defending the Reich. The History of JG1,* JAC Publication, 1992).

[35] Bristow and Marshall were shot down in DK328/V on 7 November 1942 during an operation against the 5,000 ton German ship *Elsa Essberger* in the mouth of the River Gironde. Both men survived and were made PoW.

[36] A full account of the Oslo raid can be found in Martin Bowman, *The Men Who Flew The Mosquito*, Pen & Sword, 2003 and Stuart R. Scott, *Mosquito Thunder*, Sutton 1999.

[37] 'Collie' Collins evaded capture and eventually returned home nine months later via the French underground and imprisonment in Spain. (A full accout of his adventures can be found in Martin W. Bowman, *Low Level From Swanton*, ARP, 1995.) Pilot Officer Harry J. Milford and Sergeant George Nicholls were captured almost immediately and later placed in PoW camps. Milford was sent to *Stalag Luft III*, Sagan, in Pomerania. He became heavily involved in the 'X' escape organization in the British compound and was one of those who took part in the the Great Escape on the night of 24 March 1944 when seventy-six prisoners got out of the camp through an underground tunnel. All except three were recaptured. Furious, Hitler ordered that fifty of the recaptured prisoners were to be shot and Milford was one of those executed by the *Gestapo*. Collins was awarded the DFM and went on to fly three more tours – over 100 operations – with 226 Squadron, in Mitchells. In 1945 he was awarded the DFC. On 22 September 226 Squadron lost a second Boston, flow by Flight Sergeant M. A. H. Demont, which was claimed by *Hauptmann* Klaus Mietusch, *Kommandeur* of 7./JG26, who shot his victim down at 1315hrs 1 3/4 miles east of Ostend. A career officer who had joined the *Geschwader* in 1938, it was his twenty-third victory. Demont and his crew were killed. Major Mietusch was KIA on 17 September 1944, when his Fw 190A-8 was shot down by Lieutenant William R. Beyer of the 361st Fighter Group, 8th Air Force who was flying a P-51 Mustang. Mietusch had logged 452 combat sorties and was credited with seventy-five victories (See Donald

Caldwell, *The JG26 War Diary,* Vol. 2 1943–45, Grub Street, 1998).

[38] John Bede *They Hosed Them Out* Australian Book Soc. 1965. (Published in the UK as 'Rear Gunner')

[39] See Stuart R. Scott, *Mosquito Thunder*, Sutton, 1999

[40] Eindhoven was Mike Carreck's final operation in 105 Squadron. His tour over, he was posted to 17 OTU 'on rest' as an instructor.

[41] John Bede *They Hosed Them Out*

[42] John Bede *They Hosed Them Out*

[43] Flight Sergeant Alex G. Paterson RCAF of 487 Squadron, was hit and his aircraft crashed off Oostkapelle with the loss of the whole crew.

[44] Most likely Sergeant A. M. Swan of 464 Squadron who had about 7 ft of his port wing shot away by light flak

[45] John Bede, *They Hosed Them Out*

[46] Pelly-Fry's aircraft was hit just after he released his delayed-action bombs. With much-reduced hydraulic pressure, a large hole in the starboard wing and a coughing and spluttering starboard engine, he avoided the rooftops but could not climb above 800 ft or keep up with the others on the way home. He came back alone after two Fw 190s were beaten off.

[47] Flown by Sergeant Cecil A. Maw of 107 Squadron, and shot down by 5./JG1.

[48] Kirchener had received the *Eisern Kruez II* (Iron Cross 2nd Class) shortly after his first victory, Vickers Wellington III Z1577 of 9 Squadron on an operation to Duisburg on 23 July 1942. On 11 October 1942 he destroyed a 2 Group Mosquito IV. Kirshner was killed at the controls of an He 162 Salamander jet fighter on 19 April 1945 shortly after he shot down a Spitfire. Heeson was KIA on 3 May 1943. He had twenty-eight victories to his credit. (See Eric Mombeek, *Defending the Reich: The History of JG1*, JAC Publications, 1992).

[49] John Bede, *They Hosed Them Out*

[50] Twenty-tree-year-old Sergeant Patrick. I. Stokes, his pilot, 23-year-old Canadian Flight Sergeant Alexander Gordon Paterson from Saskatchewan, and the two other crew members were KIA.

[51] One hundred-and-seven houses and ninety-six shops were completely destroyed and 107 Dutch workers and civilians living around the factory were killed and 161 wounded. Among the dead were Joanna van den Broek, wife of H. Bongaarts and their daugher Catharina, Margaretha, Wilhelmina and son Hendrik, who all died at Lijmbeekstraat 404. Lamert A. Raaijmakers, husband of M. S. Elbers and their daughters Albertina, Elisabeth, Geradina, Joanna and Sibeylla, all died at Harmoniestraat 30. Seven German soldiers were killed and eighteen wounded.

[52] *The Mossie* 18, January 1998

[53] Martin W. Bowman, *Mosquito Bomber/Fighter-Bomber Units 1942–45*, Osprey Combat Aircraft 4, 1997. A full account of the operations carried out by 2 Group Mosquitoes can also be found in Martin W. Bowman, *The Men Who Flew The Mosquito*, Pen & Sword, 2003.

[54] Arthur Eyton-Jones, *Day Bomber*, Sutton Publishing, 1998. On 30 July 1943 Christie perished after his Mitchell II FV932/Q-Queenie was shot down by Me 210s and 410s during an ASR search. Eyton-Jones and two other crew members survived and were picked up and landed at Grimsby on 3 August.

[55] 'Wutz' Galland was also credited with two Spitfires for his twenty-sixth and twenty-seventh victories.

[56] Kelch's and Kemethmüller's claims were confirmed for their first and sixty-second victories respectively. Kelch was KIA 31 July 1943. *Oberlautnant* Kemethmüller, a *Ritterkreuzträger* who had earned the Knight's Cross in Russia while a member of JG3, was twice wounded. His eight-ninth and final victory was on 17 September 1944. He was severely injured in a flying accident on 4 November 1944 and he did not return to flying status after hospitalization. (See Donald Caldwell *The JG26 War Diary*, Vol 2 1943-45, Grub Street, 1998)

[57] His claim was for a Hudson and was his final victory. After a spell as an instructor and *Saffelkapitän* in *Jagdgruppe* West from September to December 1943 *Oberleutnant* Johann Aistleitner was given command of 5./JG26. Promoted to *Hauptmann* he was KIA flying an Fw 190A-6 in combat probably with 4th Fighter Group P-47s on 14 January 1944. (See Donald Caldwell, *The JG26 War Diary*, Vol 2 1943–45, Grub Street, 1998).

[58] On 27/28 May 1943 22-year-old Peter Stanley Moore was the mid-upper gunner of a 218 Squadron Stirling flow by Flight Sergeant David Mills which was shot down during a Gardening sortie north of Terschelling by a Bf 110 of IV./NJG1 flown by *Oberfeldwebel* Karl Georg Pfeiffer and his radar operater/air gunner, Willi Knappe for their fifth victory. He had been on leave when his first crew were lost on operations and was on sick leave recovering from mumps when his second crew failed to

return from an operation. Pfeiffer finished the war with eleven victories. (See Theo Boiten and Martin Bowman, *Raiders of the Reich*, Airlife, 1996).

[59] Thompson and Horne were KIA on 1 May 1943, after take-off from Marham, while forming up for the raid on the Philips works at Eindhoven.

[60] Henk F. Van Baaren, *Bommen Vielen op Hengelo*, translated in *The Mossie* 16, April 1997.

[61] Brown, who had a similar experience six days later after taking part in an attack by fifteen Mosquitoes on the Renault works at Le Mans, was killed shortly after on a raid on the engine sheds at Malines in Belgium. His Mosquito was hit by coastal flak and finished off three minutes later by two Fw 190s.

[62] Some 9.8 tons of bombs were dropped on the John Cockerill works, Pace and Cook crashed into the Ooster Schelde off Woensdrecht. A full account of this raid is contained in 'Mosquitoes to Liège' in Michael J. F. Bowyer, *2 Group RAF*, Faber & Faber 1974 and in Stuart R. Scott, *Mosquito Thunder*, Sutton, 1998.

[63] *The Mossie* 19, April 1998.

[64] Henk F. Van Baaren, *Bommen Vielen op Hengelo*, translated in *The Mossie* 16, April 1997.

[65] On 30 July 1943 Mackenstedt crash-landed his Fw 190A-5 after being hit by return fire from an 8th Air Force B-17 and he died of his injuries in hospital. (See Donald Caldwell, *The JG26 War Diary,* Vol. 2 1943–45, Grub Street, 1998).

[66] Dennis had been awared the DFC in June 1941 for displaying 'great skill and daring' in attacks on enemy merchant ships and escorting vessels in the Mediterranean while flying Blenheims from Malta. After thirty operational sorties and a 'rest tour' at the Blenheim OCU at Bicester he had returned in July 1942 to 21 Squadron for a second tour.

[67] Three of *JG26*'s claims of four Venturas – two of them by 'Wutz' Galand were confirmed for his forty-first and forty-second victories, as were claims for two Spitfires shot down, while receiving no losses themselves. Galland was KIA on 17 August 1943 in combat with 56th Fighter Group P-47s. His score stood at fifty-four. (See Donald Caldwell, *The JG26 War Diary*, Vol. 2 1943–45, Grub Street, 1998). On 18 May David Dennis was awarded the DSO. By September 1943, having completed 34 operational sorties, he returned to the Bicester OCU as Chief Instructor this time on B-25 Mitchells.

[68] He claimed two Spitfires but JG1 lost *Feldwebel* Willi Pfeiffer of 4th *Staffel* and *Leutnant* Ernst Heesen of 5th *Staffel*, a 28-victory ace, in this combat. *Oberfeldwebel* Georg Hutter of 5th *Staffel* was shot down and wounded. Hutter was KIA on 26 December 1944. Ehlers was KIA by P-51 Mustangs of the 364th Fighter Group on 27 December 1944. At the time of his death Ehlers had fifty-five victories. (See Eric Mombeek, *Defending the Reich: The History of JG1*, JAC Publications, 1992).

[69] Wickop was KIA on 16 May 1943 when he shot down over the North Sea by a P-47 Thunderbolt of the 78th Fighter Group. In little more than three months he scored thirteen victories. *Feldwebel* Rauhaus was KIA near Caen on 31 July 1944 in combat with USAAF fighters. (See Eric Mombeek, *Defending the Reich: The History of JG1*, JAC Publications, 1992).

[70] Flight Lieutenant Harold Sutton DFC and Flying Officer John Morris, and Flying Officer Fred Opershaw and Sergeant Alfred Stonestreet, of 139 Squadron.

[71] Unable to find the target by dead reckoning Patterson identified and attacked Weimar railway station from 300 ft. He completed two tours of daylight operations on Mosquitoes and was awarded the DSO early in 1944. Squadron Leader Blessing DSO DFC RAAF was KIA on 7 July 1944 on a PFF marking sorties over Caen. A full account of the Jena raid can be found in Martin W. Bowman's, *Mosquito Bomber/Fighter-Bomber Units 1942–45*, Osprey Combat Aircraft 4, 1997

[72] Flying Officer F. M. 'Bud' Fisher, DFC, an American from Pennsylvania, and his navigator, Flight Sergeant Les Hogan DFM, were prevented from attacking the target by the balloon barrage, but bombed the town from 200 ft. (Fisher and Hogan were KIA on a night operation on 29/30 September 1943). Flying Officer Don C. Dixon, an Australian from Brisbane, and his navigator Flying Officer W. A. Christensen RAAF, attempted three runs on the target but were also prevented from bombing by the balloons and intense flak and they dropped their bombs on a goods train at Lastrup. Pilot Officer Ronald Massie and Sergeatn George Lister, who were last seen as the formation entered cloud prior to reaching the target, crashed near Diepholz and were killed.

[73] Flight Lieutenant William S. D. 'Jock' Sutherland and Flying Officer George Dean in a 139 Squadron Mosquito were seen to bomb their target but both crew were killed when they crashed at Wroxham railway station. They had flown into high-voltage overhead electric cables when attempting to land at RAF Coltishall on their return. Flying Officers Alan Rae DFM and Kenneth Bush died when their

Mosquito crashed while they tried to land at Marham on one engine.

[74] *The Mossie* 21, January 1999

[75] A full account of the part played by Mosquitoes of 8 Group and other commands can be found in Martin W. Bowman, *The Men Who Flew the Mosquito*, Pen & Sword, 2003.

[76] Eric Mombeek, *Defending the Reich: The History of JG1*, JAC Publications, 1992. The Mitchell piloted by Flight Sergeant A. R. Grindley crashed a short distance fro Maldegem airfield, the four crew members were killed.

[77] Mike Henry DFC, *Air Gunner*, Goodall, 1997.

[78] Three large-scale Ramrod operations were taking place, each one involving more than 100 aircraft. While the RAF Bostons attacked Courtrai, home of *JG26*, 18 USAAF B-26 Marauders, covered by eleven Squadrons of Spitfires and one squadron of Typhoons, would attack St Omer airfield and eight squadrons of P-47 Thunderbolts would attack Rotterdam.

[79] See Donald Caldwell, *The JG26 War Diary*, Vol. 2 1943–45, Grub Street, 1998.

[80] From September 1942 to May 1943 98 Squadron flew seventy sorties and lost two aircraft in five operational raids while 180 Squadron flew 151 sorties and lost four aircraft in nine bombing operations. The first large-scale 24 aircraft operation was flown on 12 August, Foulsham was taken over by 3 Group on 1 September and occupied by Lancaster Is of 514 Squadron.

[81] Also, 342 Squadron bombed the Chevilly transformer staion near Paris and the finale was provided by 320 Squadron's Mitchells, which flew a Ramrod operation against the Grand Quevilly power station at Rouen.

[82] A cousin of Wing Commander Bell-Irving.

[83] See Martin W. Bowman *Moskitopanik!*, Pen & Sword, 2004.

[84] The Honorable Michael J. Wedgewood Benn DFC, at twenty-two, was the eldest of three sons of William Wedgewood Benn DSO DFC Ld-H (*Legion d'Honeur*) and CdG (*Criox de Guerre*), a First World War veteran pilot and prominent politician who was created Viscount Stansgate on 22 December 1940.

[85] One of the great RAF navigators in the Second World War, after fighting in the French 61st Regiment of Artillery in the First World War and at the begining of the Second World War Livry-Level DSO DFC* CdG* DFC (USA) did at least four tours of operational flying in Coastal Command, on special duties and in 2 Group Mosquitoes. He could not be persuaded to have a break from operational flying. On 31 August 1944 'Buck' Taylor and his navigator, Flight Lieutenant Johnson were shot down on a Night Intruder to Strasbourg-Sarreborg when they attacked a train. Flak set fire to their port engine and the wing collapsed. They baled out and evaded capture, returning to England on 29 September 1944. Taylor rejoined 21 Squadron on 28 October after a spell in the RAF Hospital, Swindon. By January 1945 Squadron Leader Taylor DFC* Ld-H CdG* MID had flown a total of forty-eight low-level day and night bombing sorties.

[86] Henk F. van Baaren, *Bomman Vielen Op Hengelo*, translated into English in *The Mossie* 16, April 1997.

[87] Mike Henry DFC, *Air Gunner*, Goodall, 1997.

[88] Martin W. Bowman, *Moskitopanik!* Pen & Sword, 2004.

[89] Mike Henry DFC, *Air Gunner*, Goodall, 1997.

[90] See Martin W. Bowman, *Moskitopanik!* Pen & Sword, 2004.

[91] A full account of the Shellhaus raid can be found in Martin W. Bowman, *Moskitopanik!* Pen & Sword, 2004.

BIBLIOGRAPHY

Baaren, Henk F. Van, *Bommen Vielen op Hengelo* (Privately Published)

Bateman, John, *A War Record* (unpublished)

Bede, John, *They Hosed Them Out* (Australian Book Soc. 1965)

Boiten, Theo, *Blenheim Strike* (ARP 1995)

Boiten, Theo, *Bristol Blenheim* (Crowood Aviation Series 1998)

Bowman, Martin W., *De Havilland Mosquito* (Crowood Aviation Series 1997)

Bowman, Martin W., *Low Level From Swanton* (Air Research Publications 1995)

Bowman, Martin W., *Mosquito Bomber/Fighter-Bomber Units 1942-45* (Osprey Combat Aircraft 4 1997)

Bowman, Martin W., *RAF Bomber Stories: Dramatic first-hand accounts of British & Commonwealth airmen in WW2* (PSL 1998)

Bowman, Martin W., *The Men Who Flew the Mosquito*. (PSL 1995)

Bowyer, Chaz, *Mosquito Squadrons of the Royal Air Force* (Ian Allan Ltd 1984)

Bowyer, Michael J. F., *2 Group RAF: A Complete History 1936-1945* (Faber & Faber 1974)

Butterworth, Arthur, *We Shall Be There. A History of 107 Squadron, 1918-1963* (1990)

Caldwell, Donald, *JG26 War Diary*, The Vol. 2 1943-45 (Grub Street 1998)

Delve, Ken, *RAF Marham* (PSL 1995)

Eyton-Jones, Arthur, *Day Bomber* (Sutton Publishing Ltd 1998)

Gunn, Peter B., *RAF Great Massingham: A Norfolk Airfield at War 1940-1945* (1990)

Henry DFC, Mike, *Air Gunner* (G.T. Foulis & Co Ltd, 1964)

Henry DFC, Mike, *Air Gunner* (G. T. Foulis & Co Ltd 1964, Goodall 1997)

Hess, William N., *A-20 Boston At War*, (Ian Allan Ltd 1979)

Kloos, Jan P., *320 Squadron RAF Memorial 1940-1945* (1987)

Lambermont, Paul, *Lorraine Squadron* (Cassell & Co Ltd 1956)

Lincoln, Paul, *The Aalborg Attack* (After the Battle No 72)

McCue, Paul, *Dunsfold: Surrey's Most Secret Airfield* (Air Research Publications 1992)

Middlebrook, Martin and Chris Everitt, *The Bomber Command War Diaries: An Operational reference Book 1939-1945* (Penguin 1990)

Mombeek, Eric, *Defending The Reich. The History of JG1* (JAC Publications 1992)

Moore, Jim, *Churchill's Light Cavalry* (2 Vols.) (unpublished)

Moyes, Philip, *Bomber Squadrons of the RAF & Their Aircraft* (MacDonald 1964)

Moyes, Philip J. R., *Bombers of WW2*, Vol.2 (Hylton Lacy 1968)

Rawlings, John D. R., *Fighter Squadrons of the RAF & Their Aircraft* (MacDonald 1969)

Rijken, Kees and Paul Schepers *'Operation Oyster'* (unpublished)

Rønnest, Ole, *Aalborg 13 August 1940*, (Privately Published)

Scott, Stuart R., *Battle-Axe Blenheims: No 105 Squadron RAF at War 1940-1* (Sutton 1996)

Scott, Stuart R., *Mosquito Thunder* (Sutton 1999)

Sharp, Martin and Michael J. F. Bowyer, *Mosquito*, C. (Faber & Faber 1967)

Shores, Christopher F., *2nd Tactical Air Force* (Osprey 1970)

Spick, Mike, *Luftwaffe Fighter Aces* (Ivy Books. 1996)

The Mossie - various volumes, 1997

INDEX

254